Business and Environmental Policy

American and Comparative Environmental Policy
Sheldon Kamieniecki and Michael E. Kraft, series editors

Business and Environmental Policy
Corporate Interests in the American Political System

edited by Michael E. Kraft and Sheldon Kamieniecki

The MIT Press
Cambridge, Massachusetts
London, England

MIT Press books may be purchased at special quantity discounts for business or sales promotional use. For information, please e-mail special_sales@mitpress. mit.edu or write to Special Sales Department, The MIT Press, 55 Hayward Street, Cambridge, MA 02142.

This book was set in Sabon by SNP Best-set Typesetter Ltd., Hong Kong. Printed and bound in the United States of America.

Printed on recycled paper.

Library of Congress Cataloging-in-Publication Data
Business and environmental policy : corporate interests in the American political system / edited by Michael E. Kraft, Sheldon Kamieniecki.
    p. cm.
 Includes bibliographical references and index.
 ISBN-13: 978-0-262-11305-2 (hardcover : alk. paper)
 ISBN-13: 978-0-262-61218-0 (pbk. : alk. paper)
  1. Corporations—Political aspects—United States. 2. Business and politics—United States. 3. Legislation—United States. 4. Corporate power—United States. 5. Environmental policy—United States. 6. Industrial management—Environmental aspects—United States. I. Kraft, Michael E. II. Kamieniecki, Sheldon.
JK467.B744 2007
333.70973—dc22

                                                                2006023632

10 9 8 7 6 5 4 3 2 1

Contents

Series Foreword

The analyses presented in this edited volume focus on the role of business in environmental policy, primarily within the U.S. political system. The contributing authors examine the actions of business groups and the degree of success they enjoy within different institutional venues and at various stages of the policy process. The chapters cover policy formulation and adoption in Congress, implementation in executive agencies, intervention in the courts, and policymaking within state and local government. Two of the chapters also speak to agenda-setting activities through assessment of public opinion and the role of the media.

The book illustrates well our purpose in the MIT Press series in American and Comparative Environmental Policy. We encourage work that examines a broad range of environmental policy issues. We are particularly interested in volumes that incorporate interdisciplinary research and focus on the linkages between public policy and environmental problems and issues both within the United States and in cross-national settings. We welcome contributions that analyze the policy dimensions of relationships between humans and the environment from either a theoretical or empirical perspective. At a time when environmental policies are increasingly seen as controversial and new approaches are being implemented widely, we especially encourage studies that assess policy successes and failures, evaluate new institutional arrangements and policy tools, and clarify new directions for environmental politics and policy. The books in this series are written for a wide audience that includes academics, policymakers, environmental scientists and professionals, business and labor leaders, environmental activists, and students concerned with environmental issues. We hope they contribute to public understanding of environmental problems, issues, and policies of concern today and also suggest promising actions for the future.

Sheldon Kamieniecki, University of California, Santa Cruz
Michael Kraft, University of Wisconsin–Green Bay
American and Comparative Environmental Policy Series Editors

Preface

It is conventional wisdom that business groups are often leading players in the policymaking process. Why would one expect anything else? After all, businesses can be affected in significant and costly ways by public policy, from provisions of tax laws to regulations on environmental protection. To ensure that their interests are given proper consideration, business officials seek to influence the policy agenda as well as decisions made throughout the policy process. Similarly, knowing how central the public's views are to public policy debates, businesses and trade associations try to shape public opinion through media campaigns.

Business interests clearly have a great deal at stake when government considers taking action, and many have the resources to intervene as needed to shape policy decisions. Major energy producers in 2001, for example, played a central role in the energy policy task force established under the direction of Vice President Dick Cheney. The actions that the group recommended, which emphasized increasing energy supplies, received serious consideration in Congress during the next four years, though approval was stymied by environmentalists and other interests. In summer 2005, however, emboldened by the 2004 elections and public frustration with rising gasoline prices, Congress finally approved a far-reaching energy policy that followed the general outline of the Cheney task force recommendations. The bill provides billions of dollars in subsidies to energy producers, with oil and natural gas firms among the biggest winners.

The energy policy case is only one illustration of what critics see as the pervasive, and often detrimental, influence of business on environmental policy. By no means do business interests always win.

Yet they do seem well represented in policy debates, and they do meet with considerable success. Many examples over the past several decades could be cited in policy areas as diverse as mining, forestry, ranching, agriculture, air and water pollution control, management of toxic and hazardous chemicals, climate change, and protection of biological diversity.

It is surprising, therefore, that the role business plays in shaping public debate and in influencing the formulation, adoption, and implementation of environmental and resource policy has not been subject to as much systematic scholarly inquiry as have many other elements of environmental politics. As a result, we know little about how often business interests choose to intervene, where they intervene, what strategies and tactics they use, and especially how often they get their way in environmental policymaking. Similarly, we know little about the factors that condition their capacity to influence decision making in different government venues: the U.S. Congress, state legislatures, municipal governments, federal and state executive agencies, the courts, and multilateral international organizations. The chapters brought together in this book help fill some of these gaps in our understanding of the role and influence of business groups in environmental and natural resource policy.

In chapter 1 we provide a historical and analytic context for what follows. We review a range of studies and arguments about the role of business interests in environmental policy, and public policy more generally. We also set out what we believe are the key questions that analysts should be asking about business intervention in different political venues and the factors that condition its success. The rest of the chapters are arranged in five sections: agenda setting and elections, including the role of the media and public opinion; policy formulation and adoption in the U.S. Congress; policy implementation in administrative agencies; intervention in the courts; and policymaking at the state and local levels. In the concluding chapter we revisit the book's major findings, highlight their implications for policymaking and democratic theory, and set out suggestions for future research that could further improve our understanding of the role and impact of business in environmental and natural resource policy.

We thank the contributing authors for their cooperation and expeditious responses to our many requests for chapter revisions. It has been a pleasure to work with such a talented and dedicated group of colleagues. We also acknowledge support from the University of Wisconsin–Green Bay and the University of California, Santa Cruz. As always, we take responsibility for any errors or omissions that have escaped our notice during the writing, editing, and production of the book.

Contributors

Christopher J. Bosso is Professor of Political Science and Associate Dean, School of Social Science, Urban Affairs, and Public Policy at Northeastern University.

Gary C. Bryner is Professor of Political Science at Brigham Young University.

Cary Coglianese is the Edward B. Shils Professor of Law and Professor of Political Science at the University of Pennsylvania.

Robert J. Duffy is Associate Professor of Political Science at Colorado State University.

Scott R. Furlong is Professor of Political Science and Public and Environmental Affairs at the University of Wisconsin–Green Bay.

Deborah Lynn Guber is Associate Professor of Political Science at the University of Vermont.

Sheldon Kamieniecki is Dean of the Division of Social Sciences at the University of California, Santa Cruz.

Michael E. Kraft is Professor of Political Science and Public and Environmental Affairs and Herbert Fisk Johnson Professor of Environmental Studies at the University of Wisconsin–Green Bay.

Judith A. Layzer is Assistant Professor of Environmental Policy in the Department of Urban Studies and Planning, Massachusetts Institute of Technology.

Lettie McSpadden is Professor Emeritus of Political Science at Northern Illinois University.

Philip A. Mundo is Professor of Political Science at Drew University.

Kent E. Portney is Professor of Political Science at Tufts University.

Barry G. Rabe is Professor of Public Policy in the Gerald R. Ford School of Public Policy and Professor in the School of Natural Resources and Environment at the University of Michigan.

Paul S. Weiland is an environmental attorney at Nossaman, Gunther, Knox, and Elliott, a law firm in Southern California. Previously he worked in the Law and Policy Section, Environmental and Natural Resources Division of the U.S. Department of Justice.

I

Introduction

1

Analyzing the Role of Business in Environmental Policy

Michael E. Kraft and Sheldon Kamieniecki

Since the beginning of the modern environmental movement some thirty-five years ago, American business has played a uniquely important role in environmental policymaking. From helping to set the political agenda and formulate environmental policies to influencing decisionmaking in executive agencies and the courts, U.S. firms have been among the most significant policy actors at all levels of government. They have made a concerted effort to set out positions on a range of environmental protection, natural resource, and energy issues, influence public opinion, and advance political strategies to attain their goals.

Both scholars and journalists have given well-deserved attention to such efforts (Browne 1988; Kamieniecki 2006; Smith 2000; Vogel 1978, 1989). As a result we know much about the political activities of business and the effects they have had. Yet we think the influence of business on environmental policy merits a broader and more systematic examination. There are several key questions at the center of such an investigation. What does business try to achieve in the policy process, and what factors affect whether it succeeds in getting its way? How does such success vary from one institutional venue to another—for example, from the U.S. Congress to the executive branch, the courts, and state and local governments? We try to address these questions through a concentration on the American political system, but the research strategy we advance also could be extended to cross-national comparisons of business influence.

The relative neglect of these kinds of questions is particularly striking in light of often-heated debates in the United States over proposed new directions in environmental policy and the participation of business and environmental groups in these debates. For example, American corporations have long sought to create a business-friendly environmental policy, with mixed success. They have argued that many (if not most) environmental policies actually undermine the public welfare because of their economic inefficiency. As a result, business groups have lobbied intensively at both national and state levels for policy reforms to reduce regulatory burdens and costs and improve efficiency. Sometimes they have succeeded in these efforts and sometimes they have not. The policy approaches they have advocated include greater reliance on cost-benefit analysis, risk assessment, regulatory flexibility, public-private partnerships, and market-based incentives, among other changes (Coglianese and Nash 2006; Durant, Fiorino, and O'Leary 2004; Mazmanian and Kraft 1999; Rosenau 2000). Many of these proposals have been endorsed as well by others, inside and outside of government, who see them as a way to improve the effectiveness, efficiency, or equity of environmental policies (Dietz and Stern 2003; National Academy of Public Administration 2000).

However, not everyone is convinced. Some analysts, for example, believe that suggested policy changes of this kind are largely untested and that few empirical studies confirm they will prove to be as effective, efficient, or equitable in practice as their supporters suggest (Kamieniecki, Shafie, and Silvers 1999; Cohen, Kamieniecki, and Cahn 2005). For their part, environmentalists have campaigned actively against most of these kinds of proposals. They assert that American business is already powerful and would use any flexibility given it under such policy changes to further weaken environmental protection and resource conservation. As evidence, they point to business lobbying over the past several decades intended to modify or defeat important policy actions they believe would have benefited the environment and public health (Kamieniecki 2006; Vig and Kraft 2006). They also cite the work of business-backed research centers and "think tanks" whose reports have helped to create a pro-business and anti–environmental protection climate of opinion, particularly at the national level (Moore 2002; People for the American Way 2004).

Corporate leaders and conservative analysts, of course, challenge these assessments and question the motivation of their critics (e.g., Simon 1981, 1999; Easterbrook 1995; Wildavsky 1995; Lomborg 2001; Moore 2002). They argue that environmentalists exaggerate problems to alarm

Americans, raise money for their cause, and shape public policy to advance their own interests. They maintain that present laws, regulations, and government programs often are too expensive and are likely to result in only modest—if any—improvements in environmental quality. In their view corporations have a great deal at stake financially (as do their shareholders), and they have every right to express their positions and lobby government to protect their interests.

Business leaders also point to the progress the country has made since the early 1970s in improving air and water quality, conserving energy, preserving natural resources, and encouraging the safe transportation and disposal of chemical waste. Companies have spent billions of dollars to retool their plants and manufacturing processes to control emissions, save energy, and safely dispose of toxic waste. The timber industry has hired numerous ecologists and conservation biologists and is now managing forests more wisely by protecting critical habitats. Similarly, large agricultural firms are better managing soil erosion and containing feedlot waste and chemical runoff from cropland. Unlike in the past, firms are also cooperating more closely with government regulators and maintain that a "greening of industry" is currently taking place (Hoffman 2000; Prakash 2000; Robbins 2001; Marcus, Geffen, and Sexton 2002; Press and Mazmanian 2006). National business associations cite programs such as Energy Star, Responsible Care, and Project XL as evidence that corporations have adopted a new attitude toward protecting the environment and conserving the nation's natural resources (Marcus, Geffen, and Sexton 2002; Press and Mazmanian 2006).

Environmentalists, of course, challenge these indicators of progress as both misleading and insufficient to address the problems. They maintain that industry has taken largely symbolic steps to improve the nation's environmental quality and has not fundamentally altered its operations. They say that much more remains to be done to protect public and environmental health.

These contrasting views of the actions that business has taken to improve environmental protection, the merits of proposed policy reforms, and the purposes and success of business and environmental lobbying suggest the need for careful assessment. We focus in this book on business firms and their lobbying efforts. There is little disagreement that firms engage in diverse political activities to protect their interests and profits, yet there is considerable debate over the extent to which they get their way in deliberations over public policy (Smith 2000). Studies by Baumgartner and Leech (1998), Berry (1999), and others contend that the rapid rise of citizen groups, including environmental organizations, since the 1960s has significantly mitigated the power and influence of corporate America in Congress. Much like early studies of business power in American politics (e.g., Bauer, Pool, and Dexter 1963), their findings suggest that countervailing sources of influence in a pluralistic political system significantly constrain what business groups are able to accomplish.

There is no doubt, for example, that the major environmental groups have been successful in fundraising and have played an increasingly influential role in agenda setting, the electoral process, and issue advocacy at both national and state levels (Bosso 2005; Duffy 2003). They also use many of the same sophisticated techniques that business groups do, such as Internet-based public education and mobilization of supporters in grassroots lobbying campaigns. In addition, Smith (2000) shows that congressional decisionmaking reflects public opinion on salient policy issues even when the business community is united.

The history of environmental policy suggests much the same pattern, particularly during the 1970s and 1980s when most of the major national laws, such as the Clean Air Act and Clean Water Act, were enacted or strengthened despite business opposition (Kraft 2007). The advances in environmental protection and natural resource conservation in the 1970s and 1980s were not lost in the 1990s or even into the 2000s (Vig and Kraft 2006). Business has been ineffective in repealing the major environmental laws even if it has been more successful in modifying their implementation in the executive agencies. Given strong public support for environmental policy, it should be difficult for business to win when the issues are salient and environmental groups are able to gain sufficient media attention to mobilize supporters.

Despite such arguments and findings, business groups appear to be highly successful in getting what they want from policymakers. Some recent research supports this position. For example, Korten (1995), Clawson, Neustadt, and Weller (1998), Libby (1998), and Glazer and Rothenberg (2001) provide empirical evidence that business is still a dominant player in American politics, in general, and in environmental politics, in particular. Furlong (1997) finds that environmental and citizen groups, while active in federal rulemaking processes, rarely are as well endowed with the essential economic and political resources as business groups. McSpadden (2000) documents the role of business groups in the courts and the resources they are able to bring to litigation of environmental policy disputes. Some studies of the history of environmental and natural resource policies (e.g., Cahn 1995; Gonzalez 2001) also argue that business and other elites have exercised disproportionate influence. Specific cases of contemporary business influence on policy decisions are not hard to find, whether favorable legislative stipulations that ease regulatory requirements or award generous subsidies to industry, or the promulgation of administrative rules that provide increased corporate access to natural resources on public lands (Kamieniecki 2006; Kraft 2007; Lowry 2006).

Even these few observations about the role of business in environmental policy suggest the need for further study. Is business influence effectively balanced by the efforts of environmentalists and other citizen groups, a vigilant press, and the desire by policymakers to promote the public interest? Or, does business get its way most of the time despite these other countervailing forces? If so, how does it do that, and under what conditions does it tend to win?

There are some nettlesome methodological and theoretical concerns that need to be addressed in trying to answer such questions. For example, how should scholars study the role of business in environmental policy? Through case studies, despite their inherent limitations (Mahoney 2000)? Through surveys of policy actors to tell us about their attitudes, beliefs, motivations, and their sense of who is most influential in decisionmaking? What about examination of documentary records, which can provide substantial information on the activities of participants in the policy process, such as testimony before legislative bodies, submission of comments in executive agencies, or litigation actions? Would it be best to rely on analysis of aggregate data (e.g., on campaign contributions or lobbying reports), which can overcome some of the weaknesses of case studies, but which may not equal their potential for a rich description of business activities and their effects? Or, should students of business and environmental policy make use of a combination of quantitative and qualitative methods to benefit from the strengths of each (Kamieniecki 2006)?

The theoretical concerns have to do with how influence or power is best conceptualized, and which variables should be included in any study of business influence on environmental policy. We turn to the theoretical issues later in the chapter, following a brief review of the history of corporate development in the United States and the history of U.S. environmental policy. In a later section on the analytic framework, we pull together what seem to be pertinent variables to consider in explaining the activity of business groups and their effects.

Conceptual Overview

This book sheds light on the ongoing debate about the influence of business by analyzing the degree to which business is able to influence environmental politics and policies at different access points in the U.S. policymaking process. Businesses, as well as other interest groups, can choose various stages of the policy process to fight their battles. From a theoretical standpoint, it is not clear how corporations select where and when to try to influence environmental policy, and what variables affect such decisions (Kamieniecki 2006). It is possible that business decides to weaken or defeat environmental regulations at every access point when the issue is not salient to the public and the media, and therefore when they might expect little attention to their efforts and little opposition. Such an effort might begin, for example, at the subcommittee or committee level in Congress when bills are first being formulated, or within administrative agencies in the early stages of rulemaking. Yet even under these circumstances, businesses are likely to consider just how much is at stake in a given case and whether the investment of corporate resources in such a lobbying effort is justifiable in light of the expected benefits (Kamieniecki 2006). On salient issues companies may decide to put up limited opposition in the public arena of Congress and, instead, concentrate their time and effort fighting environmental rules within regulatory agencies such as the U.S. Environmental Protection Agency (EPA) or in the courts, where extensive media coverage is less likely. If a particular policy only affects one industry or one large company, corporate executives may choose to bypass Congress altogether and quietly approach the EPA or another agency with their grievances. Given the high stakes that are often involved, researchers can assume that firms carefully calculate at which access point they are most likely to be successful and get their way.

This chapter provides an overview of the role of business in environmental policymaking. It lays the foundation for the rest of the book by addressing central issues concerning democracy, interest-group activity, and environmental policymaking. We describe the relationship of business and government with respect to environmental policymaking, and the variables that affect it. We discuss how and under what conditions business seeks to influence government policy at different access points, and we draw from several bodies of literature to build a framework of analysis that can assist in studying such questions. We propose some practical ways scholars can assess the extent to which business succeeds in its efforts to shape political culture and to help establish a business-friendly set of environmental policies and regulations.

The book contains seven parts. Following this introductory chapter in part I, part II analyzes business and public opinion, including actions taken to frame the issues, set the political agenda, and affect election campaigns. The third part focuses on business and the legislative process in Congress, the fourth on the role of business in executive agencies, the fifth on business and the courts, and the sixth on state and local government. The last part contains the concluding chapter. While this coverage by no means exhausts the possible venues and approaches for business influence on environmental policy, it does address the most prominent activities found in the U.S. political system. We hope that students of environmental politics and policy will extend this kind of analysis to nations other than the United States to permit a broader comparison of business activities in different political venues.

As noted earlier, we find it surprising that little systematic analysis has been done on the influence of business over environmental policy, given the frequency with which corporations are the primary targets of federal environmental laws, the large amounts of money companies spend to comply with national government regulations, and the millions of dollars business spends on election campaigns, lobbyists, and attorneys each year. The studies of business and environmental policy that have been conducted tend to be relatively narrow and descriptive even where they offer intriguing and suggestive findings. Questions remain about the extent to which we can generalize from them. Most previous research focuses on a single government institution (e.g., Congress) and access point, includes only a few unique businesses as case studies, treats business as a single entity, and ignores the fact that companies belong to distinct industrial sectors. To help improve our understanding of business actions and their effects, this book examines the influence of a variety of corporations over U.S. environmental politics and policy from diverse angles and perspectives and within different governmental institutions and access points of decisionmaking.

History and Background

The role of business in the American economy has changed dramatically since the colonial days. The country moved from an agrarian economy characterized by trading and small firms to an economy dominated financially by huge, diversified firms that possess significant wealth and political influence (Lehne 2001). The role of American government changed from passively promoting economic growth to promoting selected industries (e.g., the railroads, oil companies, defense, and nuclear power) and attempting to sustain the economy. Business has long enjoyed a privileged position in our economy and in our society. Recognizing the importance of big business, government has protected and promoted its interests more often than not since the formation of the United States.

According to Vogel (1978), only in the United States did the emergence of the large corporation predate the growth of substantial government oversight. While European and Japanese leaders helped finance and establish large business enterprises, American corporations developed with less government assistance. Compared to other industrialized countries, business and American government have had an adversarial rather than a cooperative relationship with one another, particularly since World War II. This has especially been true in the environmental-issue area. The history of environmental policy illustrates this relationship well and speaks to the critical role that business has played over the past thirty-five years in policy formulation and implementation.

In what is generally considered to be the first generation of modern environmental policy actions, in the late 1960s and early 1970s the federal government greatly expanded its role in the regulation of air, water, and land, supplanting what was widely recognized as highly variable and ineffective state regulation. The new style of federal command-and-control regulation was most evident in the Clean Air Act Amendments of 1970 and the Clean Water Act of 1972, both of which set the tone for further advances in environmental protection legislation throughout the 1970s (Vig and Kraft 2006). The prevailing belief at the time was that pollution was caused primarily by callous and unthinking businesses whose behavior could be changed only through federal regulation that would compel environmentally appropriate decisions under the threat of severe penalties for noncompliance (Mazmanian and Kraft 1999).

The spurt of legislative initiatives, from the Safe Drinking Water Act of 1974 to the Comprehensive Environmental Response, Compensation, and Liability Act (Superfund) of 1980, was driven by a sharp increase in public concern about environmental threats, as well as by expanded media coverage and extensive lobbying by newly organized environmental groups (Bosso 2005; Kraft 2007). Business groups were unable to prevent these legislative enactments at either the federal or state level, although they did manage to limit their impact somewhat through provisions that required agencies to justify completely their environmental quality standards and regulations, and that permitted court challenges to such agency decisions.

One consequence of the "environmental decade" of the 1970s, as we observed earlier, was that business groups and their political allies mounted a vigorous and persistent campaign over the next twenty years to reform the regulatory process, in particular, to reduce the burdens and costs imposed on industry by these new laws. This second epoch or generation of environmental policy began in the late 1970s but was most notable during Ronald Reagan's presidency, as the White House sought to curtail implementation actions by the EPA, to reduce sharply the agency's budget, and to impose new cost-benefit tests for regulations, among other actions (Mazmanian and Kraft 1999; Vig 2006). But the regulatory reform agenda did not disappear with Reagan's departure from the presidency. It was equally visible during George H. W. Bush's presidency and during the 1990s as Bill Clinton pursued a range of reform measures, such as the EPA's Common Sense Initiative and Project XL, to head off even stronger action favored by Congress. The Republican takeover of Congress after the 1994 elections, and the election of George W. Bush in the 2000 and 2004 elections, ensured that regulatory reform would remain high on the national agenda for years to come.

The legacy of some twenty-five years of regulatory reform has been decidedly mixed. The command-and-control policies of the 1970s remain intact despite the many experiments in regulatory flexibility, collaborative decisionmaking, public-private partnerships, use of market incentives, and voluntary pollution control (Coglianese and Nash 2005; Dietz and Stern 2003; Mazmanian and Kraft 1999; Press and Mazmanian 2006; Rosenau 2000). This is chiefly because there has been insufficient political consensus at the national level to alter fundamentally the first generation of environmental policies. The result is that a new layer of reform measures has been built on the foundation of the first generation of environmental (and resource) policies without substantially changing their goals or the means used to achieve them. For this reason, business interests remain dissatisfied and continue to seek further reforms even as a third generation of environmental policies grounded in the concept of sustainable development has emerged. This latest policy agenda encompasses a wide variety of private-sector actions that are often described as voluntary "greening" of the corporation, although as we discussed earlier, scholars are divided over the degree to which such voluntary measures have worked or are likely to work in the future (Harrison and Antweiler 2003; Mazmanian and Kraft 1999; Potoski and Prakash 2005; Press and Mazmanian 2006).

As business continues to seek policy changes that favor its interests, environmental groups and their allies are often just as active in opposition to business efforts, though frequently without comparable resources or access to policymakers (Bosso 2005). Hence, it is important to ask about the roles that organized interest groups play in the policy process, both in general and specifically regarding environmental policy issues. Fortunately, a large body of work on the subject exists, though there are significant differences in assessing the effect that groups, particularly business groups, have on policy decisions.

Interest Groups and the Policy Process

During the 1950s and 1960s political scientists engaged in a vigorous debate over pluralism and the role of interest groups in democratic society. Among the questions they were most concerned about were: Do we have a system where competing groups contest one another in a fair and equitable manner, or do we have a system where a few powerful interest groups—led by a small number of elites—shape policy to further their well-being at the expense of the public good? Also, to what extent, if at all, do citizens have a meaningful say in government decisionmaking? Studies by Bauer, Pool, and Dexter (1963), Milbrath (1963), and Scott and Hunt (1965) suggested that interest groups, including those associated with business, wielded far less influence than was generally attributed to them. Yet studies by Cater (1964), McConnell (1966), and Lowi (1969) indicated that interest groups, led by "big business," were indeed undermining democracy and the public welfare.

Olson (1965) suggested that the explanation for these different appraisals lay in the nature of collective action problems and the advantages wealthy, private interest groups have in organizing and lobbying government compared to noneconomic, public interests (e.g., the young and homeless). His influential work revealed the dilemmas of organizing for collective action, and it challenged the pluralist perspective that all potential interests were equal and would have a fair chance of participating in the American political system. Olson contended that while business-oriented groups possessed significant advantages in resources and organization and were likely to mobilize, groups with many potential members seeking only collective benefits (such as consumers and environmentally concerned citizens) had a substantial disadvantage and were unlikely to unite. Hence, the battle between interest groups would never be equal and fair. Certain interests would be privileged at the expense of other interests, and this power differential would be reflected in government policy.

Olson accepted the idea that increased societal complexity led to the emergence of new interests as earlier researchers argued, but he questioned the contention that the emergence of new interests necessarily causes the creation of new organized interests. Shared interests, he maintained, are necessary but not sufficient for the establishment of organized interests. Thus, simply because a group of citizens shares an interest does not mean they will automatically organize to protect or promote that interest. According to him, significant obstacles to organized-interest formation and survival exist, including the costs involved in time, effort, and money to form and maintain a group, the free-rider problem, and the reluctance of citizens to join organized interests because of their tendency to think that one person cannot make a difference.

Although subsequent research findings challenged elements of Olson's theory of interest-group formation and survival, his recognition that there exist obstacles to organizing interests has important political implications (Moe 1980; Nounes 2002). First, his theory suggests that large portions of the broad public will remain unorganized and, therefore, unrepresented by interest groups. Second, the organized interests that do exist do not necessarily represent the various interests that comprise society. Affluent groups in America, for example, tend to have unique concerns. As recent research demonstrates, on the one hand, many more segments of society with shared interests have been able to overcome the barriers to interest-group formation and continued existence than Olson's theory would have predicted (e.g., Baumgartner and Leech 1998; Berry 1999). On the other hand, business has had no difficulty overcoming the obstacles to interest group formation and survival. On the contrary, Olson believed the largest and wealthiest corporations have enjoyed unprecedented access to the halls of power and have wielded significant influence over public policy in the United States. Unless a radical change in the American political system takes place, business will continue to hold a "privileged position" in society and will continue to exert considerable influence well into the future (Lindblom 1977).

Recent research on citizen groups and the influence of business over public policy, including environmental policy, challenges Olson's theory of collective action. Berry (1999), for example, analyzed three different sessions of Congress, specifically, 1963, 1979, and 1991, in an effort to identify which groups were active on which issues and to determine how interest-group politics and legislative policymaking have changed over time. In essence, his research attempts to document "the efforts of interest groups to influence the legislative process" (p. 8). According to Berry, it has been difficult to determine how citizen groups have fared compared with corporations and trade groups with which they contend, in part because the subject has rarely been studied. He examined 205 separate domestic social and economic policy issues that were addressed in a congressional hearing and received at least minimal attention in the press. He prepared a legislative case history for each of the issues taken up by Congress during the combined three sessions. His findings are instructive for work reported in this book. Berry found that since the early 1960s the agenda of American politics has shifted from issues that are exclusively material to a focus on issues that involve quality-of-life concerns, such as the environment. In other words, using Inglehart's (1977) terminology, he believes that over time postmaterial concerns have replaced material concerns within society. He also found that citizen groups, especially those on the left, have been the primary political force behind this trend. Citizen groups, he argues, are not only very popular but have been remarkably successful in influencing public policy. Clearly, Olson's (1965) theory would not have predicted this trend.

According to Berry (1999, 6), "most of those who have studied interest groups have concluded that there is a persistent dominance by business." Yet he finds that this was not the case during the three sessions of Congress he studied. He correctly observes that business is not unified on every policy issue and that since the 1960s the general interest group population has become larger, broader, more diverse, and increasingly influential. Indeed, Smith (2000) reports that business has been unified only on a relatively small number of bills since the 1950s. Berry argues that his findings "are important not because they improve our understanding of contemporary interest group politics but because they bear upon the level of representation that various constituencies receive in Washington" (p. 15).

Many critics maintain that interest groups subvert democracy, in part by pressing Congress to enact too much "special interest" legislation that benefits the few at the expense of the majority and, in part, by blocking legislative initiatives they oppose even when those measures are favored by, or would benefit, the general citizenry. In addition, critics contend that campaign contributions by interest groups undermine democratic government and degrade the American electoral system. In contrast, Berry (1999) rejects these arguments, saying that interest groups help to link citizens to government: "They empower people by organizing those citizens with similar interests and expressing those interests to policy-makers. In this regard, the growth of citizen groups reflects an expansion of organizing around interests that have too often received too little attention in Washington" (p. 15). Berry carefully avoids saying that business interests are no longer a force in American politics, but he does argue that their influence has significantly declined.

The Business Advantage?

Several other recent studies speak directly to this central concern about the role of business groups in contemporary policymaking. Smith's (2000) provocative investigation explores the widely held assumption that business dominates the policymaking process when it is unified on specific policy issues, thereby undermining democracy. Using the policy positions of the U.S. Chamber of Commerce as a guide, he identifies 2,364 unifying issues that were considered by Congress between 1953 and 1996. His list of unifying issues encompasses a wide range of policy areas, including employment policy, labor-management relations, and clean air regulation. Agenda building in Congress over time is his dependent variable. Among the independent variables he analyzes are "public mood" (Stimson 1999), public attitudes toward corporations, the partisan composition of Congress, "presidential leadership opening" (i.e., when partisan turnover in Congress runs in the president's favor), corporate political action committee (PAC) funding, and the state of the economy. Smith (2000, 8) finds that:

unity does not increase the direct influence of business and reduce democratic control by the citizenry. Instead, unity coincides with the opposite results. Issues marked by a common business position are precisely those for which government decisions are affected most strongly by election outcomes and the responsiveness of officeholders to their constituents. Policies match the collective desires of business only when citizens, through their policy preferences and voting choices, embrace ideas and candidates supportive of what business wants. To bolster its odds of winning in politics, business needs to seek backing from the broad public.

According to Smith, therefore, only when the public supports the unified positions of business on policy issues is business likely to achieve its legislative goals. When the public opposes the positions of business, however, Congress tends to follow the public will even though business is unified. Since all unifying policy issues are highly ideological, partisan, and salient, Congress nearly always follows the public on these issues. Smith concludes by stating, "The long-standing debates over unity among pluralists, elite theorists, and ruling class theorists have focused our attention in the wrong place. Widespread scholarly concerns about business unity are misplaced, for unifying issues are marked by the highest, rather than the lowest, degree of democratic control by the citizenry" (p. 200).

Baumgartner and Leech (1998) also ask whether business possesses a major advantage in the policymaking process. They observe that nearly all analyses of the interest-group community over time find that different types of organizations grow at different rates. Previous studies have disagreed, however, on the significance of these varying growth patterns. In their extensive study, Schlozman and Tierney (1986), for instance, find that although many new types of organizations have formed since 1960, these new groups do not comprise a more significant component in the interest-group community. In contrast, they report that the business bias in the pressure community is increasing dramatically, providing business with a bigger advantage in agenda building. They find that business groups make up nearly 50 percent of the organizations represented in Washington, D.C. In addition, more than 75 percent of the groups represent business or professional interests of some kind. In their view, "If anything, the distribution of organizations within the Washington pressure community is even more heavily weighted in favor of business organizations than it used to be" (Schlozman and Tierney 1986, 388).

Baumgartner and Leech (1998) argue that while many researchers agree with Schlozman and Tierney that business is a key player in the interest-group community, fewer agree with them that the business advantage is increasing over time (see, for example, Boyte 1980; Hadwiger 1982; Walker 1983; Browne 1988). There are two reasons for this. First, Schlozman and Tierney's own data show a growth of nonbusiness interests in Washington; these results mirror Berry's (1999) findings. Second, the two researchers do not use a complete set of comparable data on which to base their results. Therefore, "the evidence that business dominance has increased since the 1960s is limited at best" (Baumgartner and Leech 1998, 107).

Nevertheless, a number of recent studies underscore the continued special importance of business in American politics. As Libby (1998) explains, in a market economy government does everything it can to maintain good economic performance, including providing extensive "inducements" such as favorable tax, monetary, rail, highway, air, and tariff policies (also see Lindblom 1977). Libby (1998, 4) asserts, "Thus business elites are more than simple representatives of special interests: they perform a quasi-public function that political leaders regard as indispensable. In other words, business elites are first among equals in the world of interest-group politics." Korten (1995), Clawson, Neustadt, and Weller (1998), Lehne (2001), Nounes (2002), and others offer many examples of how business dominates numerous aspects of American politics, including legislative, bureaucratic, and judicial agenda building. In the environmental policy arena specifically, Glazer and Rothenberg (2001) reveal how the American automobile companies have consistently opposed government regulations to reduce emissions and increase the fuel efficiency of their vehicles. As deadlines approach, the typical response by these companies has been that meeting regulatory goals is neither technologically nor financially feasible and that, without a postponement, they will need to reduce production and lay off thousands of workers. Lindblom (1977) and others believe that despite the decline of corporate influence during the 1960s and 1970s, other interest groups still cannot compete with the wealth and other resources of business. Indeed, Rozell and Wilcox (1999) report a sharp rise in campaign contributions by corporate PACs over the last three decades, far outpacing the amount contributed by other interest groups. Therefore, Vogel (1996) contends that compared to other groups, business exerts a significant influence in American politics.

In support of Baumgartner and Leech's (1998) position, Baumgartner and Jones (1993) report significant changes in the environmental interest-group sphere, and demonstrate dramatic growth in the number of environmental groups and the resources available to them. Based on their analysis, the number of environmental organizations nearly tripled from 1960 to 1990, and the combined staff reported by those groups increased nearly tenfold. As suggested earlier, this spurt in environmental-group membership is one of the most important reasons for the enactment of so many major environmental laws during the 1970s and 1980s, often over the protests of powerful business lobbyists.

Since 1990, however, the size and resources of environmental groups have fluctuated, the competition over membership, donations, and credit for successful initiatives has intensified, and disagreements among groups have emerged (Bosso 2005). During the 1990s citizen groups became extremely sophisticated and effective at contacting Americans and persuading them to become members of their groups. Use of the Internet and advanced computer technologies aided them in this effort (Bosso and Collins 2002; Duffy 2003; Kraft and Wuertz 1996). Barring a major environmental crisis, one wonders whether the membership pool for environmental groups has bottomed out and whether there is any more room for existing groups to expand dramatically or for the addition of large environmental groups in the interest-group system. In fact, several groups have been criticized for accepting substantial funding from corporate donors, a move that may be attributed to a falling off of contributions by individuals (Bosso 2005; Dowie 1995). The Nature Conservancy, for example, accepted $140 million in corporate funding (from Cadillac, Georgia-Pacific, Merrill Lynch, and others) in 2003 alone (Nature Conservancy 2003, 74). Further, environmental groups have not always been united on major policy issues, and continued disagreements over trade, immigration, population growth, environmental justice, and other issues might undermine their ability to collaborate and influence citizens and policymakers in the future (Dowie 1995). Thus, the worst may be over for business lobbyists. Vogel (1989), McFarland (1991, 1998), and others correctly observe that the influence of business, like other interest groups, surges and declines with changes in the nature of the times. It seems, however, that business organizations have more staying power and are more resilient over time than other interest groups in American politics.

Prior to the enactment of major campaign finance reform in 2002, Clawson, Neustadt, and Weller (1998) analyzed the extent to which campaign contributions by business are a way of gaining access to elected leaders. While this access is invaluable, "it does not—and is not expected to—*guarantee* [their emphasis] a quid pro quo" (p. 6). Instead, from their standpoint:

business uses campaign contributions in a way few other groups do, as part of an "access" process that provides corporations a chance to shape the details of legislation, crafting loopholes that undercut the stated purpose of the law. Other groups do this on rare occasions; business does so routinely. Businesses are far more likely than other donors to give to *both* [their emphasis] sides in a race. (p. 13; also see Nounes 2002)

In terms of environmental legislation, Clawson and his colleagues (1998) argue that corporations have done very well politically; environmental laws have cost them a fraction of the money needed to improve air and water quality, manage the disposal of hazardous and toxic wastes, and meet federal regulatory standards. Specifically concerning the Clean Air Act of 1990, they contend that business lobbied for and got a weak, ineffective, and unenforceable law (also see Cahn 1995; Gonzalez 2001). Once the Clean Air Act was enacted, the fight continued at the EPA over specific standards, particularly those concerning acid rain regulations. According to Clawson, Neustadt, and Weller (1998), business did lose on the proposed tough new rules for soot and smog adopted during the Clinton administration, but only after an intense lobbying campaign by environmentalists and health organizations. The three investigators conclude that "the disparity in power between business and environmentalists looms large during the legislative process, but it is enormous afterward" (p. 10). As they show, business often redirects its lobbying efforts toward the EPA (or a natural resource agency) after Congress has passed and the president has signed an environmental bill. It is therefore necessary to assess the role of business once the rulemaking process begins (Kerwin 2003). As Baumgartner and Leech (1998) point out, only a few studies have pursued this line of inquiry (e.g., Furlong 1997).

Lobbying Administrative Agencies and the Courts

Lehne (2001) has closely examined the nature and extent of business lobbying in administrative agencies, and his observations have important implications for business lobbying at the EPA and the leading agencies that manage natural resources, such as the Forest Service, Bureau of Land Management, and Fish and Wildlife Service. Government agencies perform three functions in the policy process that affect companies. First, as experts, agencies frequently contribute their views and analyses when legislative programs are being formulated. Second, agencies translate statutory generalities into detailed administrative rules (i.e., through rulemaking). Third, agencies decide how administrative rules are applied to individual cases (Lehne 2001, 155). The often-technical nature of legislation and a lack of public opinion and media attention provide business with an exceptional opportunity to influence policy and rules. Further, many bureaucratic decisions affect individual companies rather than classes of firms, giving each company a better chance to triumph in front of an agency than before Congress (Godwin and Seldon 2002). Given the circumstances and conditions surrounding administrative decisionmaking, it is not surprising for Uslaner (1998, 206) to remark, "Cabinet departments and all manner of independent agencies . . . are gold mines for lobbyists." In contrast, environmental groups rarely have the level of access and resources necessary to mount an effective opposition to such business efforts in the agencies (Furlong 1997).

When important decisions by government agencies do not favor the interests of corporations, businesses will often seek litigation. The courts, therefore, are another institutional venue in which business lobbying takes place (Lehne 2001). Many large corporations boast impressive in-house legal staffs to study laws and proposed regulations, and when advantageous, to pursue litigation to protect their interests. Although litigation concerning environmental rules and regulations is fairly common, little systematic research has been done on how successful business has been in court. Scholars have found, however, that business is frequently a major player in environmental litigation and often gets its way (McSpadden 2000; O'Leary 2006). Any accurate assessment of the influence of business in the environmental policy arena should, in addition to other things, consider the success of corporations in the judicial system.

Interest Groups at the State and Local Level

In addition to an examination of interest-group activity in the various federal venues of the Congress, administrative agencies, and the courts, group activities designed to influence state and local government decisions merit careful assessment. Sadly, this is yet another area that has been relatively ignored by political scientists, both for policymaking in general and for the specific arena of environmental policy.

Over the past decade, scholarly work on environmental policymaking at the state and local level (including studies of federal-state relations) has expanded significantly and has increasingly used sophisticated methodological tools. These studies reflect the newly recognized importance of state and local governments in environmental and natural resource policies, and highlight what are often substantial differences among the states and among local governments in policy development and implementation decisions. The studies cover the territory from pollution control and conservation of watersheds and other critical lands to sustainability initiatives (e.g., Mazmanian and Kraft 1999; Portney 2003; Rabe 2006; Scheberle 2004). Yet the role of interest groups in policymaking at these levels has not been a central focus of concern. Some comparative state environmental policy studies clearly suggest that industry and environmental groups are important factors in affecting state decisions on policy adoption and implementation (Potoski and Woods 2002). We do not know, however, why business and other groups choose to get involved, the venues in which they act (e.g., the state legislature, state executive agencies, and the courts), what they do, and how often they get their way.

Even a cursory examination of recent state actions on environmental and resource issues suggests the importance of business and other groups, both currently and for the future. Parallel to regulatory reform efforts at the federal level, states have become increasingly receptive to business arguments about the need to reduce the burden associated with environmental protection. Many states have adopted such measures in recent years, for example—Wisconsin's Job Creation Act in 2004, which eased regulatory requirements on business. Commitment by federal policymakers to shift further decisions on use of public lands to the state level is certain to create new opportunities for business groups (and others) to play a strong role. One example is a Bush administration proposal of 2004 for a rule change affecting protection of roadless areas governed by the Forest Service. The new rule gives far greater discretion to state governors to expand or contract protection of the land, and critics have argued that forest products, mining, and energy companies are likely to press state governments to allow expanded access.

On the other side of the equation, a number of states have become leaders in fostering energy conservation, renewable energy use, and action to slow the rate of climate change, despite often-strong objections from business groups (Rabe 2004). Moreover, other states have adopted stringent pollution prevention initiatives, information disclosure policies related to use of toxic chemicals, and air pollution control measures that exceed federal standards, typically in opposition to the position favored by business groups (Kraft 2007; Rabe 2006). Similarly, many cities have adopted a variety of policies to promote sustainable development in their communities (Portney 2003). This book examines the actions taken by certain states and cities to protect the environment and conserve natural resources despite opposition from business interests inside their borders.

Analytic Framework

The chapters in this book focus on policy actions within each of the political venues described above—the U.S. Congress, federal executive agencies, federal courts, and state and local governments—as well as opportunities to affect public opinion and shape the policy agenda through use of the media and electoral processes. We are interested in whether, when, where, how, and why business groups choose to intervene in the policymaking process and with what degree of success. That is, we seek to learn whether these groups try to get involved in particular decisions or not, at what point they become active, in what venues they choose to act, what strategies and tactics they employ, why they make these choices, and what the consequences are—that is, whether they get their way or not. Our dependent variable is how often business influences environmental and natural resource policy and gets its way. The chapters examine both the processes of business-group involvement and the outcomes, using case studies as well as aggregate data, and they incorporate a range of explanatory variables.

We do not attempt to impose a structured analytic model to guide these investigations. But we do suggest consideration of some of the most important variables that affect these business-group choices and the outcomes. These include both endogenous and exogenous variables. Among the former are the characteristics of a particular industry or business group and its motivations, such as its size and economic resources, whether it is in the manufacturing sector or another, its competitiveness or profitability, the environmental beliefs and attitudes of senior management, regulatory cost-benefit calculations, and efforts to portray the company or business sector as socially responsible. Among the exogenous variables of note are prevailing political and economic conditions, the structure of public opinion, the extent of media coverage, and the strength of opposing interest groups, such as environmentalists.

To explain business actions and their effects, the authors draw from theories of the policy process and the institutional and political characteristics of the particular venue being studied—for example, the motivation of members of Congress to respond to constituency interests or the receptivity of state and local government officials to business groups because of their keen interest in fostering economic development. The saliency and complexity of specific environmental issues and the degree of conflict over them are also important because these conditions affect decisions by policy actors to become involved, to seek out pertinent information, and to adopt certain political strategies (Ingram and Mann 1983; Kingdon 1995; Gormley 1989).

The study of business-group involvement in the policy process faces a number of methodological hurdles. In addition to the questions we raised above, there is the long-standing challenge of measuring influence or power. That is, what kind of evidence speaks to the influence of business groups on public policy? Influence cannot be directly measured, and thus any judgment about the extent to which business or any other political actor affects policy decisions is necessarily constrained and somewhat subjective. Reasonable people might disagree about whether business groups did or did not influence a regulatory or natural resource decision. Given these limitations, the prevailing approaches within political science have been to study participation by groups, their "access" to policymakers, and perceptions of influence by policy actors. Scholars also compare what groups have sought with the subsequent policy actions by government to develop a rough measure of influence. Following this tradition, we suggest studying actions that business groups take to try to influence environmental policy decisions, and looking to decisions themselves to determine whether and, if so, to what extent business or other groups get their way.

At this stage in the study of business and environmental policy, scholars can help to clarify whether business is as dominant as some critics believe it is, or whether the influence of business groups is more subtle and complex than generally portrayed (Kamieniecki 2006). We believe we can learn much through the study of what business groups try to do, the timing and location of their interventions, and the effects.

What Follows

The chapters that follow are arranged in six sections. In chapter 2—the first of the two chapters in part II—Deborah Lynn Guber and Christopher J. Bosso examine how business seeks to shape the national policy agenda by influencing public attitudes through the use of the media and mass mobilization strategies, such as issue advocacy campaigns. They use the case of the Arctic National Wildlife Refuge to illustrate how groups can frame the issues and thus influence the way they are considered. In chapter 3, Robert J. Duffy focuses on the efforts of business organizations to influence elections, primarily through campaign contributions, and thereby affect the policymaking process. He, too, places the discussion within the context of issue framing and agenda setting.

In part III, chapters by Judith A. Layzer and Gary C. Bryner examine business lobbying of Congress. In chapter 4, Layzer analyzes the debate over climate change (human-caused global warming) to study the strategies employed by business in attempting to influence congressional decisions, both "inside lobbying" and the more visible public confrontations with its opponents in the environmental community. She also considers the role of business in framing the issue debate and challenging the scientific evidence used by advocates for climate change policy. In chapter 5, Bryner focuses on business efforts to shape decisions under the Clean Air Act (CAA), particularly the Bush administration's proposal of its Clean Skies initiative and its regulatory actions under the CAA's New Source Review provisions.

In part IV, two chapters analyze decisions within administrative agencies. In chapter 6, Scott R. Furlong examines the role that business and trade associations play in this venue, including the different strategies employed by business groups to influence the rulemaking process. In addition to utilizing case studies, he relies on surveys conducted in 2002 that describe the techniques groups use to influence regulatory policymaking. Cary Coglianese focuses on the EPA and its rulemaking process in chapter 7, with special attention to the agency's need for information about environmental risks and technology, and the opportunity that need creates for business groups to shape EPA decisions. He draws on a sample of recent EPA rulings as well as interviews with both agency staff and business groups to illuminate this process.

In part V, two chapters analyze business influence in the courts. In chapter 8, Paul S. Weiland examines the advantages and disadvantages of trying to influence environmental policy through the courts, and highlights how the structure and operation of the federal courts condition the strategies that business groups and others use and the success they enjoy. In chapter 9, Lettie McSpadden provides a historical account of the role of business and environmental groups in the courts, and uses a number of cases to examine industry challenges to executive-agency decisions in the areas of pollution control and land use. She pays particular attention to the political context in which the courts operate, and the opportunity afforded to business groups to affect appointment of justices to the courts.

In part VI, Barry G. Rabe and Philip A. Mundo along with Kent E. Portney turn to state and local governments. In chapter 10, Rabe and Mundo offer a broad examination of the role of business in state-level environmental policy decisions, including the adoption of innovations in selected states in the areas of pollution prevention, greenhouse gas emissions, and renewable energy portfolios. They also underscore the importance of state ballot propositions because they offer interest groups a unique opportunity to shape public policy. In chapter 11, Portney examines the role of business groups in local policymaking, especially in cities and particularly for land-use decisions and in promotion of local economic development agendas. He places this analysis into the broad context of changes that have occurred in cities around the country that have affected the local political landscape and the kinds of policies and programs that are possible, such as recent smart-growth initiatives and brownfield redevelopment.

The work presented in the chapters that follow advances knowledge of the role that business plays in environmental policy. The authors also point toward a rich and varied agenda for future research on critically important questions. Part VII ties the threads of the book together. In chapter 12—the final chapter—we turn to an assessment and integration of what the earlier chapters have told us and the implications for future study of business and environmental policy.

References

Bauer, Raymond A., Ithiel de Sola Pool, and Lewis Anthony Dexter. 1963. *American Business and Public Policy: The Politics of Foreign Trade.* New York: Atherton Press.

Baumgartner, Frank R., and Bryan D. Jones. 1993. *Agendas and Instability in American Politics.* Chicago: University of Chicago Press.

Baumgartner, Frank R., and Beth L. Leech. 1998. *Basic Interests: The Importance of Groups in Politics and in Political Science.* Princeton, NJ: Princeton University Press.

Berry, Jeffrey M. 1999. *The New Liberalism: The Rising Power of Citizen Groups.* Washington, DC: Brookings Institution.

Bosso, Christopher J. 2005. *Environment, Inc.: From Grassroots to Beltway.* Lawrence: University Press of Kansas.

Bosso, Christopher J., and Michael Thomas Collins. 2002. "Just Another Tool? How Environmental Groups Use the Internet." In Allan J. Cigler and Burdett A. Loomis, eds., *Interest Group Politics*, 6th ed., 95–114. Washington, DC: CQ Press.

Boyte, Harry C. 1980. *The Backyard Revolution.* Philadelphia: Temple University Press.

Browne, William. 1988. *Private Interests, Public Policy, and American Agriculture.* Lawrence: University of Kansas Press.

Cahn, Matthew A. 1995. *Environmental Deceptions: The Tension between Liberalism and Environmental Policymaking in the United States.* Albany: State University of New York Press.

Cater, Douglass. 1964. *Power in Washington.* New York: Random House.

Clawson, Dan, Alan Neustadt, and Mark Weller. 1998. *Dollars and Votes: How Business Campaign Contributions Subvert Democracy.* Philadelphia: Temple University Press.

Coglianese, Cary, and Laurie K. Allen. 2004. "Does Consensus Make Common Sense? An Analysis of EPA's Common Sense Initiative." *Environment* 46 (January/February): 10–25.

Coglianese, Cary, and Jennifer Nash, eds. 2006. *Leveraging the Private Sector: Management-Based Strategies for Improving Environmental Performance.* Washington, DC: Resources for the Future.

Cohen, Steven, Sheldon Kamieniecki, and Matthew A. Cahn. 2005. *Strategic Planning in Environmental Regulation: A Policy Approach That Works.* Cambridge, MA: MIT Press.

Dietz, Thomas, and Paul C. Stern, eds. 2003. *New Tools for Environmental Protection: Education, Information, and Voluntary Measures.* Washington, DC: National Academy Press.

Dowie, Mark. 1995. *Losing Ground: American Environmentalism at the Close of the Twentieth Century.* Cambridge, MA: MIT Press.

Duffy, Robert J. 2003. *The Green Agenda in American Politics: New Strategies for the Twenty-First Century.* Lawrence: University Press of Kansas.

Durant, Robert F., Daniel J. Fiorino, and Rosemary O'Leary, eds. 2004. *Environmental Governance Reconsidered: Challenges, Choices, and Opportunities.* Cambridge, MA: MIT Press.

Easterbrook, Gregg. 1995. *A Moment on the Earth: The Coming Age of Environmental Optimism.* New York: Viking.

Engler, Robert. 1977. *The Brotherhood of Oil: Energy Policy and the Public Interest.* Chicago: University of Chicago Press.

Furlong, Scott R. 1997. "Interest Group Influence on Rulemaking." *Administration and Society* 29 (July): 325–347.

Glazer, Amihai, and Lawrence S. Rothenberg. 2001. *Why Government Succeeds and Why It Fails.* Cambridge, MA: Harvard University Press.

Godwin, R. Kenneth, and Barry J. Seldon. 2002. "What Corporations Really Want from Government: The Public Provision of Private Goods." In Allan J. Cigler and Burdett A. Loomis, eds., *Interest Group Politics,* 6th ed., 205–224. Washington, DC: CQ Press.

Gonzalez, George A. 2001. *Corporate Power and the Environment: The Political Economy of U.S. Environmental Policy.* Lanham, MD: Rowman and Littlefield.

Gormley, William T. Jr. 1989. *Taming the Bureaucracy: Muscles, Prayers, and Other Strategies.* Princeton, NJ: Princeton University Press.

Gunningham, Neil, Robert A. Kagan, and Dorothy Thornton. 2003. *Shades of Green: Business, Regulation, and Environment.* Stanford, CA: Stanford University Press.

Hadwiger, Don F. 1982. *The Politics of Agricultural Research.* Lincoln: University of Nebraska Press.

Harrison, Kathryn, and Werner Antweiler. 2003. "Incentives for Pollution Abatement: Regulation, Regulatory Threats, and Non-Governmental Pressures." *Journal of Policy Analysis and Management* 22 (3): 361–382.

Hoffman, Andrew J. 2000. Integrating Environmental and Social Issues into Corporate Practice. *Environment* (June): 22–33.

Inglehart, Ronald. 1977. *The Silent Revolution.* Princeton, NJ: Princeton University Press.

Ingram, Helen M., and Dean E. Mann. 1983. "Environmental Protection Policy." In Stuart S. Nagel, ed., *Encyclopedia of Policy Studies,* 687–724. New York: Marcel Dekker.

Kamieniecki, Sheldon. 2006. *Corporate America and Environmental Policy: How Often Does Business Get Its Way?* Palo Alto, CA: Stanford University Press.

Kamieniecki, Sheldon, David Shafie, and Julie Silvers. 1999. "Forming Partnerships in Environmental Policy: The Business of Emissions Trading in Clean Air Management." *American Behavioral Scientist* 43 (September): 107–123.

Kerwin, Cornelius M. 2003. *Rulemaking: How Government Agencies Write Law and Make Policy*. 3rd ed. Washington, DC: CQ Press.

Kingdon, John W. 1995. *Agendas, Alternatives, and Public Policies*. 2nd ed. New York: Longman.

Korten, David C. 1995. *When Corporations Rule the World*. West Hartford, CT: Kumarian Press.

Kraft, Michael E. 2007. *Environmental Policy and Politics*. 4th ed. New York: Pearson Longman.

Kraft, Michael E., and Diane Wuertz. 1996. "Environmental Advocacy in the Corridors of Government." In James G. Cantrill and Christine L. Oravec, eds., *The Symbolic Earth: Discourse and Our Creation of the Environment*, 95–122. Lexington: University Press of Kentucky.

Lehne, Richard. 2001. *Government and Business: American Political Economy in Comparative Perspective*. New York: Chatham House.

Libby, Ronald T. 1998. *Eco-Wars: Political Campaigns and Social Movements*. New York: Columbia University Press.

Lindblom, Charles E. 1977. *Politics and Markets: The World's Political-Economic Systems*. New York: Basic Books.

Lomborg, Bjørn. 2001. *The Skeptical Environmentalist: Measuring the Real State of the World*. Cambridge: Cambridge University Press.

Lowi, Theodore J. 1969. *The End of Liberalism*. New York: Norton.

Lowry, William, R. 2003. "A New Era in Natural Resource Policies?" In Norman J. Vig and Michael E. Kraft, eds., *Environmental Policy*, 5th ed., 325–345. Washington, DC: CQ Press.

———. 2006. "A Return to Traditional Priorities in Natural Resource Policies." In Norman J. Vig and Michael E. Kraft, eds., *Environmental Policy*, 6th ed., 311–332. Washington, DC: CQ Press.

Mahoney, James. 2000. "Strategies of Causal Inference in Small-N Analysis." *Sociological Methods and Research* 28 (4) (May): 387–424.

Marcus, Alfred A., Donald A. Geffen, and Ken Sexton. 2002. *Reinventing Environmental Regulation: Lessons from Project XL*. Resources for the Future: Washington, DC.

Mazmanian, Daniel A., and Michael E. Kraft, eds. 1999. *Toward Sustainable Communities: Transition and Transformations in Environmental Policy*. Cambridge, MA: MIT Press.

McConnell, Grant. 1966. *Private Power and American Democracy*. New York: Knopf.

McFarland, Andrew S. 1991. "Interest Groups and Theories of Power in America." *British Journal of Political Science* 21:257–284.

————. 1998. "Social Movements and Theories of American Politics." In Anne N. Costain and Andrew S. McFarland, eds., *Social Movements and American Political Institutions: People, Passions, and Power.* Lanham, MD: Rowman and Littlefield.

McSpadden, Lettie. 2000. "Environmental Policy in the Courts." In Norman J. Vig and Michael E. Kraft, eds., *Environmental Policy*, 4th ed., 145–164. Washington, DC: CQ Press.

Milbrath, Lester W. 1963. *The Washington Lobbyists.* Chicago: Rand McNally.

Moe, Terry M. 1980. *The Organization of Interests: Incentives and the Internal Dynamics of Political Interest Groups.* Chicago: University of Chicago Press.

Moore, Curtis. 2002. "Rethinking the Think Tanks: How Industry-Funded 'Experts' Twist the Environmental Debate." *Sierra* 87:56–59, 73.

National Academy of Public Administration. 2000. *Environment.Gov: Transforming Environmental Protection for the 21st Century.* Washington, DC: NAPA.

Nature Conservancy. 2003. "Financials." *Nature Conservancy Magazine* 53:74.

Nounes, Anthony J. 2002. *Pressure and Power: Organized Interests in American Politics.* Boston: Houghton Mifflin.

O'Leary, Rosemary. 2006. "Environmental Policy in the Courts." In Norman J. Vig and Michael E. Kraft, eds., *Environmental Policy*, 6th ed., 148–168. Washington, DC: CQ Press.

Olson, Mancur. 1965. *The Logic of Collective Action: Public Goods and the Theory of Groups.* Cambridge, MA: Harvard University Press.

People for the American Way. 2004. *Buying a Movement.* Available on the organization's website: www.pfaw.org/pfaw/general/default.aspx?oid=2052. The document itself is undated.

Portney, Kent E. 2003. *Taking Sustainable Cities Seriously: Economic Development, the Environment, and Quality of Life in American Cities.* Cambridge, MA: MIT Press.

Potoski, Matthew, and Aseem Prakash. 2005. "Green Clubs and Voluntary Governance: ISO 14001 and Firms' Regulatory Compliance." *American Journal of Political Science* 49:235–248.

Potoski, Matthew, and Neal D. Woods. 2002. "Dimensions of State Environmental Policies: Air Pollution Regulation in the United States." *Policy Studies Journal* 30 (2): 208–226.

Prakash, Aseem. 2000. *Greening the Firm: The Politics of Corporate Environmentalism.* New York: Cambridge University Press.

Press, Daniel, and Daniel A. Mazmanian. 2006. "The Greening of Industry: Combining Government Regulation and Voluntary Strategies." In Norman J. Vig and Michael E. Kraft, eds., *Environmental Policy*, 6th ed., 264–287. Washington, DC: CQ Press.

Rabe, Barry G. 2004. *Statehouse and Greenhouse: The Emerging Politics of American Climate Change Policy.* Washington, DC: Brookings Institution Press.

Rabe, Barry G. 2006. "Power to the States: The Promise and Pitfalls of Decentralization." In Norman J. Vig and Michael E. Kraft, eds., *Environmental Policy*, 6th ed., 34–56. Washington, DC: CQ Press.

Robbins, Peter Thayer. 2001. *Greening the Corporation: Management Strategy and the Environmental Challenge*. London: Earthscan.

Rosenau, Pauline Vaillancourt. 2000. *Public-Private Policy Partnerships*. Cambridge, MA: MIT Press.

Rozell, Mark J., and Clyde Wilcox. 1999. *Interest Groups in American Campaigns: The New Face of Electioneering*. Washington, DC: CQ Press.

Scheberle, Denise. 2004. *Federalism and Environmental Policy*. 2nd ed. Washington, DC: Georgetown University Press.

Schlozman, Kay Lehman, and John T. Tierney. 1986. *Organized Interests and American Democracy*. New York: Harper and Row.

Scott, Andrew M., and Margaret A. Hunt. 1965. *Congress and Lobbies: Image and Reality*. Chapel Hill: University of North Carolina Press.

Shaiko, Ronald G. 1999. *Voices and Echoes for the Environment: Public Interest Representation in the 1990s and Beyond*. New York: Columbia University Press.

Simon, Julian. 1981. *The Ultimate Resource*. Princeton, NJ: Princeton University Press.

———. 1999. *Hoodwinking the Nation*. New Brunswick, NJ: Transaction Publishers.

Smith, Mark A. 2000. *American Business and Political Power: Public Opinion, Elections, and Democracy*. Chicago: University of Chicago Press.

Stimson, James A. 1999. *Public Opinion in America: Moods, Cycles, and Swings*. 2nd ed. Boulder, CO: Westview Press.

Uslaner, Eric M. 1998. "Lobbying the President and the Bureaucracy." In Paul S. Herrnson, Ronald G. Shaiko, and Clyde Wilcox, eds., *The Interest Group Connection: Electioneering, Lobbying, and Policymaking in Washington*. Chatham, NJ: Chatham House.

Vig, Norman J., and Michael E. Kraft, eds. 2006. *Environmental Policy*. 6th ed. Washington, DC: CQ Press.

Vogel, David. 1978. *Lobbying the Corporation: Citizen Challenges to Business Authority*. New York: Basic Books.

———. 1989. *Fluctuating Fortunes: The Political Power of Business in America*. New York: Basic Books.

———. 1996. *Kindred Strangers: The Uneasy Relationship between Politics and Business in America*. Princeton, NJ: Princeton University Press.

Walker, Jack L. Jr. 1983. "The Origins and Maintenance of Interest Groups in America." *American Political Science Review* 77:390–406.

Wildavsky, Aaron. 1995. *But Is It True? A Citizen's Guide to Environmental Health and Safety Issues*. Cambridge, MA: Harvard University Press.

II

Agenda Setting: Public Opinion, the Media, and Elections

2

Framing ANWR: Citizens, Consumers, and the Privileged Position of Business

Deborah Lynn Guber and Christopher J. Bosso

Introduction

On the morning of March 16, 2005, a narrowly divided U.S. Senate prepared to vote on a key amendment to a budget resolution designed to block oil and gas exploration in Alaska's Arctic National Wildlife Refuge (ANWR). While previous attempts to open the area to energy development had failed time and again, the momentum that day shifted. As correspondents in Washington struggled to explain the complex legislative maneuvers involved, crude oil futures on the New York Mercantile Exchange rose to more than $56 a barrel, the highest price on record since 1983.[1] With both stories breaking the news, President George W. Bush took advantage of a scheduled press conference in the White House briefing room. "I am concerned about the price of energy," he said. "I'm concerned about what it means to the average American family when they see the price of gasoline go up." After attributing the problem to an imbalance of supply and demand, and explaining the substance of his own stalled energy plan, the president added: "I hope Congress passes ANWR. There's a way to get some additional reserves here at home on the books."[2]

By the time the Senate voted later that day—fifty-one to forty-nine in favor of opening portions of the ANWR coastal plain to drilling—rhetoric on the subject had escalated into a war of words. Senator Lisa Murkowski of Alaska embraced the outcome as a "healthy balance between production and conservation," while Secretary of the Interior Gale Norton said the chamber had "cast a vote for America's energy security."[3] But it was a stinging defeat for environmentalists, who had blocked the measure repeatedly and passionately for more than two decades. The author of one Resources for the Future (RFF) study on ANWR declared the vote "a victory for the oil lobby," while the Sierra Club charged that it was "another example of the extraordinary disconnect between public opinion and Congressional action."[4] As advocates on both sides braced for the next public relations battle in the ANWR campaign, one group with a vested interest in the outcome was noticeably absent from the debate. The oil industry had decided to stay silent.

The chapters aligned in this book address, in varying ways, the conditions under which business groups influence environmental policy, and the opportunities and constraints that influence their success. Within that context, the ANWR case offers a worthy and fascinating challenge. While those in the environmental community may interpret the Senate vote as a triumph of interest-group politics over democratic institutions, the deliberate decision of major oil companies like British Petroleum (BP), ChevronTexaco, and ConocoPhillips to back away from open participation in the ANWR policy arena suggests a more complicated story. Indeed, we believe that the pragmatism of that decision speaks volumes about the fluid nature of business influence over political decisions. In an era where business no longer assumes what Lindblom (1977) once called a "privileged position" in American politics, today's corporations must work relentlessly to position their arguments in the public mind (Vogel 1989; Smith 2000). By drawing on research on agenda setting and issue framing, we use the ANWR case to illustrate how corporations and their ideological allies have tried to exploit the entwined issues of energy security, availability, and cost to their advantage. In the end, we argue that the public's ambivalence on energy and the environment, embodied in a tension between the public-minded "citizen" and the self-regarding "consumer," enabled the oil lobby to step back from ANWR and pursue a strategy of triangulation instead, where advertising campaigns and high-profile donations to mainstream environmental groups were used to mend corporate reputations, while distracting attention away from quieter efforts to direct the agenda of government in their favor.

A Policy Window on ANWR

Within months of his inauguration in January 2001, President George W. Bush placed as a centerpiece of his energy policy a long-standing goal of the oil industry and its largely Republican allies to allow drilling in the previously off-limits coastal plain of the Arctic National Wildlife Refuge. Indeed, mainly Democratic opposition to drilling in ANWR derailed energy legislation pushed by the president's father, George H. W. Bush, in 1991, just months after conclusion of the Persian Gulf War. Only after the elder Bush took ANWR off the table did a much watered-down energy bill pass a year later, and the Clinton administration stead-fastly opposed drilling in the region throughout the 1990s.[5] A decade later, however, opening up ANWR to oil production had returned as a key element in an administration's announced drive to foster energy independence by maximizing use of the nation's oil, coal, and natural gas.

Advocates of wilderness preservation and wildlife protection had always regarded drilling in the refuge as both unnecessary and reckless, given what they argued were its limited proven reserves and the potential for irreversible damage to sensitive tundra and resident wildlife.[6] But environmentalists had little influence over the new president's proposal. While their expectations of this Bush administration were low given the president's environmental record as governor of Texas and his long-standing ties to the oil industry—similar to those of Vice President Richard Cheney—they were shocked nevertheless to find themselves completely shut out of meetings of the administration's National Energy Policy Development Group. The administration even refused to release a list of task force participants, prompting the Sierra Club, Natural Resources Defense Council (NRDC), and other advocacy organizations to sue under the Freedom of Information Act to gain access to the records. The long legal tussle over the energy task force, ultimately decided along narrow legal grounds in the administration's favor, only reinforced perceptions about the extent to which its energy and environmental policies simply refracted industry priorities, and the degree to which the White House was eager to conceal those ties from public scrutiny.[7]

With no effective access to an administration dominated by former energy industry executives to an extent not seen since the Reagan administration, environmentalists could hope only to mobilize their own supporters and other sympathetic constituencies to obstruct action in Congress. Registered lobbyists representing the National Audubon Society and the National Wildlife Federation, among others, worked with their largely Democratic allies to shape a legislative blocking strategy even before the administration's proposal went to Capitol Hill. NRDC lawyers led the legal effort to open up the records of the energy task force in hopes that evidence of industry dominance over the process might provoke a public backlash. Staff at the Wilderness Society and other organizations mined federal records for data and reports to counter the administration's public arguments about the extent of proven reserves and the possible impacts of drilling on the preserve's ecosystem.

In spite of coordinated and well-organized opposition, an unexpected convergence of events soon opened a window of opportunity to strengthen the president's hand. First, arguments in favor of drilling in ANWR gained traction in the wake of the terrorist attacks of September 11, 2001, which renewed public debate over the nation's reliance on oil imports from the volatile Middle East. Within weeks, proponents were linking ANWR to energy independence, to national security, and to the administration's economic stimulus package. In remarks to labor union leaders, President Bush argued: "This energy bill that we're working on is a jobs bill. And when we explore for power, U.S. power, U.S. energy in ANWR, we're not only helping us become less dependent on foreign sources of crude oil and foreign sources of energy, we're creating jobs for American workers, jobs so that men and women can put food on the table."[8]

Members of Congress pushed the argument even further. "It is appropriate for Americans to examine again our increasing dependence on foreign oil, especially Mideast oil," argued Senator Frank Murkowski (R-Alaska), a key proponent of drilling in ANWR. "Each senator is going to have to recognize his obligations to our national security as opposed to environmental extremists."[9] Senator James Inhofe (R-Oklahoma) went so far as to attach an ANWR amendment to an October 2001 defense authorization bill, arguing that energy independence was now a component of national security policy. That tactic failed to generate sufficient support, but it signaled a new level of intensity in a debate framed by proponents in increasingly patriotic terms.[10] Environmentalists countered that national security would be better served through a strategy of aggressive energy conservation, including raising the average fuel economy on automobiles, sport utility vehicles (SUVs), and light trucks, but such proposals had little traction within an administration agenda typified by Vice President Cheney's view, expressed previously, that while conservation was a laudable "private virtue," under the circumstances it could hardly be considered serious public policy.[11]

Several other exogenous events likewise strengthened the case, at least rhetorically, for increasing domestic oil production. A massive electrical blackout in August 2003, which temporarily cut power to 50 million residential customers in the upper Midwest and Northeast, highlighted the vulnerability of the country's energy grids. Even though very little of the nation's electricity is generated from oil, and drilling in ANWR would do nothing to modernize the patchwork system of transmitting electricity that allowed the outage to occur, the emergency nevertheless gave new momentum to the administration's energy plan.[12] Representative Billy Tauzin (R-LA), chair of the House Energy and Commerce Committee, described the need to open up ANWR as a "moral obligation," and suggested that critics should try to "live in the dark and see how they like it."[13]

Meanwhile, the retail price of a gallon of gasoline began to surge, surpassing the $2 mark in spring 2004, then spiking again to more than $3 in the aftermath of Hurricane Katrina, which damaged oil industry infrastructure along the Gulf Coast in August 2005. House Republicans and their ideological allies at think tanks like the National Center for Policy Analysis and the Competitive Enterprise Institute used the trend to press their agenda in the media, insisting that "the latest gas spike [was] more evidence of the need to pass an energy bill that would boost domestic supplies by opening the Arctic National Wildlife Refuge in Alaska to oil drilling."[14] Like the blackout, the connection between ANWR and gasoline prices was theoretical at best—dependent first on finding meaningful reserves, and even then on a delay of five to ten years in extracting them—but the issue played squarely to the public's increasingly anxious mood. As Smith (2002) notes, when people perceive an energy "crisis" they typically demand government action and changes in policy to manage the problem. The president was prepared to offer both.

Finally, proponents of drilling in ANWR gained even stronger partisan and ideological control of government in the November 2004 elections. Not only was President Bush elected to a second term in office, but Republicans also strengthened their control over both chambers of

Congress, most critically the Senate, where they secured a net gain of four seats.[15] Equally important were the Democratic losses, chief among them Senate Minority Leader Thomas Daschle (D-SD), whose role in blunting the administration's drive to open up ANWR had become a part of his opponent's campaign theme that Daschle was a partisan obstructionist.[16]

This strengthened Republican majority used its advantage to dictate the formal approval process on ANWR when the 109th Congress convened in early 2005. In particular, the March 16 vote was embedded strategically in an amendment to the budget bill, which according to Senate deficit-control rules adopted in the mid-1990s was subject to a vote by simple majority. As a result, Senate Democrats were unable to wield, or even threaten to use, their only effective tactical weapon, the filibuster. More important, the proposal's inclusion in a larger budget bill reduced its saliency to the broader public and thereby lessened the capacity of environmentalists to mobilize against it.

Students of agenda setting have long pointed to the creation of "policy windows" to explain the timing of key legislative decisions. While early accounts likened the process, quite memorably, to a "garbage can" (Cohen, March, and Olsen 1972), later studies pointed to a less chaotic metaphor, emphasizing the convergence of various "streams" that flow independently through the political system: problems in need of a solution, policy proposals waiting for action, and political events that demand attention, including external crises, election results, and shifts in public mood. According to Kingdon (1995), a "policy window" opens at the moment in which a recognized problem is coupled with a viable solution, and the political climate is ripe for change. "Policy entrepreneurs" are responsible for gaining the attention of important people, for coupling solutions to problems, and for linking both problems and solutions to politics. Ultimately in the case of ANWR, the window of opportunity created by the aftermath of September 11, energy blackouts, soaring gasoline prices, and Republican majorities in Washington worked to the benefit of drilling proponents, giving oil companies their best chance in years to realize a long-standing goal to expand their efforts in Alaska beyond the North Slope. Indeed, if the fortunes of business fluctuate over time (Vogel 1989), the political arena in 2005 offered, in the words of one observer, "the most business-friendly climate since the days of President McKinley."[17]

As a result of this convergence of forces, overt lobbying by the oil industry or other major elements of the business community on ANWR was notably absent in the months preceding the Senate vote. They were content, instead, to allow the administration and congressional Republicans to take the lead. In fact, most major oil companies gave the distinct impression that they had grown disinterested in ANWR altogether. On the one hand, industry insiders claimed to be more skeptical than the administration about ANWR's proven reserves.[18] When compared to other contested areas for exploration, including Florida's Gulf Coast, they seemed to question its long-term economic viability. On the other, the issue had become such a political "hot potato" that oil companies already sensitive about their public image wanted nothing to do with another open fight over what environmentalists called "one of our greatest national treasures."[19] ChevronTexaco, British Petroleum (BP), and ConocoPhillips cut their public ties to the prominent pro-drilling consortium, Arctic Power, and crafted their press releases carefully so as not to ignite concern about despoiling nature. ExxonMobil reiterated its support for "environmentally responsible development within the Coastal Plain of the Arctic National Wildlife Refuge," while BP said in its official statement that "we have taken the view that it is up to the people and the U.S. government to decide whether drilling should occur there. If drilling is authorized, we will then decide whether to bid on the acreage on offer" based on a determination of what "can be explored and developed without adverse impact to wildlife."[20] That the oil industry felt it necessary to avoid controversy and to express diffidence to the outcome of the political process speaks volumes about the degree to which the influence of business is constrained by popular opinion (Smith 2000), particularly on salient issues.

Molding Public Opinion

Just one week prior to the Senate's March 16 vote on the ANWR budget amendment, respondents in a Gallup survey were asked to select the statement about energy and the environment with which they most agreed: "Protection of the environment should be given priority, even at the risk of limiting the amount of energy supplies—such as oil, gas, and coal—which the United States produces," or the "development of U.S. energy supplies—such as oil, gas, and coal—should be given priority, even if the environment suffers to some extent." When pressed, 52 percent of those responding prioritized environmental protection, while 39 percent opted for greater development of energy supplies.[21] In light of the ongoing war in Iraq, and mounting concern over gasoline prices, the clarity of that preference seemed impressive. But it was hardly indisputable.

Survey researchers frequently ask Americans whether they support an increase in domestic oil production. The results range wildly, and are conditioned by a number of factors. When presented as a way "to reduce the country's dependence on imports of Middle East oil," 73 percent approve of "increasing oil drilling in the U.S."[22] However, support for drilling erodes when national security concerns are balanced against reminders of environment impacts, or when respondents are encouraged to consider "other solutions," including energy conservation.[23] Interest in expanded oil production also wanes when attention is shifted from the general to the specific.[24] While respondents are quick to endorse drilling when the location is defined vaguely within U.S. borders, they are reluctant to support it in any number of places mentioned by name, including the Great Lakes, Florida's Gulf Coast, public lands in the Rocky Mountains, or, most significant of all, Alaska's Arctic National Wildlife Refuge.[25]

In summer 2001, when the president began his push on ANWR, Americans were inclined to believe that energy had become a "very serious" issue—more serious, in fact, according to poll trends, than at any time since 1977.[26] In response, 63 percent supported the broad goals of "drilling for natural gas on public lands," and 64 percent backed "investing in more gas pipelines."[27] A combined 70 percent warned that it was either "very important" or "extremely important" that the president and Congress do something to *increase* oil and gas production, and 53 percent were willing to offer tax breaks to corporations to provide incentives for drilling to be done.[28] Nevertheless, there was stubborn resistance to the idea of "opening up the Alaskan Arctic Wildlife Refuge for oil exploration." Just 38 percent of those polled supported the plan as a way "to deal with the energy situation."[29]

Four years later the verdict seemed less certain. Dueling polls featured prominently in the press seemed to swing wildly in one direction, then the other, giving an impression of confusion and volatility. In January 2005, a Luntz Research Group study conducted on behalf of a consortium of pro-drilling interests known as Arctic Power, found 53 percent in favor of "exploration, development, and production of oil and natural gas" in ANWR as "one of the ways to increase our nation's energy supply," while a December 2004 Zogby International survey funded by the Wilderness Society found 55 percent *opposed* when asked if they thought "oil companies should be allowed to drill for oil in America's Arctic National Wildlife Refuge." Meanwhile, Harris Interactive found 53 percent in support of allowing companies "the ability to drill for oil in certain areas" such as ANWR "to decrease our reliance on foreign oil," while according to Gallup 53 percent believed the region "should not be opened up for oil exploration."[30] To take the evidence at face value meant that the public either supported drilling in ANWR by up to a seventeen-point margin, or opposed it by an identical margin. As David W. Moore, a senior Gallup poll editor, wondered: "Can opinion be that vague?"[31]

The answer was "almost certainly yes," Moore explained, since the public's knowledge on the subject was shockingly low. According to the Luntz Research Group poll, 87 percent could not name a single word found in the acronym ANWR, while the same proportion failed to accurately place its location within the state of Alaska. When the issue was narrowly focused, respondents seemed to take their cue from the name that was read to them, which allowed the phrase "wildlife refuge" to tap into a latent store of environmental concern. Yet without a clear understanding of the issue to anchor their responses, most were willing to be persuaded by the arguments they were offered. Hence, when the issue was "implicitly framed as one of reducing U.S. dependence on foreign oil and dealing with the high price of oil and gas," people were willing to support drilling in ANWR by a "decisive margin."[32] When a range of other alternatives (including energy conservation) were emphasized instead, the margin swung like a pendulum in the opposite direction. Not surprisingly, such dualities offered advocates on both sides ample opportunity to shape their discursive arguments.

Experiments in question wording have demonstrated time and again how minor alterations in survey design can produce dramatically different results (Schuman and Presser 1981). As Zaller and Feldman (1992, 582) point out, polls do not simply *measure* public opinion, "they also shape and channel it by the manner in which they frame issues, order the alternatives, and otherwise set the context of the question." They believe that on a wide range of issues, people hold in their heads opposing considerations, which under varied circumstances might lead them to one decision or another. When interviewed by pollsters they call to mind a sample of those ideas: some that have been made salient by recent experiences or events, and others that they have been primed to consider by the questionnaire itself. Since most respondents are ambivalent about most issues in the first place, their answers can be particularly vulnerable to "framing effects" that are created—whether intentionally or not—by the order in which questions are presented, the language that is used, or the response options that are offered.

In this sense, public sentiment on the issue of drilling in ANWR should come as no surprise. If policy preferences can be swayed with relative ease by the context in which an issue is described, the Arctic National Wildlife Refuge might be said to offer a "self-activating" frame. The name itself invokes an image of public land permanently set aside for wildlife protection, while the nearly unavoidable mention of Alaska is likely to trigger memories of the *Exxon Valdez* oil spill in Prince William Sound in 1989. Ten years later, 62 percent of those polled by Gallup correctly recalled, without prompting, the name of the oil company involved in the accident, 66 percent believed that there was "still oil left in the water and on the beaches," and nearly everyone—a staggering 91 percent—believed that a similar accident was likely to happen again in the future.[33]

In short, environmental groups like the Wilderness Society, which financed the Zogby International poll on ANWR, had every incentive to craft their questions narrowly, and in strictly preservationist terms. After all, asking respondents whether they supported drilling for oil in Alaska was likely to bring emotive images of oil-soaked seals and birds to mind, pressing even ill-informed respondents into opposition. In contrast, for the Luntz Research Group and its client Arctic Power, counteracting that frame required either removing the name itself by referring to the obscure acronym ANWR, or juxtaposing it with frames of equal value by directing attention to energy prices or national security.[34] The results proved so changeable in the end that the staff at the Environmental News Service complained, quite simply, "you get what you poll for."[35]

Crafting an Issue Frame

If, as Walter Lippmann (1922) so famously wrote, people respond to the "pictures in their heads" rather than to some objective reality, the role that politicians, corporations, and interest groups play in constructing those images warrants careful attention. The capacity to frame an issue strategically by controlling the cues and symbols cognitively linked to it may be one of the most important tools that these groups have at their disposal (Jacoby 2000). Whether in the limited context of a questionnaire or in the broader realm of political debate, issue framing allows elites to exploit seemingly inconsistent attitudes held by average Americans to their advantage.

When the narrow subject of drilling in ANWR failed to attract popular support in early 2001, President Bush changed course. He directed attention to a broader set of concerns by reference to a weakening U.S. economy and an emerging "energy crisis," reminding Americans of soaring gasoline prices and electrical blackouts, both of which in his view provided defensible ground for a rollback of environmental regulations. By summer 2004, according to the Pew Research Center, "the high price of gasoline" had come to dominate public attention. Legal sovereignty had been transferred to a new Iraqi government just weeks before, and violent conflict involving U.S. soldiers stationed in the region continued, but far more respondents said they followed news stories on gasoline prices "very closely."[36] The president used the opportunity to press to open more federal lands to oil drilling to reduce American dependence on reserves abroad. "These measures have been repeatedly blocked by members of the Senate," he said, "and American consumers are paying the price."[37]

The administration's overall strategy was crafted, in part, on the advice of Republican pollster Frank Luntz, president of the Luntz Research Group. In a lengthy 2002 memorandum to party leaders, Luntz advised them to assure voters that they were committed to "preserving and protecting" the environment, but that it could be done "more wisely and effectively."[38] He told Republicans to emphasize that "exploring" for oil in ANWR—not drilling—was just "one component of a comprehensive energy policy," and not to "allow the radical environmentalists to force you into talking about only this one component."[39] In the end, the rhetorical strategy succeeded by creating a coherent bundle of issues "stronger than the sum of its parts."[40] As William Saletan, writing for the liberal online magazine *Slate*, had warned in May 2001:

> Right now, most Americans oppose drilling in ANWR. But the more we discuss that idea in terms of energy rather than the environment, the more the political equation changes. Economic considerations enumerated by Bush and Cheney— "sharp increases in fuel prices from home heating oil to gasoline," electrical threats to "the high-tech industry," strangled economic growth and layoffs—add weight to the pro-drilling side of the equation. National security concerns—the dependence on foreign oil that, in Cheney's words, makes it "easy for a regime such as Iraq to hold us hostage"—enter the debate, as well.[41]

Four months later, the administration's response to the September 11 terrorist attacks, and its recasting of ANWR as a national security issue, would demonstrate Saletan's prescience.

If Luntz's advice to Republicans was to enlarge the debate over drilling in Alaska to energy policy in general, a converse decision was made to narrow simultaneously the range of possible solutions. As Stone (1989, 282) argues, "problem definition is a process of image making, where the images have to do fundamentally with attributing cause, blame, and responsibility." When promoting issues in need of government redress, she says, political actors "*deliberately portray* them in ways calculated to gain support for their side . . . all the while making it seem as though they are simply describing facts." By largely ignoring the value of energy conservation and prioritizing accelerated production instead, the administration—and Vice President Cheney, in particular—encouraged American consumers to believe that they were "on the same team" as the oil companies themselves, driven by the same shared impulse.[42] It was a strategy that on the one hand adroitly reversed the public's usual suspicions about the greed and culpability of Big Oil in raising gas prices (Farhar 1994), and on the other muted criticism of the president's close ties to industry executives. After all, says Saletan, during an energy crisis "Bush and Cheney's careers in the oil industry begin to look more like expertise than like a conflict of interest."[43]

Finally, since those in the oil industry were acutely sensitive to the fragile nature of their corporate reputations, they pursued an aggressive public relations strategy, funding advertising campaigns that promoted good deeds to an audience of Americans eager for both affordable gas and pristine landscapes (Alsop 2004). BP's "Beyond Petroleum" and "Plug the Sun" ads, Shell Oil's "Profits or Principles" philosophy, and Chevron's "People Do" campaign all advanced corporate and environmental responsibility. While such self-promotion may have seemed absurd and even comical at times, as in the case of one DuPont television commercial that depicted sea lions applauding a passing oil tanker with their flippers to the strains of Beethoven's "Ode to Joy," the subtle, cumulative effects on popular opinion of what some term "greenwashing" cannot be underestimated.[44]

Business as a Strategic Player

We believe that the Senate's vote in favor of drilling in ANWR in March 2005 was not a result of direct business lobbying per se, but rather the culmination of its long-term efforts to shape the overall composition and direction of government, and its success in framing the broader public debate. In this sense, we concur with Smith (2000, 10), who argues in his detailed and long-term study of corporate influence in American politics that the reasons "business positions either win or lose are traceable not to any kind of direct leverage that business exerts, but rather result most importantly from the impacts of public opinion and election outcomes." Within that context, three long-term strategies in particular stand out.

Supporting the Party of Business

Other chapters in this book address corporate electoral and lobbying strategies, but it is worth noting here that the "fluctuating fortunes" of business (Vogel 1989) depend in no small part on Republican dominance over the institutions of government. Business in the general sense can be more or less unified (Smith 2000), and it can be more or less in favor with the American people but, ultimately, the primacy of a business agenda in American politics is linked to the capacity of the GOP to refract those values and goals through the systems of representation and governance.

In this regard, the resurgence of business since the mid-1970s, at least in comparison to environmental and other progressive values, reflects the broader regional and ideological realignments of and ideological polarization between the two major parties, especially on issues related to role of government (Shipan and Lowry 2000). More than forty years ago Schattschneider (1960, 42–42) observed that the success of business in politics owes less to any "pressure" it puts on Congress than to the fact that "Republican members of Congress are committed in advance to a general pro-business attitude." What has changed in four decades is the degree to which Republicans are unified by libertarian conservative values on environmental and natural resource matters, as well as their overall capacity to deliver on their beliefs. Republicans have not only held onto the presidency for all but eight of the twenty-four years since the election of Ronald Reagan—thereby ushering in a reshaping of the federal judiciary—they have also controlled one or more chambers of Congress for sixteen years, and almost entirely since their big breakthrough in 1994. The cumulative result is a far cry from the days when a Democratic Congress dueled with Richard Nixon over which of the institutions on opposite ends of Pennsylvania Avenue could lead on the environment (Jones 1975, 175–210). The 2004 elections only reinforced Republican, and by extension, business dominance in Washington. The March 16 vote on ANWR "only happened because Americans elected a larger [Republican] majority," said Jim DeMint (S.C.), one of seven new GOP senators who supported oil drilling.[45]

Issue Framing

Business interests are not simply content to support Republicans, of course. Corporations also see their influence tied directly to a widespread and fundamental societal fealty to their core belief system, one rooted in the discursive elements of free-market capitalism, private property rights, freedom of individual choice, and minimal government—the language and belief system of the consumer.

"Consider the possibility that businessmen achieve an indoctrination of citizens so that citizens' volitions serve not their own interests but the interests of businessmen," Lindblom (1977, 202) advised. "Citizens then become allies of businessmen. The privileged position of business comes to be widely accepted. In electoral politics, no great struggle needs to be fought." This dimension of Lindblom's often-criticized argument bears serious consideration since it speaks to the broader argument about the importance of problem definition and issue framing in politics (Stone 1988; Bosso 1994b). Indeed, the privileged position of business can be said to hold so long as its core values dominate public discourse. The famous Luntz memorandum underscores the importance of language, and reminds us that rhetoric, classically understood, is key to winning policy debates. Positive value frames like "choice" and "freedom" lie at the core of any discursive argument made by business, forcing opponents to devise frames that speak to similarly potent values of "equity" or, in the case of ANWR, an iconic image of undisturbed "beauty."

Business works hard to shore up its preferred discursive frames, directly through public relations and advertising campaigns, indirectly through financial support for libertarian conservative think tanks like the American Enterprise Institute, Hudson Institute, Competitive Enterprise Institute, Heritage Foundation, and Cato Institute, not to mention their many state and regional brethren. Such strategic, long-term support for the generation and dissemination of libertarian ideas has paid off with the clear dominance of the market frame in virtually every area of the environmental and energy policy debate, to the point that environmentalists invariably are forced to start out by defending any government "intrusion" into the market (Smith 2000). Business also maintains its own array of peak associations like the Business Roundtable, Chamber of Commerce, and National Federation of Independent Businesses. Even if different elements of the business community and their respective peak associations disagree occasionally on specific policy proposals (e.g., universal health care), they typically align on core values and agendas. More important, those values are promoted as naturally "American."

Greenwashing

Constrained by popular opinion on the one hand, and emboldened by political allies on the other, business interests find it profitable to play both ends against the middle by pursuing their goals privately with allies in Washington while simultaneously maintaining a green image to a citizenry that wants to balance environmental values with consumer preferences. As Alsop (2004) argues, Americans want to believe that they can have both. Business plays on that desire through donations to moderate environmental organizations and, more cynically, through "front" organizations like the trade association–backed Global Climate Coalition.

The issue of corporate money is explosive within organized environmentalism (Bosso 1994a, 2005). The studiously apolitical land conservancies (e.g., Nature Conservancy and Conservation International) are by far the most successful seekers of direct corporate support, followed by more traditional wildlife organizations (e.g., National Wildlife Federation and Ducks Unlimited) and more market-oriented groups like the Izaak Walton League. In fiscal year 2004, for example, direct corporate donations comprised 8 percent of Conservation International's over $92 million in revenues and 6 percent of the Nature Conservancy's $865 million. These donations came from a wide array of corporations, among them oil giants British Petroleum, ChevronTexaco, and ConocoPhillips, automobile makers Ford and General Motors, and major utility companies like American Electric Power and Cinergy.[46] The relative importance of direct corporate support seems modest compared to other sources (e.g., individual contributions and foundations), but it has tremendous symbolic value for environmental organizations that seek to project a "responsible" and "nonpartisan" image.

For environmental activists on the left in particular, corporate donations are little more than cynical ploys to "greenwash" their public images. The World Wildlife Fund, for example, accepts donations from, among others, DuPont, ChevronTexaco, Alcoa, Philip Morris, and Home Depot, the nation's largest home-improvement store operator. Meanwhile, each of these corporations was targeted for its behavior by another environmental group. Home Depot, for example, was the object of a global boycott organized by the Rainforest Action Network until it agreed to stop selling lumber harvested from endangered forests in the United States and abroad.[47] Similar charges of corporate "greenwashing" have been aimed at the Nature Conservancy for including on its board executives from American Electric Power, branded the nation's worst power company by the NRDC for its record on air pollution, and General Motors, which Environmental Defense called "Global Warmer Number One."[48]

Corporate money is, if nothing else, good public relations, especially when the company or industry in question might be under public scrutiny. Donations to the Nature Conservancy or World Wildlife Fund by Home Depot or Chevron cannot help but burnish a company's image. To critics, however, this money is an outright bribe, and some wonder how any environmental group that takes it can speak critically of corporate behavior when events warrant. For example, in 2000 the Ford Motor Company Fund (not to be confused with the Ford Foundation) gave out $14 million in grants to environmental organizations, including $5 million to Conservation International for a center for environmental leadership in business and another $5 million to Audubon for bird monitoring and public education.[49] Meanwhile, Ford was being assailed by other environmental organizations for the poor fuel efficiency of its sport utility vehicles. In one particularly notable instance, a coalition of environmental groups ran advertisements in major newspapers that prominently portrayed company chairman Bill Ford as a grotesque Pinocchio, the wooden puppet whose nose grew each time he told a lie. Ford's fib, according to the advertisement, was his pledge in 2000 to improve fuel efficiency of his company's SUV fleet by 25 percent in five years, a goal toward which no progress had been made.[50]

Politics and Markets

Whether through direct or indirect means, business gains its "greatest returns" in politics when it successfully influences the public mood. "Policies desired by business," says Smith (2000, 167), "would then become a byproduct of the strong linkages between the opinions of citizens and the behavior of elected officials." But if public opinion on issues like ANWR is ill-informed, ambivalent, and confused, *which* opinion do policymakers follow, and *which* does business seek to shape?

Scholars have long recognized that decisions reached in the voting booth differ from those made in the marketplace. In general, consumer choices are thought to reflect a miserly self-interest, while citizens are motivated by more altruistic concerns when making collective decisions for society at large (Buchanan 1954; Buchanan and Tullock 1962; Wilson and Banfield 1964, 1965; Martinez-Vazquez 1981; Sagoff 1988). When

Americans are polled on energy and environmental issues, those expectations are frequently met. If the subject is placed in a *political* context—by comparing interest in a variety of news stories, by ranking political priorities, or by considering a range of policy options—environmental concern tends to rank high in the public's consciousness. However, when those same topics are positioned in a *market* context, where the cost of gasoline or home heating fuel is borne by the individual alone, the citizen quickly gives way to his or her alter ego, the consumer.

As the ANWR case demonstrates, however, those positions are far from static. Because of the ambivalence of public opinion and the power of issue framing, energy issues often span the chasm between public and private, blurring lines of distinction between the citizen and the consumer. On the one hand, a well-defined frame might encourage consumers to view the purchase of a fuel-efficient automobile as a patriotic act.[51] On the other, an altogether different frame might persuade citizens to personalize the benefits of domestic oil production in a way that amplifies demand for lower gasoline prices. The very fluidity of those boundaries means that the *psychology* of choice matters more than its location (Guber 2003).

In the end, we argue that business enjoys a privileged position in American politics if and when its interests align with those of the consumer. Such an alignment does not happen naturally given the individual's wariness of corporate power in the abstract. It is, instead, continuously cultivated and maintained. Business works hard to foster rhetorical arguments that merge politics and markets, citizens and consumers, on issues like ANWR that fall somewhere in between. For example, one week prior to the March 2005 vote in the U.S. Senate, David O'Reilly, chairman and chief executive of ChevronTexaco, said in an interview with the *Washington Post*: "We'd like to see it developed. It's just another opportunity to meet a consumer need from within the country and reduce imports by a comparable amount." Carl Pope, executive director of the Sierra Club, was quick to counter that drilling there "would not save consumers a dime at the pump," but the very fact that he responded through a market frame on ANWR showed how much the terms of the debate had been shaped by the other side.[52]

The public debate over ANWR brings to mind Schattschneider's (1960, 68) famous dictum that "the definition of the alternatives is the supreme instrument of power." A generation of scholarly literature on agenda setting and problem definition (e.g., Cobb and Elder 1972; Rochefort and Cobb 1994; Baumgartner and Jones 1993) underscores Schattschneider's fundamental argument. Indeed, for those who want to shape public discourse—and by extension, public policy—on energy and the environment, negotiating the boundary that divides the citizen from the consumer may present the biggest challenge of all. For instance, in buying a new automobile, the consumer makes choices based on preferences any behavioral economist can explain—price, quality, convenience, and performance, even simplistic attributes like cupholders and tilting steering wheels. Nowhere do those preferences easily include ecosystem preservation, energy independence, or a host of other factors not included on the side-window pricelist. Consumers seldom consider such matters, but citizens do. Of course, as Tullock (1976, 5) reminds us, "voters and consumers are essentially the same people. Mr. Smith buys and votes; he is the same man in the supermarket and the voting booth." But he is, increasingly, pulled in one direction or another by the appeals of competing elites.

To the extent that the consumerist frame wins the discursive war on issues like ANWR, Lindblom is at least half right. It is not business that enjoys a privileged position in American politics. It is the *consumer*. Corporations and their Republican allies just happen to speak the language. The practical effect on environmental policy, however, is one and the same.

Conclusions

By the end of 2005, the momentum enjoyed by drilling proponents was challenged once again. In November, Democratic victories in the governors' races in New Jersey and Virginia hinted at the public's growing dissatisfaction with Republican majorities in Washington. Anxious to avoid the appearance of party unrest before the 2006 midterm elections, GOP leaders in the House and Senate deleted authorization for oil exploration in ANWR from the omnibus budget bill when it became clear that it and other controversial provisions—in particular, cuts in Medicare spending, farm subsidies, and student loans—were eroding support for the entire bill among a small but pivotal group of moderate northern Republicans.[53] The following month, Senator Ted Stevens (R-Alaska) attempted to append the decision on ANWR to a defense spending bill. However, late in the night of December 21, it too was blocked in order to ensure the success of the party's other priorities, including Hurricane Katrina relief and funding for an avian flu vaccine.[54] Members of the environmental lobby, who had monitored the outcome from a reception area outside the Senate chamber, rejoiced in what the Sierra Club called "a victory for all Americans."[55] But Murkowski, showing the strain of a long and bitter struggle, said simply: "It is the shortest day of the year, and it feels like it has gone on and on and on."[56]

Republican leaders in the House and Senate vowed to revive authorization on ANWR early in 2006, arguing that rising oil prices, the need to provide alternatives to oil production along the hurricane-exposed Gulf of Mexico, growing demand in China and India, and fears of potential disruption in global oil supplies linked to a dispute over Iran's nuclear program, made such a move imperative.[57] As if to underscore these arguments, in January 2006 the Interior Department announced that it would open up for drilling nearly 400,000 acres previously off limits in the National Petroleum Reserve, about 150 miles west of ANWR, in the process reversing a Clinton-era compromise intended to protect migratory bird habitats and native hunting grounds.[58] Environmentalists vowed to continue their fight on both fronts.

Ultimately, these recent events underscore and reinforce the basic dynamics at play. We believe that the future of ANWR will depend not only on the lobbying efforts of business and industry, or the increasingly defensive pressure applied by environmental groups. It will hinge as well—if not more—on the degree to which the consumerist frame continues to dominate discourse on energy policy overall, and the extent to which the Republican Party maintains and expands its control over the instruments of government decisionmaking.

Notes

1. Justin Blum, "OPEC Move Fails to Stop Oil Price Rise," *Washington Post*, March 17, 2005, E03.

2. White House Press Release, "President's Press Conference," March 16, 2005, www.whitehouse.gov/news/releases/2005/03/20050316–3.html.

3. Lisa Murkowski, "Speech to the Alaska Legislature," March 30, 2005, http://murkowski.senate.gov/speech_033005.html; Department of the Interior, "Statement by Secretary of the Interior Gale Norton," March 16, 2005, www.doi.gov/news/05_News_Releases/050316d.

4. Resources for the Future, "Author Responds to Senate Vote Allowing Oil Drilling in Arctic National Wildlife Refuge," *RFF Press*, March 17, 2005, www.rff.org/rff/RFF_Press/CustomBookPages/loader.cfm?url=/commonspot/ security/getfile.cfm&PageID=17125; Sierra Club, "Statement on Passage of Budget Resolution Conference Report," April 29, 2005, www.sierraclub.org/ pressroom/releases/pr2005-04-29.asp.

5. Clifford Krauss, "Energy Bill Is Derailed in Senate," *New York Times*, November 2, 1991, A37.

6. Editorial, "The Iraq Gambit for Drilling in ANWR," *Seattle Times*, April 15, 2002, B4.

7. David Stout, "Appeals Court Backs Cheney in Secrecy Case," *New York Times*, May, 11 2005, A1.

8. White House Press Release, "Remarks by the President in Meeting with Labor Leaders, International Brotherhood of Teamsters, Washington, D.C.," January 17, 2002, www.whitehouse.gov/news/releases/2002/01/20020117-5.html.

9. Miguel Llanos, "Green Issues Sidelined by September 11: How the Tragedy Changed the Environmental Landscape," *MSNBC*, November 14, 2001, www.msnbc.com/news/649869.asp.

10. Editorial, "Oil Opportunism," *Boston Globe*, September 27, 2001, A13.

11. Geneva Overholser, "Cheney's Swagger a Waste of Energy," *Boston Globe*, May 7, 2001, A19.

12. Bill Walsh, "Blackout Adds Fuel to Energy Debate," *Times-Picayne*, September 3, 2003, 6.

13. Juliet Eilperin, "GOP Renews Hopes for Alaska Oil Drilling: Blackout Boosts Energy Bill's Prospects, but Democrats Stand Firm on Keeping Refuge Off-Limits," *Washington Post*, August 26, 2003, A4.

14. Zachary Coile, "Rocketing Gas Prices Worry White House," *San Francisco Chronicle*," March 31, 2004, A3; H. Sterling Burnett, "The Drive for Solutions: Drilling Would Ease U.S. Dependence," *Milwaukee Journal Sentinel*, May 23, 2004, J1; Ben Lieberman, "If You Really Want to Reduce Gas Prices, Here's How," *Chicago Sun-Times*, May 31, 2004, 47.

15. Helen Dewar, "GOP Gains Boost Chances of Alaska Drilling: Supports of Exploration in Wildlife Refuge Appear to Have Majority in New Senate," *Washington Post*, December 16, 2004, A2.

16. Dirk Lammers, "Daschle, Thune, Debate Campaign Tactics," *Associated Press*, September 20, 2004, via Lexis-Nexis.

17. Gail Russell, "Washington More Open to Business Than Usual," *Christian Science Monitor*, June 9, 2005, 1; David Lightman, "Business Winning Victories in D.C.," *Hartford Courant*, March 27, 2005, A1.

18. Jeff Gerth, "Big Oil Steps Aside in Battle Over Arctic," *New York Times*, February 21, 2005, A12.

19. Bruce Alpert, "Senate OKs Drilling in Alaskan Refuge," *Times-Picayne*, March 17, 2005, 1; Jonathan Waterman, "What We Would Lose in Alaska," *Washington Post*, June 6, 2005, A19.

20. Charles Pope, "Senate OKs Oil Drilling in Arctic Refuge," *St. Louis-Post Dispatch*, March 17, 2005, A1; British Petroleum statement on ANWR, www.bp.com/genericarticle.do?categoryId=2011285&contentId=2016579.

21. Gallup Organization, March 7–10, 2005 [datafile], n = 1,004 adults nationwide.

22. Opinion Dynamics, for Fox News, April 16–17, 2002 [datafile], n = 900 national registered voters: Q15.

23. For example, respondents in an NBC News poll were asked: "Do you think that the higher prices for electricity, gasoline, and other sources of energy during the past year are a good reason to allow new oil exploration in some federally protected areas, such as the Alaskan wilderness, or should the federal government keep these areas off limits and consider other solutions?" Fifty-six percent of those polled preferred the latter. Hart and Teeter Research Companies, for NBC News, March 1–4, 2001 [datafile], n = 2,024 adults nationwide: Q83.

24. See Prothro and Grigg 1960.

25. Greenberg Quinlan Research & Tarrance Group, for the League of Conservation Voters Education Fund, May 21–23, 2001 [datafile], n = 1,000 national adult likely voters: Q39–Q43.

26. Lydia Saad, "Americans Mostly 'Green' in the Energy vs. Environment Debate," *Gallup Poll Monthly* 126 (2001): 35.

27. Riley E. Dunlap and Lydia Saad, "Only One in Four Americans Are Anxious about the Environment," *Gallup Poll Monthly,* 127 (April 2001): 13.

28. Gallup Organization, June 8–10, 2001 [datafile], n = 1,011 adults nationwide: Q21.

29. Gallup Organization, May 7–9, 2001 [datafile], n = 1,005 adults nationwide: Q5.

30. Harris Interactive, January 11–16, 2005 [datafile], n = 2,209, http://www.harrisinteractive.com/harris_poll/index.asp?PID=539; Gallup Organization, March 7–10, 2005 [datafile], n = 1,004 adults nationwide: Q722.

31. David W. Moore, "Conflicting Polls Show an Uncertain Public on ANWR," *Poll Talk*, March 8, 2005, www.gallup.com/poll/content/login.aspx?ci=15178.

32. Moore, "Conflicting Polls Show an Uncertain Public on ANWR."

33. Gallup Organization, March 19–21, 1999 [datafile], n = 1,018 adults nationwide: Q2–Q4.

34. Moore, "Conflicting Polls Show an Uncertain Public on ANWR."

35. "ANWR: You Get What You Poll For," *Environmental News Service*, February 2005, www.findarticles.com/p/articles/mi_kmens/is_200502/ai_n13275104.

36. "Democratic Party Image Improvement: Democrats More Confident, Kerry Faring Better in Battleground States," *Pew Center for the People and the Press*, July 21, 2004, http://people-press.org/reports/display.php3?ReportID=220.

37. Neela Banerjeen, "Would More Drilling in America Make a Difference?", *New York Times*, June 20, 2004, 14.

38. Luntz Research Companies, *Straight Talk* (Alexandria, VA: Luntz Research Companies, 2002), 107.

39. Luntz Research Companies, *Straight Talk*, 116.

40. William Saletan, "Is There an Energy Crisis? It Depends on Who You Ask," *Milwaukee Journal-Sentinel*, May 13, 2001, J2.

41. Saletan, "Is There an Energy Crisis?"

42. Saletan, "Is There an Energy Crisis?"

43. Saletan, "Is There an Energy Crisis?"

44. David Helvarg. "Perception Is Reality," *E: The Environmental Magazine*, 7 (1996): 38–41.

45. Jim VandeHei, "Business Sees Gain in GOP Takeover: Political Allies Push Corporate Agenda," *Washington Post*, March 27, 2005, A1.

46. Conservation International, *Annual Report, 2004*: 23, 30; Nature Conservancy, *Annual Report, 2004*, http://nature.org/joinanddonate/corporatepartnerships/.

47. Tom Price, *Cyber-Activism* (Washington, DC: Foundation for Public Affairs, 2000), 18.

48. Editorial, "Big Green Blues," *Washington Post*, May 12, 2003, A18.

49. Michelle Cole, "Environmental Gifts Bring Ford a Truckload of Trouble," *The Oregonian*, June 16, 2001, A1.

50. "Fara Warner, "Environmental Group Depicts Ford's Chief as Pinocchio," *New York Times*, February 26, 2004, C8. The advertisement ran on February 11, 2004, A11.

51. "POLL—Americans See Fuel Efficient Cars as 'Patriotic,' " *PlanetArk: World Environmental News*, March 18, 2005, www.planetark.com/avantgo/dailynewsstory.cfm?newsid=29988.

52. Quoted in Justin Blum and Jim VandeHei, "Bush Steps Up Pitch for Drilling in Alaska Refuge," *Washington Post*, March 10, 2005, A2.

53. Robert Pear, "Arctic Drilling Push Is Seen as Threat to Budget Bill," *New York Times*, November 3, 2005, A23; Carl Hulse, "House Shelves Plan for Alaska Drilling," *New York Times*, November 10, 2005, A23.

54. Carl Hulse, "Senate Rejects Bid for Drilling in Arctic Area," *New York Times*, December 22, 2005, A1.

55. Sierra Club, "Arctic Refuge Victory for All Americans," December 21, 2005, www.sierraclub.org/pressroom/releases/pr2005–12–21.asp.

56. Hulse, "Senate Rejects Bid for Drilling in Arctic Area."

57. Zachary Cole, "GOP to Renew Push to Drill for Arctic Oil: Selling Points Are Higher Prices and Tensions over Iran," *San Francisco Chronicle*, January 26, 2006, A3.

58. Felicity Barringer, "U.S. Reverses Accord and Opens 389,000 Acres in Alaska to Explore for Oil," *New York Times*, January 13, 2006, A13.

References

Alsop, Ronald J. 2004. "Corporate Reputation: Anything but Superficial." *Journal of Business Strategy* 25 (6): 21–29.

Baumgartner, Frank R., and Bryan D. Jones. 1993. *Agendas and Instability in American Politics*. Chicago: University of Chicago Press.

Bosso, Christopher J. 1989. "Setting the Public Agenda: Mass Media and the Ethiopian Famine." In Michael Margolis and Gary Mauser, eds., *Manipulating Public Opinion: Essays on Public Opinion as a Dependent Variable*. Monterey, CA: Brooks-Cole.

Bosso, Christopher J. 1994a. "The Color of Money: Environmental Groups and the Pathologies of Fund-Raising." In Allan Cigler and Burdett Loomis, eds., *Interest Group Politics*, 4th ed. Washington, DC: CQ Press.

Bosso, Christopher J. 1994b. "The Contextual Bases of Problem Definition." In David A. Rochefort and Roger W. Cobb, eds., *The Politics of Problem Definition*. Lawrence: University Press of Kansas.

Bosso, Christopher J. 2005. *Environment, Inc.: From Grassroots to Beltway*. Lawrence: University Press of Kansas.

Buchanan, James M. 1954. "Individual Choice in Voting and the Market." *Journal of Political Economy* 62:334–343.

Buchanan, James M., and Gordon Tullock. 1962. *The Calculus of Consent: Logical Foundations of Constitutional Democracy*. Ann Arbor: University of Michigan Press.

Cobb, Roger, and Charles Elder. 1972. *Participation in American Politics: The Dynamics of Agenda Building*. Boston: Allyn and Bacon.

Cohen, Michael D., James G. March, and Johann P. Olsen. 1972. "A Garbage Can Model of Organizational Choice." *Administrative Science Quarterly* 17 (1): 1–25.

Farhar, Barbara C. 1994. "Trends: Public Opinion about Energy." *Public Opinion Quarterly* 58 (4): 603–632.

Guber, Deborah Lynn. 2003. *The Grassroots of a Green Revolution: Polling America on the Environment*. Cambridge, MA: MIT Press.

Jacoby, William G. 2000. "Issue Framing and Public Opinion on Government Spending." *American Journal of Political Science* 44 (4): 750–767.

Jones, Charles O. 1975. *Clean Air: The Policies and Politics of Pollution Control*. Pittsburgh: University of Pittsburgh Press.

Kingdon, John. 1995. *Agendas, Alternatives, and Public Policies.* 2nd ed. New York: HarperCollins.

Lindblom, Charles E. 1977. *Politics and Markets.* New York: Basic Books.

Lippmann, Walter. 1922. *Public Opinion.* New York: Macmillan.

Martinez-Vazquez, Jorge. 1981. "Selfishness versus Public 'Regardingness' in Voting Behavior." *Journal of Public Economics* 15:349–361.

Prothro, James W., and Charles M. Grigg. 1960. "Fundamental Principles of Democracy: Bases of Agreement and Disagreement." *Journal of Politics* 22:276–294.

Rochefort, David, and Roger Cobb. 1994. *The Politics of Problem Definition.* Lawrence: University Press of Kansas.

Sagoff, Mark. 1988. *The Economy of the Earth: Philosophy, Law, and the Environment.* New York: Cambridge University Press.

Schattschneider, E. E. 1960. *The Semisovereign People: A Realist's View of Democracy in America.* New York: Holt, Rinehart and Winston.

Schuman, Howard, and Stanley Presser. 1981. *Questions and Answers in Attitude Surveys: Experiments on Question Form, Wording, and Context.* New York: Academic Press.

Shipan, Charles R., and William R. Lowry. 2000. "Environmental Policy and Party Divergence in Congress." *Political Research Quarterly* 54 (2): 245–263.

Smith, Eric R. A. N. 2002. *Energy, the Environment and Public Opinion.* Lanham, MD: Rowman & Littlefield.

Smith, Mark A. 2000. *American Business and Political Power: Public Opinion, Elections, and Democracy.* Chicago: University of Chicago Press.

Stone, Deborah A. 1988. *Policy Paradox and Political Reason.* New York: HarperCollins.

Stone, Deborah A. 1989. "Causal Stories and the Formation of Policy Agendas." *Political Science Quarterly* 104:281–300.

Tullock, Gordon. 1976. *The Vote Motive.* Hobart Paperback No. 4. London: Institute of Economic Affairs.

Vogel, David. 1989. *Fluctuating Fortunes: The Political Power of Business in America.* New York: Basic Books.

Wilson, James Q., and Edward Banfield. 1964. "Public Regardingness as a Value Premise in Voting Behavior." *American Political Science Review* 4:876–887.

Wilson, James Q., and Edward Banfield. 1965. "Voting Behavior on Municipal Public Expenditures: A Study in Rationality and Self-Interest." In Julius Margolis, ed., *The Public Economy of Urban Communities.* Baltimore: Johns Hopkins University Press.

Zaller, John, and Stanley Feldman. 1992. "A Simple Theory of the Survey Response: Answering Questions versus Revealing Preferences." *American Journal of Political Science* 36 (3): 579–616.

3
Business, Elections, and the Environment

Robert J. Duffy

The first television ad in the 2004 general election for the U.S. Senate in Colorado aired in early August, just after the state's primary. The advertisement criticized Democratic candidate Ken Salazar, the state's attorney general and former head of Colorado's Department of Natural Resources, for his handling of a cyanide spill at the Summitville mine. The ad accused Salazar of "lax oversight" of the spill and alleged that later, as attorney general, Salazar cut a deal with the "foreign millionaire responsible" for the spill, which resulted in "sticking taxpayers with a bill of more than $100 million." The advertisement concluded by asking viewers to "call Ken Salazar and tell him to fight for Colorado taxpayers for a change."

This and other advertisements, which cost somewhere between $500,000 and $1 million, were the handiwork of Americans for Job Security (AJS), a secretive nonprofit 501(c)(6) trade organization.[1] Although IRS regulations allow such organizations to engage in public education and issue-advocacy campaigns, electioneering may not constitute their primary purpose. Since its inception in 1996, however, virtually all of the group's budget has been spent on political advertising, the bulk of which has occurred in the months preceding elections. In just the last three election cycles, AJS has spent more than $17 million, all of it on behalf of Republican candidates. The group contends, however, that its advertisements are grassroots lobbying designed to educate the public about issues, and are not aimed at influencing elections. As a result, AJS has reported making no political expenditures in the last three election cycles. Although AJS has not disclosed its funding sources, published reports have noted that more than 500 corporations and individuals have contributed up to $100,000 each, and that both the American Forest and

Paper Association and the American Insurance Association contributed $1 million in "seed money" to the group (Isikoff 2000).

The group's Colorado advertisements are noteworthy for several reasons. First, they offer one of the few examples in recent years of a business organization raising environmental issues in an electoral context. Typically, television advertisements and direct mail by business groups, including AJS, focus on other issues. A Public Citizen (2004) study shows that in both 2004 and in previous cycles, for example, other AJS advertisements criticized Democratic candidates on taxes, job creation, fair-trade practices, prescription drug benefits, education, tort reform, estate taxes, Social Security, term limits, health insurance, and without a trace of irony, accepting money from "special interests," including polluters.

The avoidance of environmental issues is relatively easy to explain: as any pollster knows, the environment is a consensual issue that enjoys broad, although not necessarily deep, public support (Guber 2003). To attack a candidate for voting to protect the environment would likely be counterproductive, especially if the attack came from a business organization, whose motives would be easy to question. Perhaps that is why when AJS does raise environmental issues, it is more likely to criticize candidates for not doing enough to protect the environment than for doing too much. In short, the leaders of business groups understand the need to depict their organizations as socially responsible.

Given public support for environmental protection, business groups know that it is more effective to talk about other issues, like medical tort reform, in their campaign advertising. After all, candidates who support tort reform, or lower taxes, are also likely to support other issues of importance to business, including the environment. Thus, one virtue of trying to frame the debate on these other issues, at least from the perspective of business groups, is that the environment becomes a nonissue for most voters.

The AJS advertisements are also noteworthy because they illustrate the growing importance of independent expenditures and issue advocacy by narrow interests, including groups that seek to mask their identity. Who could be against job security, after all? As a result, business money has flowed into organizations like AJS, Citizens for Sensible Energy Choices,

Freedom Works, and Progress for America, all of whom have waged expensive issue-advocacy campaigns in recent years. Business PACs continue to provide financial support to candidates, of course, but they have supplemented their efforts with the newer, less regulated forms of political spending. In this sense, business groups are merely part of the broader trend among interest groups of all stripes that have followed the same path.

As noted in chapter 1, it is widely agreed that American corporations routinely engage in a diversity of political activities designed to advance and protect their interests. There is disagreement, however, on the effectiveness of these efforts. Baumgartner and Leech (1998) and Berry (1999), for example, argue that citizen groups are now significant countervailing sources of power, while environmentalists and others contend that business continues to enjoy a privileged position in policy deliberations (Libby 1998; Gonzalez 2001). This chapter reports and analyzes trends in how American business groups approach electoral politics.[2] Conventional wisdom holds that American business uses its superior wealth to influence elections by supporting pro-business candidates. What is not so clear, however, is what business groups are actually doing to influence elections, whether what they are doing differs significantly from the actions taken by other interest groups, including environmental organizations, and which factors influence business decisions on how and when to get involved in elections. This chapter seeks to shed some light on these issues. I argue that business groups have become more active in recent election cycles, and have channeled their abundant financial resources into a variety of tools to educate and mobilize their employees and the general public in a seamless effort to influence policymakers. My central argument is that business-group electioneering is but one part of their broader efforts to shape public policy. Indeed, groups' financial support of candidates and parties, in the form of direct contributions from PACs, soft money, independent expenditures, or election-oriented issue advertisements from affiliated 501(c) or 527 organizations, is part of a strategy that seeks to frame issues before elections, and to then support candidates who back their positions on those issues.[3] After the election, the groups then sponsor issue advertisements designed to persuade the public to support legislation sponsored by the beneficiaries of their electoral activities. Corporations recognize that electing more business-friendly public officials is an essential step toward creating a more business-friendly environmental policy.

Interest-Group Electioneering

Interest-group political strategies are affected by both internal and external factors (Rozell and Wilcox 1998). Among the internal factors that matter are a group's resources, its goals, the ideology of its leadership, its beliefs about electioneering, its organizational maintenance needs, and the characteristics of its membership. PACs representing individual firms, for example, may behave differently than trade associations or umbrella organizations representing a more diverse membership. Similarly, business groups with ample financial resources will be able to pursue multiple electoral activities in multiple races; they can at least consider conducting expensive independent-expenditure or issue-advocacy campaigns. Lack of money, on the other hand, forces businesses to be more selective in deciding whether and where to get involved and limits their options as to how to get involved. Thus, they may be more likely to join coalitions that enable firms in similar straits to pool their resources on behalf of preferred candidates. Businesses with relatively narrow interests, such as those engaged in natural resource extraction, may support incumbents with positions on the committees with jurisdiction over their specific policy concern, while diversified companies may spread their money more widely. Finally, business groups whose leaders hold strong ideological beliefs may be more likely to support candidates of one party rather than contribute to both.

Organizational maintenance concerns can also affect a group's electoral activities. Bosso (2005) has argued that the structure of the advocacy community within which a particular group operates can affect its strategic choices. A crowded advocacy community creates incentives for groups to find their own unique niche; those that fail to do so may cease to exist. Over time, the community matures and groups settle into a rough division of labor, with each group specializing in its own substantive or tactical niche. Some groups, for example get involved in elections, while others do not. Some of those who do get involved limit themselves to forming PACs and making direct contributions to candidates; others conduct voter-education campaigns and seek to mobilize the grassroots.

External factors may also shape the constraints and opportunities facing interest groups. Relevant here are economic conditions, election results, the shape of public opinion, and the strength and strategies of opposing forces (Stimson 2004). Also important is the framework within which groups conduct their electoral efforts, notably the legal rules and common practices that govern electoral activity (Rozell and Wilcox 1998). Shifts in any of these factors may alter the constraints and opportunities facing particular groups, leading them to change course. For example, the Republican takeover of Congress fundamentally altered the context of both policymaking and electioneering. Environmental groups could no longer count on a sympathetic majority to defend their interests, and business groups no longer needed to contribute to Democratic incumbents to maintain access. Similarly, a business downturn may leave groups with less money for activities that are perceived as discretionary.

Electoral strategies may also change in response to the actions of opposing groups. Interest groups that are the first to exploit a new strategy often enjoy a "honeymoon" period in which their opponents are caught off guard (Pralle 2003). This is the case with the use of independent-expenditure, issue-advocacy, and voter-education campaigns by labor unions, environmentalists, and other progressive groups. When these efforts were perceived as successful, some business groups followed suit with similar campaigns.

The Changing Context of Interest-Group Electioneering

The framework in which interest groups operate has changed dramatically in recent decades. The institutional upheaval of the 1960s and 1970s fundamentally altered the context in which policymaking occurred, creating an environment that is more crowded and competitive, and that rewards different types of group behavior. Browne (1998), for example, has argued that direct or "inside" lobbying is no longer sufficient for groups seeking to influence policy. Success in contemporary policymaking, he suggests, requires that groups lobby everyone, all the time. In addition to policymakers, this "all-directional lobbying" encourages groups to lobby one another, the media, and the public, and to devote considerable energy to framing issues.

Today, there are now more groups, spending more money, in new ways in efforts to influence elections (Duffy 2003; Rozell and Wilcox 1999). The proliferation of organized interests, the increasing use of nonprofit groups, and the explosive growth of independent expenditures and issue advocacy by interest groups are examples of this trend. The net effect of these changes, according to Cigler and Loomis (1998), is a "blurring" of the traditional roles of political parties and organized groups in elections. Political parties now act as group patrons, directing donors to allied interest groups so they may conduct voter-registration drives and telephone banks. In another sign of the blurring of traditional roles, it is not uncommon for interest groups to engage in activities that had previously been carried out by the parties, including candidate recruitment, fundraising, campaign advertising, as well as voter education and mobilization (Duffy 2003).

Of particular importance here are the increasingly sophisticated electoral activities of environmental organizations, notably the League of Conservation Voters and the Sierra Club. In the aftermath of the 1994 elections, environmental groups found themselves without direct access to the majority party in either chamber. In response, both organizations became significantly more active and strategic. They raised and spent more money, began conducting independent-expenditure, issue-advocacy, and voter-education campaigns, and concentrated their efforts on competitive races. Environmental groups also began registering, targeting, and mobilizing voters; moreover, they increased efforts to coordinate their activities with one another and with other progressive organizations.

Electoral Strategies

Like other interest groups, business organizations have adapted to changes in the political opportunity structure. When Supreme Court interpretations of the Federal Election Campaign Act (FECA) opened the door to PAC creation, the number of business-sponsored PACs mushroomed. When it became apparent that the FEC was turning a blind eye to large soft-money contributions, businesses moved to exploit that opening as well. In the mid-1990s, when the near total collapse of the federal election campaign finance regime opened the door to a flood of independent expenditures and issue advocacy by nonprofits, some business associations joined in.[4] Finally, after the passage of the Bipartisan Campaign Reform Act (BCRA) and its subsequent validation by the Supreme Court, some business interests created new 501(c) and 527 organizations and shifted their spending to these. In light of the new law's restrictions on broadcast advocacy, many groups increased their "ground-war" activities, placing greater emphasis on voter education and mobilization (Magleby, Monson, and Patterson 2005).

Students of political action committees generally agree that although a variety of factors shape contribution decisions, most PACs follow an access strategy and contribute to incumbents who are in a position to advance the group's policy goals (Sorauf 1988; Clawson, Neustadt, and Waller 1998; Conway, Green, and Currinder 2002). Corporate PACs often have very specific issue concerns, so they typically give to incumbents in order to cultivate and maintain access. According to West and Loomis (1999), this preference for incumbents shows that corporate PACs are involved in elections to advance their lobbying goals. They note "that is especially true for corporations in concentrated industries, in which investment—by either one firm or a tightly knit trade association—will provide tangible dividends" (p. 29).

In explaining the preference for incumbents, Herrnson (1998) notes that the decision rules guiding corporate PAC contributions are first to support likely winners, and second to support those who have the potential to influence legislation of interest to the PAC and its parent organization. In practice, these rules translate into supporting the congressional leadership, committee chairs and ranking members, and members of committees that have jurisdiction over their areas of concern. Furthermore, most corporate and trade-association PACs have tended to avoid involvement in primaries and in voter-mobilization campaigns (Rozell and Wilcox 1999), although there is evidence that such involvement is increasing.

Business organizations that seek broader policy goals, such as the Chamber of Commerce, the National Federation of Independent Business (NFIB), and the Business Industry Political Action Committee

(BIPAC) are more likely to support Republicans and to try to increase their numbers in Congress (Rozell and Wilcox 1999). As a result, these groups are more likely to follow an electoral strategy and contribute to Republican challengers and candidates for open seats. In the pivotal 1994 midterm elections, in which Republicans gained control of the House for the first time in forty years, NFIB contributed $371,625, 84 percent of which went to Republican candidates. Overall, 60 percent of the group's contributions went to challengers or to open-seat races, most of which were competitive. The NFIB shifted gears in 1996 in an effort to defend vulnerable Republican incumbents, giving half of its contributions to incumbents, 30 percent to candidates for open seats, and 20 percent to challengers (Shaiko and Wallace 1999).

In making their contribution decisions, groups like NFIB and BIPAC are quite strategic. When giving to challengers or candidates for open seats, for example, the NFIB looks at the candidate's fundraising potential, their political viability, and available polling data (Shaiko and Wallace 1999). BIPAC uses three criteria for determining whether and how to get involved in a race: the preponderance of the candidate's support for business interests, a competitive race, and the candidate's need for money (Nelson and Biersack 1999). In the aftermath of the 1994 elections, moreover, BIPAC worked to convince industry leaders that continued electoral activity was needed to reelect a sympathetic Congress. As Nelson and Biersack (1999) argue, this was an explicit recognition of the link between elections and policymaking.

With the recent upsurge in the formation of 501(c) and 527 organizations, documented below, individual firms can now pursue both contribution strategies simultaneously. Their corporate PAC can follow an access strategy and contribute mostly to incumbents of both parties. At the same time, if they choose to contribute to the Chamber of Commerce, the NFIB, BIPAC, or others, they can pursue an electoral strategy aimed at increasing the number of pro-business candidates in Congress, most of whom are Republicans.

The Republican takeover of Congress in 1994 had a profound effect on the political opportunity structure confronting PACs and led to a dramatic shift in their contribution patterns. For most of the 1980s and early 1990s, corporate and trade-association PACs favored Democrats, because Democrats controlled both chambers of Congress. The change in partisan control after 1994, however, altered the incentives for corporate PACs, which no longer needed to give to as many Democrats. Instead, they could align their political giving with their ideological preference for Republicans (Nelson 1998). To illustrate, 57 percent of corporate PAC contributions to House candidates in 1994 went to Democrats, but two-thirds went to Republicans in 1996. In the Senate, corporate PAC contributions to Republicans increased from 59 percent in 1994 to 81 percent in 1996. Similarly, trade-association PACs increased their contributions to Republican candidates from 54 to 75 percent. Much of the shift can be explained by business support for the Republican agenda (Herrnson 1998), but as Rozell and Wilcox (1999) note, the Republican leadership also pressured business groups to increase their contributions to the party and its candidates. In addition, the increasing electoral salience of taxes, tort reform, and other economic issues may help explain why businesses opened their coffers to Republican candidates.

Direct Contributions to Federal Candidates

Corporate PACs have routinely contributed far more than other types of PACs, and as table 3.1 indicates, their contributions dwarf those from PACs affiliated with environmental organizations. Since 1990, for example, forestry-industry PACs alone have contributed more than twice the amount given by environmental PACs. The disparity becomes even more lopsided when PACs from selected other business sectors are taken into account, demonstrating that at least with respect to PAC contributions, environmental groups cannot hope to match the money business brings to bear on federal elections.

It is clear that external factors play an important role with respect to direct contributions from business. Table 3.2 documents the pronounced shift in business contributions to Republicans after the 1994 elections. Most energy and natural resource PACs favored Republicans even before they gained majority status, but their spending has since tilted even more heavily to the GOP. The partisan change had a more noticeable effect on those sectors, like electric utilities, that had previously contributed most of their money to Democrats (Center for Responsive Politics 2005d). The sudden drop in support for Democrats shows that firms in these sectors

Table 3.1
PAC contributions by sector, 1990–2004

Election cycle	Environment	Forestry	Mining	Chemical	Oil and gas	Utilities	Automobile manufacturing
2004	$384,263	$1,337,581	$1,489,566	$2,532,516	$5,831,847	$9,915,875	$1,764,240
2002	$790,032	$1,847,909	$1,955,176	$2,195,785	$6,546,683	$10,568,428	$1,455,424
2000	$551,221	$2,226,795	$1,657,070	$2,069,087	$7,039,043	$8,251,609	$1,529,750
1998	$400,662	$1,837,937	$1,503,871	$1,607,506	$6,850,891	$6,480,424	$1,505,504
1996	$700,664	$2,042,656	$1,314,472	$1,745,825	$6,615,583	$5,316,476	$1,264,730
1994	$1,311,051	$1,364,274	$1,091,279	$1,719,239	$6,531,529	$4,470,411	$920,243
1992	$1,201,203	$1,743,201	$1,086,304	$1,842,298	$6,669,404	$4,689,456	$851,600
1990	$651,343	$1,608,822	$953,987	$1,670,402	$6,002,274	$3,964,531	$828,945
TOTALS	$5,990,799	$14,009,175	$11,051,725	$15,382,658	$52,087,254	$53,657,210	$10,120,436

Source: Center for Responsive Politics, "Long-Term Contribution Trends," www.opensecrets.org/industries.indus.asp?

Table 3.2
Partisan contributions by sector, 1990–2004

Election cycle	Natural gas pipelines Rep-Dem %	Forestry Rep-Dem %	Mining Rep-Dem %	Chemical Rep-Dem %	Oil and gas Rep-Dem %	Utilities Rep-Dem %	Automobile manufacturing Rep-Dem %
2004	73–27	80–20	85–15	78–22	80–20	66–34	65–35
2002	73–27	76–24	82–18	79–21	80–20	66–34	63–37
2000	75–25	83–17	86–14	80–20	79–21	68–32	69–31
1998	75–25	81–19	76–24	78–22	77–23	65–35	70–30
1996	75–25	80–20	74–26	77–23	77–23	66–34	74–26
1994	47–53	72–28	64–36	67–33	63–37	46–54	53–47
1992	45–55	75–25	63–37	73–27	66–34	44–56	53–47
1990	42–58	75–25	60–40	73–27	62–38	46–54	47–53

Source: Center for Responsive Politics, "Industry Profiles," www.opensecrets.org/industories/index.asp.

were pursuing an access strategy, shifting their contributions to support incumbents in the new majority party.

Furthermore, business PACs tend to contribute heavily to members of committees with jurisdiction over their policy interests. Members of the Senate Environment and Public Works Committee, which oversees many environmental programs, have received just under $425,000 from environmental donors, but they have received far more from industry sources. In fact, according to the Center for Responsive Politics (2005a), individuals and PACs affiliated with the oil and gas, electric utility, automotive, chemical, and mining industries contributed more than $11.5 million to committee members in the 2002 and 2004 election cycles. When other manufacturing and business donors are included, the ratio of business-environmental contributions becomes even more lopsided. In a pattern repeated on other committees, the bulk of business money went to Republicans, with the utility sector again being the most even-handed.

As table 3.3 indicates, similar patterns are evident with respect to other committees with jurisdiction over environmental policy. In the last two election cycles, electric utility, oil and gas, mining, and forestry interests have contributed more than $12.75 million to members of the Senate Energy and Natural Resources Committee, compared to just $235,000 from environmental donors (Center for Responsive Politics 2005c). All four commodity interests, of course, are affected by the committee's decisions on the public lands.

During the same period on the House side, oil and gas, mining, and forestry interests have contributed just under $3 million to members of the Resources Committee, while environmental interests donated slightly more than $200,000 (Center for Responsive Politics 2005c). Members of the Energy and Commerce Committee received more than $13.4 million from donors affiliated with the real estate, electric utility, oil and gas, and automotive industries; environmental interests were not in the top twenty sectors contributing to committee members (Center for Responsive Politics 2005c).

The figures from the last two election cycles are representative of previous cycles as well. Thus, if one accepts the presumption that campaign contributions increase access to policymakers, then clearly business enjoys greater access than environmentalists.

Table 3.3
Individual and PAC contributions to environmental committees, 2002–2004 election cycles

Sector	House Resources	House Energy and Commerce	Senate Energy and Natural Resources	Senate Environment and Public Works	Total committee contributions
Oil and gas	$2,131,900	$3,008,926	$4,480,006	$3,973,416	$13,594,248
Mining	$510,559		$1,495,134	$1,437,028	$2,005,693
Electric utilities		$4,702,991	$4,215,218	$2,811,017	$11,729,226
Forestry	$403,613		$1,478,743		$1,882,356
Automotive	$2,214,285			$1,849,855	$4,064,140
Chemicals				$1,588,895	$1,588,895
Environmental groups	$202,856		$235,270	$423,772	$861,898

Source: Center for Responsive Politics, "Committee Profiles," www.opensecrets.org/cmteprofiles.

Soft-Money Contributions

Although direct contributions from business interests far outpaced those of environmental organizations, the disparity was even greater when it came to so-called soft-money contributions.[5] Until the Bipartisan Campaign Reform Act (BCRA) outlawed the practice, interest groups and corporations could use funds from their general treasuries to make potentially unlimited contributions to party committees. In theory, the money was to be used for party-building activities, such as voter registration, get out the vote, and generic party advertising. Ostensibly, soft money was to be used only for state and local activities and not to aid in the election of candidates to federal office. This distinction was, however, difficult to maintain in practice; money used by state party officials to mobilize voters in state elections would likely benefit that party's federal candidates as well. The major problem with soft money, though, was that it allowed donors to evade the contribution limits and disclosure requirements in the Federal Election Campaign Act. Critics of the practice worried that large donors would at a minimum enjoy greater access to party leaders and public officials, and could perhaps exercise undue influence over election results.

Consistent with the theory that most business groups follow an access strategy, a significant number of firms made soft-money contributions to both political parties, especially in the early to mid-1990s. That way, they would have friends on both sides of the aisle. A review of soft-money contributions from businesses most directly affected by environmental issues, however, reveals a distinct preference for the Republican Party. More than 90 percent of the soft-money contributions from the mining, automotive, forestry, and electric utility sectors went to the GOP, while oil and gas and agribusiness interests gave 75 percent to Republicans.

As table 3.4 illustrates, business interests donated extraordinary sums of soft money between 1992 and 2002. While environmental interests gave just over $460,000, soft-money contributions from forestry, oil and gas, electric utilities, mining, and agribusiness interests totaled more than $180 million, the vast majority of which went to the Republican Party. The agribusiness and oil and gas sectors were by far the largest donors; as an example, Chevron itself contributed more than $4.6 million, ten times the amount given by environmentalists.

Table 3.4
Trends in soft-money donations, 1992–2002

	1992	1994	1996	1998	2000	2002	TOTALS
Environment	$3,815	$1,167	$31,500	$0	$217,250	$208,500	$462,232
Forestry	$243,191	$552,430	$1,433,332	$961,523	$3,504,790	$1,176,776	$7,872,042
Oil and gas	$5,282,081	$4,609,015	$10,047,475	$8,701,003	$16,180,200	$10,079,938	$54,899,712
Utilities	$560,609	$807,352	$3,811,713	$4,157,223	$8,440,510	$8,802,735	$26,580,142
Mining	$102,063	$256,450	$1,049,655	$1,114,454	$2,727,572	$2,166,257	$7,406,451
Automobile manufacturing	$95,610	$142,750	$663,160	$257,560	$267,730	$331,873	$1,758,683
Agribusiness	$7,288,067	$6,315,222	$16,046,575	$13,202,019	$20,942,199	$19,572,330	$83,366,412
Chemical	$1,218,418	$1,687,879	$3,690,697	$2,297,837	$4,952,814	$2,614,548	$16,462,193

Note: The term *soft-money donations* refers to the unregulated and potentially unlimited contributions to party committees, ostensibly for party-building activities such as voter registration and generic advertising for the party, or to help state and local candidates.

Source: Center for Responsive Politics, "Long-Term Contribution Trends," www.opensecrets.org/industries.indus.asp?

Independent Expenditures, Issue Advocacy, and 527 Organizations

The rise of independent spending by interest groups and political parties has had a significant effect on American elections (Magleby and Monson 2004). This spending has typically taken the form of either independent expenditures or issue advocacy. Independent expenditures encompass spending made without prior consultation with a candidate. Groups making such expenditures face no spending limits; they may call for the election or defeat of specific candidates, but may not coordinate their actions with any candidate's campaigns. Independent expenditures must be disclosed to the FEC.

Groups engaged in issue-advocacy advertising may also spend unlimited amounts but, unlike independent expenditures, the advertisements may not expressly advocate the defeat or election of a particular candidate, and the spending need not be disclosed to the FEC. So long as the advertisements do not use words such as *vote for*, *elect*, *support*, *defeat*, or *vote against*, they are not considered election advertisements and thus cannot be regulated under federal election laws. There are two basic types of issue advertisements. The first, sometimes referred to as "genuine" issue advertisements, are those whose primary purpose is to advocate an idea or policy; such advertisements usually focus on important policy issues or pending legislative matters. The second type of issue advertisement is often impossible to distinguish from the commercials aired by candidates, and is designed to influence election results. Electioneering issue advertisements tend to focus on individual candidates rather than issues, and they often seemed aimed at shaping the viewer's image of candidates. Electioneering issue advertisements also tend to air in the weeks and months before elections, while "genuine" issue advertisements air throughout the year (Holmes and McLaughlin 2002).

Since 1996, both types of issue advertisements have become increasingly common. Although business groups have frequently employed issue-advocacy advertising to influence public policy, its use has become more common in recent years as business has sought to counter the efforts of environmental groups, labor unions, and other Democratic-affiliated organizations. Business groups do this for the same reasons as the other groups—independent expenditures and issue advocacy allow them to spend unlimited amounts on behalf of issues and candidates they like or against those they dislike, while evading responsibility for those efforts. In addition, such spending allows business groups to have greater control over the content and timing of their message; in essence, the groups can spend heavily in an effort to force their issues onto the public agenda and into the discourses of campaigns, while trying to keep other issues out (Duffy 2003; West and Loomis 1998).

Corporate advertising can serve multiple goals—it can help sell products, boost a company's image, shape public policy, and even influence election results (Sethi 1979). Consequently, it is often difficult to determine an issue ad's primary goal. Consider, for example, the full-page newspaper advertisements the Coors Brewing Company took out in most of the state's newspapers in the final two weeks of the 2004 election. The advertisements, which did not even mention the election, touted the firm's commitment to Colorado's people and environment and stressed its contribution to the state's economy, as well as its charitable giving. A company spokesman explained the very expensive ad buy as a necessary response to attacks on the company's environmental record and citizenship by the League of Conservation Voters and others during the campaign. Given that the firm's CEO, Pete Coors, was also the Republican candidate for the U.S. Senate in a very close race, reasonable people might wonder if the advertisements were designed to boost his candidacy, the firm's tarnished reputation, or both (Saunders and Duffy 2005).

An examination of issue advocacy by business organizations suggests that although they have sponsored electioneering issue-advertisement campaigns since at least 1996 (Shaiko and Wallace 1999), such advertisements rarely focus on environmental issues. In 2004, for example, Progress for America Voter Fund, a 527 organization established to help George W. Bush's reelection campaign, spent $35 million on an issue-advocacy, voter-mobilization, and grassroots effort. Its advertisements focused on terrorism (Magleby, Monson, and Patterson 2005). That same year the U.S. Chamber of Commerce spent $7 million in an effort "to educate voters about the devastating impact of a runaway legal system on the American way of life." Most of its television commercials and direct mail addressed the need for medical liability reform, which had tested well in focus groups (Magleby, Monson, and Patterson 2005). The Chamber also supported The November Fund, a 527 organization that seeks to raise public awareness of lawsuit abuse. Their campaign focused on seven states through a program of television, radio, and print advertising, direct mail, Internet, and earned media.

Similarly, in 2000 and 2002 the Chamber of Commerce and the Business Roundtable were involved in a number of House and Senate races where they ran cookie-cutter spots accusing the Democratic candidates of supporting a "big government prescription drug plan." The Chamber's actions were not unique; in 2002 other business groups sponsored issue-advocacy campaigns focusing on Medicare, Social Security, the death penalty, the estate tax, tort reform, and the need for less government. In fact, with the exception of the handful of AJS advertisements mentioned above, business-group issue advocacy seemingly addressed every issue but the environment. Undoubtedly, the groups' own polling and focus groups told them that the other issues were more effective in persuading voters, which is, after all, at least one of the goals of issue-advocacy advertisements.

Of course, the absence of the environment as a focus of business advertising does not mean that they think the issue is unimportant. A more plausible explanation is that business groups know that their preferred candidates will stand a better chance of winning if environmental issues are absent from the campaign debate. The leaders of business groups know as well as anyone else that voters trust Democrats much more than Republicans when it comes to protecting the environment—and that this applies to Republican voters as well (Cushman 1996). So given public sentiment on the environment, why bring it up? As noted in chapter 1, it is harder for business to prevail in Congress when environmental issues are salient and environmental groups are able to mobilize their supporters. The same logic applies in elections: business' preferred candidates win when environmental issues are not center stage.

An examination of business-group issue advocacy also shows that corporate actors typically do not sponsor advertisements in their own name—they create front organizations with names that often seem designed to disguise their identity. Businesses know that corporate issue advertising is undermined by the perception that such commercials are self-serving, and the public is more likely to perceive advertisements from nonprofits as credible (Coe 1983; Haley 1996; Falk 2003). The activities of Freedom Works, a 501(c)(4) organization, are illustrative. The group, whose stated purpose is to "fight for lower taxes and less regulation," has close ties to the Republican Party leadership and to energy interests. In 1998, the group received donations of almost $1 million from Philip Morris, at least $200,000 from DaimlerChrysler, Emerson Electric, General Electric, and Florida Crystals Corporation; it also received contributions of at least $100,000 from U.S. Sugar, Georgia Pacific, and Exxon. Former House Majority Leader Dick Armey serves as the organization's chair. The group's cofounder is David Koch, vice president of Koch Industries, an oil and gas firm with obvious interests in environmental policy. Koch Industries contributed $374,000 to the group in 1998. Other board members with ties to companies interested in environmental policy include C. Boyden Gray, former White House counsel to President George H. W. Bush and a spokesperson for the Electric Reliability Coordinating Council, an industry group that has sought relaxed emissions standards for power plants under the Clean Air Act (Public Citizen 2004).

Freedom Works includes the environment as one of its many concerns. The group's website notes that it supports "a free-market approach to environmental protection," including the protection of private-property rights, and claims that "one-size-fits-all regulations from Washington are not appropriate for addressing environmental challenges." Of the Environmental Protection Agency (EPA), the group says "the regulations they impose and the penalties they dispense are among the most restrictive in the world" (Freedom Works 2005).

Freedom Works has also conducted electioneering issue-advocacy campaigns. In fact, the group spent more than $16.5 million on direct mail, telemarketing calls, radio commercials, and e-mail in the 2000 and 2002 election cycles. In addition to addressing Social Security, tort reform, and tax issues, the group has raised environmental issues on just two occasions. In October 2002, it sent more than 75,000 pieces of direct mail claiming that New Hampshire Democratic Senate candidate Jeanne Shaheen "jeopardizes America's energy security," and noted how her "extreme environmental views" would endanger people's economic security. That same year the group sent 20,000 e-mails to South Dakota voters noting Democratic Senate candidate Tim Johnson's opposition to drilling in the Arctic National Wildlife Refuge and his vote to raise gas taxes (Public Citizen 2004).

Although business has shied away from environmental issue advertisements in elections, there are many examples of "genuine" environmental issue advertisements. In these spots, business groups typically seek to put a green face on their actions and preferred policies. Many of the issue-advertisement campaigns are tied to pending legislative proposals and, because many advertisements appear only in the nation's capital, are clearly designed to shape elite thinking on the specific proposals at hand. Advertisements that appear outside of Washington are often directed at generating public pressure on elected officials on pending legislation or to shape public perceptions of issues.

According to one study, more than $15.4 million was spent on issue advertising related to the Bush administration's National Energy Plan in 2001–1002; of this, fully 94 percent of the spending came from business organizations (Falk 2003). In fact, energy/environmental issues were the focus of more issue advertisements than any other topic during that same period, and Americans for Balanced Energy Choices (ABEC), a coalition of coal, mining, and utility firms, was the top spender overall. Indeed, ABEC accounted for nearly 20 percent of all television issue advertising during the 107th Congress, with virtually its entire ad buy on national cable (Falk 2003).[6] Other energy interests spending more than $1 million to discuss aspects of the energy plan were the Nuclear Energy Institute, BP, ExxonMobil, and the Alliance for Energy and Economic Growth (Falk 2003).

Consider as well the many organizations that conducted issue-advocacy campaigns urging the designation of Yucca Mountain in Nevada as the nation's only permanent high-level nuclear waste repository. One of the groups, the Alliance for Energy and Economic Growth (AEEG), was established in 2001 by the U.S. Chamber of Commerce and an assortment of nuclear power, coal, oil, and natural gas associations to promote the Bush administration's national energy plan. According to a study by the Annenberg Public Policy Center (Falk 2003), AEEG paid for six print advertisements and three television commercials in 2001 and 2002, all of which were aimed at the Washington, D.C., market. All of the advertisements urged support for a comprehensive national energy policy, with expanded domestic energy production as a key element. Many of the advertisements also noted the importance of ensuring reliable supplies of domestic energy, while one television advertisement endorsed the Bush energy plan for supporting "increased production of clean affordable energy." In declaring their support for "clean" as well as "affordable" energy, AEEG was seeking to establish its environmental bona fides, which was critical because most people had probably never heard of the group before seeing their advertisements.

Another organization, the Alliance for Sound Nuclear Policy, is actually a coalition of nuclear industry groups and others who supported opening the Yucca Mountain repository. The group ran newspaper advertisements in May 2002 in Delaware, Oregon, Rhode Island, and Washington, and television commercials in Wyoming. The four print spots were tailored for each location, but each claimed that Yucca Mountain was the permanent solution to the waste problem, noting that "it just makes sense nuclear waste should be permanently disposed at a secure, specially designed facility far away from our waterways, towns, and cities." The advertisements were scheduled on the eve of a June vote on Yucca Mountain in the Senate Energy and Natural Resources Committee, and were aimed at persuading senators in the respective states to vote in favor of the facility (Grove 2002). The industry position was that the waste would be more secure at one central location than spread across the nation at many reactors.

Other business groups advertising in support of opening Yucca Mountain were the Nuclear Energy Institute (NEI), the industry's lobbying group in Washington, and the Chamber of Commerce (U.S. Chamber of Commerce 2002a). NEI paid for print and television commercials in 2001 and 2002, some supporting the storage of nuclear waste at Yucca Mountain, and others promoting nuclear power as a solution to climate change, calling it a clean alternative to fossil fuels (Falk 2003).

Considered collectively, the advertisements by the various groups serve multiple purposes. In the short term, some sought to influence pending votes in Congress. Others were designed to frame perceptions of the industry's product as an environmentally desirable source of energy, while still others were intended to cast the nuclear industry itself in a more favorable light. After all, how could an industry that supports clean air be all that bad? Both of these are clearly long-term goals that have, in point of fact, been ongoing for more than two decades (Duffy 1997).

All told, Yucca Mountain was the subject of more than $570,000 of issue-advocacy advertising, with 96 percent of that total in support of the repository. Groups opposing the site spent a total of $20,000, while the Nuclear Energy Institute alone spent $260,000 in support. President Bush signed the legislation designating Yucca Mountain as the nation's sole permanent high-level nuclear waste repository in July 2003 (Falk 2003).

Voter-Education and Voter-Mobilization Campaigns

It is a cliché that imitation is the sincerest form of flattery. In interest-group politics, it also happens to be true. When labor unions, environmental organizations, the National Rifle Association, and other ideological groups saw results from putting more money and emphasis on grassroots voter-education and voter-mobilization efforts, business organizations were not far behind. Compared to just four years ago, business groups are paying considerably more attention to the so-called ground war in an attempt to spread their message widely. These efforts have been spearheaded by the Business Industry Political Action Committee (BIPAC), the Chamber of Commerce, and the National Federation of Independent Business (NFIB), which have all had programs to turn out more voters by educating business owners about political activity and the finer points of federal election laws.[7]

One of the most notable developments in recent years has been a dramatic increase in internal communications from business associations to both members and employees. When communicating to company executives, managers, and shareholders, business owners can endorse candidates, but they cannot advocate the election or defeat of any candidate to their employees. Owners may, however, talk to employees about the issues that matter to the company and where the candidates stand on those issues. When labor unions concluded that internal communications were more effective in mobilizing voters than broadcast issue advocacy, other groups followed suit. The first major corporate effort took place in 2000, when the Chamber of Commerce joined with state and local chambers to provide access to three million businesses; one study estimated that much of the Chamber's $15 million in spending that year was for internal communications (Conway, Green, and Currinder 2002).

Business organizations have also begun conducting voter-education and voter-mobilization campaigns. In 2002, for example, the Chamber of Commerce put fifty people on the ground in thirty-two states, sent two million pieces of mail, made one million telephone calls, organized fundraisers for candidates, educated voters, conducted GOTV efforts, and launched a web-based tool to "inform and motivate employees." In explaining his organization's actions, U.S. Chamber of Commerce President and CEO Thomas Donohue said that "we took a page from our opponent's playbook and made sure every voter knew where the candidates stood on our issues" (U.S. Chamber of Commerce 2002b).

The Chamber put even more emphasis on its grassroots program in 2004, when it reported putting 215 people on the ground in 31 states, sending 3.9 million pieces of mail and more than 30 million e-mails, making 6.8 million telephone calls, and distributing more than 36,000 Get-Out-The-Vote kits to corporations and chambers to help them run their own campaigns. To put the Chamber's efforts into context, the 56 unique mail pieces it sent were more than any other group in 2004 (Magleby, Monson, and Patterson 2005). In addition to its federal efforts, the Chamber also continued its work on state elections involving attorneys general and Supreme Court justices (U.S. Chamber of Commerce 2004a).

According to Dirk Van Dongen, president of the National Association of Wholesalers-Distributors, the effort in the 2004 election "was truly huge. It was several times bigger and broader than anything done by business before." To illustrate, 91 of the Business Roundtable's 160 member companies participated in a program to provide employees with access to political information via the Internet. The U.S. Chamber of Commerce coordinated a similar program for 75 companies, 230 local chambers, and 95 trade associations. Similarly, the NFIB sent out millions of postcards, e-mails, and faxes, and made telephone calls to remind business owners to vote early and to vote for small-business candidates (Birnbaum and Edsall 2004).

There were common elements to the grassroots programs run by BIPAC, the NFIB, and the Chamber of Commerce. All developed "voter-education" websites with downloadable tools for voter education, voter registration, absentee ballots, finding polling places, and information on early voting.[8] The Chamber's website also featured a scorecard rating candidates on issues like medical liability reform, free trade, and energy. All three endorsed the view expressed on the Chamber's election website (U.S. Chamber of Commerce 2004b) that most "workers want information from their employers about candidates, issues, and elections. In fact, employees cite their employer as the single most trusted source of this information."

BIPAC's grassroots effort, now known as the Prosperity Project, began in 2000 as part of an effort "to protect and extend" the Republican majority in Congress by mobilizing the business community. By the 2002 election, half of the Fortune 50 were engaged in the project, which sought to develop "an integrated national political strategy for American business." Like the Chamber's program, the Prosperity Project was designed to help members educate and mobilize employees about their stakes in campaigns and elections. By 2004, BIPAC's "political toolkit" could be customized by each firm, who had their choice of an Internet or intranet site with candidate voting records, payroll stuffers, buttons, and posters. There were also options to download registration forms, absentee ballots, and the mechanics of voting (BIPAC 2004). After the 2004 elections, BIPAC reported sending 30 million e-mail messages through its website, and claimed that approximately 800,000 voter-registration and early-voting forms were downloaded from the site, more than double the previous cycle (Magleby, Monson, and Patterson 2005).[9] Besides creating the federal program, BIPAC also worked to establish similar programs in the states, which focused on state issues and candidates.

Conclusions

This chapter has analyzed trends in how American business groups approach electoral politics. Business organizations have significantly increased the scope and sophistication of their electoral efforts over the past ten years. Business groups have tried to maximize their electoral influence by mobilizing their grassroots supporters, by forging alliances with one another, and by raising and spending more than ever before. In the last decade, much of the spending has taken new forms, as business aggressively tried to set the agenda in numerous campaigns nationwide. These new tactics demonstrate that business groups, like labor unions, environmental groups, and others, are adapting to the new "rules of the game" in campaign finance, which allow virtually unlimited and unregulated spending by those seeking to influence elections. For groups trying to get the most from their political spending, independent expenditures and issue advocacy are clearly attractive options. Business groups typically have much more money than environmental organizations, and have always been able to contribute far more to candidates and parties. The new forms of spending enable business groups to extend that advantage, while the grassroots mobilization efforts have the potential to provide business with a counterweight to the mass membership of environmental groups.

This chapter also set out to determine which factors influence business decisions on when and how to get involved in elections. As we have seen, both internal and external factors shape electoral activity by business groups. Changes in partisan control of Congress, public opinion on the environment, the actions of environmental and other progressive groups, and changes in campaign finance rules and practices have influenced business decisionmaking. Internal variables are also important. We have seen that individual firms, interested in maintaining access to key legislators, may make direct contributions to candidates of both parties, while umbrella organizations such as NFIB follow a more ideological path and conduct issue-advertisement campaigns on behalf of Republican candidates. Firms that are concentrated geographically seem to behave differently than those spread across the country (Golden 1998; Kamieniecki 2006). Finally, the need to appear socially responsible leads business groups to avoid raising environmental issues directly in elections and to focus instead on other issues.

At the same time, much remains to be known about the role business groups play in American elections. Most obviously, although their superior resources allow business groups to spend more money, in more ways, and in more races, it is very difficult to assess systematically the effectiveness of their electioneering. For example, do independent-expenditure, issue-advocacy, and voter-education campaigns actually work? Business-backed candidates have done very well in recent election cycles but, given the many variables involved in any election, it is hard to say whether business groups played a decisive role. Similarly, additional research is needed to learn more about the internal factors that influence business activities in this arena. For example, are particular types of firms more or less likely to participate in elections, or to engage in certain types of electoral activity? Currently, aggregated campaign finance data, which often lump businesses into very broad categories, do not lend themselves readily to nuanced analyses of patterns in business spending. Finally, we do not know enough about business actions in state and local elections, including initiative and referendum campaigns. This will become increasingly important as more environmental authority is devolved to state and local governments.

Notes

1. Although tax laws limit electoral and lobbying activity by 501(c) nonprofits, they also permit such groups to engage in a wide range of political actions. 501(c)(3) organizations may not engage in express advocacy, while 501(c)(4), 501(c)(5), and 501(c)(6) groups may, so long as political activity is not the group's primary purpose. In recent years, a growing number of interest groups have changed their organizational structures by creating separate entities that allow them to participate in a broader range of activities.

2. Admittedly, business is not monolithic. Given the wide range of businesses in the United States, disagreements over environmental policy are inevitable, even within one industry. Corporations have different interests, which can limit their ability to cooperate on specific policy issues. Support for clean air regulations, for example, may hinge on the ability of individual firms to meet the proposed standards.

3. Organized under section 527 of the tax code, such organizations are tax exempt and yet may engage in a range of political activities. The term is usually used to refer to groups that are created primarily to influence elections but that are not regulated by the Federal Election Commission. These 527 organizations are allowed to engage in issue advocacy and voter mobilization campaigns, but may not engage in express advocacy in federal elections.

4. The Business Industry Political Action Committee (BIPAC), which operated primarily as a PAC from its establishment in 1963 until November 2000, when its board established a 501(c)(3) organization, called Friends of Adam Smith, to "reintroduce the important of free enterprise to a broad audience and to increase the understanding that political freedom without economic freedom is neither." See BIPAC, "Electing Business to Congress," http://www.bipac.org/detail.asp?id=302.

5. The term refers to the unregulated and potentially unlimited contributions to party committees, ostensibly for party-building activities such as voter registration and generic advertising for the party, or to help state and local candidates. In practice, soft-money donations allowed donors to bypass the contribution limits and disclosure requirements in the Federal Election Campaign Act.

6. Falk 2003, 9, 18.

7. The National Federation of Independent Business (NFIB) is the nation's largest small-business lobbying group, with over 600,00 members in 50 states. According to the organization's mission statement, its purpose is to "affect public policy at state and federal level" and to be a key business resource for small business in America. As the group's website makes clear, the NFIB also has a distinct interest in environmental policy: "Next to taxes and the associated paperwork requirements, complex environmental regulatory requirements are the most troublesome to NFIB's members." The NFIB has special concerns about "the burdens associated" with programs administered by several federal agencies: the Environmental Protection Agency's Toxics Release Inventory and Superfund programs, the Army Corps of Engineers' wetlands programs, and the Fish and Wildlife Service's endangered species programs. Like the NFIB, BIPAC has an interest in environmental and energy issues, which is not surprising because at least six of the group's chairs have headed energy or utility firms. In describing the business agenda, the group's website states that "government should minimize the cost and scope of the regulatory burden it imposes, take from the private sector only those tax revenues it truly needs, and exercise fiscal restraint in its own spending practices." Moreover, BIPAC asserts that the federal government should shy away from "overly aggressive federal regulation," and notes that environmental protection "should be attained with a sound and balanced regulatory regimen." Like other business organizations, BIPAC expresses a strong preference for "tax and other incentives to promote voluntary environmental policies rather than prescriptive broad-based regulations." With respect to the public lands and energy, BIPAC supports "the balanced use of natural resources on public and private lands," and the implementation of "a comprehensive market-based national energy policy that uses all forms of energy to meet consumer demand for reliable energy, while at the same time ensuring the quality of the environment." See BIPAC, "The Business Agenda," http://www.bipac.org/agenda/agenda.asp.

8. NFIB's program was called "Get Out the Vote Project "1-3-10," and could be downloaded from its website. NFIB also published "Volunteers Organized to Influence Congress and Elections: A Political Grassroots Action Manual," which included many tips on how to lobby public officials, how to deal with the media, and how to assist candidates in elections through phone banks, doorhangers, rides to the polls, and so on. See NFIB, "Voter Info," www.nfib.com/page/polVoterInfo.

9. Magleby, Monson, and Patterson 2005, 25.

References

Baumgartner, Frank R., and Beth L. Leech. 1998. *Basic Interests: The Importance of Groups in Politics and in Political Science*. Princeton, NJ: Princeton University Press.

Berry, Jeffrey M. 1999. *The New Liberalism: The Rising Power of Citizen Groups*. Washington, DC: Brookings Institution.

BIPAC. 2004. "About the Prosperity Project." www.bipac.org/project/about.asp.

Birnbaum, Jeffrey H., and Thomas B. Edsall. 2004. "At the End, Pro-GOP '527s' Outspent Their Counterparts." *Washington Post*, November 6, A6.

Bosso, Christopher J. 2005. *Environment, Inc.: From Grassroots to Beltway.* Lawrence: University Press of Kansas.

Browne, William P. 1998. "Lobbying the Public: All-Directional Advocacy." In Allan J. Cigler and Burdett A. Loomis, eds., *Interest Group Politics*, 5th ed., 343–364. Washington, DC: CQ Press.

Center for Responsive Politics. 2005a. "Committee Profiles." www.opensecrets. org/cmteprofiles.

Center for Responsive Politics. 2005b. "Donor Profiles." www.opensecrets.org/ orgs/summary.asp?ID=D000000110.

Center for Responsive Politics. 2005c. "Long-Term Contribution Trends." www.opensecrets.org/industries/indus.asp.

Center for Responsive Politics. 2005d. "PAC Contributions to Federal Candidates." www.opensecrets.org/pacs/sector.asp.

Cigler, Allan J., and Burdett A. Loomis. 1998. "From Big Bird to Bill Gates: Organized Interests and the Emergence of Hyperpolitics." In Allan J. Cigler and Burdett A. Loomis, eds., *Interest Groups Politics*, 5th ed., 391–399. Washington, DC: CQ Press.

Clawson, Dan, Alan Neustadt, and Mark Waller. 1998. *Dollars and Votes: How Business Campaign Contributions Subvert Democracy.* Philadelphia: Temple University Press.

Coe, Barbara J. 1983. "The Effectiveness Challenge in Issue Advertising Campaigns." *Journal of Advertising* 12 (4): 20–41.

Conway, M. Margaret, Joanne Connor Green, and Marian Currinder. 2002. "Interest Group Money in Elections." In Allan J. Cigler and Burdett A. Loomis, eds., *Interest Group Politics*, 6th ed., 117–140. Washington, DC: CQ Press.

Cushman, John. 1996. "GOP Backing Off from Tough Stand over Environment." *New York Times*, January 26, A1.

Duffy, Robert J. 1997. *Nuclear Politics in America: A History and Theory of Government Regulation.* Lawrence: University Press of Kansas.

Duffy, Robert J. 2003. *The Green Agenda in American Politics: New Strategies for the Twenty-First Century.* Lawrence: University Press of Kansas.

Dwyre, Dianne. 2002. "Campaigning Outside the Law." In Allan J. Cigler and Burdett A. Loomis, eds., *Interest Group Politics*, 6th ed., 144–160. Washington, DC: Q Press.

Falk, Erika. 2003. *Legislative Issue Advertising in the 107th Congress.* Washington, DC: Annenberg Public Policy Center. Available at "Issue Ads @ APPC: Organizations," www.annenbergpublicpolicycenter.org/issuead.

Freedom Works. 2005. "Environment: Issue Homepage." www.freedomworks .org/informed/key_template.php?issue_it=8.

Golden, Marissa Martino. 1998. "Interest Groups in the Rule-Making Process: Who Participates? Whose Voices Get Heard?" *Journal of Public Administration Research and Theory* 2:245–270.

Gonzalez, George A. 2001. *Corporate Power and the Environment: The Political Economy of U.S. Environmental Policy.* Lanham, MD: Rowman & Littlefield.

Grove, Benjamin. 2002. "Yucca Advertising War Heats Up," *Las Vegas Sun*, May 30.

Guber, Deborah Lynn. 2003. *The Grassroots of a Green Revolution: Polling America on the Environment.* Cambridge, MA: MIT Press.

Haley, E. 1996. "Exploring the Construct of Organization as a Source: Consumers' Understandings of Organizational Sponsorship of Advocacy Advertising." *Journal of Advertising* 25 (2): 19–25.

Helvarg, David. 1997. *The War against the Greens: The "Wise-Use" Movement, the New Right, and Anti-Environmental Violence.* San Francisco: Sierra Club Books.

Herrnson, Paul S. 1998. "Interest Groups, PACs, and Campaigns." In Paul S. Herrnson, Ronald G. Shaiko, and Clyde Wilcox, eds., *The Interest Group Connection: Electioneering, Lobbying, and Policymaking in Washington*, 37–51. Chatham, NJ: Chatham House.

Holmes, Craig B., and Luke P. McLoughlin. 2002. *Buying Time 2000: Television Advertising in the 2000 Federal Elections.* New York: Brennan Center for Justice.

Isikoff, Michael. 2000. "The Secret Money Chase." *Newsweek*, June 5, 23.

Kamieniecki, Sheldon. 2006. *Corporate America and Environmental Policy: How Often Does Business Get Its Way?* Palo Alto, CA: Stanford University Press.

Libby, Ronald T. 1998. *Eco-Wars: Political Campaigns and Social Movements.* New York: Columbia University Press.

Magleby, David B. 2000. "Interest Group Election Ads." In David B. Magleby, ed., *Outside Money: Soft Money and Issue Advocacy in the 1998 Congressional Elections*, 41–62. Boulder, CO: Rowman & Littlefield.

Magleby, David B., and J. Quin Monson, ed. 2004. *The Last Hurrah? Soft Money and Issue Advocacy in the 2002 Congressional Elections.* Washington, DC: Brookings Institution Press.

Magleby, David B., J. Quin Monson, and Kelly D. Patterson, ed. 2005. *Dancing without Partners: How Candidates, Parties, and Interest Groups Interact in the New Campaign Finance Environment.* Provo, UT: Center for the Study of Elections and Democracy.

Nelson, Candice J. 1998. "The Money Chase: Partisanship, Committee Leadership Change, and PAC Contributions in the House." In Paul S. Herrnson, Ronald G. Shaiko, and Clyde Wilcox, eds., *The Interest Group Connection:*

Electioneering, Lobbying, and Policymaking in Washington, 52–64. Chatham, NJ: Chatham House.

Nelson, Candice J., and Robert Biersack. 1999. "BIPAC: Working to Keep a Probusiness Congress." In Robert Biersack, Paul S. Herrnson, and Clyde Wilcox, eds., *After the Revolution: PACs, Lobbies, and the Republican Congress*, 36–46. Boston: Allyn and Bacon.

Pralle, Sarah. 2003. "Venue Shopping, Political Strategy, and Policy Change: The Internationalization of Canadian Forest Policy." *Journal of Public Policy* 23 (3): 233–260.

Public Citizen. 2004. "The New Stealth PACs: Tracking 501(c) Non-Profit Groups Active in Elections." www.stealthpacs.org/profile.

Rozell, Mark J., and Clyde Wilcox. 1999. *Interest Groups in American Campaigns: The New Face of Electioneering*. Washington, DC: CQ Press.

Saunders, Kyle, and Robert Duffy. 2005. "The 2004 Colorado U.S. Senate Race." In David B. Magleby, J. Quin Monson, and Kelly D. Patterson, eds., *Dancing without Partners: How Candidates, Parties, and Interest Groups Interact in the New Campaign Finance Environment*, 178–194. Provo, UT: Center for the Study of Elections and Democracy.

Sethi, S. Prakash. 1979. "Institutional/Image Advertising and Idea/Issue Advertising as Marketing Tools: Some Public Policy Issues." *Journal of Marketing* 43 (January): 68–78.

Shaiko, Ronald G., and Marc A. Wallace. 1999. "From Wall Street to Main Street: The National Federation of Independent Business and the New Republican Majority." In Robert Biersack, Paul S. Herrnson, and Clyde Wilcox, eds., *After the Revolution: PACs, Lobbies, and the Republican Congress*, Boston: Allyn and Bacon.

Sorauf, Frank. 1988. *Money in American Politics*. Glenview, IL: Scott, Foresman.

Stimson, James. A. 2004. *Tides of Consent: How Public Opinion Shapes American Politics*. Cambridge: Cambridge University Press.

Switzer, Jacqueline Vaughn. 1997. *Green Backlash: The History and Politics of Environmental Opposition in the U.S.* Boulder, CO: Lynne Rienner.

U.S. Chamber of Commerce. 2002a. Press Release of July 2. www.uschamber.com/press/releases/2002/july/02-110.htm.

U.S. Chamber of Commerce. 2002b. Press Release of November 6. www.uschamber.com/press/releases/2002/November6.htm.

U.S. Chamber of Commerce. 2004a. "Elections 2004: Vote for Business." www.uschamber.com/sb/focus/election.

U.S. Chamber of Commerce. 2004b. www.voteforbusiness.com.

West, Darrell M., and Burdett A. Loomis. 1999. *The Sound of Money: How Political Interests Get What They Want*. New York: Norton.

Wright, John R. 1996. *Interest Groups and Congress: Lobbying, Contributions, and Influence*. New York: Longman.

III

Policy Formulation and Adoption: The U.S. Congress

4

Deep Freeze: How Business Has Shaped the Global Warming Debate in Congress

Judith A. Layzer

It is widely assumed that corporate America plays an important role in crafting business-friendly environmental policies in Congress. As noted in the introductory chapter, however, scholars have found that business's legislative fortunes vary, depending on the breadth and cohesiveness of the business coalition as well as the salience of the environmental problem. On the one hand, the broader and more cohesive the business coalition, the better able its members are to fend off costly regulations (Vogel 1989, 1996). On the other hand, the more salient the issue, the less able even a unified business coalition is to dictate the goals and form of regulation (Smith 2000). Recognition of these realities shapes the lobbying strategies of both business and environmental interests, and the interaction among those strategies, in turn, creates incentives for legislators to respond to or ignore environmental problems.

In this chapter I argue that when faced with a newly identified environmental problem, affected businesses typically respond by trying to prevent the issue from becoming widely salient, in hopes of deterring Congress from enacting regulations to address it. They do this by undermining environmentalists' definition of the problem and redirecting attention to the costs of policy. Over time, however, increasing scientific certainty as well as environmentalists' campaigns to shape media coverage, public opinion, and business preferences can shift the perceptions of senior managers regarding the costs and benefits of regulation. As a result, some companies may redirect their lobbying efforts from preventing regulation to ensuring that Congress enacts the policies they prefer. The legislative debate reflects this evolving interplay among science, environmental activism, and business lobbying. At first, efforts by a unified business coalition to prevent a newly identified environmental problem from becoming salient are likely to discourage risk-averse legislators from addressing it. But if environmentalists succeed in fracturing the business coalition by converting some senior managers, aspiring legislative leaders are likely to adopt the issue and turn congressional attention to designing rules that provide the flexibility and regulatory certainty business desires.

To illustrate this argument, I trace the evolution of the fossil-fuel, utility, and automobile industries' efforts to influence the legislative debate over global warming.[1] This case offers a prime opportunity to observe the strategy business adopts in response to the identification of a new, high-stakes environmental problem. In addition, because addressing global warming threatens to impose costs on some of the world's largest corporations, the case allows us to control for several of the key variables posited in the book's conceptual framework as determining business's political strategy—size, profitability, economic resources, and the desire to maintain a socially responsible reputation—and focus on the impact of a single factor: senior managers' perception of the costs and benefits of regulation. In particular, we can see how those perceptions evolve in response to changes in the science and in environmentalists' tactics. Finally, because global warming has been on the political agenda for nearly two decades, we can discern how the interaction among business, science, and environmental activism affects legislative decisionmaking over time.

Business and the Environment in Congress

Organized interests can influence legislative decisionmaking in two ways: through inside and outside lobbying. Inside lobbying involves personal contact with lawmakers and is enormously important in shaping the details of bills. By contrast, outside lobbying, the focus of this chapter, entails activities such as grassroots mobilization, advocacy advertising, and media campaigns—all of which aim to influence both public opinion and legislators' perception of public concern about an issue (Kollman 1998). Proponents of policy change use outside lobbying to stimulate and convey the salience of a problem and hence create incentives for leaders and rank-and-file legislators to address it. By contrast, defenders of the status quo use outside lobbying to *prevent* an issue from becoming salient. Their goals are to create public confusion, make the costs of addressing the problem concrete and personal, and furnish their legislative allies with plausible explanations for opposing policy change—thereby reducing the likelihood that risk-averse legislators will expend political capital on the issue.

Although its role in financing campaigns gives business a clear advantage with respect to inside lobbying (Birnbaum 1992; Clawson, Neustadt, and Weller 1998), the balance of power with respect to outside lobbying is more complicated, particularly in environmental politics. Environmentalists have been extremely effective at defining problems in ways that raise their salience because they bring important political resources to bear. They enjoy the backing of most of the world's scientists, many of whom have become increasingly outspoken about the human impact on the natural environment. In addition, they benefit from the pervasiveness of environmental ideas in American culture (Dunlap 1995; Kempton, Boster, and Hartley 1995). Moreover, they are generally perceived as more credible and public-spirited than their business adversaries (Berry 1999). Furthermore, the media have abetted environmentalists' efforts by using ecological language to describe environmental problems (Schoenfeld, Meier, and Griffin 1979).

Although environmentalists have been extraordinarily successful, business has figured out how to counter their influence with outside-lobbying campaigns of its own. When faced with the prospect of an environmental regulation that threatens their bottom line, businesses adopt a three-pronged strategy in hopes of preventing the problem from becoming salient. First, they discredit the science that underpins environmentalists' claims by portraying it as highly uncertain and distorted by biased scientists and advocates. Second, they portray environmentalists as elite, misanthropic extremists who frighten the public in order to fill their own coffers. Third, they draw attention to the economic costs of addressing the problem, particularly the impact of regulation on jobs and consumer prices. To enhance their credibility, businesses have funded sympathetic experts and think tanks that provide technical backing for their arguments.

Large corporations, with their deep pockets, have been particularly adept at crafting and disseminating alternatives to environmentalists' storyline (West and Loomis 1999). But, as environmentalists have recognized, the same entities that are best equipped to counter their message are also politically vulnerable. Large corporations are sensitive to their public image and therefore to the popularity of the positions they take. Furthermore, because they typically operate in multiple states and often have operations in other countries, they find a heterogeneous regulatory environment burdensome. Environmentalists have capitalized on these vulnerabilities by adopting a variety of tactics aimed at changing senior managers' perceptions of the costs and benefits of—and hence their corporate interest in—protective policy. They have launched consumer boycotts and negative publicity campaigns that exploit companies' desire to appear green. For example, the Rainforest Action Network's boycott of the Home Depot prompted the company to stop buying and selling wood from endangered forests overseas and old-growth forests in the United States (Vogel 2005). Similarly, a boycott of tuna caught using methods that kill dolphins convinced canners to support a dolphin-safe labeling law (Layzer 2006). Environmentalists also have instigated state-level policymaking, which results in the creation of an onerous patchwork of regulations, in hopes of prompting business to seek federal rules. This tactic was extremely effective in the acid rain debate because it pitted utilities from "clean" states against those from "dirty" ones (Layzer 2006). Finally, environmentalists have employed collaboration and persuasion, emphasizing a growing scientific consensus on the magnitude and importance of an environmental problem to make it harder for image-conscious companies to resist. For instance, when the science linking chlorofluorocarbons to ozone loss became sufficiently certain, DuPont reversed its position and began to support the Montreal Protocol (Parson 2003).

Once their perceptions of the costs and benefits of regulation shift, senior managers may elect to throw their support behind new legislation and even work with environmentalists to devise a solution. Their motives vary: some believe that properly designed regulations can confer a competitive advantage; others aim to create a positive image by adopting a pro-regulatory stance; still others view regulatory tightening as inevitable and hope that, as early movers, they can win a seat at the table when rules are chosen (Gunningham, Kagan, and Thornton 2003). A business-environmentalist coalition can, in turn, provide a powerful spur to legislators to act on an issue. For environmentalists, however, this kind of politics comes at a price: legislative action becomes more likely, but the resulting policies often accommodate the concerns of business at the expense of environmental stringency.

The Global Warming Debate

The evolution of the global warming debate exemplifies the complex interplay between the outside-lobbying efforts of business and the tactics of environmentalists as each struggles to shape the legislative debate over a new environmental issue. At first, scientists and environmentalists defined the problem of global warming, and the media dutifully repeated their story: greenhouse gas emissions caused by deforestation and fossil-fuel combustion were raising the global temperature, with potentially disastrous consequences. But the issue's emergence on the political agenda prompted a coalition of fossil-fuel-based industries to mobilize and devote enormous sums to defusing public concern about climate change. They accomplished this end by sowing doubt about the science underpinning the global warming hypothesis and drawing attention to the economic costs of curbing greenhouse gas emissions. Throughout the 1990s, a broad and unified coalition of industries and their conservative allies succeeded in preventing global warming from becoming widely salient; as a result, despite scientific and international alarm, legislative leaders in the United States declined to address the issue. Over time, however, business unity fractured as increasingly certain scientific assessments, environmental activism, and the response to these developments by states and the international community caused shifts in some business leaders' perceptions of the costs and benefits of federally mandated emissions limits. Although many senior managers staunchly denied the seriousness of global warming, others began publicly acknowledging the problem and taking voluntary actions to curb their greenhouse gas emissions. Still others endorsed mandatory federal limits, as long as any new regulation was tailored to their needs. As a result of these changes in the political context, in 2003 the Senate began seriously debating the details of a regulatory approach that would provide the certainty and flexibility that business demanded.

The Road to Kyoto: 1988–1997

Although the global warming hypothesis received serious scientific attention beginning in the 1970s, the U.S. media did not publicize the issue until the extraordinarily hot, dry summer of 1988, when NASA scientist James Hansen told the Senate Energy and Natural Resources Committee that human-induced global warming was imminent and sufficiently well understood that policymakers should act to address it. There was an immediate surge in media coverage, which in turn raised public awareness, and politicians responded. In a speech in Detroit on August 31, presidential candidate George H. W. Bush said that "those who think we are powerless to do anything about the 'greenhouse effect' are forgetting about the 'White House Effect'" and vowed to act on the issue during his first year in office (Vig 1994, 81). In Congress Senators Tim Wirth (D-CO) and Al Gore (D-TN), as well as Representative Claudine Schneider (R-RI), drafted comprehensive global warming bills, even though the passage of these measures was highly unlikely.

That fall the United Nations and the World Meteorological Organization jointly sponsored the creation of the Intergovernmental Panel on Climate Change (IPCC), whose purpose was to provide policymakers with a scientific foundation for international negotiations to address the issue of global warming. In 1990 the IPCC released its first report, which concluded that emissions resulting from human activities were substantially increasing the atmospheric concentrations of greenhouse gases; doubling of carbon dioxide (CO_2), the most abundant greenhouse gas, was likely to increase the global temperature by 1.4 to 4.5 degrees Celsius; and an immediate 60 percent reduction in emissions would be needed to stem the buildup of CO_2 in the atmosphere (IPCC 1990).[2]

Members of the fossil-fuel-based industries quickly perceived the financial implications of defining global warming as a serious problem: oil and coal are the main sources of CO_2; coal-fired utilities are the largest emitters of CO_2 (40 percent of total U.S. emissions), while the transportation sector is a close second (30 percent). From the outset these industries' primary goal was to prevent global warming from becoming widely salient and thereby ensure there would be insufficient domestic support for an international treaty to address it. To this end, in 1989 the National Association of Manufacturers spun off the first major organization aimed at coordinating business participation in the climate change debate, the Global Climate Coalition (GCC)—an amalgamation of fifty-four industry and trade-association members representing electric utilities, automobile manufacturers, and oil and coal producers (as well as railroads and other manufacturers). In hopes of defusing public concern about global warming the GCC launched an attack on the scientific basis for the global warming hypothesis: coalition members financed the publication and distribution of books, pamphlets, and articles by a handful of skeptics who challenged the scientific understanding of the climate and the evidence for asserting that humans were having an impact on it (Gelbspan 1997). The GCC's second objective was to shift public attention to what it claimed would be the overwhelming economic impact of policies to curb greenhouse gas emissions. To accomplish this the coalition sponsored and disseminated dozens of economic studies projecting the exorbitant costs of a worldwide energy transition (Layzer 2006).[3]

In a separate endeavor, in 1991 the National Coal Association, the Western Fuels Association, and Edison Electric Institute (the largest utility trade association) joined forces to establish the Information Council on the Environment (ICE), whose mission was to conduct a publicity campaign to discredit the scientific consensus on global warming. Three prominent skeptics—University of Virginia climatologist Patrick Michaels, University of Arizona climatologist Robert Balling, and soil scientist Sherwood Idso—served as the campaign's scientific advisors. The initiative called for placing scientific skeptics in broadcast appearances, editorial pages, and newspaper interviews, particularly in districts that received their electricity from coal and had a representative on the House Energy Committee. ICE disbanded after environmentalists exposed it to the media, but its efforts to create public confusion about global warming had already borne fruit. For example, Western Fuels had spent $250,000 creating a video that was widely shown in Washington, D.C. Titled *The Greening of Planet Earth*, the video's message was that a warmer, wetter, CO_2-enhanced world would benefit the United States.

The industry campaign was extremely effective at deterring presidential leadership. The George H. W. Bush administration, although sensitive to international pressures to address global warming, was heavily influenced by industry arguments. In a February 1990 speech, President Bush acknowledged the issue but said he did not believe the scientific evidence justified major new proposals or spending programs and emphasized the importance of ensuring that any policies adopted would not deter economic growth and were consistent with free-market principles. In 1992 the president signed the Framework Convention on Climate Change (FCCC), whose primary goal is "the stabilization of greenhouse gas concentrations in the atmosphere at a level that would prevent dangerous anthropogenic interference with the climate system." But he did so only after threatening to boycott the Rio Earth Summit if the convention contained any specific goals or deadlines for reducing CO_2 emissions.

With the election of President Bill Clinton just a month after the Senate ratified the FCCC, environmentalists hoped the United States would take a more proactive approach to global warming. In his first Earth Day speech Clinton promised to restructure energy use in the United States, converting the nation from fossil-fuel dependence to reliance on renewables and clean-burning sources. But after failing to convince Congress to adopt his Btu tax proposal, Clinton's zeal evaporated: the 1993 White House Climate Change Action Plan included about fifty voluntary federal energy conservation programs but did not deal directly with greenhouse gas emissions.

Clinton's reluctance to take a strong stand on global warming reflected a shrewd reading of the public, which was hardly clamoring for him to address the issue. After a brief period of heightened attention in 1988 and 1989, media interest in the issue had waned, partly because environmentalists lacked a compelling story: the villains were ordinary Americans, with their profligate lifestyles; the most likely victims were small island nations; and the crisis appeared at least a generation away. Furthermore, any effort to reduce greenhouse gas emissions would produce immediate costs while promising distant benefits. As important, though, media coverage had begun to reflect the impact of the industry campaign: in 1988 and 1989 the vast majority of media coverage emphasized human-made contributions to global warming and suggested immediate, mandatory action was warranted; by 1990, however, journalists were regularly quoting skeptics to "balance" their reporting on global warming (Boykoff and Boykoff 2004). Opponents' efforts appeared to be paying off among the public as well: public concern dwindled as media coverage declined and lost its urgency; furthermore, a 1994 poll by Cambridge Reports found that just 28 percent of respondents perceived a scientific consensus that "global warming exists and could do significant damage," while 58 percent believed scientists were divided (www.pipa.org).

Although they were faring well domestically, opponents of global warming policies were incensed by two international developments that occurred in 1995. First, the IPCC released its second assessment, which concluded with even more certainty than its predecessor that "the balance of the evidence suggests that there is a discernible human influence on global climate." The report also reiterated that a 60–80 percent reduction in CO_2 emissions would be necessary just to stabilize atmospheric concentrations of greenhouse gases (IPCC 1996). Second, international negotiators agreed that any legal instrument to come out of the formal negotiations scheduled for Kyoto, Japan, in 1997 would impose emissions reductions only on developed countries.

To frame these events for their domestic audience, fossil-fuel-based industry leaders initiated another round of outside lobbying. They tried to discredit the IPCC report by launching personal attacks on its senior authors, charging them with down playing scientific uncertainty and creating the perception of consensus where none existed. In addition, they challenged the idea of exempting developing countries, pointing out those countries were deforesting their land, thereby eliminating carbon sinks, and in the future would be the major carbon emitters. Furthermore, industry spokespeople argued that such an approach would put American businesses at a competitive disadvantage and prompt jobs to move overseas. The Coalition for Vehicle Choice, a Washington-based group financed by the automobile industry, initiated a campaign to recruit white-hat allies by convincing small-business, labor, and local civic groups throughout the United States that the Kyoto Protocol would be "bad for America." Similarly, the Center for Energy and Economic Development, whose $4 million annual budget was furnished by the coal industry, targeted business and civic groups in eleven states and forged an alliance with the United Mine Workers union, which also opposed the treaty.

The arguments made by these broad industry-labor coalitions fell on receptive ears in Congress: the 1994 elections had produced Republican majorities in both the House and Senate, and skeptical claims about the

Kyoto Protocol provided political cover for conservative Republicans to pursue their ideological preferences. Newly elevated legislative leaders immediately moved to reinforce efforts to undermine climate change science. For instance, in September 1995 California Republican Representative Dana Rohrabacher convened a series of subcommittee hearings titled "Scientific Integrity and the Public Trust," whose purpose was to highlight contrary views and thereby discredit mainstream climate change science in general and the IPCC in particular. Similarly, hearings held by the House Science Committee in March 1996 to determine the budget for U.S. climate change research featured three prominent scientific skeptics: Patrick Michaels, Robert Balling, and S. Fred Singer. Even environmentally concerned members of Congress felt compelled to respond to industry's widely publicized arguments. On July 25, 1997, the Senate unanimously passed a nonbinding resolution, the Byrd-Hagel amendment, which echoed industry's position: it stipulated the Senate would not give its advice and consent to any international agreement that failed to require developing countries to reduce their emissions or that would result in "serious harm to the economy of the United States."

In October President Clinton unveiled a moderate plan to reduce the nation's greenhouse gas emissions to 1990 levels between 2008 and 2012 using a $5 billion package of tax breaks and other incentives. Conservative Republicans in Congress immediately denounced the proposal, expressing their opposition in precisely the terms employed by the industry coalition. House Majority Whip Tom DeLay (R-TX) said: "Before we do anything that hurts children, hurts our nation's competitiveness, hurts the taxpayer, and hurts economic growth, we need to know all the facts." Thomas Bliley (R-WV), chair of the House Commerce Committee, was equally derisive: "It will inevitably cause a massive increase in what Americans pay for electricity and natural gas, and a slowing of our economic growth by at least a full percentage point." The president's proposal, Bliley added, "is unilateral disarmament by the United States. The result will be a treaty that isn't global and which won't work, and that ultimately will cost American jobs and raise American taxes" (Freedman 1997).

Despite congressional belligerence, President Clinton pledged to bring to the Kyoto meeting "a strong American commitment to realistic and binding limits that [would] significantly reduce our emissions of greenhouse gases" (Molitor 1999, 220). The president enjoyed some support among business leaders: backing the administration were the International Climate Change Partnership, comprising a handful of Fortune 500 companies—such as DuPont, General Electric, and AT&T—that hoped to shape U.S. policy on the issue; the Business Council for Sustainable Energy, which consisted of producers of natural gas and alternative energy producers and manufacturers of energy-saving devices; and some members of the insurance industry, which feared catastrophic losses if scientists' predictions were borne out. But the vast majority of the business community remained firmly opposed to greenhouse gas emissions limits. More important, as *Wall Street Journal* reporter John Fialka (1997a) pointed out, business supporters of the White House were newly mobilized, while "the big guns from the other side [had] been booming away for years."

Furthermore, to counteract the White House effort to drum up public and business support in advance of the Kyoto meeting, in the fall of 1997 industry opponents of the treaty launched an all-out media blitz. The GCC alone spent $13 million on an advertising campaign that warned television viewers that "strict reductions in greenhouse gases would have catastrophic economic consequences, endangering the lifestyle of every American. Gasoline would shoot up by 50 cents or more a gallon; heating and electricity bills would soar, while higher energy costs would raise the price of almost everything Americans buy. The livelihoods of thousands of coal miners, auto-workers, and others employed in energy-related fields were on the line" (Christiansen 1999, 258). To reinforce this message, conservative think tanks such as the Competitive Enterprise Institute and the National Center for Policy Analysis sponsored a series of press conferences and delivered speeches throughout the summer and fall of 1997. They also sent representatives to Kyoto to issue daily bulletins and promote their views in the media (McCright and Dunlap 2000).

The impact of these countervailing efforts to shape public opinion and legislators' perceptions was mixed. For example, a widely cited poll taken by the Pew Research Center for the People and the Press in November found that nearly three-quarters of respondents would pay 5 cents more for gasoline, and 60 percent said they would pay 25 cents more, to combat global warming (www.people-press.org). Pew noted that public opinion was still quite malleable, however, since most people had not fully engaged with the issue. A Gallup poll conducted immediately prior to the Kyoto talks suggested that public fears about global warming had declined substantially from 1992 levels. While 42 percent said scientists mostly believed global warming was a serious threat, 44 percent believed scientists were mostly divided on the issue (Moore 1997).

These survey data were sufficiently ambiguous that elected officials could discern no clear signal on climate change. Muddled public opinion, in turn, allowed conservative Republicans to express their skepticism about the Kyoto protocol without fear of political repercussions and inhibited moderate Republicans and Democrats, who discerned few incentives to expend their political capital promoting measures to tackle global warming. In early December, when negotiators agreed to a treaty requiring the United States to reduce its greenhouse gas emissions by 7 percent by 2012, conservatives responded by competing to see who could forecast the direst consequences. Former presidential candidate Malcolm "Steve" Forbes Jr. said the treaty would amount to a $2,000 tax increase for every American family and called it a "government power grab." Even Vice President Gore, perhaps the government's most ardent environmentalist, was in a bind. As journalist Ronald Elving observed: "If Gore tries to push his vision of sacrifices for planetary ecology on the Senate, the vision will be rejected. If he tries to sell it to voters (who will be subjected to fearsome degrees of counter-programming), he himself will be rejected. And if he transmits this identity to his party, he will divide the ranks and burden every Democratic candidate with the kind of anti-growth, anti-consumption baggage they had to drag behind them through the 1970s and 1980s" (Elving 1997).

Debating Greenhouse Gas Emissions Limits: 1998–2005

In early 1998 industry opponents geared up to ensure that the Kyoto Protocol stood no chance of Senate ratification. Because there was little scientific disagreement about rising global temperature, industry operatives turned to debunking claims about the role of human activity, emphasizing the uncertainty of scientists' models, and touting the ostensible benefits of increased atmospheric CO_2. In addition, they argued that complying with the treaty would hamper U.S. competitiveness, cause jobs to move overseas, and dampen economic growth. With allies in leadership positions in both the House and Senate, and the 2001 inauguration of George W. Bush, defenders of the status quo were well positioned to resist global warming policies.

Even as opponents of global warming policy gained control of the federal policymaking apparatus, however, the political context of the issue was changing: scientific support for the global warming hypothesis was solidifying, and U.S. scientists were becoming increasingly outspoken; environmental advocates were targeting businesses directly; and the states were enacting global warming policies in response to scientific and environmental activism. These developments, in turn, changed some senior managers' perceptions of the costs and benefits of regulation, and some CEOs began endorsing mandatory emissions limits. In 2003, sensing the issue's rising salience and a softening of industry opposition, aspiring legislative leaders proposed the nation's first-ever greenhouse gas emissions controls. But they made sure to tailor their proposals to the requirements of business supporters.

Opposition to Kyoto

Virtually all executives from the industries whose profitability was threatened by the Kyoto Protocol initially were outspoken in their opposition to its ratification. They called it costly, ineffective, and inequitable, and they insisted that any policy adopted by the United States rely instead on voluntary programs. For example, Chrysler Corporation Chair Robert Eaton said: "For months we have urged the administration not to bind this country to reductions of greenhouse-gas emissions with arbitrary deadlines. Innovation and invention don't often come with dates certain." Red Cavaney, president of the American Petroleum Institute, claimed that the treaty could force oil companies and others with high energy costs to move plants and jobs to countries not working under emissions-reduction requirements. He doubted that technology could achieve the kinds of reductions being discussed and said the result would be energy rationing, "which means less energy for everyone," or "dramatically and artificially" raising prices through taxes. Thomas Kuhn, president of the Washington-based Edison Electric Institute, described the agreement as "economic suicide" and said it would cost electric utilities with coal-fired generating facilities as much as $30 billion (Fialka 1997b).

In April 1998 a group led by the American Petroleum Institute and including representatives of Exxon, Chevron, and the massive utility, the Southern Company, circulated a memorandum containing a Global Climate Science Communications Action Plan, which aimed to defuse support for the Kyoto Protocol. The document began by summarizing industry's claims that "signing such a treaty will place the U.S. at a competitive disadvantage with most other nations, and will be extremely expensive to implement. Much of the cost will be borne by American consumers who will pay higher prices for most energy and transportation." The authors proposed that treaty opponents adopt an action plan to make climate change a "nonissue" by "inform[ing] the American public that science does not support the precipitous actions Kyoto would dictate, thereby providing a climate for the right policy decisions to be made" (Adams et al. 1998). The plan recommended identifying, recruiting, and training a team of five independent scientists to participate in media outreach; developing a global science kit for the media; producing and distributing a steady stream of climate science information; convincing a major national TV journalist to produce a report examining the scientific underpinnings of the Kyoto treaty; and organizing, promoting, and conducting a series of campus and community workshops and debates on climate science.

Environmentalists exposed the plan to the media, so like the 1991 ICE plan it was never formally implemented. But its authors continued to coordinate their activities and promote their views through a variety of think tanks, organizations, and websites. For example, to celebrate Earth Day 1998 the Western Fuels Association launched the "Greening Earth Society," a self-described "grassroots movement" dedicated to the proposition that "having more CO_2 in the atmosphere will be good, not bad. It will lead to a greater diversity of plants, more abundant crops, more animals" (Fialka 1998). And the Cooler Heads Coalition—an umbrella group of seventeen prominent conservative, industry-funded think tanks and advocacy organizations—coordinated efforts to "dispel the myths of global warming by exposing flawed economic, scientific, and risk analysis" (www.globalwarming.org).

Legislative Leaders Protect the Status Quo

Industry opponents of climate change policies hoped their campaign would be sufficient to bolster conservative allies in Congress and intimidate potential leaders. Sure enough, recognizing that he lacked Senate support, President Clinton declined to submit the Kyoto Protocol for ratification. Furthermore, instead of proposing emissions limits, he unveiled a five-year, $6.3 billion package of tax breaks and research spending in pursuit of the treaty's emissions-reduction goals. Even that was too much for Republican leaders in Congress, who were determined to squelch any effort to comply with the treaty, and in April 1998 the Senate Budget Committee deleted the 1999 portion of the president's spending package. Senator Chuck Hagel, whose committee planned to hold hearings to assess the protocol's economic impact, crowed: "What we're saying is there will be no implementation of the Kyoto Protocol and no funds expended. Boom. It's that simple" (Fialka 1998). To put an exclamation point on their opposition, for the next three years Republicans attached riders to a variety of appropriations bills explicitly prohibiting the use of funds "to propose or issue rules, regulations, decrees, or orders for the purpose of implementing, or in preparation for the implementation of, the Kyoto Protocol."

Global warming policy opponents were overjoyed when President George W. Bush took office in January 2001, thereby further cementing their advantage. The new president quickly reversed himself on a campaign pledge to regulate CO_2 emissions and instead announced his opposition to the Kyoto Protocol, which he characterized as unfair and ineffective. According to the *New York Times*, the president reversed his position under "strong pressure from conservative Republicans and industry groups" (Suskind 2004, 127).[4] In a letter explaining his views, Bush echoed the themes articulated by industry: energy production was a top priority; coal, the workhorse that produced half the country's power, needed protection; lifting the burden of environmental regulations from business was essential; and CO_2 emissions limits were a harmful constraint on American commerce. To appease Republican moderates, in February 2002 Bush announced a domestic plan to reduce the economy's "carbon intensity" (the ratio of greenhouse gases to gross domestic product) by 18 percent over ten years.[5] The centerpiece of the plan was a voluntary program to encourage industrial polluters to reduce their emissions. The plan also included $4.6 billion in tax credits over five years. In presenting his proposal the president made it clear that economic growth was his primary concern, and that he believed a thriving economy would provide the resources to invest in clean technologies.

Changes in the Political Context

Even as conservative leaders in Congress and the White House adopted the arguments of global warming policy opponents, several aspects of the political context were changing in ways that divided the business community. First, the scientific consensus on the existence of, human contribution to, and threats posed by climate change was becoming unassailable. In January 2001, atmospheric concentrations of CO_2 reached a historic high of 370 ppm, and the IPPC released its third and most unequivocal report on the dangers of global warming. The report documented the unprecedented warming of the second half of the twentieth century and emphatically rejected skeptics' primary counterargument—that solar activity, not human activities, was responsible for the earth's increasing temperatures. In addition, a growing mountain of scientific studies documented the impacts of global warming—from melting glaciers to changes in species' mating habits and migration patterns—many of which were occurring even faster than scientists had predicted.

Second, in the face of determined political resistance environmentalists had adjusted their tactics and begun lobbying business directly. Some of their efforts were confrontational: Greenpeace and the Rainforest Action Network launched consumer boycotts and campaigns to tarnish the reputation of big companies whose policies failed to reflect concern about global warming. In addition, environmentalists joined forces with religious groups and began submitting shareholder resolutions demanding that corporations reveal their global warming liability. Others adopted a collaborative approach: in May 1998 the Pew Center on Climate Change established a Business Environmental Leaders Council, whose primary objective was to bolster the credibility of climate change science by increasing the visibility of business leaders' support. By 2002 the group had thirty-eight members, including AEP, Entergy Corp., Sunoco, Boeing, Toyota, and Lockheed Martin. In March 2000 the World Wildlife Fund announced a partnership with six heavyweights, such as Johnson & Johnson and IBM, in its Climate Savers Program, an audit program whose goal was to show that companies could voluntarily achieve reductions that equaled or exceeded those called for under the Kyoto Protocol. Also in 2000 Environmental Defense began working with Pew, the Nature Conservancy, and at least thirty large companies to hammer out an international emissions trading scheme under its Partnership for Climate Action program.

Third, states were responding to the scientific consensus and environmental activism by enacting global warming policies of their own (Rabe 2004). In 1997 Oregon limited CO_2 emissions for new or expanded power plants to a level 17 percent below the most efficient natural-gas-fired plant in the United States. In 1999 Texas established a requirement that utilities achieve a certain percentage of their portfolio using renewable energy sources, and other states quickly followed suit. By 2002 Massachusetts and New Hampshire had imposed CO_2 limits on power plants, and in 2003 they joined forces with seven other Northeastern states and five Eastern Canadian provinces to plan a regional cap-and-trade system. In July 2002 California passed a bill that made it the first state to limit greenhouse gas emissions by automobiles and light trucks. And, in 2003, Maine passed the nation's first law calling for specific cuts in greenhouse gas emissions.

CEOs' Perceptions and Strategies Diverge

More certain science and new approaches to environmental activism, as well as action by the states, changed some senior managers' perceptions of the costs and benefits of enacting a federal global warming policy. As a result, by the fall of 1998 the oil, automobile, and utility company coalitions were showing signs of strain. As the scientific consensus grew stronger, some CEOs began to believe that carbon limits were inevitable and that being early movers would earn them a prominent role in designing the rules. Others, concerned about maintaining a green corporate image, feared that environmentalist-backed boycotts and shareholder resolutions portrayed them as environmentally unfriendly. Some preferred uniform federal rules to the emerging hodgepodge of state-level requirements. So while most executives remained opposed to mandatory emissions limits, senior managers in a handful of prominent companies began to see advantages in changing their position on the issue. Furthermore, although CEOs' motives varied, there was virtually unanimous support for a cap-and-trade system that would provide both regulatory certainty and flexibility. Therefore, they shifted their focus from blocking legislation to ensuring that Congress would adopt a market-based system whose rules would give them credit for both emissions (carbon source) reductions and forestland (carbon sink) acquisition.

In the oil industry, there was a dramatic split, with two of the largest firms—ExxonMobil and BP—taking opposite positions. On taking office in 1995 ExxonMobil's CEO, Lee Raymond, established himself as a vocal critic of global warming science and a staunch opponent of greenhouse gas emissions reductions, which he said would lead to widespread economic harm. In October 1997 Raymond urged developing countries to avoid environmental controls that would hinder their development and jeopardize foreign investment. He encouraged them not to curtail but increase their use of fossil fuels, pointing out that nature was to blame for most global warming and that changes in the Earth's temperature were commonplace. In 2002, at the Seventh Annual Asia Oil & Gas Conference in Kuala Lumpur, Raymond told attendees that "we in ExxonMobil do not believe that the science required to establish this linkage between fossil fuels and warming has been demonstrated—and many scientists agree" (Cassady 2005, 7). To promote its position, between 1998 and 2004 ExxonMobil gave more than $15 million to conservative organizations working to influence public and policymakers' views about global warming (Cassady 2005). The company also spent $55 million between 1999 and 2004 on direct lobbying and worked closely with the White House to craft its position on global warming and the Kyoto pact (Mooney 2005).

By contrast, BP withdrew from the GCC in 1997, because, according to CEO John Browne, "The time to consider policy dimensions of climate change is not when the link between greenhouse gases and climate change is conclusively proven, but when the possibility cannot be discounted and is taken seriously by the society of which we are a part" (Johnson 1997). As former BP executive Steve Percy explains, large multinationals like BP recognize they have to comply with the Kyoto Protocol overseas; moreover, they prefer uniform federal regulations to an assortment of state laws. Percy also emphasizes the potential for profitable innovation, the extent to which emissions cuts to reduce energy waste could pay off, and the importance of maintaining a positive environmental image with both customers and shareholders (E&E TV 2005). To demonstrate the effectiveness of its preferred approach, BP devised an internal cap-and-trade system that enabled it to reduce its emissions by 10 percent, at a savings of $650 million (Carey 2004).[6] To publicize its commitment, the company undertook a $200 million public relations campaign and, in 2000, changed its corporate symbol from a shield to a sunburst and began promoting itself with the slogan "Beyond Petroleum."

The utility industry saw a split among its CEOs as well. Although a handful of utilities in Southern California, New England, and New York began curbing their CO_2 emissions voluntarily in the early 1990s, the vast majority remained skeptical about global warming science and implacably opposed to taking any action to address it. In the early 2000s, however, a number of utilities began adopting new policies to reduce their greenhouse gas emissions. For example, in 2001 the New Orleans–based Entergy Corp. announced it would hold its CO_2 emissions to 2000 levels through 2005 in order to convey to the public its seriousness on global warming and send a message to politicians that trading credits was the most efficient way to encourage industry to cut its greenhouse gas output. In August 2002 Entergy donated 600 acres of land along Louisiana's Red River to the federal government in hopes of getting credit if the United States decided to regulate CO_2 emissions, since the trees planted on the land would (theoretically) absorb and store an estimated 275,000 tons of CO_2 (Fialka 2002).

The Ford Motor Co. shook up the U.S. automobile industry with its highly publicized efforts to cultivate a green image. Led by its new chair, William Clay Ford Jr., a self-described environmentalist, in early December 1999 Ford withdrew from the GCC saying that it had begun to see its membership in the group as an impediment to pursuing its environmental initiatives credibly. On global warming, a Ford spokesperson said "there is enough evidence that something is happening that we ought to look at this seriously" ("Ford Leaves Coalition That Opposes Treaty on Global Warming," 1999). In July 2000 Ford announced it would improve the average fuel economy of its SUV fleet 25 percent over five years (though it did not say how, and it infuriated environmentalists by continuing to lobby with the rest of the industry against increased CAFE standards).[7] General Motors immediately promised to beat Ford's improvements, and DaimlerChrysler said it would meet or beat any Ford SUV fuel economy gains. In spring 2001 Ford announced it had dropped its long-held skepticism about global warming and said that of all the ways the company would be judged in the coming years, "None will be greater than our response to climate change." Ford then took out full-page newspaper ads in the United States and Europe in May 2001 that said: "Global warming. There. We said it. Some find our stand on global warming rather unique. Mostly due to the fact that we actually have one" (Ball 2001, A1).

Adding to the chorus, a handful of companies in energy-dependent industries undertook an initiative aimed at demonstrating that a cap-and-trade system could work. In January 2003 American Electric Power (AEP), Ford, and ten other companies, along with the city of Chicago, announced the creation of the Chicago Climate Exchange. Each participant in the exchange promised to cut its greenhouse gas emissions by 1 percent in 2003, 2 percent in 2004, 3 percent in 2005, and 4 percent in 2006, from a baseline determined by its average annual emission levels between 1998 and 2001. These companies hoped to generate a currency of credits, including credits for carbon sinks, that would become internationally tradable. Leading the charge was DuPont, which had spent heavily to cut its greenhouse gas emissions by 40 percent between 1990 and 2000. Stung by its experience a decade earlier, when its resistance to the science linking chlorofluorocarbons and ozone loss had sparked bitter protests against the company, DuPont officials had decided to take a different tack when the global warming issue emerged.

Ideological conservatives were appalled by CEOs' defections. As early as June 2000, the conservative Marshall Institute's William O'Keefe recognized the political implications of the business coalition's dissolution and rebuked business leaders for their squeamishness in the face of environmentalist coercion: "Prior to Kyoto, the business community was focused, united and forceful," he said.

Our support for S.R. 98 [Byrd-Hagel] and our willingness to openly debate the climate change issue and undertake a major advertising campaign was a significant achievement. Momentum was on our side. Unfortunately, we did not sustain it because many in the business community do not understand perseverance. . . . Because of this failure, the [Clinton] Administration and its environmental allies have regained the momentum. They have succeeded in fracturing out unity and putting industry on the defensive. (www.marshall.org)

Ironically, the conservative Bush administration may have exacerbated the industry split by promising credit for any voluntary emissions reductions made. As Thomas Lyons (2003, 40) explains, "Early reduction credits create a constituency for mandatory measures because the credits only pay off if regulations are imposed."

Congress Takes Up Climate Change

Activity on global warming in Congress reflected changes in the political context and the breakup of the industry coalition. Between 1998 and 2002, partly in response to the early actions of some businesses, Democrats and moderate Republicans introduced dozens of bills that purported to address climate change—by giving credit for early action to reduce emissions, promoting research on climate change and technologies to reduce or sequester carbon emissions, promoting voluntary emissions reductions or automotive fuel efficiency, establishing tax incentives for energy efficiency, and adding CO_2 limits for utilities to the Clean Air Act rewrite—but they did not vigorously promote these measures. By 2003, however, continuing efforts by environmentalists and scientists to raise public concern about global warming, combined with public advocacy by some powerful corporate leaders, created incentives for aspiring leaders to make a serious attempt at instituting mandatory, economy-wide greenhouse gas emissions limits. The 2003 Climate Stewardship Act failed, and a similar bill lost by an even larger margin in 2005, reflecting rank-and-file senators' continuing reluctance to act in the face of serious political uncertainty. Nevertheless, the momentum for mandatory emissions limits appeared to be growing. By the summer of 2006, many thought that greenhouse gas regulation was inevitable, and Senate leaders were trying to construct an approach that would pass muster with business and gain the endorsement of a congressional majority.

The Climate Stewardship Act, 2003 In 2003 Republican John McCain (AZ), chair of the Senate Commerce Committee, teamed up with Democrat Joe Lieberman (CT) to sponsor the nation's first-ever limit on greenhouse gas emissions. Their bill, the Climate Stewardship Act (S 139), required the electricity, transportation, industrial, and commercial sectors—which together account for 85 percent of U.S. emissions—to cut their greenhouse gas emissions to 2000 levels by 2010 and to 1990 levels by 2016. Consistent with industry preferences, the bill imposed a cap on overall emissions and then allowed businesses to trade credits with one another to achieve the required reduction. As leading businesses had also hoped, the bill included language allowing companies to offset their obligations with carbon sinks and overseas reductions. In justifying his sponsorship of the measure, McCain cited both IPCC and National Academy of Sciences reports that said human actions were at least partly responsible for the recently observed warming trend. He added that the United States faced "substantial ecological disruption" unless it did more to curb its greenhouse gas emissions. He also pointed out that other countries were already preparing to impose emissions limits, states and companies were moving forward, and Americans' concern about climate change had "increased dramatically."

The bill faced staunch opposition from the president, however, who argued that more research was needed before taking steps to control greenhouse gases and that, in any case, his program of incentives for voluntary action was sufficient. The bill also faced determined resistance within the Senate. In late July 2003, James Inhofe (R-OK) tried to muddy the debate by again inviting two scientific skeptics to debunk the global warming hypothesis before the Senate Environment and Public Works Committee. Inhofe himself gave a two-hour speech on the Senate floor in which he said: "With all of the hysteria, all of the fear, all of the phony science, could it be that man-made global warming is the greatest hoax ever perpetrated on the American people? It sure sounds like it."[8]

Moreover, although the Climate Stewardship Act attracted a handful of business supporters, the majority of business leaders backed the opposition. Utility giant AEP was officially neutral on the Climate Stewardship Act—a switch from its traditional opposition to CO_2 caps—because the bill's sponsors had revamped the measure to make its cuts less onerous than those AEP had already agreed to make under the Chicago Climate Exchange. But a host of powerful trade associations lobbied furiously against the bill. The American Petroleum Institute, the Alliance of Automobile Manufacturers, the National Mining Association, the Portland Cement Association, the American Iron and Steel Institute, the American Chemistry Council, and the Aluminum Association publicly expressed their support for the president's voluntary approach. Just before the vote the Edison Electric Institute, the American Public Power Association, the National Mining Association, and the National Rural Electric Cooperative Association sent a letter to senators urging them to vote against the Climate Stewardship Act. "The bill's mandatory cap-and-trade and mandatory reporting approaches are the wrong ways to address global climate change," the letter said. The authors instead advocated an emphasis on technology-based approaches as exemplified by the pending energy bill. It concluded by noting that "our industries and many others have been active participants in voluntary greenhouse gas reduction programs for nearly a decade" (Kuhn et al. 2003).

Despite the controversy, in October—after rebuffing a jurisdictional challenge from Senator Inhofe—McCain and Lieberman made an unusual parliamentarian deal with Senate Majority Leader Bill Frist (R-TN) to force a vote on their bill. Just prior to the vote McCain displayed a series of satellite photos showing reduction of the Arctic ice cap, the disappearing snow pack on Africa's Mount Kilimanjaro, and the loss of most of the glaciers in Glacier National Park. But fellow Republicans continued to articulate the industry position, firing back with statistics showing projected job losses that would have occurred if the United States had ratified Kyoto Protocol. "I can hear the giant sucking sound of jobs leaving our country every time I return to Ohio," said Republican Senate George V. Voinovich (Fialka 2003, B2).

For fence-sitting senators the divisions among their colleagues and within the business community over voluntary versus mandatory emissions reductions made support of the Climate Stewardship Act politically risky. Even though its authors relaxed the bill's goals by stripping the provision requiring additional emissions reductions (to 1990 levels by 2020), the 2003 Climate Stewardship Act lost by a vote of 43–55. The defeat came along party lines, with forty-six Republicans and nine Democrats (mostly from coal and agricultural states) opposed and six Republicans (mostly from New England) voting yes. An exuberant Senator Inhofe gloated: "The science underlying this bill has been repudiated, the economic costs are far too high, and the environmental benefits are non-existent" (Jalonick 2003).

The Climate Stewardship Act Redux, 2005 Although they lost four of their original supporters in the 2004 elections, McCain and Lieberman persisted, and in spring 2005 they proposed a modified version of the Climate Stewardship Act as an amendment to the Senate energy bill. In an effort to convey his belief in the issue's growing salience, McCain

suggested that low polling numbers of President Bush and other prominent Republicans might be partly due to their position on climate change.
In fact, since the late 1990s virtually all polls had found that around
three-quarters of Americans believed global warming was a real problem;
a large majority believed that human activities were causing climate
change; and a substantial majority believed there was consensus among
scientists on the issue. However, industry's efforts to divert attention to
the costs of curbing global warming had clearly been effective as well:
an overwhelming majority thought the government should address
global warming, but the public was sharply divided as to whether it
should take gradual or immediate steps (www.pipa.org).

The polls did not provide a clear mandate, but they did suggest much
of the public believed some action was warranted. Moreover, since the
2003 vote several business leaders had become even more vocal in their
support of federal emissions limits in general, and a cap-and-trade policy
in particular. In September 2004, the Conference Board—a nonprofit
organization comprising about 2,000 major corporations—issued a
report citing increased scientific consensus that humans were contributing to the warming of the planet and predicting "increased pressure" on
corporate boards to address the issue. Although the group's membership
had taken varying positions on global warming, the board concluded its
report by saying that businesses ignored the global warming debate "at
their peril." The report predicted that despite continuing debate over the
Kyoto Protocol, "governments and markets are likely to act on their perception of the science. Increasingly, this perception is swinging toward a
belief that climate change is an urgent priority that must be addressed
through a variety of measures" (Ball 2004b, A2).

CEOs of some of the largest U.S. companies clearly agreed and set out
to influence the form of those regulations. In December 2004 Cinergy
Corp., one of the nation's biggest electric utilities, endorsed the idea of
a national cap on greenhouse gas emissions. "As we look out, I believe
that it's more likely than not that we'll live in a carbon-constrained
world," said James E. Rogers, Cinergy's chair and CEO. "We think we
have a significant risk because we burn so much coal, so we want to start
hedging our bets" (Ball 2004a, A8). The Cincinnati utility urged Congress to enact a policy that would "take the unnecessary uncertainty out
of national environmental policy." It added that because several states

were already moving on the issue, "it makes sense that any U.S. solution be national in nature" (Ball and Regalado 2004, A6). Shortly after Cinergy's announcement Exelon Corp.'s CEO John Rowe (2004, B2) ran a piece in the *Wall Street Journal* that said: "At Exelon, we believe that the science of global warming is overwhelming. We believe that greenhouse-gas emissions will be regulated here in the United States in the near future. We believe that the U.S. can and should do something about global climate change without waiting for China or the Third World, but in a way that encourages them to follow."

In May 2005 General Electric CEO Jeffrey Immelt announced that GE would spend $1.5 billion by 2010 on clean technologies R&D, reduce its greenhouse gas emissions by 1 percent by 2012, and increase its energy efficiency by 30 percent by 2012. "If you look to the future, there is going to be a day when we have standards of some kind pertaining to carbon," Immelt said. "I think most business people are planning for that implicitly, even without doing anything that's overt." He anticipated that global warming would be good for GE and its shareholders because the company sells low-emissions technologies. "We're at a tipping point where energy efficiency and emissions reductions also equal profitability," he said (Kranhold and Ball 2005, A2). Immelt pushed the White House to clarify energy policy and to commit to "market mechanisms." Although he did not endorse the Climate Stewardship Act specifically, he said a cap-and-trade system would make sense.

To highlight the position of business leaders, Representative Sherwood Boehlert (R-NY) invited four prominent executives to a House Science Committee hearing in early June about business's efforts to reduce greenhouse gas emissions and their desire for a policy that would give them credit for their actions. Jim Rogers of Cinergy testified that his company's decision to reduce greenhouse gas emissions was made because states were taking action on climate change, and shareholders were demanding a response from energy companies. Furthermore, as the Kyoto Protocol went into effect around the world in February 2005, U.S. multinationals had to comply with overseas regulations and faced the prospect of a trade complaint from European nations. Mack McFarland of DuPont pointed out that "as various greenhouse gas emissions policy regimes develop around the world, there seems to be little effort to take account of the actions of early movers like ourselves. This can place the early movers at a competitive disadvantage and act as a disincentive to other entities that step up with bold voluntary actions" (Stempeck 2005).

With prominent industry leaders adopting positions in favor of mandatory emissions limits and the public apparently convinced that climate change was a problem, if not necessarily an urgent one, opposition to emissions curbs began to soften in the Senate. For example, Nebraska's Senator Hagel, once a vocal detractor of Kyoto but now widely seen as a presidential candidate in 2008, thought climate change held some credit-claiming potential. In February 2005 he introduced three bills that would provide tax benefits and government-backed loans to U.S. companies that export or invest in equipment to reduce CO_2 emissions. In addition, Pete Domenici (R-NM), a longtime global warming skeptic and—because of his seniority and his position as chair of the Senate Energy and Natural Resources Committee—a crucial defector from the antiregulatory position, expressed a newfound willingness to consider endorsing mandatory emissions limits. Although he ultimately declined to cosponsor a climate change amendment proffered by Democrat Jeff Bingaman (NM), Domenici did acknowledge a change of heart on the issue: "I have come to accept that something is happening with the Earth's climate," he said. "I am looking for a solution" (Kriz 2005, 2504).

The Bush administration continued to express its unwillingness to support any greenhouse gas emissions curbs, however. In the middle of the 2005 energy policy debate, the White House Office of Management and Budget issued a Statement of Administrative Policy that said: "The administration is not convinced of the need for additional legislation with respect to climate change and will oppose any climate amendments that are inconsistent with the president's climate change strategy" (Samuelsohn 2005). Senator Inhofe also devised a new strategy to counter CO_2-limiting amendments: to discourage utilities from supporting such legislation, he introduced the "Ratepayers Protection Act," which would have the Congressional Budget Office study the effects of reducing CO_2 emissions on consumers and, if those costs were substantial, prevent utilities from passing them on to low-income ratepayers. House Republican Joe Barton of Texas, chair of both the Energy and Commerce Committee and the energy conference committee, also made plain his unwillingness to endorse any energy bill that contained greenhouse gas emissions limits.

When the Senate finally did vote on the Climate Stewardship Act, on June 22, the proposal lost 38–60. Some senators still felt uncomfortable moving on an issue marked by so much highly visible controversy; others who had previously supported the bill withdrew their backing in response to provisions creating $500 million in incentives to build nuclear power plants. Despite the defeat, however, the Senate seemed to be gearing up for a carbon trading system: only two hours after voting against the Climate Stewardship Act, the chamber approved a "Sense of the Senate" resolution put forward by Bingaman that (1) officially acknowledged that greenhouse gases are contributing to global warming, and (2) urged Congress to "enact a comprehensive and effective national program of mandatory, market-based limits on emissions of greenhouse gases that slow, stop and reverse the growth of such emissions." At the same time, in deference to continuing conservative and industry opposition, the resolution also said that any approach adopted by Congress should not significantly harm the U.S. economy and should encourage comparable actions by other nations.

By the end of 2005, the atmospheric concentration of CO_2 had reached 381 ppm, which was 2.4 ppm above 2004 levels and 100 ppm above the preindustrial average. Numerous polls conducted throughout the spring of 2006 suggested the American public was convinced that global warming was occurring and supported government action to address it (Morello 2006). At an April conference on climate change convened by the Senate Energy and Natural Resources Committee, executives from Exelon, Duke Energy, General Electric, Shell Oil, Wal-Mart, and other corporations once again urged Congress to approve a mandatory cap on U.S. greenhouse gas emissions. Nevertheless, the Bush administration—notwithstanding its newfound interest in alternative energy technologies—continued to oppose greenhouse gas emissions limits. Furthermore, although senators Bingaman, McCain, and Lieberman continued to try to build support for their proposals, few observers expected a climate bill to pass in the Senate in 2006. Prospects were even bleaker in the House, where Republican leaders easily quashed an effort to attach a sense of the Congress resolution, similar to the one passed in the Senate the previous spring, to the fiscal 2007 U.S. EPA and Interior Department spending bill. In short, although supporters of emissions limits were optimistic that Congress was moving closer to passing global warming legislation, in the absence of an obvious crisis, opponents clearly retained the upper hand.

Conclusions

The global warming story illustrates both the ability of industry to resist protective environmental legislation and the ability of scientific and environmental activism to change business's perceptions of its interests and thereby shift the legislative debate. For years a unified industry coalition publicly disputed climate change science and highlighted the costs of an energy transition. Ultimately, though, the convergence of overwhelming science and new tactics by environmentalists led prominent members of the business community to defect, thereby opening up the possibility of a policy shift.

But although environmentalists succeeded in breaking up the business coalition, they did so in exchange for accepting a narrow view of the plausible solution: business will only support the approaches that offer the regulatory certainty and flexibility it desires. As a result, although Congress is likely to pass mandatory greenhouse gas emissions in the coming years, its approach almost certainly will not bring about the transformation in energy use and hence the dramatic reductions in greenhouse gas emissions that most scientists say are necessary to avert the consequences of global warming. The Bush administration's lukewarm support for developing and adopting alternative fuel sources and its dogged pursuit of fossil-fuel-based energy supplies will further dampen progress. And the absence of an aggressive U.S. policy will undermine international efforts to persuade developing countries to pursue clean-energy-based growth.

More generally, for environmentalists, the ability of business to counter their campaigns creates a genuine quandary: should they continue to work within the conservative ideological framework established during the late 1970s and 1980s, which pits environmental protection against economic growth, or should they engage in a more fundamental campaign to persuade Americans that long-run economic vitality depends on a healthy environment? While the former promises immediate results, the policies chosen are likely to offer only marginal environmental improvements. By contrast, the latter has the potential to deliver genuinely protective policies—but almost certainly at the expense of short-term, and potentially irreversible, environmental losses.

Notes

1. In referring to global warming rather than climate change, I adopt the Environmental Protection Agency's definition of *global warming* as the human-caused trend of increasing global temperatures and other climate change phenomena. This is to distinguish the problem from *climate change*, which is used to refer to all climate variability, the causes of which are both natural and human activities, such as the burning of fossil fuels and deforestation.

2. Scientists noted that because CO_2 and other greenhouse gases remain in the atmosphere for 100 years, early action is imperative, and some buildup of gases— and therefore some warming—is inevitable.

3. As Ross Gelbspan observes, because of corporations' privacy rights it is impossible to determine precisely how much industry has spent on its public relations efforts. Based on records of corporations' nonprofit subsidiaries, Gelbspan reports that in 1994 and 1995 the GCC spent more than $1 million to downplay the threat of climate change. In 1992 and 1993 the National Coal Association spent more than $700,000 on climate change–related efforts. The American Automobile Manufacturers Association spent nearly $100,000 in 1993 on "global climate change representation and membership dues to the GCC. In 1993 the American Petroleum Institute paid $1.8 million to the public relations firm of Burston-Marsteller, which spearheaded the drive to defeat Clinton's fossil fuel tax proposal" (Gelbspan 1997, 55–56).

4. Ironically, Bush had originally pledged to regulate CO_2 emissions after being lobbied by a group of utility executives who argued that regulatory certainty was vital to their interests (Adams 2001).

5. As many observers have noted, this policy does little beyond affirming the longstanding trend of reducing the United States economy's carbon intensity.

6. BP met its target in 2002, nine years ahead of schedule, at which point it dismantled its internal trading system because pursuing emissions reductions threatened to distort the company's capital allocation and investment strategies (Vogel 2005).

7. Ford failed to achieve its objectives. The fuel efficiency of its fleet has improved only marginally, and in fact Ford's vehicles remain the most carbon-intensive of any manufacturer (Vogel 2005).

8. The quotation its taken from Inhofe's Web page: http://inhofe.senate.gov/.

References

Adams, A. John, Candace Crandall, David Rothbard, Jeffrey Salmon, Lee Garrigan, Lynn Bouchey, Myron Ebell, Peter Cleary, Randy Randol, Robert Gehri, Sharon Kneiss, Steve Milloy, and Joseph Walker. 1998. "Global Climate Science Communications Action Plan." April 3. www.environmentaldefense.org.

Adams, Rebecca. 2001. "Bush's Decision Not to Curb Carbon Dioxide Casts Shadow on Emission Control Legislation." *CQ Weekly*, March 17.

Ball, Jeffrey. 2001. "Warming Trend: Auto Makers Juggle Substance and Style in New Green Policies." *Wall Street Journal*, May 15, A1.

———. 2004a. "AEP and Cinergy to Outline Ways to Cut Emissions." *Wall Street Journal*, February 19, A8.

———. 2004b. "Conference Board Stiffens Global-Warming Stance." *Wall Street Journal*, September 8, A2.

Ball, Jeffrey, and Antonio Regalado. 2004. "Cinergy Backs U.S. Emissions Cap." *Wall Street Journal*, December 2, A6.

Berry, Jeffrey. 1999. *The New Liberalism: The Rising Power of Citizen Groups*. Washington, DC: Brookings Institution.

Birnbaum, Jeffrey. 1992. *The Lobbyists: How Influence Peddlers Get Their Way in Washington*. New York: Times Books.

Boykoff, Maxwell T., and Jules M. Boykoff. 2004. "Balance as Bias: Global Warming and the U.S. Prestige Press." *Global Environmental Change* 14: 125–136.

Carey, John. 2004. "Global Warming: Consensus Growing among Scientists, Governments and Businesses That They Must Act Fast to Combat Climate Change." *Business Week*, August 16, 60–68.

Cassady, Alison. 2005. "ExxonMobil Exposed: More Drilling, More Global Warming, More Oil Dependence." July. www.exxposeexxon.com/.

Christiansen, Gale E. 1999. *Greenhouse: The 200-Year Story of Global Warming*. New York: Penguin Books.

Clawson, Dan, Alan Neustadt, and Mark Weller. 1998. *Dollars and Votes: How Business Campaign Contributions Subvert Democracy*. Philadelphia: Temple University Press.

Dunlap, Riley E. 1995. "Public Opinion and Environmental Policy." In James P. Lester, ed., *Environmental Politics and Policy: Theories and Evidence*. Durham, NC: Duke University Press.

E&E TV. 2005. "Former BP CEO Percy Discusses Corporate Reaction to Climate, Ecosystems Report." July 20.

Elving, Ronald D. 1997. "Saving the Earth, Losing Peoria." *CQ Weekly*, December 13, online edition.

Fialka, John. 1997a. "Clinton's Effort to Curb Global Warming Draws Some Business Support, but It May Be Too Late." *Wall Street Journal*, October 22, 1.

————. 1997b. "Global-Warming Treaty Is Approved." *Wall Street Journal*, December 11, 1.

————. 1998. "Global-Warming Debate Gets No Consensus in Industry." *Wall Street Journal*, April 16, 1.

————. 2002. "Entergy Gives Land to Create Refuge, Win Emissions Credits." *Wall Street Journal*, August 26, A4.

————. 2003. "Senate Rejects Mandatory Curbs on Gas Emissions in 55–43 Vote." *Wall Street Journal*, October 31, B2.

"Ford Leaves Coalition That Opposes Treaty on Global Warming." 1999. *Wall Street Journal*, December 7, 1.

Freedman, Allan. 1997. "Clinton's Global Warming Plans Take Heat from Congress." *CQ Weekly*, October 25, online edition.

Gelbspan, Ross. 1997. *The Heat Is On*. Reading, MA: Perseus Books.

Gunningham, Neil, Robert A. Kagan, and Dorothy Thornton. 2003. *Shades of Green: Business, Regulation, and Environment*. Stanford: Stanford, CA: University Press.

IPCC Working Group I (IPCC). 1990. *Climate Change: The IPCC Scientific Assessment*. Ed. J. T. Houghton, G. J. Jenkins, and J. J. Ephraums. New York: Cambridge University Press.

IPCC Working Group I (IPCC). 1996. *Climate Change 1995: The Science of Climate Change*. Ed. J. T. Houghton, L. G. Meira Filho, B. A. Gallander, N. Harris, A. Kattenberg, and K. Maskell. New York: Cambridge University Press.

Jalonick, Mary Clare. 2003. "Defeat of Senate Global Warming Bill Highlights Worries over Economic Impact." *CQ Weekly*, November 1, online edition.

Johnson, Ian. 1997. "Exxon Urges Developing Nations to Shun Environmental Curbs Hindering Growth." *Wall Street Journal*, October 14, 1.

Kempton, Willett, James S. Boster, and Jennifer A. Hartley. 1995. *Environmental Values and American Culture*. Cambridge, MA: MIT Press.

Kennamer, J. David. 1992. "Public Opinion, the Press, and Public Policy: An Introduction." In J. David Kennamer, ed., *Public Opinion, the Press, and Public Policy*. Westport, CT: Praeger.

Kingdon, John W. 1989. *Congressmen's Voting Decisions*. 3rd ed. Ann Arbor: University of Michigan Press.

Kollman, Ken. 1998. *Outside Lobbying: Public Opinion and Interest Group Strategies*. Princeton, NJ: Princeton University Press.

Kranhold, Kathryn, and Jeffrey Ball. 2005. "General Electric Plans Broad Push on Green Issues." *Wall Street Journal*, May 9, A2.

Kriz, Margaret. 2005. "Heating Up." *National Journal*, August 6, 2504–2508.

Kuhn, Thomas R., Jack Gerard, Alan H. Richardson, and Glenn English. 2003. Letter to senators, October 29 (on file with author).

Layzer, Judith A. 2006. *The Environmental Case: Translating Values into Policy.* 2nd ed. Washington, DC: CQ Press.

Lyons, Thomas P. 2003. " 'Green' Firms Bearing Gifts." *Regulation* (fall): 36–40.

McCright, Aaron M., and Riley E. Dunlap. 2000. "Challenging Global Warming as a Social Problem: An Analysis of the Conservative Movement's Counter-Claims." *Social Problems* 47 (4): 499–522.

Molitor, Michael. 1999. "The United Nations Climate Change Agreement." In Norman J. Vig and Regina S. Axelrod, eds., *The Global Environment: Institutions, Law and Policy.* Washington, DC: CQ Press.

Mooney, Chris. 2005. "Some Like It Hot." *Mother Jones* 30 (3) (May/June), 36–45.

Moore, David. 1997. "Greenhouse Warming: Fears Have Declined, but Still Viewed as a Major Problem for the Next Generation." *Gallup Poll Archives.* www.gallup.com.

Morello, Lauren. 2006. "Polls Find Groundswell of Belief in, Concern about Global Warming." *Greenwire*, April 21.

Parson, Edward. 2003. *Protecting the Ozone Layer: Science and Strategy.* New York: Oxford University Press.

Pope, Charles. 1998. "Fresh Focus on Global Warming Does Not Dispel Doubts about Kyoto Treaty's Future." *CQ Weekly*, June 6.

Rabe, Barry G. 2004. *Statehouse and Greenhouse: The Emerging Politics of American Climate Change Policy.* Washington, DC: Brookings Institution Press.

Rowe, John. 2004. "The Time to Address Climate Change Is Now." *Wall Street Journal*, December 28, B2.

Samuelsohn, Darren. 2005. "McCain-Lieberman Support Eroding over Nuclear Provisions." *E&E Daily*, June 15. http://www.eenews.net/EEDaily/2005/06/15/archive/2/?terms=climate%20change.

Schoenfeld, A. Clay, Robert F. Meier, and Robert J. Griffin. 1979. "Constructing a Social Problem: The Press and the Environment." *Social Problems* 27:38–61.

Smith, Mark A. 2000. *American Business and Political Power.* Chicago: University of Chicago Press.

Stempeck, Brian. 2005. "Executives Detail Greenhouse Gas Reduction Plan." *E&E Daily*, June 9, 2005. http://www.eenews.net/EEDaily/2005/06/09/archive/8/?terms=climate%20change.

Suskind, Ron. 2004. *The Price of Loyalty: George W. Bush, the White House, and the Education of Paul O'Neill.* New York: Simon & Schuster.

Vig, Norman J. 1994. "Presidential Leadership and the Environment: From Reagan and Bush to Clinton." In Norman J. Vig and Michael E. Kraft, eds., *Environmental Policy in the 1990s: Toward a New Agenda*, 2nd ed., 71–95. Washington, DC: CQ Press.

Vogel, David. 1989. *Fluctuating Fortunes: The Political Power of Business in America*. New York: Basic Books.

————. 1996. *Kindred Strangers: The Uneasy Relationship between Politics and Business in America*. Princeton, NJ: Princeton University Press.

————. 2005. *The Market for Virtue: The Potential and Limits of Corporate Social Responsibility*. Washington, DC: Brookings Institution Press.

West, Darrell M., and Burdett A. Loomis. 1999. *The Sound of Money: How Political Interests Get What They Want*. New York: Norton.

5

Congress and Clean Air Policy

Gary C. Bryner

The Clean Air Act (CAA) provides a useful vehicle for examining in detail the role of business in congressional policymaking, and its ability to shape the policy agenda. More importantly, an assessment of how Congress has dealt with the CAA illuminates how business groups help to mold the details of environmental laws in ways that protect their interests and minimize adverse regulatory effects on business goals. The act is one of the most complex laws ever enacted by Congress. Over time, the various versions of the act have grown from 8 pages in 1965 to 450 pages in 1990, its mandates have reached to nearly every sector of the economy, and the costs and benefits of compliance with the act have had a major impact on the U.S. economy. The CAA is championed by environmental advocates as a model of how Congress can establish expansive goals and specific deadlines and provisions to compel federal agencies and states to take aggressive steps to achieve environmental goals. At the same time, its market-based acid rain regulatory program is widely cited by economists as the kind of regulatory approach that should be embraced, and it has become a model for innovative climate change and other environmental policies (Bryner 1997). For all these reasons, the CAA can be viewed as emblematic of the modern regulatory state. The act has to some extent become symbolic of environmental law in general, and criticisms of the CAA often apply to the broader set of environmental laws.

This chapter begins with a discussion of how business groups typically seek to influence decisions within Congress and the strategies and tactics they employ, some of the distinguishing features of Congress as a policymaking institution, the incentives that shape the way members engage in policymaking, and the institutional conditions that affect the success of business in influencing policy. It then examines a case study of business efforts to influence decisions within Congress in the evolution of clean air policy. The chapter concludes with a discussion of how business influence in the case of clean air applies to other environmental policy issues.

I argue that environmental policymaking in Congress is a paradox, although a familiar one after more than three decades of policy action. Because of the importance of economic growth and the health of the economy, members of Congress are very attentive to the demands of business. Business interests dominate campaign contributions to members (see chapter 3), and they enjoy unparalleled access to members of Congress (see chapter 4). Nevertheless, Congress has enacted ambitious environmental laws that business has largely opposed. Each time a sweeping new environmental law has been proposed, business has aggressively lobbied against the measure, arguing it will lead to a loss of jobs, increases in prices, and other economic disruptions.

Congress typically does not retreat from the ambitious goals set in these laws. Rather it responds to business demands in other ways. It adjusts the details of legislation, such as extending deadlines for compliance, providing for business influence in the administrative rulemaking process, and authorizing limited enforcement resources to agencies, which minimizes disruption of business operations. The paradox results from conflicting demands on members of Congress. They are caught between strong public support for ambitious goals that promise to secure public health and environmental quality and strong business opposition to provisions that might harm economic growth and employment. It is no surprise that the policies resulting from such cross-pressures fall short of achieving their goals.

Although the clean air compromises have worked politically in Congress for decades, they have not been successful in reducing air pollution to safe levels (U.S. EPA 2005). The EPA has been caught in the vice of competing pressures, and has been set up for frequent policy failure because it has been unable to satisfy the expectations created by environmental laws. The most successful reductions in pollution have largely come the relatively few times when Congress has been willing to mandate specific emissions-reduction targets or other requirements, rather than giving the agency broad delegations of power. Congressional willingness

[handwritten margin note at top: "⊕ laws have "failed to reduce air pollution to →↓ safe safe levels"—"]

to delegate responsibility to the EPA to make the hard choices required to reduce pollution and members' responsiveness to business demands for delayed implementation and reduced regulatory burdens have come at a price. Despite considerable progress in reducing air pollution, thousands of Americans continue to die from air pollution and millions suffer from the adverse health effects it causes. This is a theme to which I return later in the chapter. To understand these outcomes one has to examine how business groups have mastered the art of political influence.

Business Groups and Congress in Environmental Policymaking

Throughout this book the authors ask similar questions in an effort to understand how business groups influence environmental policy. How do these groups decide where and when to try to influence policy decisions? In what venues, such as Congress or regulatory agencies, do they choose to act? What strategies and tactics, such as direct lobbying or framing of the issues, do they employ? What are the consequences of all of these efforts? Do business groups in fact get their way much of the time, only some of the time, or only under certain limiting conditions? *[handwritten margin note: "questions about Big."]*

   In their introductory chapter, Kraft and Kamieniecki suggest that among the major variables affecting business actions and success are the characteristics of a particular industry (such as its size, resources, and profitability), the qualities of relevant political institutions (such as the incentives that motivate members of Congress or state and local government officials to act), prevailing political and economic conditions, the strength of environmental groups and other opposing interests, and the political saliency of the issues. They also argue that influence by business and others can be assessed in one of two ways: by examining the perceptions of influence of policymakers and by comparing what groups have sought and gained from government. *[handwritten margin note: "variables affecting influence"]*

   It should be said that none of this is easy to do. As the editors note in chapter 1, a variety of methodological questions arise in any such enterprise. What kinds of data would be necessary to provide credible answers to such questions? The use of extensive empirical data would be ideal, but few sources of pertinent data on business lobbying and its effects are available. A single case study would not likely suffice because it may not be typical of environmental policy actions. Multiple case studies would be better, but they still face similar criticism as possibly not being representative of the great diversity of environmental policy actions, from national energy policy and climate change to protection of biological diversity and water resources. Each policy area attracts a somewhat different set of actors, including different kinds of business groups. For these reasons, the cases offered in this chapter, which focus on the Clean Air Act, can only be suggestive. However, the arguments advanced here can be tested with other cases that go well beyond air pollution, and perhaps eventually with a broader set of data.

Group Access to Congress: The Privileged Position of Business

A fundamental feature of the policymaking process within Congress is the dominant role that organized interests play. Since Congress itself occupies such a critical position in environmental policymaking in general, and air pollution policy in particular, focusing on unique features of the congressional structure and the legislative process is essential in examining business strategy and tactics.

One of the most important features of Congress is its fragmented and decentralized, committee and subcommittee system. Almost all policymaking decisions are made in the committees and subcommittees rather than on the floor of Congress, and this structure increases access to interest groups. The committees are fairly specialized and their actions typically do not attract the level of attention in the press that accompanies floor debate on controversial issues such as Social Security reform or national energy policy. Interest groups gravitate to the committees, where they attempt to persuade members and their staff to modify proposed legislation to their liking, often long before the issues gain much visibility (Rosenbaum 2005, 37). As Robert Duffy notes so well in chapter 3, interest groups help to ensure their access to the committees by targeting their campaign contributions to members of pertinent committees. At this stage groups can affect the way the issues are defined or framed (see chapters 2 and 4), the formulation of proposed legislation, the conduct of committee hearings, and voting on amendments and final legislation. They can also try to influence oversight hearings that review executive-agency implementation decisions and decisions on how agencies are to be funded each year, and therefore whether agencies are able to implement programs as thoroughly as the law requires.

Defenders of this system of interest-group access to Congress say it is pluralistic and open, with all interests having the potential to organize into groups and vie for influence in shaping policy. The critics argue, to the contrary, that not all interests are represented or enjoy equal resources as they seek to influence policymaking (Lowi 1979). They also say that historically business groups have enjoyed a privileged position in Congress and in the executive branch as well (Lindblom and Wood-house 1993). Business groups, they say, have greater financial resources to participate in lobbying, financing of elections, and other politicking than do other interests. More importantly, members of Congress recognize how dependent their political careers are on a healthy economy and on productive and successful businesses, and therefore how important it is for them to ensure that their policies contribute to economic growth. Environmental groups enjoy considerable resources as well, ranging from their access to the media to their ability to label proposals as good or bad for the environment to their capacity to mobilize public opinion to support or oppose legislative proposals (Bosso 2005; Duffy 2003). Nevertheless, the "formidable advantages" that business enjoys in the policymaking process have often been enough "to give a decisive edge in competitive struggles with environmental or other interests" in shaping environmental policy in Congress (Rosenbaum 2005, 38).

Congressional Action on Environmental Policy: Partisan Differences Widen

Despite these trends of business dominance, Congress nevertheless enacted an impressive array of environmental protection and natural resource laws from the late 1960s to 1990. These include the Clean Air Act, Clean Water Act, Endangered Species Act, Resource Conservation and Recovery Act, Safe Drinking Water Act, and Superfund, among many others. Democrats provided the leadership for most of these laws, but influential Republicans in the House and Senate also played key roles in supporting ambitious environmental laws. In fact, most bills passed with strong support from both parties (Kraft 2006). Not only did environmentalism enjoy bipartisan support, but industry groups found strong allies among Democrats as the majority party in Congress for most of this time. The party helped to ensure that environmental laws would be implemented in ways that were responsive to business concerns through the opportunities discussed above, such as oversight hearings and annual appropriations for the agencies. Moreover, the Democrats were eager to claim credit for a healthy economy and were wary of legislative actions that could impose unreasonable burdens on industry— even if they were not generally so preoccupied with such concerns as Republican lawmakers were.

Environmental politics in Congress underwent an important transition in 1994 when Republicans won control of the House of Representatives for the first time in forty years. Republican members, led by Newt Gingrich (R-GA), had fashioned a "Contract with America" that unified congressional races around a number of issues. These included reducing the burden of environmental and other regulations by shrinking unfunded mandates (federally imposed regulatory responsibilities on state and local governments), compensating landowners for complying with environmental regulations ("takings" legislation), and requiring federal agencies to justify regulations through cost-benefit and risk analyses.

When they took office in 1995, House leaders, enthusiastically supported by business interests, became even more ambitious, targeting environmental laws like the Clean Water Act, the Endangered Species Act, and Superfund for a major retrenchment of federal regulatory power, and proposing generic bills on risk assessment, takings, and unfunded mandates. Industry officials worked closely with then Majority Whip Tom DeLay (R-TX) to mount several efforts to weaken environmental laws. Among these was Project Relief, a lobbying group with close ties to the National Federation of Independent Businesses (representing small businesses), which focused on reducing paperwork and other compliance costs of environmental laws. Another group, Americans for Reasonable Regulation, was closely associated with the National Association of Manufacturers; it championed risk assessment as a way to reduce regulatory requirements such as the demand for expensive pollution control equipment. These groups largely bypassed the traditional media and focused on talk radio, community newspapers, conservative activists, and the Internet to mobilize pressure on members of Congress to support the regulatory relief effort (Schulzke 2002).

The aggressive tone and radical changes in policy proposed by the newly empowered congressional leaders provoked a backlash that even-

* E groups /ramed Rep. efforts as "relief" rather
than to "reform"
Congress and Clean Air Policy 133

tually sank most reform efforts. Environmental and other public interest groups effectively rebutted the charges of business groups and their
House Republican allies, forming a coalition of 230 groups called Citizens for Sensible Safeguards that challenged the Republican anecdotes of
regulatory overreach. Federal agencies also tried to rebut the criticism of
excessive regulatory power, and the mainstream media produced exposés
of dubious industry claims. Environmentalists and their allies were very
successful in framing Republican efforts as regulatory relief rather than
reform. They also were effective in targeting moderate Republicans in
the House and Senate through grassroots and media campaigns that
focused on the threats to public health and environmental protection
from Republican initiatives. House regulatory relief bills were blocked
in the Senate, and by November 2005, moderate House Republicans
began joining Democrats to defeat similar measures proposed by House
leaders. The leadership abandoned most wholesale legislative changes
and concentrated instead on modest changes to be achieved through the
use of riders attached to appropriations bills. Some of these were vetoed
by President Bill Clinton and others survived (Kraft 2006; Schulzke
2002).

By 1996, the Republican anti–environmental regulation insurgency
was defeated, an outcome widely viewed as a result of hubris and overreach and a remarkable political miscalculation about strong public
support for environmental protection. In 1996 Congress enacted amendments to the Safe Drinking Water Act and rewrote pesticide policy (the
Food Quality Protection Act). However, for most other major environmental laws the pattern was persistent gridlock as increasingly sharp differences between the two major parties on environmental issues became
common (Kraft 2006; Lazarus 2004). As measured by congressional
voting scores compiled by the League of Conservation Voters, for
example, the two parties showed a widening gulf from the early 1970s
through the late 1990s (Shipan and Lowry 2001). This gap remained just
as evident by 2005 as party polarization continued to be a dominant
feature of congressional policymaking. In short, in the aftermath of the
1994 elections, Congress proved largely incapable of enacting major new
environmental laws. The congressional deadlock in environmental policymaking has lasted over a decade, despite great economic and environmental changes and major advances in environmental science. The

authorizing authority under which many environmental laws operate has formally expired, and nearly all policy experts believe that these laws need to be amended and updated for them to succeed in the twenty-first century (National Academy of Public Administration 2000; Vig and Kraft 2006). Yet action by Congress is difficult at best in light of polarized party politics and continued battles between business groups and environmental and other interests who oppose their positions.

It is misleading to lump all businesses together. As the editors argue in chapter 1, business groups are not always united in their policy views (for example, over nuclear power). In addition, large corporations are more likely than small businesses to have the technical and legal resources required to ensure compliance with complicated regulatory provisions. They may even come to embrace regulation as a way to reduce competition from small counterparts. State and local governments are also subject to pollution control and natural resource regulation, and their views may intersect tightly with those of business in opposing pollution control and natural resource regulations or may diverge in the face of strong local political pressure. Businesses that sell control technologies may be among the most influential proponents of new environmental laws, and their views carry significant weight with some members of Congress.

Corporate views on environmental issues also have evolved. Some businesses have found that environmental regulations help them to reduce waste and save money (Prakash 2000). Many corporations have institutionalized environmental programs and made corporate environmental performance a priority. Business does not always oppose new environmental protection programs and some companies have supported regulatory initiatives. However, business is largely united in supporting voluntary environmental protection programs and policies that protect business flexibility and decisionmaking autonomy (Press and Mazmanian 2006; Shabecoff 1993, 142–145).

Clean Air and Congressional Policymaking: The Role of Business Groups

To explore the general propositions about the role of business in environmental policymaking raised by the editors of this book, it is helpful to examine the evolution of clean air policy in Congress as well as current controversies that illustrate the patterns described above. As noted earlier, the influence of business groups varies from one environmental policy area to another, so no case study can offer definitive conclusions that allow one to generalize to other areas. Nevertheless, a case study of the CAA can provide considerable insight into how business groups have been so successful in getting what they want from Congress.

The first Clean Air Act, enacted in 1963, established a legal process for cities, states, and the federal government to take regulatory action against polluters. Much of the focus was on emissions from motor vehicles, and the act authorized the federal government to issue emissions standards for hydrocarbons and carbon monoxide; standards were issued in 1966 and took effect in the 1968 model year. The emergence of environmentalism as a powerful political issue in the late 1960s, celebration of the first Earth Day in 1970, and broad public support for environmental protection measures led to the creation of the U.S. Environmental Protection Agency (EPA) in 1970 and to a new Clean Air Act, passed that same year.

The 1970 and 1977 Clean Air Acts
The 1970 act promised that the nation's air would be clean by 1975. Congress took two very different approaches in pursuit of that goal. It delegated broad authority to the EPA to issue national ambient air quality standards and to the states to develop and enforce plans to bring them into compliance with those standards. In contrast, it specified by law that motor vehicle emissions were to be reduced by 90 percent from 1970 levels, beginning with the 1975 models. Nitrogen oxide was to be cut by 90 percent by 1976. The most contentious issue in Congress was the tailpipe emissions standards, and the automobile industry vigorously opposed Congress setting the standards, arguing instead that the task should be delegated to the EPA. Members of the Interstate and Foreign Commerce Committee who drafted the bill were responsive to industry demands. However, other members of Congress proposed even more stringent tailpipe standards when the bill reached the House floor. The Senate's provisions were also more stringent that those in the House bill, and the Senate's tailpipe standards were included in the final bill (Bryner 1995).

Lobbying by the automobile industry has been evident throughout the history of clean air laws, and the industry has won major concessions from lawmakers. According to one account, "Every time Congress ordered the automotive companies to cut down on their tailpipe emissions or to improve fuel efficiency, they complained that such improvements were not technologically feasible or would make their cars too expensive" (Shabecoff 1993, 142). When the nation failed to meet the 1975 deadline for attaining air quality standards, Congress began revising the Clean Air Act. Motor vehicle emissions continued to be the most vexing problem. The automobile industry had lost the 1970 skirmish but eventually won the war. Congress amended the act four times in subsequent years in order to give automobile makers more time to meet emissions standards for new vehicles. Congress also gave the EPA the authority to waive stricter standards if control technologies did not materialize.

Other industries, notably electric power generating plants, have proved to be as influential as automobile makers. In the 1977 Clean Air Act, Congress set new clean air deadlines of 1982 (1987 for areas with severe ozone and carbon monoxide problems). It then turned attention to power plants and in a key compromise, began requiring new fossil-fuel-fired power plants to use the "best technological system of continuous emission reduction," widely understood to require the installation of "scrubbers" that removed sulfur dioxide from power plant emissions. Scrubbing of sulfur dioxide emissions was required even if companies used low-sulfur coal, removing much of the incentive to replace high- with low-sulfur coal and thus protecting the high-sulfur coal industry that had effectively persuaded Congress that it would suffer massive job losses if utilities shifted to low-sulfur coal (Ackerman and Hassler 1981).

Industry officials also had argued that retrofitting old equipment would be prohibitively expensive and that the plants should be allowed to operate until they were retired and replaced by the next generation of cleaner facilities. As a result, Congress exempted power plants put in operation before the 1977 law was enacted from the standards required of new plants. As the evolution of clean-air legislation demonstrates, this was a fateful decision by Congress. Exempted or grandfathered power plants continued to operate well past their expected lifetime since it was much cheaper to operate them than to build new plants that met much more stringent, environmentally protective standards. Utility industry officials were successful in convincing members of Congress that voters' utility bills would increase if new plants were forced to clean up, and congressional fears of being blamed for high energy prices kept these old, dirty power plants operating long after they could have been replaced by cleaner, more efficient plants.

The 1990 Clean Air Act Amendments

Throughout most of the 1980s, industry groups worked with the Reagan administration to try to weaken the stringency of Clean Air Act provisions. Congress resisted rollbacks in regulatory programs, and a decade of legislative deadlock resulted. Authorization for the act technically expired in 1981 and Congress provided for clean air programs to continue through appropriations laws. Geographic and ideological forces made compromise difficult. Proposals from Northeast states to reduce acid rain and the emissions from Midwest power plants that were responsible for the problem were largely stymied by Democrats from states producing high-sulfur coal and the states that relied on the coal to fuel their power plants. Republicans were opposed to these actions as well, but for different reasons. They objected to stringent environmental regulations on ideological grounds, much as they opposed other federal regulatory efforts. The logjam was broken when Reagan's vice president, George H. W. Bush, campaigned for the presidency in 1988 on an environmentally friendly platform, distancing himself from the Reagan administration's widely criticized environmental policies.

During the campaign, Bush promised a new Clean Air Act, and his administration proposed an ambitious acid rain program that was even more aggressive than Democratic versions in Congress. The centerpiece of the law was a program aimed at reducing power plant emissions blamed for acid rain. Instead of traditional direct command-and-control regulation opposed by industry, this would be done by capping allowable emissions from major plants and then permitting them to buy and sell their emissions allowances. Plants able to make the cheapest reductions could go beyond their requirements and generate credits for excess cleanup, which they could sell to companies who found it cheaper to offset their emissions with these credits rather than make the expensive emissions-reduction investments themselves. By adopting this approach, environmental goals could be achieved at much lower total costs. The administration received credit for keeping its campaign promise and industry was able to significantly reduce compliance costs. Part of the breakthrough was also due to the perception in Congress that the electric power industry had been particularly intransigent during the 1980s, blocking any effort to break the logjam in Congress, and deserved to bear a major burden in reducing air emissions (Bryner 1995).

Developments in the regulation of automobile emissions also demonstrate the power that regulated industries enjoy in Congress even when they are caught misleading members. The automobile and oil industries, in particular, have regularly overstated compliance costs and difficulties, and their credibility has suffered. Easterbrook, for instance, argues that one of the lessons from air pollution regulation is to "*never* believe Detroit." For instance, after the 1990 CAA Amendments, states began considering legislation to require a new round of emissions controls on new motor vehicles. In 1991, Ford executives told Maryland legislators that such standards would be a "nightmare" since "there are no cars in existence that could meet the standard," and the legislature defeated the proposal. Three weeks later, Ford unveiled a production car that met the new standards at an increased price of only $100 (Easterbrook 1995, 187; emphasis in original).

Another clean air initiative demonstrates the oil industry's credibility. The Bush administration supported an amendment to the CAA that would require that, by 1998, 10 percent of vehicles run on alternative fuels. Oil companies opposed this measure as they did others. One company, Arco, however, began working on reformulating gasoline. In less than ninety days company chemists had come up with a reformulated gas that cut smog precursors by 37 percent. The additional cost per gallon quickly fell to 4.3 cents. An Arco vice president reported in an interview that the company could have developed the cleaner fuel years before but "we were already selling all the gasoline we could make and there was no government requirement for a low-pollution product, so what was our incentive?" (Easterbrook 1995, 196–197). Congress quickly responded by including a reformulated gas mandate that was included in the 1990 amendments, and Arco suffered the wrath of the

American Petroleum Industry, the oil companies' trade association, for breaking ranks (Bryner 1995).

Congressional Clean Air Deadlock

Clean air resurfaced on the congressional agenda in the late 1990s, and this period affords another look at the power of industry groups in Congress. In the mid-1990s, the federal government and subsequently many states began to deregulate the traditional monopolies of electricity companies. In 1997, after considerable groundwork had been laid by environmental groups in meetings with state officials and by providing technical assessments, attorneys general from several states in the Northeast petitioned the EPA to require major emissions reductions from stationary sources in downwind states. Old coal-fired power plants, however, seemed poised to be able to maintain their insulation from pressure to modernize and reduce emissions (Clean Air Network 1997). Environmental groups, led by the Boston-based Clean Air Task Force (2000), eventually joined the policy debate and argued for a strategy to level the playing field among competing electricity-generating firms. The competitive "leveler" was a concept known as "environmental comparability"—the idea that clean air rules should apply equally to all power plants, not just to new plants. Energy efficiency and renewable technology advocates sought to combine support for environmental comparability with efforts to deregulate electricity. The problem was that competitive pressures for cheap power encouraged power companies to keep operating their old coal-fired plants well beyond their typical life span. This stymied the expectation underlying the Clean Air Act that old, relatively dirty and inefficient power plants would be phased out and replaced by cleaner, more efficient facilities. This was a remarkable achievement by environmental groups who were able to place power plant emissions on the state and national policy agendas, despite industry opposition to any new legislation.

However, the Republican takeover of the House of Representatives made new clean air legislation to address the problem of grandfathered power plants quite unlikely. The new House leadership gave unprecedented access to regulated industries and was sympathetic to their concerns. House leaders proposed radical revisions to environmental laws and the Clean Air Act in general (one leader even called for the CAA's repeal). Yet Senate and Clinton administration opposition to these legislative rollbacks caused House leaders to retreat. The EPA eventually issued new rules for fine particles and ozone in 1997 that put additional pressure on power plants as a major source of these pollutants. With congressional efforts to repeal parts of the Clean Air Act blocked by environmentalists and Democrats, industry groups shifted the venue and challenged the new regulations in court (see chapter 9). Here they argued not only that the EPA regulations were unjustified but that the Clean Air Act itself was unconstitutional because it delegated excessive authority to the EPA to make policy decisions. The Supreme Court eventually rejected industry's constitutional challenge; it also upheld the agency's authority to issue clean air regulations.[1] This brief history suggests some of the conditions under which industry may not get its way, such as when Congress and the executive branch are controlled by different parties and Democrats are unsupportive of industry's position.

The EPA also began aggressive enforcement of the Clean Air Act's New Source Review provisions, which require installation of the same pollution controls as new plants when power plants modernize and upgrade. EPA officials targeted a number of large plants that the agency believed had modernized without installing new source control equipment. Some utilities negotiated agreements to install new control equipment while others resisted. Litigation ensued as industry groups continued to challenge every major regulation the agency issued.

The climate for power plant cleanup cooled considerably in 2001 because of the Bush administration's overall approach to environmental policy and, in particular, President George W. Bush's reversal of his campaign pledge to reduce carbon dioxide emissions from power plants. The administration gave priority to energy policy over clean air, arguing in its National Energy Plan that regulators must reduce barriers for power companies to produce more power to meet growing demand. The EPA eventually issued revised New Source Review rules that made it easier for old power plants to continue to operate without investing in new emissions control equipment and scaled back enforcement efforts. The rules allowed utilities to undertake maintenance and other projects that cost up to 20 percent of the total cost of the plant without triggering requirements that they install the stringent emissions controls required of new sources. The new rules reflected a major policy victory by industry and effectively ended some of the enforcement actions started in the Clinton administration to require utilities to install the new control technologies when making operational changes (Shogren 2004).

The Clear Skies Initiative

The Bush administration also issued a proposed set of amendments to the Clean Air Act, labeled "Clear Skies," that was later introduced in Congress as the Clear Skies Act of 2003. Clear Skies would require power plants to reduce nitrogen oxide, sulfur dioxide, and mercury emissions by 70 percent by 2018. Its defenders argued that the act would produce greater reductions more cheaply and more quickly than through simply implementing the Clean Air Act's existing provisions through regulations (Holmstead 2005; Easterbrook 2005). Emissions trading was a key element of the program. The intended effect was to reduce compliance costs as industries met emissions-reduction targets through a cap-and-trade system, based on the 1990 acid rain market system, rather than requiring that all facilities employ state-of-the-art control technologies. Democrats in Congress introduced their own bills to reduce power plant emissions, but included carbon dioxide as a fourth emission to be reduced.

Critics argued that Clear Skies was an industry-based effort to kill the New Source Review program. The initiative, if adopted, would allow them to put off new controls on power plants for years. They said if the EPA implemented the existing law and simply required plants to install state-of-the-art control technologies (called Maximum Achievable Control Technologies in the Clean Air Act), it could reduce emissions by a larger percentage and much sooner than what would be achieved by the Bush proposal (Campbell 2005). A National Academy of Science report issued in early 2005 concluded that the provisions of Clear Skies would likely result in less emissions reduction than if the New Source requirements were implemented. Yet the EPA and Bush administration officials argued that the certainty promised by new legislation outweighed the benefits from the piecemeal, power plant-by-power plant approach that characterized the existing New Source Review program (Eilperin 2005). A study by Abt Associates, a consulting firm used by the

EPA to evaluate policy options, compared Clear Skies with two competing legislative initiatives and found that the administration's proposal would produce the fewest benefits from power plant cleanup. Clear Skies would likely result in 14,000 saved lives, while the two bills would likely save 16,000 lives in one case and 22,000 lives in another (Janofsky 2004).

There has been very little support in Congress for Clear Skies, perhaps because it has not been a policy priority of the administration. In addition, the utility industry has not lobbied aggressively for the measure. Apparently it preferred instead the current system of delayed compliance requirements. In December 2003, the Bush administration proposed two rules to control power plant emissions—one for nitrogen oxides and sulfur dioxide and another for mercury—in the event Clear Skies was not enacted.[2] These regulations follow the well-trod pattern of imposing new cleanup standards and extended dates. The mercury rules were particularly targeted by environmentalists because, in at least three different instances, passages in the proposal mirrored almost word for word portions of memorandums written by industry lobbyists (Eilperin 2004). They also were concerned because of the growing evidence that mercury is accumulating in the tissue of humans at increasing rates and poses a significant risk to human health. Nevertheless, the administration issued final rules in 2005, and environmental groups immediately challenged them in federal court.

In addition, the Clear Skies bill languished in Congress because Democrats and a few Republicans demanded that any legislation regulating power plants include carbon dioxide controls in an effort to control climate change. Several bills were introduced in the early 2000s. By 2003, senators from twenty-six states supported legislation that would limit emissions of nitrogen oxides, sulfur dioxide, mercury, and carbon dioxide from power plants. As might be expected, business groups lobbied against these bills, as did the White House, and they were quite successful in keeping them from moving forward. Most Republicans in Congress, except those from the Northeast, supported the administration's clear opposition to the bills, but the Bush administration was not able to convert that opposition into support for its competing initiative, Clear Skies. The level of support for these measures reflects the gridlock characteristic of current environmental policymaking in general, where both industry groups and environmentalists are able to block most measures they strongly oppose, but neither is able to move legislation forward (Kraft 2006).

Assessing the Role of Business in Clean Air Policymaking

Congressional action on clean air policy can be considered to be both successful and unsuccessful as measured against political and environmental quality criteria. That is, one can judge any policy a success politically if it meets the needs of the key policy actors, particularly members of Congress. Students of Congress typically look to public popularity, support by key interests, a flow of campaign contributions, and ultimately electoral victory as indicators of such political success. Policy actions also can be evaluated in terms of whether they satisfy public needs, such as whether they improve environmental quality and reduce risks to public health (Bennear and Coglianese 2005).

As the case studies of the Clean Air Act suggest, the pattern of clean air politics and policymaking has been quite consistent for thirty-five years. Members of Congress, in response to strong public support for clean air and lobbying by environmental groups, select ambitious goals that promise to eliminate the problem and ensure everyone eventually breathes clean air. They can claim success in addressing an issue of great importance to the public. Business groups, even if united, are not successful in convincing Congress to pass legislation that conflicts with clear public sentiment (Smith 2000). Industry groups regularly warn that such goals are unrealistic and inconsistent with available technologies and practices, and business lobbying compels Congress to extend deadlines far into the future. The justification is plausible. Industries need time to develop new control technologies and processes. Yet pollution control equipment usually turns out to be less expensive than industry warnings suggest. Once companies have an incentive to invent new control technologies, actual costs are much lower (Easterbrook 1995).

Regulated industries have lobbied aggressively on every clean air issue, but they usually get only part of what they demand during the policy development and legislative stage. Nevertheless, they end up playing a dominant role in the implementation of clean air laws in the administrative process. As indicated above, once laws are enacted, business challenges virtually every major regulation the EPA proposes, and litigation regularly delays implementation and thus the imposition of compliance costs even when business groups are unsuccessful in the courts in challenging agency regulations. In this way, equilibrium is reached. The public sees strong laws on the books, industry rewards members of Congress for their responsiveness to business needs, and incumbents are reelected (Schoenbrod 2005). All of these outcomes suggest successful policymaking as measured by the political criteria discussed above. Some environmental progress also occurs, but clean air goals remain largely unrealized (U.S. EPA 2005).

The variables suggested by Kraft and Kamieniecki in chapter 1 help explain this broad pattern in clean air politics. Environmental groups, working effectively with the media, have largely been successful in framing clean air regulation as a public health imperative that requires ambitious goals. Industries affected by clean air regulation include the largest and most influential corporations and trade associations. They have a long history of issuing dire warnings concerning the adverse economic consequences of aggressive regulation whenever new initiatives are opposed, but those warnings typically fail to deter Congress in formulating ambitious clean air goals. However, industry warnings about job loss, higher prices, and other economic consequences of regulation resonate strongly in Congress. They are the most potent arguments business can offer, but they do not deter members of Congress from embracing strong goals. Still, they do prompt members to ensure that the path to achieving those goals is shaped by industry concerns.

A primary factor that affects the ability of industry to obtain what it seeks has been the extent of Republican control of Congress and the White House. But Republican-led institutions are not by themselves a guarantee of business success. The ability of Senate Democrats and Republicans from Northeastern states to block proposals they believe go too far in weakening environmental protections is a significant barrier to industry efforts to repeal provisions of existing environmental laws or to enact laws more to their liking. Conversely, Democratic control of government does not guarantee environmentalist success. Democrats controlled both houses of Congress in the 1980s, for example, but were deadlocked among themselves over how to amend the Clean Air Act.

Democrats representing high-sulfur coal-producing states and states with old coal-burning plants often locked horns over clean-air legislation with their counterparts who favored strict emissions controls. The Clinton administration did not issue many of its most important environmental and natural resource initiatives until its last days, evidence that it was wary of imposing new regulatory requirements on industry (Vig and Kraft 2006). Environmental initiatives have been strongest, and industry influence weakest, when political leaders from the two parties have competed for leadership on environmental issues.

Even when industry has issued inflated and inaccurate statements, such as the assertions made by the oil and automobile industry as Congress wrote the 1990 CAA, congressional support has not diminished. The reason is that industry can rely on key supporters to rally to its defense. For example, the automobile industry has long had the enthusiastic support of Representative John Dingell (D-MI), who has represented the Detroit area in Congress for half a century. For many years Dingell headed the important House Energy and Commerce Committee when Democrats controlled the House. With the House under Republican control since 1995, Dingell has served as the ranking minority member on the committee. In either capacity, Dingell needs no prodding to come to the defense of the industry. The automobile industry is able to count on Dingell and to rally its other supporters in Congress to block what it considers to be ill-advised legislative proposals, such as raising automobile fuel efficiency standards. Similar representation can be found in both the House and Senate for many other industries.

Beyond Clean Air: Business Influence in Environmental Policymaking

Business influence in environmental policymaking in Congress, of course, extends well beyond its actions on clean air policy. In recent years, one major focus has been on regulatory reform initiatives that are designed to constrain the way administrative agencies implement the law, whether the CAA or any other environmental laws. I have argued that a key compromise in Congress was a decision to limit the resources granted to the EPA to help ensure that business can effectively intervene in administrative and judicial processes to protect its interests (Bryner 1987; Smith 2005). Because courts are oriented toward giving those materially affected by government action an opportunity to challenge those actions, business can almost always slow down the implementation process even if it does not win in the courts.

During the past decade, members of Congress, prompted by industry demands for more independence from regulation, have found additional ways to slow down regulatory activity without directly amending environmental laws. They do so by imposing generic requirements on the EPA and other regulatory agencies, such as cost-benefit analysis and paperwork-reduction requirements. Recent presidents have issued a series of executive orders aimed at specifying when and how agencies are to take into account and balance the costs and benefits of the actions they propose.[3] These efforts have been motivated by a variety of goals, such as reducing the cost of compliance with regulations in order to foster economic growth, increasing the cost-effectiveness of regulations so that benefits are maximized, and ensuring that agency actions are consistent with administration policy objectives. But Congress has gone further.

Under the Unfunded Mandates Reform Act, for example, each agency must prepare a benefit-cost analysis for any proposed and final rule "that may result in the expenditure by State, local, and tribal governments, in the aggregate, or by the private sector, of $100,000,000 or more (adjusted annually for inflation) in any one year." In its analysis, the agency must also "identify and consider a reasonable number of regulatory alternatives and from those alternatives select the least costly, most cost-effective or least burdensome alternative that achieves the objectives of the rule."[4] Under the Paperwork Reduction Act, the Office of Information and Regulatory Affairs (OIRA), an office within the Office of Management and Budget (OMB), reviews and approves or disapproves "each collection of information by a Federal agency, including information required to be provided under federal agency regulations."[5]

Similarly, the Information Quality Act (sometimes called the Data Quality Act) authorizes the OMB to ensure the "quality, objectivity, utility, and integrity of information . . . disseminated by federal agencies."[6] Industry and trade associations have used these laws to challenge regulatory agencies and slow down the regulatory process. The Information Quality Act was approved by Congress with no public hearings and was inserted as twenty-seven lines of text within a massive appropriations bill that President Bill Clinton had no choice but to sign (Kraft 2006, 137). The act has been used by regulated businesses to challenge agency policies and delay their implementation under the guise of "correcting" scientific and technical information. Defenders of the act argue that it is available for anyone to challenge agency information and is consistent with the public's right to know what government is doing in an "understandable way" (Greenwood 2005). Critics charge, however, that the act has been used chiefly by business groups to "slow regulation and bypass or amend existing standards" (Shapiro 2005).

Conclusions

As the chapters in this book demonstrate clearly, business and environmental interests collide in Congress, the courts, and the executive-branch agencies as both aggressively seek to shape public policy. Yet the environmental protection imperative that resonated strongly in Congress during the 1970s and even much of the 1980s, and drove the balance between strong goals and delayed implementation, is now uncertain. As I have argued, the last ten years of Republican control of Congress, reinforced by the first term of the George W. Bush administration, suggest that the balance may be shifting toward a diminution in environmental goals as well as even longer lag times before modest goals are to be achieved. The administration's fixation on a national energy policy that emphasizes expanded production necessarily requires that clean air regulation will decline in importance. Sharp increases in the price of gasoline and other oil-based fuels may also put pressure on government to relax current strict clean air standards.

Patterns of industry influence in other areas of environmental policy might differ from that of clean air regulation. The critical importance of energy policy complicates the creation of clean air policy in important ways, because policymakers give higher priority to securing a stable and relatively low-cost supply of energy than most other policy goals. Environmental policies that do not hinder energy production may allow for less industry influence. As suggested early in the chapter, future research might compare other cases of business influence in environmental policy to the pattern reported here. Of special interest is research that can identify the conditions under which business influence can be minimized, or where business groups have proved willing to support environmental policy advances.

In light of the political constraints on clean air and other environmental policies highlighted in the chapter, what alternatives exist for redesigning policy for the future? Since environmental goals are rarely achieved, perhaps a more realistic approach would include less ambitious objectives and sufficient resources to accomplish them. Such an approach would also be attractive as a way to reinforce the integrity of law. Yet a risk with this strategy is that it could lead to a retreat in environmental goals by starting from a lower target before making the inevitable compromises. Moreover, the consequences of the aggressive regulatory relief campaign by Republican House leaders and their industry allies in the mid-1990s continue to shape environmental politics, because there is little trust among environmentalists that the current Congress could reform environmental law in ways that would secure strong environmental protection and natural resource conservation. For its part, as long as business enjoys such an influential role in the implementation and enforcement of environmental laws, it is not motivated to invest in another major campaign for radical legislative changes.

Another alternative in light of the national policy deadlock in clean air and other environmental policy areas, is to look to state- and local-level regulatory innovation, as discussed by Rabe and Mundo in chapter 10 of this book. It is no exaggeration to say that some of the most promising environmental policy advances of recent years have occurred at this level (Mazmanian and Kraft 1999; Rabe 2006). Even so, many air pollution problems cross political boundaries and will require some creative ways to bring states together.

The greater challenges for both national and state and local policymaking in addressing persistent air pollution problems lie in figuring out how to design the next generation of environmental policies. They will need to go beyond pollution control to a more integrated and comprehensive effort to create sustainable communities and economies (Mazmanian and Kraft 1999). To achieve these goals, however, requires a number of political developments. One of them is likely new congressional leaders and a new administration willing to undertake such a broad reexamination of environmental policy. Another is support for clean air that goes beyond traditional environmentalists to labor, civil

rights, and other progressive groups, and to an even wider array of mainstream interests. A third is more governors who pressure the national
government for action and encourage industry to preempt growing state
regulation with national standards. A fourth is creation of a sense of
urgency that carbon dioxide emissions from power plants and other
sources need to be regulated as part of an effort to reduce the threat of
disruptive climate change. Finally, a fifth is the development of a new
public ethic that demands a more cautious, protective stewardship of the
Earth so that succeeding generations will be able to enjoy a hospitable
world in which to live.

Notes

1. *Whitman v. American Trucking Associations*, 531 U.S. 457 (2001).

2. The NO_x and SO_x rule would reduce power plant emissions in twenty-nine
Eastern states and the District of Columbia in two phases. Sulfur dioxide emissions would drop by 3.6 million tons in 2010 (a cut of approximately 40 percent
from current levels) and by another 2 million tons per year when the rules are
fully implemented (a total cut of approximately 70 percent from today's levels).
NO_x emissions would be cut by 1.5 million tons in 2010 and 1.8 million tons
annually in 2015 (a reduction of approximately 65 percent from today's levels).
The mercury rule would reduce emissions by nearly 70 percent from current
levels by 2018. These rules are discussed in detail in a special issue of the Air
and Waste Management Association's publication, *EM* (August 2005).

3. The most important presidential actions have been Exec. Order 12,291, 3
C.F.R. 127 (1982); Exec. Order 12,498, 3 C.F.R. 323 (1986); and Exec. Order
12,866, 3 C.F.R. 638 (1994).

4. Public Law 104-4, section 202 (March 22, 1995).

5. 44 U.S.C. chapter 35.

6. Sec. 515 of Title V of Treasury and General Government Appropriations Act
for FY 2001, Public Law 106-554, 44 USC 3516 (note).

References

Ackerman, Bruce A., and William T. Hassler. 1981. *Clean Coal/Dirty Air*. New
Haven, CT: Yale University Press.

Bennear, Lori Snyder, and Cary Coglianese. 2005. "Measuring Progress: Program
Evaluation of Environmental Policies." *Environment* 47 (2) (March): 22–39.

Bosso, Christopher J. 2005. *Environment, Inc.: From Grassroots to Beltway*.
Lawrence: University Press of Kansas.

Bryner, Gary C. 1987. *Bureaucratic Discretion: Law and Policy in Federal Regulatory Agencies*. New York: Pergamon Press.

———. 1995. *Blue Skies, Green Politics: The Clean Air Act Amendments of 1990 and Their Implementation.* 2nd ed. Washington, DC: CQ Press.

———. 1997. "Market Incentives in Air Pollution Control." In Sheldon Kamieniecki, George A. Gonzalez, and Robert O. Vos, eds., *Flashpoints in Environmental Policymaking.* Albany, NY: SUNY Press.

Campbell, Bradley. 2005. "Too Little, Too Late, Too Few." *The Environmental Forum* (March–April): 42.

Clean Air Network. 1997. "Poisoned Power: How America's Outdated Electric Plants Harm Our Health & Environment." Washington, DC: CAN.

Clean Air Task Force. 2000. "Death, Disease & Dirty Power: Mortality and Health Damage Due to Air Pollution from Power Plants." Boston: CATF.

Duffy, Robert J. 2003. *The Green Agenda in American Politics: New Strategies for the Twenty-First Century.* Lawrence: University Press of Kansas.

Easterbrook, Greg. 1995. *A Moment on the Earth: The Coming Age of Environmental Optimism.* New York: Viking.

———. 2005. "Clear Skies, No Lies." *New York Times*, February 16.

Eilperin, Juliet. 2004. "EPA's Wording Found to Mirror Industry's." *Washington Post*, September 22, A 29.

———. 2005. "Plan Lowers Clean-Air Standard." *Washington Post*, January 14, A07.

Greenwood, Mark. 2005. "A Statute for All of Us." *The Environmental Forum* (July-August): 29.

Holmstead, Jeff. 2005. "Leadership, Action—Not Regs, Litigation." *The Environmental Forum* (March–April): 43–44.

Janofsky, Michael. 2004. "Study Ranks Bush Plan to Cut Air Pollution as Weakest of 3." *New York Times*, June 10, 1.

Kraft, Michael E. 2006. "Environmental Policy in Congress." In Norman J. Vig and Michael E. Kraft, eds., *Environmental Policy: New Directions for the Twenty-First Century*, 6th ed. Washington, DC: CQ Press.

Lazarus, Richard J. 2004. *The Making of Environmental Law.* Chicago: University of Chicago Press.

Lindblom, Charles E., and Edward J. Woodhouse. 1993. *The Policy-Making Process.* 3rd ed. Englewood Cliffs, NJ: Prentice Hall.

Lowi, Theodore J. 1979. *The End of Liberalism.* New York: Norton.

Mazmanian, Daniel A., and Michael E. Kraft, eds. 1999. *Toward Sustainable Communities: Transition and Transformations in Environmental Policy.* Cambridge, MA: MIT Press.

National Academy of Public Administration (NAPA). 2000. *Environment.gov: Transforming Environmental Protection for the 21st Century.* Washington, DC: NAPA.

Prakash, Aseem. 2000. *Greening the Firm: The Politics of Corporate Environmentalism.* Cambridge: Cambridge University Press.

Press, Daniel, and Daniel A. Mazmanian. 2006. "The Greening of Industry: Combining Government Regulation and Voluntary Strategies." In Norman J. Vig and Michael E. Kraft, eds., *Environmental Policy*, 6th ed. Washington, DC: CQ Press.

Rabe, Barry G. 2006. "Power to the States: The Promise and Pitfalls of Decentralization." In Norman J. Vig and Michael E. Kraft, eds., *Environmental Policy*, 6th ed. Washington, DC: CQ Press.

Rosenbaum, Walter A. 2005. *Environmental Politics and Policy*. Washington, DC: CQ Press.

Schoenbrod, David. 2005. *Saving Our Environment from Washington: How Congress Grabs Power, Shirks Responsibility, and Shortchanges the People*. New Haven, CT: Yale University Press.

Schulzke, Eric. 2002. "Defining Issues, Defining People: Actor Uncertainty and the Framing of Environmental Politics." Doctoral dissertation, University of California, Berkeley.

Shabecoff, Philip. 1993. *A Fierce Green Fire: The American Environmental Movement*. New York: Hill and Wang.

Shapiro, Sidney. 2005. "The Case against the IQA." *The Environmental Forum* (July–August): 26–33.

Shipan, Charles R., and William R. Lowry. 2001. "Environmental Policy and Party Divergence in Congress." *Political Research Quarterly* 54 (June): 245–263.

Shogren, Elizabeth. 2004. "EPA Is Lax on Coal Power Rule, Report Says." *Los Angeles Times*, October 1, 1.

Smith, Mark A. 2000. *American Business and Political Power: Public Opinion, Elections, and Democracy*. Chicago: University of Chicago Press.

Smith, Joseph. 2005. "Congress Opens the Courthouse Doors: Statutory Changes to Judicial Review under the Clean Air Act." *Political Research Quarterly* 58 (March): 139–149.

U.S. EPA. 2005. "Air Emissions Trends—Continued Progress through 2004." http://www.epa.gov/airtrends/econ-emissions.html.

Vig, Norman J., and Michael E. Kraft, eds. 2006. *Environmental Policy: New Directions for the Twenty-First Century*. 6th ed. Washington, DC: CQ Press.

IV

Policy Implementation in Administrative Agencies

6

Businesses and the Environment: Influencing Agency Policymaking

Scott R. Furlong

Public policy changes that can have significant effects on the environment and public health often occur well outside of the public eye and with little knowledge on the part of anyone other than well-connected individuals. It is not hard to find examples from recent years. A prominent one concerns the "buffer-zone" rule for surface mining, which has had major effects on water quality in coal-mining states such as West Virginia. While often ignored by the mining industry, under this rule companies are not to mine within 100 feet of a stream. In 2004, the George W. Bush administration proposed a change in the policy. The proposed new rule stated that mining could occur within 100 feet of a stream if the companies "could show that they took measures to 'the extent possible' to protect water quality and avoid harm to fish and wildlife" (Warrick 2004, A1). This somewhat minor change leaves open to interpretation the meaning of "the extent possible" and favors mining companies, so it may adversely affect the surrounding environment. A reasonable assumption is that the new rule and similar changes in mining regulations are in part a reflection of the close relationship between the Bush administration and the coal and mining industry—a relationship that appears to provide a significant advantage to the industry when it attempts to lobby administrative officials. It is easier to approach such officials with requested changes when they are predisposed to favor industry's position. In contrast, environmental groups enjoy no similar warm reception in the Bush administration.

This example illustrates well the critical role of both executive-branch agencies and the presidency itself in the U.S. policy process. This is nowhere more visible than in the Bush administration. As many accounts of policymaking within the administration have demonstrated, it has made exceptional use of the administrative process to bring about policy change, most often in support of the positions taken by the business community (Goldstein and Cohen 2004; Weiss 2004; Warrick 2004). In particular, the administration has found that it could most effectively advance its conservative, pro-business agenda in this manner because the policy changes were generally not visible to the public but were clearly known to and appreciated by the beneficiaries (such as coal-mining companies). The administration has tended to avoid high-profile and potentially high-conflict actions such as proposing major changes to popular environmental laws that would require congressional approval. Instead, it has concentrated on the relative obscurity of administrative policy change that is far less likely to be covered by the press or to stimulate public disapproval. This course of action gives it greater control over the way the issues are framed and the way the policy debate takes place. The proposed changes invariably can be defended as promoting efficiency, economic growth, job expansion, reliance on domestic energy supplies, or other equally positive social goals. Thus, any potential conflict over rule changes can usually be reduced.

Because of these qualities of administrative policy change, the Bush administration has been able to rely heavily on "clarifications" to existing rules and reversal of rules from the Clinton administration that it opposed. It has benefited from congressional approval in 2000 of the little-known Data Quality Act, which greatly expands the opportunities for interest groups (especially business groups) to challenge the quality of the information used by agencies in developing rules (Andrews 2006; Weiss 2004). Through these "under-the-radar" methods, the Bush administration has been highly effective in rolling back social regulation, including environmental policies. Most of these actions have not aroused much public or congressional opposition, presumably because media coverage has been minimal and the general public is unaware of the decisions.

The common view of the role that businesses play in influencing environmental policy focuses on congressional lobbying. This view of interest-group influence is not limited to environmental policy. Most of the research conducted on the role of interest groups in the policy process and journalistic accounts concentrate on how organizations get what they want from legislatures. As a result, much less is known about how groups participate in agency policymaking. This omission is unfortunate because much policymaking generally, and environmental policymaking in particular, occurs through the actions taken by executive agencies. One would expect that business interests are keenly aware of the potential to influence federal agency decisions, and that they take appropriate actions in that venue as well as in Congress and the states and localities.

This chapter examines the role that businesses, and the trade associations representing these businesses, play in attempting to influence environmental policy within federal agencies, particularly the U.S. Environmental Protection Agency (EPA). Much as the congressional committee system reflects the high degree of policy specialization within Congress and provides numerous points of access for groups trying to influence public policy, executive agencies offer a complex and specialized institutional venue, and equally numerous points of access. Sophisticated groups are well aware that the enactment of statutes signals not the end of lobbying efforts but a new beginning. In fact, many more opportunities for policy influence arise once federal agencies are charged with implementation of congressional statutes. For example, while many interest groups actively sought to mold the Clean Air Act Amendments of 1990 as they moved through the legislative process, the resulting legislation required the EPA to develop hundreds of rules and regulations, the formulation of which could be, and was, subject to extensive lobbying by diverse groups. Interest groups are also intimately familiar with the often-striking differences between the characteristics of rulemaking within the EPA and what one finds in natural resource agency rulemaking. The former typically deals with public health issues (e.g., an acceptable level of mercury emissions), whereas the latter involves commodity or land-use issues (e.g., permitted use of snowmobiles in national parks). Hence, different kinds of interest groups are involved and different strategies may be used to influence agency decisions.

Chapter 1 highlights the often-distinctive institutional venues where business groups may seek to influence environmental policy decisions, and argues that we have very limited knowledge of how business groups decide whether to intervene in any particular venue, when, and how. This chapter focuses on business lobbying efforts directed at federal agencies responsible for environmental policy implementation. As chapter 1 notes, some analysts suggest that business groups enjoy a significant advantage in lobbying federal agencies (e.g., Webb Yackee and Webb Yackee 2004) whereas others challenge that assertion (e.g., Golden 1998; Kamieniecki 2006). This chapter speaks to these arguments by exploring several sets of data that can help to answer the kinds of questions set out in chapter 1 related to business strategies for lobbying agencies and their effectiveness. These questions include the following:

• To what extent are business interests involved in attempting to both gain access to the agencies and influence their decisions on environmental regulatory policy? Is this involvement any different from what is attempted by other kinds of groups, such as public interest groups?
• How effective are such lobbying efforts by business in affecting decisions made by administrative agencies responsible for implementing environmental policy? Do businesses have a disproportionate influence in regulatory policymaking?

Delegation of Authority, Bureaucratic Discretion, and the Role of the Executive Branch

In general, one thinks of the executive branch primarily as the collection of agencies, bureaus, and offices responsible for implementing laws passed by Congress. While this characterization captures important elements of the bureaucratic role, it is also critical to recognize the potent lawmaking power that many agencies possess and the impact they can have on U.S. society. As a result of congressional delegation of authority, agencies within the executive branch can have significant discretion in the implementation of public policy, and hence considerable ability to shape policy direction and effects.

This exercise of agency discretion is especially notable in the implementation of regulatory policy, which typically involves the issuance of detailed regulations that have the effect of law. Eisner, Worsham, and Ringquist (2000) define regulation as "an array of public policies explicitly designed to govern economic activity and its consequences at the level of the industry, firm, or individual unit of activity." These regulations often set the specific requirements that must be followed by a variety of regulated entities (often businesses). The specific regulatory actions are evident daily in the *Federal Register*, the federal government's publication of executive actions and policies. For example, although the Safe

Drinking Water Act was enacted to ensure the quality of drinking water, it is up to the EPA through rulemaking to set the National Primary Drinking Water Standards for different contaminants to ensure this quality. These are the actual legal requirements that must be met to ensure safe water quality.

Understanding delegation of authority and the role of the bureaucracy in making policy through the regulatory process is crucial in order to appreciate the role of interest-group and business activities in the making of environmental policy. Experienced interest groups, including businesses, recognize the policymaking role of the executive branch and, therefore, pursue lobbying activities much as they do with Congress. Indeed, one could say that congressional delegation of authority to the executive agencies has created a whole new venue for lobbying for those who lose their fight in Congress. Berry (1984) refers to this as "appeals court lobbying." As the editors say in chapter 1, one would expect resourceful interest groups to seek out the most appropriate venues to achieve their policy goals. Often the result is executive-agency lobbying.

While delegation of authority provides the executive-branch agencies with the ability to make policy, Congress and the president continually develop mechanisms to limit the discretion that unelected agency officials have in making policy. These mechanisms, such as administrative procedures, not only limit the procedural and substantive decisions made within the agencies, but also provide a way for represented interests to become involved in the administrative process. As will be discussed later, for example, the Administrative Procedure Act (APA) mandates a process requiring agencies to seek public input when developing regulations. In reality, the public input often consists largely of advice and comments by organized interests that are directly affected by the agency decisions.

Another recent example of limits placed on discretion was approval of the Data Quality Act referred to earlier. The law was approved as a rider to a large appropriations bill without any congressional debate. It was backed by business interests concerned with how information can be used (or misused) by executive agencies such as the EPA. The law directs the OMB to ensure that information disseminated by the federal government is reliable (Weiss 2004, A1). In essence, the act is both an administrative and oversight tool that can be used to limit agency discretion. On the surface, the act appears to be an innocuous stipulation that encourages use of quality information. But as Weiss (2004, A1) observes, its interpretation "could tip the balance in regulatory disputes that weigh the interests of consumers and business." The law allows organizations to petition the government to stop action by calling into question the information and data being used by an agency. A strict interpretation can tie up regulatory actions for significant periods of time. While the petition process is open to all, historically over 80 percent of the significant petitions have been filed by business interests, and it appears that environmental actions are among those that are petitioned most frequently (Weiss 2004).[1]

Interest Groups and the Executive Branch: Theoretical Perspectives

Some scholars debate whether individual businesses should be considered interest groups at all (Baumgartner and Leech 1998). For purposes of this chapter, any organization (whether membership or not) that attempts to influence public policy should be considered an interest group. Businesses are interest groups because they attempt to influence policy in order to achieve their goals. Individual businesses or trade associations may be characterized as economic interest groups because they are lobbying primarily to promote their own self-interests, even if they also sometimes have larger ideological interests as well. In contrast, public interest groups typically back efforts that will benefit not only their membership but potentially any member of society.

Scholars have examined the interaction that occurs between interest groups and the executive branch from a number of different perspectives. Agency-capture theory states that agencies act as servants of the organized interests that they regulate rather than of the general public (Bernstein 1955; Stigler 1971; Golden 1998). In some cases, policies are said to be made by the very groups most directly affected by these requirements (Lowi 1987). Generally, scholars discuss capture theory in association with economic or business interests. That is, it suggests a level of undue influence by singular economic interests over the agencies responsible for policymaking. In the area of environmental policy, businesses obviously represent a major lobbying interest attempting to influence agencies such as the EPA, but not the only interest. Issues in the environmental policy area are complex and typically include a wide range of interests seeking to be heard. This complexity of interest has led most political scientists to dismiss capture as inadequate for an explanation of policymaking systems because it is highly unlikely that an agency would be beholden to only one set of interest groups (Heclo 1978).

Examining the role of interest groups through the various theories describing issue networks (Heclo 1978), subgovernments, policy subsystems, or advocacy coalitions (Sabatier 1988) is also common. In these theories there are a variety of government and nongovernmental actors interested in a particular policy issue. The interactions occurring within these systems help to explain developments in the policy process such as problem definition, alternative selection, and implementation. Recognizing the importance of the subsystem model, Eisner, Worsham, and Ringquist (2000) examine regulatory policies by using the two dimensions of saliency and complexity associated with a particular policy area. Environmental policy, according to the authors, is representative of a policy area that is highly salient and complex. The level of complexity dictates a need for expertise that often occurs within subsystems. Only actors that have the ability to specialize in a particular policy are likely to be involved in its development. Yet, the level of saliency of environmental policies (often high) encourages participation by a number of different participants. Thus, according to Eisner, Worsham, and Ringquist (2000, 151), you get "two competing advocacy coalitions divided by traditional ideological core beliefs." Within these coalitions are a variety of interest groups attempting to influence policy. The politics of the U.S. government process dictate the relationships between businesses and trade associations within this coalition and the executive agencies implementing policy. During Republican administrations, one would expect that business interests would have both more access and influence because Republicans are also more likely to support and pursue the ideas of economic rationality; conversely, during Democratic administrations they would have less access and influence (Kamieniecki 2006).

This latter political situation is well illustrated by the EPA's adoption of new rules in 1997 that tightened the standards for ozone and fine particulates. Under the Clean Air Act, the agency is required to review its National Ambient Air Quality Standards for each of the major pollutants covered by the act every five years. Where necessary (for example, based on new scientific evidence), it is to revise the standards. In response to a court order to issue new particulate standards, the agency proposed revised standards for both ozone and fine particulates that were stringent and costly. In June 1997, it then gained approval by the Clinton White House for the new standards despite strong opposition by industry and the president's own economic advisers, both of whom worried that the costs would be unreasonably burdensome (Cushman 1997). To soften the blow on industry, the agency allowed a generous time frame for states to comply with the new standards, permitting up to fifteen years. Nonetheless, this is clearly a case where business groups lost and environmental and health interests were successful.

Not surprisingly, business groups went on to challenge the standards in court, supplying a fitting example of the concept of litigation strategies as "appeals court lobbying" (Berry 1984; O'Leary 2006). In February 2001, the Supreme Court unanimously and decisively rejected industry's arguments that the EPA action was unjustified, grounding its opinion in the language of the Clean Air Act. The act stipulates that the agency must consider only the requirement to protect public health and safety and that it is not required to balance the benefits and costs of such regulations.[2]

While most of this chapter discusses situations where business interests are successful in their lobbying efforts, this case shows that an important variable affecting the outcome is which party or president controls the executive branch. Industry groups might well have been more successful in a Republican administration. Indeed, many of the environmental policy decisions of the Bush administration were decidedly more friendly to business interests than was the case during the Clinton administration (Vig and Kraft 2006).

There is a distinct difference between political access and political influence. One can measure access through a number of means, depending on the political institution being studied. For example, Langbein (1986) examines congressional access through the number of minutes that members of Congress spend with representatives of organized interests. In the executive branch, there are several ways that scholars can examine access. Researchers have examined participation in rulemaking (Furlong 1997; Golden 1998; Kerwin 2003; Kamieniecki 2006; Yackee

2006), membership on advisory committees (Balla and Wright 2001), and contacts made with presidential management offices (Berry and Portney 1995). But access does not guarantee influence in the political process. While access is likely a necessary condition for influence to occur, it is not a sufficient condition.

Interest-group scholars have had a difficult time trying to measure influence and whether it occurs in the political process. Furlong (1997) and Kerwin (2003) examine group influence on the executive branch indirectly through surveys by asking lobbyists working for interest groups if they believe they are influential. Golden (1998) and Kamieniecki (2006) attempt to examine differences between proposed and final rules to see what changes were made and then to connect these changes to comments made during the notice-and-comment process. In all of these cases, however, it remains unclear if the agency decisions are a direct result of what interest groups do in their lobbying efforts or are explained by some other factors.

Interest Groups and the Executive Branch
Studying interest-group lobbying of the executive branch raises challenging questions, in part, because the executive branch includes a number of quite different institutions; these range from diverse cabinet and independent executive agencies (e.g., the Department of Transportation or the EPA) to independent regulatory commissions (e.g., the Federal Trade Commission) to White House offices (e.g., the OMB) to the president himself. It is safe to say that all of these institutions are open to lobbying by interest groups as they seek to influence policy, but both the lobbying strategies and their effectiveness differ. Moreover, the different institutions are interrelated in ways that are sometimes difficult to study. A good illustration comes from the old Council on Competitiveness in the administration of George H. W. Bush. Berry and Portney (1995), for example, linked business access to the council with subsequent efforts to influence agency policies and rules in general, and EPA policies in particular. Yet it would be hard to demonstrate just how the council and its staff influenced the EPA.

As these challenges suggest would be the case, the literature on interest-group lobbying of the executive branch is not as empirically developed as similar lobbying research on the legislative branch. In fact, often scholars discuss interest-group activity of the executive branch as a tangent to legislative lobbying (Schlozman and Tierney 1986). There have been some efforts to learn more about the role that interest groups play in agency policymaking. A few analyses have employed case studies to examine the influence of rulemaking. For example, Magat, Krupnick, and Harrington (1986) examined rulemaking for EPA water pollution rules. The authors find that those industries most affected by the rules were more likely to comment on the standards, again showing the predominance of business interests. While such studies of the world of rulemaking are important, as Golden (1998) has pointed out, they also could be limited because of their focus on interest-group activity in Washington, D.C. (also see Kamieniecki 2006).

Kerwin (1994, 2003) was the first to systematically examine the role that groups play in rulemaking. His initial study, conducted in 1993 and updated in 2003, surveyed interest groups specifically on their participation in the rulemaking process. In both surveys, it was apparent that organizations considered participation in the rulemaking process to be an extremely important avenue in influencing public policy, rating it on a par with their participation in lobbying the legislature. Organizations lobby executive agencies in a number of ways, including providing written comments on proposed rules, attending and participating in public hearings, informally contacting agency officials prior to or after the notice of the proposal, and participating on advisory committees. More recently, we can also add a variety of electronic formats, such as the use of electronic policy dialogues and e-mail, through which interest groups can contact officials in an agency (Furlong and Kerwin 2005).

As noted earlier, while accessing and lobbying executive agencies is one thing, an equally important question is the ability of these groups to actually influence agency decisions. In the area of rulemaking, the most common form of participation is likely through notice-and-comment rulemaking administered through the APA and other statutes enacted since the passage of the APA in 1946. The APA provides for minimal procedural requirements for agencies conducting informal rulemaking, which offer opportunities for interested parties to comment on notices of proposed rules being developed by regulatory agencies.

In reviewing the effects of these procedures by others, West (2004) gives three reasons for their existence. First, they provide for a meaningful opportunity for those interested in the rules to have their voices heard and potentially influence the agencies' policies. Second, these procedures "promote responsiveness indirectly by strengthening political oversight of the bureaucracy" (p. 67). In essence, the notice that agencies provide through the *Federal Register* can act as a cue to the affected interests that might then lobby the legislature or the White House in an attempt to influence the bureaucracy indirectly. This reason corresponds to theories by a number of researchers regarding indirect control and oversight over the bureaucracy. Congress can use the interest groups to "pull the alarm" when something goes wrong within the bureaucracy, then conduct oversight on these agencies (McCubbins and Schwartz 1984) and establish administrative procedures to control what the agencies are doing (McCubbins, Noll, and Weingast 1987, 1989). Third, the procedures are symbolic and in West's words a "legitimate" delegation of authority, but have no real effect on changing agency policy. Agencies, in other words, ask for public comments because they are required to do so. They believe they are the experts, and it is rare for them to make significant changes based on outside comments. The first and second reasons for these procedures get at the question of interest-group influence on agency policymaking. What does the research say about this?

Kerwin's surveys (2003; see also Furlong 1997) asks interest groups to rate their effectiveness in influencing rulemaking. According to the respondents, they were successful in influencing rulemaking on a regular basis. While self-assessments such as these are problematic, they provide one perspective on ability to influence. From the agency perspective, it appears that groups may overstate their ability to influence. West (2004) interviewed a number of agency officials regarding the role of public comment in the rulemaking process. His analysis suggests that there are limited opportunities for these public comments to have a major direct effect on agency regulations because of the way these rules are developed.[3] This is not to say that groups cannot influence agency policies. On the contrary, West confirms through his interviews that agencies often seek informal participation prior to publishing a proposed rule. Kerwin's

(2003) surveys of interest groups bear out the importance of such informal agency contacts, which may occur off the record. Organizations place a great emphasis on such contacts, and they are considered one of the most effective techniques.

The EPA's rules governing mercury pollution from power plants demonstrate the potential that such access prior to the proposal can have for an interest group. Not only did the EPA take into consideration input from industry interests regarding this proposal, but in certain blatant cases it lifted exact language from memorandums provided by industry representatives. According to Pianin (2004, 31), "A side-by-side comparison of one of the three proposed rules and the memoranda prepared by Latham & Watkins—one of Washington's premier corporate environmental law firms—shows that at least a dozen paragraphs were lifted, sometimes verbatim, from the industry suggestions." What is particularly interesting in this case is that the assistant administrator for EPA's Office of Air and Radiation, the political appointee primarily responsible for this regulation, worked for Latham & Watkins prior to his appointment to the EPA. This illustration of the "revolving door" between government and interest groups is typically discussed as a problem of agency personnel moving into business and using their former contacts unethically to influence policymaking. But this case demonstrates that the revolving door turns both ways and the entrance into the agency can be just as problematic. As this relates to the influence of business, a comment from Martha Keating of the Clean Air Task Force perhaps states the concern best: "It just illustrates the inside track the industry groups and some of these law firms have with the administration" (Pianin 2004, 31).

Trying to measure organizational influence on rules directly is difficult. Are changes to regulations made as a result of the comments submitted by the general public or specific interest groups? Are they due to additional data and analysis being presented, or perhaps from marching orders being provided by the White House or OMB? Golden (1998) and Kamieniecki (2006) measure interest-group influence by examining changes that occur between the proposed and final rule. While they find that agencies are willing to change rules based on public comment, most of these changes are inconsequential, and major changes to rules are rare. Another study by Webb Yackee and Webb Yackee (2004) and Yackee

(2006) finds that not only are business interests participating more frequently in rulemaking, but their comments are significantly more likely to change agency rules than any other organizational type.[4]

Many of these studies comment on the role of business interests and what appears to be their advantage in the rulemaking process. Why might there be such an advantage? To use James Q. Wilson's (1980) typology, organizations interested in concentrated costs or benefits are more likely to participate in policymaking because of the recognition of the inherent benefits of their participation. Regulations have a direct affect on them. Public interest groups, however, are less likely to participate because either they do not perceive any benefit or the benefit is distributed very broadly among many, making collective action more difficult because of the free-rider problem (Olson 1965). Rulemaking actions typically increase the costs of doing business. Therefore, one would expect increased participation by businesses or trade associations seeking to protect their operations. Environmental regulations, which often have concentrated costs and disbursed benefits, are thus more likely to engender business participation than are other proposed regulations. Additionally, Wright (1996) suggests that businesses and trade associations will be more active in executive-branch lobbying because of their greater expertise in legal and administrative issues compared to public interest groups. Finally, the substantial differences in resources between business groups and public interest groups can affect participation.

Communicating with and Influencing the Bureaucracy

Direct lobbying of the executive branch and the access associated with it can be quite different from lobbying the legislature. Legal requirements, such as the APA and the Federal Advisory Committee Act, often require open access to decisionmaking within the executive branch. These requirements were implemented in order to prevent the appearance of undue influence on agency decisionmaking. When these procedures are not followed, as was the case with Vice President Cheney's National Energy Policy Development Group, critics often raise concerns regarding who is participating and question whether unfair access has been provided to important decisionmakers. An "All Things Considered" program on National Public Radio even parodied the creation and inclusion of this task force by suggesting that the environmental organization's invitations must have been "lost in the mail" (Kluger and Slavin 2002).

In the area of legislative lobbying, researchers often examine the role that campaign contributions play in interest-group access (Langbein 1986; Baumgartner and Leech 1998) and influence (Hall and Wayman 1990; Langbein 1993; Wright 1990). Since providing political contributions to executive agencies is illegal, one might question its applicability to executive lobbying. Yet contributions are made to presidential candidates and, as recent presidential administrations have shown, they do appear to provide some additional access to a president or the president's personal staff. How this might affect specific agency policies or individual rules is open to conjecture, but it can raise eyebrows. For example, some have suggested that a change to an EPA regulation was based on the fact that the individual who would benefit from the change was one of the Bush Pioneers, a group of people who raised at least $100,000 for the 2000 campaign (Grimaldi and Edsall 2004). In this situation, a Clinton-proposed rule would have increased regulatory requirements for shop towels used to clean up chemical spills. After the election of George W. Bush in 2000, industry lobbyists were able to get the agency to propose less stringent requirements, saving the industry millions of dollars. This action raises the possibility of a link between campaign contributions made by the Pioneer and the access provided to him and the related industry lobbyists that led to changes to the regulation and other policies initiated by the Bush White House.

As mentioned earlier, there are a variety of mechanisms used by interest groups trying to lobby agency rulemaking, but probably the one used most often is providing written comments to proposed rules. Under the APA, organizations can participate in informal or notice-and-comment rulemaking. Agencies developing informal regulations typically must provide an opportunity for interested parties to submit comments on proposed actions. As an example, the EPA's recent air emissions standards governing mercury pollution from utility plants received nearly 540,000 public comments (Eilperin 2004). In the case of such a high-profile regulation, one expects a large number of public comments from a variety of sources. These sources range from environmental groups concerned about environmental protection and public health as well as about the effect such a cap-and-trade approach proposed by the administration may have on these issues, to electrical utility interests concerned about the costs of implementation and wanting as much flexibility as possible.

Theoretically, the comments that agencies receive help in formulating the final regulation. While some rules such as the one on mercury emissions generate a large number of public comments, sometimes these comments are more political than informational.[5] As such, it is also important to note that the agency is not merely counting the "votes" for or against a proposed rule. In fact, the purpose of notice-and-comment is for agencies to receive additional substantive information that would help improve their final rules. This kind of information—rather than the quantity of particular comments—is supposed to guide rule writers (Kamieniecki 2006). Yet, from a political perspective, it may be difficult for agencies to ignore thousands of comments even if they do not necessarily provide new data or information. It should also be noted that with the advent of electronic communication, e-rulemaking is much more prevalent within many agencies.

Most rulemakings tend to deal with relatively specific areas of policy. As a result, the types of organizations likely to participate will be those having some specialized knowledge of the policy arena. Organizations with the necessary substantive and procedural resources may be at an advantage in such a process. One study of rulemaking participation specifically related to environmental policy shows that there are inter-agency differences that affect participation. The EPA rules studied had a large percentage of the comments come from business organizations (Golden 1998).

Participation in bureaucratic policymaking can also occur through offices within the Executive Office of the President. Offices such as the OMB can influence what goes on within executive agencies so one would expect interest groups to attempt to lobby here as well. Some presidential administrations have been accused of selective access in these organizations. As noted earlier, the Council on Competitiveness created by President George H. W. Bush, for example, served as a "super-OMB," reviewing agency policies of particular importance. Critics of the council argued that it provided access to businesses and others friendly to the administration's concerns about the regulatory environment (Triano and

Watzman 1991). Vice President Dick Cheney's energy task force, also mentioned earlier, received a great deal of press coverage, especially in relation to access to and membership of the task force. There were claims that the members of the task force, mainly representatives of the oil and gas industry, had undue influence over the administration's energy policy and that pro-environmental organizations were excluded from this process.

One particular idea that appears to have been broached by industry participants in this task force dealt specifically with the EPA's New Source Review (NSR) program and proposals by energy interests to gut it. Under the NSR program, energy companies were expected to bring older plants into compliance with the Clean Air Act through nonroutine updates of their equipment. As the EPA began to crack down on these violations, the energy industry stalled, and was able to take advantage of the access provided by the more favorable Bush administration that took office in January 2001. Through their contacts on the energy task force and the sympathetic Bush appointees, the energy interests were able to obtain favorable treatment in regard to the New Source Review. One telling example was that the EPA initially attempted to adopt a regulation that would allow generating plants to spend up to 20 percent of a unit's replacement cost without meeting the NSR threshold. This 20 percent compares to the 0.75 percent that was recommended by EPA civil servants.[6]

More recently, the OMB has provided another access point by requesting nominations from the outside to reform regulations. In a February 20, 2004, notice in the *Federal Register*, the OMB requested nominations for regulatory reforms that may affect the manufacturing industry (U.S. Office of Management and Budget 2004). While such nominations can potentially come from anywhere, it appears clear that the intent on OMB's part is getting input from businesses and similar interests, which have submitted a number of candidates for reform. Public interest groups, such as Public Citizen, see this activity as inappropriate. According to Joan Claybrook, president of Public Citizen, "What OMB has become for business is the special-interest pleader. Each company and industry has its own set of particular [rules] they don't want" (Skrzycki 2004). All of these examples provide those privileged with access the ability to influence regulatory policy by communicating with organizations closely tied to the White House. In these examples, the access does not appear to be equal and is heavily tilted toward business interests.

Business Participation in Environmental Regulatory Policy

While participation and lobbying occur through direct interactions between groups and the agencies primarily responsible for the development and implementation of these polices, indirect pressure can also occur through White House offices or Congress in order to achieve similar goals. This section examines some of these methods and also explores data regarding group participation in this branch of government.

Kerwin (1994) conducted the first systematic data collection on how organizations participate in rulemaking, probably one of the most common forms of executive-branch lobbying, and presented his results in his first edition of *Rulemaking* (see also Furlong 1997). The survey examined a wide range of issues regarding how interest groups receive information regarding rulemaking and also how they access this process in attempts to influence regulations coming from executive agencies. Ten years later, Furlong and Kerwin (2005; see also Kerwin 2003) updated this survey to see if any changes had occurred in rulemaking participation and the perceived influence of organizations on agency policy.[7] To provide some context to business participation in environmental policy, it is helpful to show general interest-group participation in regulatory rulemaking. Table 6.1 summarizes some of the devices used by all interest groups surveyed and the frequency of their use. Table 6.2 provides information regarding how effective interest groups perceived these methods to be for influencing rulemaking.

These general data on interest-group participation in rulemaking provide several conclusions worth emphasizing. First, groups are not using written comments in response to a proposed rule as often as they did during the first survey conducted in 1992. This is interesting because this form of participation could be considered the most formal and widely accepted since it was established in the APA. Participation in the hearing process, however, increased between the two survey dates, and there are somewhat smaller increases in contacting an agency before and

Table 6.1

Methods used by interest groups to influence rules, by frequency of use (percentages from 1992 and 2002 surveys)

Frequency	Comments to proposed rules		Attendance at public hearings		Informal contact with agency before NPRM		Informal contact with agency after NPRM	
	1992	2002	1992	2002	1992	2002	1992	2002
Never	1.5	5.3	7.0	1.7	8.4	2.7	4.6	3.6
Sometimes/ frequently	45.1	65.6	77.6	89.4	61.8	86.8	66.2	79.7
Always	53.4	29.2	15.5	8.8	29.8	10.7	29.2	17.0

Source: Adapted from Cornelius Kerwin, *Rulemaking: How Government Agencies Write Law and Make Policy*, 3rd ed. (Washington, DC: CQ Press, 2003).

Table 6.2

Interest-group perspectives on the effectiveness of methods to influence rules (percentages from 1992 and 2002 surveys)

Effectiveness	Comments to proposed rules		Attendance at public hearings		Informal contact with agency before NPRM		Informal contact with agency after NPRM	
	1992	2002	1992	2002	1992	2002	1992	2002
Less effective	16.1	14.3	36.7	16.9	15.1	10.4	32.0	22.9
Effective	29.8	31.4	30.5	33.0	13.6	21.7	18.8	35.2
More effective	54.2	54.3	32.9	50.0	71.2	68.0	49.2	41.9

Source: Adapted from Cornelius Kerwin, *Rulemaking: How Government Agencies Write Law and Make Policy*, 3rd ed. (Washington, DC: CQ Press, 2003).

after the proposal. One of the largest increases was for the amount of contact prior to the proposal. Based on these results, organizations seemed to want to use participation methods that provide direct access to agency policymakers. Written comments are somewhat passive, and groups do not have the same assurance that they are being heard.

Table 6.2 examines the effectiveness of these techniques as perceived by the organizations. While there are no major changes during the ten-year period, it is interesting to note that organizations perceived themselves as being more effective generally.[8] The results of these two tables provide meaningful background information about group participation in regulatory policy. It is clear that organizations generally consider such participation important in their lobbying activities, and perhaps as important as legislative lobbying. The question is how such participation in general bureaucratic policymaking relates to businesses and environmental policy.

The data from the Furlong and Kerwin study do not specifically examine environmental policy, but generally economic organizations such as trade associations and businesses participated in more rulemakings than the other organizational types. Individual businesses participated in over twice the number of rulemakings than did public interest groups. This general result is also borne out by studies by Golden 1998 and Webb Yackee and Webb Yackee 2004, showing a propensity of business interests involved in rulemaking compared to other forms of interest groups.[9] In addition, my own research points to a large discrepancy in business-interest participation in agency rulemaking. Business interests submitted many more comments in response to proposed regulations compared to other interests (Furlong 2004).

Participating in the notice-and-comment process is probably the most common way for organizations to get their voices heard regarding agency policies, but participation occurs in other ways—often outside of the public eye. Informal contacts between groups and agencies are quite common, and can be very effective forms of lobbying, yet the general public knows little about these contacts and how they may influence agency policy. With the passage of the Lobbying Disclosure Act, it is now possible to examine some of this activity that in the past was not well documented. I conducted a study on this informal lobbying for both the executive and legislative branches that shows a similar bias in economic interests. In general, economic organizations were more active in lobbying informally than public interest groups were. This discrepancy was even more pronounced in the area of executive lobbying (Furlong 2004). Do these discrepancies change when looking at environmental issues?

To examine only environmental issues, I used the Lobbying Disclosure Reports for all of 1996. These reports were obtained and put into a usable dataset through a project conducted by Baumgartner and Leech. As discussed by Furlong (1998) and Baumgartner and Leech (1999), there are some questions about the data collected under this law, yet they represent one of the only ways to examine what interactions occur between interest groups and policymakers generally, and agency officials specifically.[10] The data provided by Baumgartner and Leech contain approximately 19,000 reports. For purposes of this study, I narrowed down the number of reports used by focusing on environmental and natural resource issues. Of the seventy-six issue areas listed, five are clearly environmental related: Clean Air & Water, Environment/ Superfund, Natural Resources, Real Estate/Land Use Conservation, and Waste (hazardous/solid/interstate/nuclear). This subset represents 2,213 registrants—a group that files a Lobbying Registration form with Congress.

With these data we can examine the role that business interests play in informal lobbying generally and executive branch lobbying specifically, through a number of different lenses. Table 6.3 shows all of the registrants by the type of interest groups reporting that lobby both the legislative and executive branches. It indicates a large discrepancy in lobbying by business interests and other groups. Business interests, which include organizations categorized by "Business" and "Trade Association," represent over 94 percent of all of the organization registrants on environmental issues. In contrast, only about 3 percent of the registrants are public interest groups.[11]

Another way to study these data is by examining clients rather than registrants. By looking at the client variable, one can see not only individual organizations representing themselves but also what types of interests lobbying firms are representing. Individual interest groups can represent themselves, but in the case of lobbying firms, it is possible for them to represent multiple clients. As an example, one can look at the Wexler Group in the data and see that its clients included Eastman

Table 6.3
Registrants for environmental issues by organizational type

Organizational type	Frequency	Percent	Cumulative percent
Business[1]	1842	83.3	83.3
Trade association[2]	241	10.9	94.1
Union	12	0.5	94.6
Public-interest group	69	3.1	97.8
Other[3]	49	2.2	100.0
Total	2213	100.0	100.0

[1] Business groups include individual corporations and professional lobbying firms.
[2] Trade associations also include professional associations such as the American Medical Association (AMA).
[3] "Other" represents the remainder of registrants such as government entities, universities, and unknown classifications.

Kodak (individual business) and the American Forest and Paper Association (trade association), among others. Table 6.4 shows the client distribution.

Once again we see a large discrepancy between business interests and all other group types. In the case of the clients represented in the database, over 73 percent are business interests compared to about 6 percent of public interest groups. The major change seems to be with organizations in the "other" category.[12] As mentioned, these data examine lobbying of both the legislative and executive branches, but does this discrepancy between business interests and other organizational types remain when one just examines executive-branch lobbying? Additional analyses were conducted of lobbying information similar to analyses conducted based on data in tables 6.3 and 6.4, except in these cases only interest groups that stated that they lobbied the executive branch were examined. Subsequent analyses of the data show that business interests continue to dominate environmental lobbying in the executive branch compared to other group types, much as they did with overall lobbying efforts. While there is a slight increase in public interest group registrants and clients representing groups that lobby the executive branch, there continues to be a large discrepancy between these organizations and business interests.

Table 6.4
Clients for environmental issues by organizational type

Organizational type	Frequency	Percent	Cumulative percent
Business	1,171	52.9	52.9
Trade association[1]	451	20.4	73.3
Union	20	0.9	74.2
Public-interest group	140	6.3	80.6
Other[2]	430	19.4	100.0
Total	2,212	100.0	100.0

[1] Trade associations also include professional associations such as the AMA.
[2] "Other" represents the remainder of registrants such as government entities, universities, and unknown classifications.

A few aspects of executive-branch lobbying are not made clear by this data analysis. First, does the discrepancy between business interests and other group types represent more active lobbying by business groups generally, or is it an illustration of the current interest-group population? In other words, if business interests represent 75 percent or more of the interest-group population in this policy arena, then one might expect the registrant and client numbers to follow. Other research by Furlong (2004) and Baumgartner and Leech (2001) has shown such an increase in the percentage of business-type organizations. Second, these data show the amount of lobbying that occurs and not necessarily the amount of influence these organizations are having on agency policymaking. A number of studies show that organizations that participate in agency decisionmaking have the ability to influence these policies (Furlong 1997; Kerwin 2003; Webb Yackee and Webb Yackee 2004; Yackee 2006). One may be able to infer that the participation shown above is leading to some level of influence. It is also clear that in order to be able to influence agency policy, one must have access. The data above show that business interests appear to have significantly more access in the environmental arena.

As noted earlier, access does not guarantee policy influence, but it is clear that it is a necessary condition in order for influence to occur. As the different data sources show, business interests have some significant advantages when it comes to accessing government in general and the executive branch in particular. The empirical analyses all point to a system whereby business interests are much more active in participating in the administrative process. The various case studies discussed throughout this chapter support the data's contention of unequal levels of participation, but perhaps more importantly also suggest that this participation is leading to situations where business interests have the ability to shape environmental policy through executive-branch implementation. Chapter 1 states that one of the purposes of this book is to obtain a better understanding of the influence business may have on environmental policy, and specifically if it is as dominant as many believe, or whether this influence is more subtle than is usually assumed. The findings reported in this chapter seem to support both positions. These results raise questions regarding the development of environmental policy in the context of a democratic society. Are all voices being heard? Is elitism alive and well in this policy arena, especially in an era in which Republicans control the legislative and executive branches?

Conclusions

This chapter discusses some of the theoretical and empirical research regarding the role that interest groups may play in influencing bureaucratic policy. The background regarding delegation of authority from Congress to the executive branch and the procedures put in place to control bureaucratic discretion is important to understand when examining organizational influence of bureaucratic policy generally, and environmental policy specifically. The technological complexity of environmental policy dictates quite a high level of substantive delegation to the agencies involved in making this policy. However, the saliency and conflict associated with environmental policy often lead Congress and the president to develop procedural mechanisms to monitor and control the implementation of these policies. These mechanisms are often the route through which interest groups are afforded access to the executive branch and attempt to influence its policies.

Within the environmental policy arena, access is particularly important where a great many actual policy decisions are left to the discretion of agencies as they implement the myriad environmental statues. The data in this analysis clearly show a large discrepancy in the types of organizations that are accessing the executive branch in their attempts to influence policy. In just about every case, businesses, and like-minded organizations such as trade associations, represent over 75 percent of the organizations accessing agencies generally, and environmental issues specifically. The data above do not provide as clear an answer regarding the effectiveness of such access in influencing policy. Recent research suggests that organizations believe that they are somewhat effective in using a variety of techniques in affecting agency policy generally (Furlong and Kerwin 2005; Kerwin 2003; Webb Yackee and Webb Yackee 2004). There is no reason to believe that these results would be any different within the environmental arena.

Chapter 1 discusses a variety of studies by interest-group scholars of the important role that citizen groups (Berry 1999) and public opinion (Smith 2000) play in environmental policymaking. I tend to agree. But many of these studies have examined environmental policymaking in the congressional arena. Given the electoral motives of members of Congress, one should expect responsiveness to changes in the interest-group environment and shifts in public opinion. Executive-branch policymaking, though, does not necessarily rely on popular support for changes as much as on expertise and data. In addition, the evolution of presidential management of rulemaking and of other executive-branch policymaking mechanisms provides a certain level of control over what goes on within the executive agencies. Finally, in an era of unitary government controlled by Republicans, it is unlikely that congressional oversight will be conducted on policy shifts away from environmental protection. These conditions underscore the need to understand how decisions are made within the executive-branch agencies.

The cases discussed throughout the chapter would appear to support the idea that business groups, in particular, have been very successful in influencing environmental policies within executive-branch agencies, especially during the recent Bush administration. Journalistic accounts suggest greater access to bureaucratic policymakers from the highest levels in the case of the vice president's energy task force or the revolving door that has brought former industry officials into decisionmaking roles as political appointees, to lower-level areas where industry-provided language is making its way into specific rulemakings. While it is unlikely that anyone could seriously argue that environmental regulatory agencies are "captured" by business interests, it is clear that these groups can and do play a pivotal role in shaping agency policy. As the Clinton 1997 air quality regulation discussed earlier suggests, business does not always win. This is true even during Republican administrations where, for example, we have seen energy interests unsuccessful in opening up the Arctic National Wildlife Refuge in Alaska, and General Electric's inability to keep the Hudson River off the EPA's Superfund National Priorities List.

If the access provided to organizations is equitable and all viewpoints are being taken into consideration, then the ideals of the APA and other laws and procedures put in place to ensure fair decisionmaking should not be a concern. Likewise, if agencies are making changes based on better information and data that ultimately should lead to effective policies, then again goals of the administrative process to gather the most accurate and up-to-date information should be met. The major concern arises in regard to unequal access by certain players or categories of groups because of their ideological beliefs, partisan loyalties, or economic self-interest and power. This same concern must also be raised in terms of why changes might be occurring in public policies. Is it because of the quality of the data, or is favoritism entering into the decision process? McKay and Webb Yackee (2004) ask the question "Does the squeaky wheel get the grease?" in terms of influencing federal rulemaking; they conclude that, in fact, agencies appear to alter final rules to match the dominant interests. The data in this chapter tend to support the fact that business interests are active players in the rulemaking process and potentially have a greater ability get their views heard and considered—or get their wheels greased—than others do.

Notes

1. One example was that logging groups were able to challenge the Forest Service calculations used to justify restrictions on timber harvest (Weiss 2004, A01).

2. The case is *Whitman v. American Trucking Association*, 531 U.S. 457 (2001).

3. I asked a similar question in earlier research and found similar results. In this case, agency respondents were asked to estimate on a scale of 0 (never) to 10 (always) the frequency with which they made changes in rules under development as a result of comments from interest groups. See Furlong 1992.

4. According to the Webb Yackee and Webb Yackee study (2004) that examined forty rules from the Department of Labor's Occupational Safety and Health Administration and Employment Standards Administration, as well as the Department of Transportation's Federal Railroad Administration and Federal Highway Administration, over 57 percent of the comments from the forty rules studied came from business interests compared to 19 percent from government interests and 22 percent from nonbusiness/nongovernment interests. In addition, while business interests submitted comments for all of the rules, almost 50 percent of the rules received no comments from public interest groups, which again shows the disparity in participation by organizational type.

5. As an example, the League of Conservation Voters generated 20,000 Internet comments that likely are lacking in strong scientific rationale, but provide a political context in which to evaluate the proposal. See Eilperin, 2004.

6. See Barcott 2004 for additional information on this issue.

7. For the initial study, Kerwin and Furlong surveyed over 2,000 organizations and had a response rate of less than 20 percent. Their 2003 study surveyed approximately 550 organizations, and there was a response rate of about 25 percent. In each survey, the proportion of the different types of interest-group organizations was representative of other interest-group surveys.

8. For a complete discussion of these survey results, see Kerwin 2003 as well as Furlong and Kerwin 2005.

9. While Golden does report that business interests are very involved in rule-making, she states that these interests do not appear to have undue influence over the process.

10. For more information on the quality of the data in these reports and some of the potential issues associated with them, see Furlong 1998 and Baumgartner and Leech 1999.

11. I also examined these data after removing lobbying firms—which are classified as businesses—from the dataset. Even by removing a large number of these registrants from the analysis, business interests (businesses and trade associations) still represent close to 85 percent of the registrants compared to about 8 percent for public interest groups (the next highest number).

12. This category likely contains more organizations such as hospitals that may not conduct lobbying as a regular activity and therefore employ "hired guns."

References

Andrews, Richard N. L. 2006. "Risk-Based Decision Making: Policy, Science, and Politics." In Norman J. Vig and Michael E. Kraft, eds., *Environmental Policy*, 6th ed. Washington, DC: CQ Press.

Balla, Steven J., and John R. Wright. 2001. "Interest Groups, Advisory Committees, and Congressional Control of the Bureaucracy." *American Journal of Political Science* 45:799–812.

Barcott, Bruce. 2004. "Changing All the Rules." *New York Times*, April 4, section 6, 38.

Baumgartner, Frank R., and Beth L. Leech. 1998. *Basic Interests: The Importance of Groups in Politics and in Political Science*. Princeton, NJ: Princeton University Press.

————. 1999. "Studying Interest Groups Using Lobbying Disclosure Reports." *VOXPOP* 17 (3): 1–3.

————. 2001. "Interest Niches and Policy Bandwagons: Patterns of Interest Group Involvement in National Politics." *Journal of Politics.* 63:1191–1213.

Bernstein, Marver. 1955. *Regulating Business by Independent Commission.* Westport, CT: Greenwood Press.

Berry, Jeffrey M. 1984. *The Interest Group Society*. Boston: Little, Brown.

Berry, Jeffrey M. 1999. *The New Liberalism: The Rising Power of Citizen Groups*. Washington, DC: Brookings Institution.

Berry, Jeffrey M., and Kent E. Portney. 1995. "Centralizing Regulatory Control and Interest Group Access: The Quayle Council on Competitiveness." In Allan J. Cigler and Burdett A. Loomis, eds., *Interest Group Politics*, 4th ed. Washington, DC: CQ Press.

Cushman, John H. Jr. 1997. "Clinton Sharply Tightens Air Pollution Regulations Despite Concern over Costs." *New York Times*, June 26, 1, A18.

Eilperin, Juliet. 2004. "Comment Period on Mercury Emissions to End." *Washington Post*, June 29, A02.

Eisner, Marc A., Jeff Worsham, and Evan J. Ringquist. 2000. *Contemporary Regulatory Policy*. Boulder, CO: Lynne Rienner.

Furlong, Scott R. 1992. "Interest Group Influence on Regulatory Policy." Doctoral dissertation, School of Public Affairs, American University.

————. 1997. "Interest Group Influence on Rule Making." *Administration and Society* 29:325–348.

————. 1998. "The Lobbying Disclosure Act and Interest Group Lobbying Data: Two Steps Forward and One Step Back." *VOXPOP* 17 (3): 4–6.

————. 2004. "Lobbying the Executive Branch: Exploring Interest Group Participation in Executive Branch Policymaking." In Paul S. Herrnson, Ronald G. Shaiko, and Clyde Wilcox, eds., *The Interest Group Connection*, 2nd ed. Washington, DC: CQ Press.

Furlong, Scott R., and Cornelius M. Kerwin. 2005. "Interest Group Participation in Rulemaking: What Has Changed in Ten Years." *Journal of Policy Administration Research and Theory* 15:353–370.

Golden, Marissa. 1998. "Interest Groups in the Rule-Making Process: Who Participates? Whose Voices Get Heard?" *Journal of Public Administration Research and Theory* 8:245–269.

Goldstein, Amy, and Sarah Cohen. 2004. "Bush Forces a Shift in Regulatory Thrust." *Washington Post*, August 15, A01.

Grimaldi, James V., and Thomas B. Edsall. 2004. "Fundraiser Denies Link between Money, Access." *Washington Post*, May 17, A01.

Hall, Richard L., and Frank W. Wayman. 1990. "Buying Time: Moneyed Interests and the Mobilization of Bias in Congressional Committees." *American Political Science Review* 84:797–820.

Harter, Phillip. 1982. "Regulatory Negotiation: A Cure for the Malaise." *Georgetown Law Review* 71:1–113.

Heclo, Hugh. 1978. "Issue Networks and the Executive Establishment." In Anthony King, ed., *The New American Political System*. Washington, DC: American Enterprise Institute.

Kamieniecki, Sheldon. 2006. *Corporate America and Environmental Policy: How Often Does Business Get Its Way?* Palo Alto, CA: Stanford University Press.

Kerwin, Cornelius M. 1994. *Rulemaking: How Government Agencies Write Law and Make Policy*. Washington, DC: CQ Press.

———. 2003. *Rulemaking: How Government Agencies Write Law and Make Policy*. 3rd ed. Washington, DC: CQ Press.

Kluger, Bruce, and David Slavin. 2002. "Cheney Satire." *All Things Considered*. Washington, DC: National Public Radio. www.npr.org/templates/story/story. php?storyId=1138967.

Langbein, Laura I. 1986. "Money and Access: Some Empirical Evidence." *Journal of Politics* 48:1052–1062.

———. 1993. "PACs, Lobbies, and Political Conflict: The Case of Gun Control." *Public Choice* 75:254–271.

Lowi, Theodore. 1987. "Two Roads to Serfdom: Liberalism, Conservatism and Administrative Power." *American University Law Review* 36:295–322.

Magat, Wesley, Alan Krupnick, and Winston Harrington. 1986. *Rules in the Making*. Washington, DC: Resources for the Future.

McCubbins, Mathew, Roger Noll, and Barry Weingast. 1987. "Administrative Procedures as Instruments of Political Control." *Journal of Law, Economics and Organization* 3 (2): 243–277.

———. 1989. "Structure and Process, Politics and Policy: Administrative Arrangements and the Political Control of Agencies." *Virginia Law Review* 75 (3): 431–482.

McCubbins, Mathew, and Thomas Schwartz. 1984. "Congressional Oversight Overlooked: Police Patrols versus Fire Alarms." *American Journal of Political Science* 28:165–179.

McKay, Amy, and Susan Webb Yackee. 2004. "Does the Squeaky Wheel Get the Grease? Interest Group Participation and Influence on Federal Rulemaking."

Paper presented at the annual meeting of the Midwest Political Science Association, Chicago, April 14–17.

O' Leary, Rosemary. 2006. "Environmental Policy in the Courts." In Norman J. Vig and Michael E. Kraft, eds., *Environmental Policy*, 6th ed., 148–168. Washington, DC: CQ Press.

Olson, Macur. 1965. *The Logic of Collective Action: Public Goods and the Theory of Groups.* Cambridge, MA: Harvard University.

Pianin, Eric. 2004. "Thanks for the Memos." *Washington Post National Weekly Edition,* February 9–15, 31.

Sabatier, Paul. 1988. "An Advocacy Coalition Framework of Policy Change and the Role of Policy-Oriented Learning Therein." *Policy Sciences* 21 (2–3): 129–168.

Schlozman, Kay Lehman, and John T. Tierney. 1986. *Organized Interests in American Democracy.* New York: Harper & Row.

Skrzycki, Cindy. 2004. "Business Groups Jump at Chance to Scratch Regulatory Itches." *Washington Post,* June 15, E01.

Smith, Mark A. 2000. *American Business and Political Power: Public Opinion, Elections, and Democracy.* Chicago: University of Chicago Press.

Stigler, George J. 1971. "The Theory of Economic Regulation." *Bell Journal of Economics and Management Science* 2 (1) (spring): 3–21.

Triano, Christine, and Nance Waltzman. 1991. *All the Vice President's Men: How the Quayle Council on Competitiveness Secretly Undermines Health, Safety and Environmental Programs.* Washington, DC: OMB Watch/Public Citizen.

U.S. Office of Management and Budget. 2004. "Draft 2004 Report to Congress on the Costs and Benefits of Federal Regulations." *Federal Register,* vol. 69, no. 34, 7987.

Vig, Norman J., and Michael E. Kraft, eds. 2006. *Environmental Policy: New Directions for the Twenty-First Century.* Washington, DC: CQ Press.

Warrick, Joby. 2004. "Appalachia Is Paying Price for White House Rule Change." *Washington Post,* August 17, A01.

Webb Yackee, Jason, and Susan Webb Yackee. 2004. "Strength in Numbers? Assessing Equality of Participant Influence in the Informal Rulemaking Process." Paper presented at the 2004 annual meeting of the Midwest Political Science Association, Chicago.

Weiss, Rick. 2004. " 'Data Quality' Law Is Nemesis of Regulation" *Washington Post,* August 16, A01.

West, William F. 2004. "Formal Procedures, Informal Processes, Accountability, and Responsiveness in Bureaucratic Policy Making: An Institutional Policy Analysis." *Public Administration Review* 64:66–80.

Wilson, James Q. 1980. *The Politics of Regulation.* New York: Basic Books.

Wright, John R. 1990. "Contributions, Lobbying and Committee Voting in the U.S. House of Representatives." *American Political Science Review* 84:417–438.

———. 1996. *Interest Groups and Congress: Lobbying Contributions and Influence.* Boston: Allyn and Bacon.

Yackee, Susan Webb. 2006. "Sweet-Talking the Fourth Branch: The Influence of Interest Group Comments on Federal Agency Rulemaking." *Journal of Public Administration Research and Theory* 16:103–124.

7

Business Interests and Information in Environmental Rulemaking

Cary Coglianese

Over the past decade and a half, the Environmental Protection Agency (EPA) has imposed regulations on over 150 industrial sectors with the aim of reducing toxic air pollution. In setting its emissions standards for air toxics, the EPA needed to gather vast amounts of detailed information about the industrial processes used within each sector, as well as information about the technological fixes available to reduce toxic emissions. Yet the EPA did not have most of the information it needed. Even though EPA engineers were generally familiar with industrial operations in a few highly regulated sectors, they did not know as much as the managers and engineers running the very firms the EPA intended to regulate. Of course, on its own, industry certainly has little incentive to share information that would make it easier for the EPA to impose costly new regulations. How, then, did EPA acquire the information it needed to develop workable air toxics regulations? This chapter sets out to answer this question. In doing so, it shows how important information is to the regulatory game between business and government. Business seeks to use its informational advantage to try to affect government decisions, while regulators seek to counteract industry's desire to deploy information selectively in pursuit of its interests.

Although Bauer, Pool, and Dexter (1963) noted some years ago that lobbyists trade on information, most contemporary accounts of business lobbying continue to describe lobbying in terms of resources, pressure, and campaign contributions. While these are surely part of the overall picture, information also plays a key role in business lobbying (Leone 1986, 211), just as it does in other areas of politics (Krehbiel 1991). Indeed, in regulatory policymaking, information plays a particularly vital role because the development of regulation calls for making fine-grained, technical judgments about how to control the behavior of private-sector organizations and the design of major industrial operations.

Business interests struggle to use information strategically to affect environmental policy. To show how information figures into the regulatory game, this chapter begins by explaining why government needs business information and describing industry's incentives to keep from revealing adverse information to regulators. The chapter next presents two main strategies regulators use to break through industry's silence and acquire information they need to develop effective regulations. The chapter then examines the specific informational challenges the EPA encountered when implementing the air toxics provisions of the 1990 Clean Air Act Amendments. To implement these amendments, the EPA had to become expert in the detailed operations of hundreds of industrial sectors and thousands of facilities across the country. This chapter analyzes how the EPA regulators managed to acquire substantial amounts of necessary information, showing the important role that information played in business lobbying and policymaking over air toxics.

Business Information and Public Policy Decisionmaking

Since regulatory policy aims to solve problems, regulators need detailed information about the problems they intend to solve as well as about various alternative solutions to those problems (Breyer 1982, 109; Hawkins and Thomas 1989, 14). This is especially true for environmental regulation, which demands an understanding of the health risks from exposure to contaminants, the options for reducing those risks, and the expected health and economic consequences of various risk-reduction options or regulatory standards (Esty 2004).

This need for information stems in part from professional norms that lead most engineers, scientists, and other regulatory officials to want to make reasonably good public policy decisions. Even if some regulators are not interested in good public policy but instead seek to advance their own agenda and interests, they still have incentives to understand the consequences of different regulatory proposals, because they need to know who such policies will help and hurt.

Furthermore, the need for extensive information in making regulatory policy is reinforced by a variety of legal and political norms that place the burden of proof on the regulator to demonstrate that new regulations are needed and well crafted (Wagner 2004). The larger political and constitutional culture in the United State generally supports free markets, such that government intervention into private affairs is typically thought to require a justification (OMB 2003). For example, the Administrative Procedure Act of 1946 (APA), which sets forth the procedures that agencies must follow in developing new regulations, authorizes courts to set aside any regulation deemed "arbitrary and capricious."[1] Courts read this language in the APA to demand that agencies provide careful reasons for their policy decisions—reasons backed up, of course, with credible information.[2] Similarly, since at least the early 1980s, both Democratic and Republican White Houses have required regulatory agencies to develop elaborate benefit-cost analyses before issuing any significant new regulations (Adler and Posner 2001; Johnston 2002; Morgenstern 1997). These required analyses also dictate that regulators gather information before issuing a new regulation.

Although government agencies need accurate and extensive information to make regulatory decisions, sometimes the information they need is held only by the very businesses they seek to regulate. Admittedly, for many purposes government can learn as much as, if not more than, industry. For example, laboratory studies and epidemiological research conducted by government agencies, university scientists, or outside consulting firms may reveal as much about the health effects of certain pollutants as anything known to industry. But since businesses know more about the products they produce, as well as precisely how they produce them, firms are often better positioned than government regulators to know important details about the environmental risks created by their production processes (Coglianese and Lazer 2003). Businesses will also often be better positioned to understand how environmental risks can be mitigated. Private-sector managers typically know more about which pollution control measures will be effective in their facilities, as well as the extent to which certain measures would create unintended consequences or undesirable costs (Coglianese, Zeckhauser, and Parson 2004; Michael 1996; Wagner 2004).

Despite the superior information they often hold, businesses do not generally have any incentive to share all their relevant information with government, especially if doing so would make it easier for regulators to impose costly standards on industry (Breyer 1986; Noll and Owen 1983). To be sure, industry does have an incentive to share self-serving information with government, such as information showing that the likely costs of a new regulation would be higher than government anticipates or that the likely benefits would be lower (Quirk 1981). Such information can certainly be helpful to government, but in many cases that information alone will be selective, if not biased (Croley 2003; Leone 1986, 211). Government also needs information that industry has a strong interest in keeping confidential, such as information showing that the costs would be lower than expected or benefits higher.

Industry's incentives for disclosing adverse information are affected in important ways by the nature of information. One important feature about information is that once it is disclosed it cannot generally be retrieved. Any individual firm therefore has a good incentive to keep adverse information closely under wraps. Moreover, since most regulations apply to a number of different firms in the same industrial sector, these firms often have a collective interest in keeping adverse information away from the regulator. This will generally be the case whenever information disclosed by any individual firm allows the regulator to make a credible generalization about a variety of firms in the industry, and thereby to use that information to justify a costly regulation applicable to all such firms.

Since the disclosure of information by any single firm can be adverse to the interests of all similar firms in that same industry, it is in the entire industry's interests to have every firm keep from disclosing certain information to the government. The maintenance of "collective silence" throughout an industry is relatively easy if all the firms share the same interests, such as if they all produce their products in exactly the same way or market them to exactly the same markets (Coglianese, Zeckhauser, and Parson 2004).[3] For example, the tobacco industry for many years shared an interest in, and managed to maintain, collective silence about the health hazards and addictive properties of tobacco products (Derthick 2002). In such cases, government regulators face great difficulty in eliciting voluntary disclosure of broadly relevant information from any given firm.

At times, firms within an industry sector will not all share the same interests, which will make it harder for industry to maintain collective silence and easier for government to extract adverse information from industry. For example, some firms may use up-to-date equipment that pollutes less than older equipment used by other firms in the same sector. The former firms might not be as harmed by disclosure of information about production hazards as the latter firms.

When there are different interests in the disclosure of adverse information about the costs or benefits of regulation, firms may try to keep others from sharing that information with government. The ongoing, albeit competitive, relationships between firms in the same sector provide an opportunity for firms to exact retribution on those who "squeal" to the regulators. Those who disclose can be forced to leave the industry's trade association or find themselves without support of the rest of the industry on other important policy issues (Coglianese, Zeckhauser, and Parson 2004).[4] These kinds of pressures tend to offset the ready disclosure of information, even when firms' interests diverge slightly. In short, regulators simply cannot expect that businesses will readily volunteer what they know to help government justify more stringent and costly regulations.

How Do Regulators Gain Information from Business?

To obtain information needed for new regulations, regulators must take affirmative steps to penetrate an industry's veil of silence. Given the incentives faced by business, regulators have two general strategies available to them. They can either exploit differences in firms' interests or create new incentives for disclosure.[5]

Regulators' first main strategy is to exploit the differences that exist in firms' interests, seeking to find the weak points in any united front that any industry tries to present. While industry may try collectively to counteract any tendency that an individual firm could have to disclose, firms do differ in terms of how new regulations will affect them, depending on the firms' technologies and production processes, manufacturing costs and market conditions, levels of research and development into alternative technologies, and the degree to which environmental leadership brings them a competitive advantage (Leone 1986; Wilson 1990; Golden 1998; Hart 2002). Individual firms will be more inclined to cooperate with the regulator if they will be less adversely affected than their competitors (Melnick 1998).[6]

Regulators exploit firms' varied interests when they ask firms to disclose information on a voluntary basis. This can take place through a formal request, such as when the agency sends a letter asking a firm to allow regulators to visit one of its facilities or distributes a voluntary survey to all firms within a sector. It also frequently takes place informally, such as when a regulator picks up the telephone to talk with someone from business or has a conversation in the hallway at a professional conference or advisory committee meeting. Such voluntary information requests provide an opportunity for firms to self-select according to their propensity to disclose information to the regulator. Firms that provide adverse information in response to such voluntary requests for information will often be those that have interests different from those of other firms in the industry. For example, in the 1970s the S.C. Johnson Wax Company broke with the rest of industry and voluntarily acknowledged the feasibility of eliminating chlorofluorocarbon (CFC) propellants from aerosol products in order to protect the ozone layer. But S.C. Johnson clearly was not as threatened by a ban on CFCs as were other firms, since only a small fraction of its aerosol products used CFC propellants (Coglianese, Zeckhauser, and Parson 2004).

There are other differences regulators can exploit, namely, differences in interests between employees and the firms that employ them. For instance, the environmental or safety and health personnel within companies may at times have goals more aligned with the objectives of government regulators than with those of the firms for which they work. Through relationships with individual informants, regulators may gain information they can use to justify requiring industry to undertake additional investments.

Of course, even though employees' interests are not fully aligned with those of their employers, individual informants will not openly share adverse information with government, for doing so would put them at risk of losing their jobs. The same is likely to be the case for individual firms that may face the risk of other forms of retribution by other firms in the industry (Coglianese, Zeckhauser, and Parson 2004). To make the "exploit differences" strategy work the best, then, regulators need to pursue this strategy as privately as possible, ensuring confidentiality to their sources. At times regulators need to keep the information provided voluntarily by informants entirely to themselves, using it instead as a basis for finding the same information in ways that can then be used in the agency's analyses and rulemaking documents.

Regulators' second major strategy is to create incentives for businesses to disclose information. These incentives can take the form of punishment for failing to disclose information or rewards for disclosure. In terms of punishment, some regulatory agencies possess formal subpoena power, which gives them authority to back up mandatory requests for information with the threat of civil fines. Another, more tacit punishment available to regulators is the imposition of an excessively burdensome regulation in the absence of further information submitted by business. If regulators are able to signal credibly that they will impose a draconian rule in the absence of additional information, firms will have good reason to come forward with information that will enable the regulator to adopt a more reasonable rule. Once businesses see the regulators' default option as a new regulation that is exceedingly onerous, information that once had been considered adverse (when the default position was the status quo) is effectively transformed into self-serving information and will therefore be disclosed to stave off stringent regulation. Legislators sometimes provide a highly credible threat by enacting so-called hammer provisions that can impose costly statutory obligations in the absence of timely action by EPA to adopt more reasonable administrative standards.

In addition to resorting to threats of punishment, regulators can also induce firms to turn over needed information by the selective use of rewards. Admittedly, regulators cannot outright pay firms to reveal information. But sometimes they can craft new regulations in ways that subtly work to the comparative advantage of firms that cooperate. Firms that cooperate with regulators can also be rewarded over the longer term, whether through favorable treatment on other regulatory matters or by gaining increased access to and information about the inner workings of the government agency, something that can be of great help to business lobbyists (Coglianese, Zeckhauser, and Parson 2004).

Regulatory agencies like the EPA have also created recognition programs designed to reward cooperating firms. Through the EPA's National Environmental Performance Track, for example, the government has recognized and rewarded several hundred private-sector facilities that the agency has determined exhibit superior environmental management. From interacting with these so-called leadership businesses, EPA regulators learn more about best practices in private-sector environmental management.

Regulators can use both strategies—exploit differences and create incentives—in the same regulatory proceeding. They first may try to exploit any differences in firms' interests in disclosure, and then try to direct rewards or penalties toward those firms already inclined to disclose. Regulators do find it useful to pursue information from multiple sources, for this not only maximizes the chances that *some* firm will disclose adverse information, but it also gives the regulator the ability to assess the accuracy of information by comparing what different firms disclose. When approaching different firms for pieces of the informational puzzle, regulators will typically downplay or obscure the significance of any specific piece of information in its development of a new regulation, so that the firms are less likely to view the release of that specific information as adverse to their interests (Coglianese, Zeckhauser, and Parson 2004).

EPA's Air Toxics Regulations

Few issues have presented as large a challenge in terms of collecting information from industry as has the EPA's regulation of toxic air pollutants. Regulation of air toxics is a major public policy issue, with air pollution making up the vast majority of all the toxic chemical releases tracked by the EPA.[7] To regulate in this area, government needs a lot of information—not merely about air pollutants, but also about how businesses create those pollutants and what options exist to reduce their emissions.

Congress responded to the problem of air pollution by passing the Clean Air Act of 1970, the first major piece of modern federal environmental legislation regulating private business (Andrews 1999; Coglianese 2001b; Graham 1999; Vig and Kraft 2006). The Clean Air Act of 1970 created a framework for air pollution regulation that has imposed, and continues to impose, enormous costs on industry. The central feature of the Clean Air Act was the creation of National Ambient Air Quality Standards (NAAQS) that drive the regulation of so-called criteria air pollutants (Portney 2000). These NAAQS form the backbone of a regulatory system that consists of an extensive array of state emissions standards for business and federal requirements for motor vehicles and transportation fuels.

Over the past several decades, the EPA has declared six substances to be criteria air pollutants: carbon monoxide, lead, nitrogen dioxide, ozone, particulate matter, and sulfur dioxide. These substances are defined under the act as ones that "may reasonably be anticipated to endanger public health or welfare [and which are emitted from] numerous or diverse mobile or stationary sources."[8] Yet far more substances than just these six have a negative effect on public health.

In recognition of the risks posed by other air pollutants, section 112 of the 1970 Clean Air Act authorized the EPA to adopt uniform National Emissions Standards for Hazardous Air Pollutants (NESHAPs). Unlike NAAQS, which are standards governing the overall or ambient quality of the air, the NESHAPs are emissions standards governing what businesses may discharge from their smokestacks, vents, and industrial equipment. According to the act, hazardous air pollutants (also called air toxics) were pollutants to which no NAAQS applied but that could be "reasonably anticipated to result in an increase in mortality or an increase in serious irreversible, or incapacitating reversible, illness."[9] Substances are considered toxic or hazardous when they are suspected of causing cancer, birth defects, or immunological, reproductive, or neurological health problems.

In the 1970 Clean Air Act, Congress directed the EPA to set NESHAPs at levels that protected the public health and provided an "ample margin of safety," taking into account the economic costs of emissions control.[10] Operating under this standard, the EPA listed only seven air pollutants as hazardous during the two decades following passage of the act. For environmentalists and others concerned about public health, the EPA's progress was insufficient. Citizens were exposed to hundreds of potential toxic air pollutants from industrial operations. The EPA had even "estimated that emissions of toxic air pollutants may cause some 1,600 to 3,000 cancer cases a year" (Conference Committee 1990).

During the 1980s, public concern about toxic chemicals grew. During the first half of the decade, Congress enacted the Superfund law and passed major amendments to the Resource Conservation and Recovery Act, both laws addressing different aspects of the toxic waste problem (Coglianese 2001b; Vig and Kraft 2006). Furthermore, when Congress amended the Superfund law in 1986, it also imposed reporting requirements on companies that used certain toxic chemicals, requiring them to report publicly their release of these toxic substances into the environment (Hamilton 2005; Karkkainen 2001).

The Clean Air Act Amendments of 1990 were debated against this backdrop of concern. The problem of air toxics was foremost on the agenda of a coalition of national environmental groups, as well as of considerable concern to key members of Congress involved in the reauthorization of the act, such as Representative Henry Waxman (D-CA). Many were frustrated by the EPA's pace in listing substances as hazardous air pollutants and developing the NESHAPs (Bryner 1995). Although the EPA's relatively slow progress was due at least in part to the Reagan administration's general antipathy to environmental regulation, the design of the hazardous air pollutant provisions of the 1970 Clean Air Act may also have been a factor. By requiring the EPA first to make a determination that a substance was hazardous and then to establish a NESHAP for that substance, the act left the agency vulnerable to contestation over both sets of decisions. More significantly, even though the NESHAPs were supposed to be based on a determination of a "safe" level of exposure plus an ample margin of safety, it was not easy to determine a safe level for the hundreds of chemicals suspected of causing cancer and other health problems. Sound risk assessment called for animal studies of the toxicological effects of substances, as well as epidemiological studies of the effects of exposure on humans. Furthermore, setting a "safe" level was complicated by the suspicion that many chemicals had no level of exposure that did not cause some observable health effects, however trivial. Setting toxic air pollutant standards at zero, though, would have effectively forced the closure of much of the economy.

Congress responded in 1990 by making two major changes to the air toxics provisions in section 112 of the Clean Air Act. First, Congress added a list of 189 chemical substances that it deemed to be hazardous air pollutants. In doing so, it removed the EPA's responsibility for determining whether the listed substances were indeed truly hazardous.[11] Second, for each of the listed substances, Congress directed the EPA to establish the NESHAPs based on existing technology—specifically, the maximum achievable control technology (MACT)—rather than based on health risk. In other words, instead of setting a level that would be "safe" with an adequate margin of safety, the EPA now needed to set emissions standards at the lowest levels that could be attained with existing technology.

For all "source categories"—basically, all the industrial sectors generating air toxics—the EPA needed to establish its NESHAPs based on its determination of the MACT.[12] Congress gave the EPA discretion in defining source categories and subcategories, but each was to encompass similar types of industrial operations. For new firms within any category, the NESHAP needed to reflect the degree of emissions attainable by the best-controlled source in that same category.[13] For existing firms, the NESHAP was to be set, at a minimum, at the level of the average emissions from the best 12 percent of existing sources in the same category, or at the level of the average emissions from the best five sources for categories with less than thirty sources.[14] After the EPA issued the NESHAPs for a given source category and chemical, sources had up to three years to come into compliance, although the agency could grant one-year extensions to individual facilities.

The 1990 legislation also imposed a strict timetable on the EPA for issuing the NESHAPs. Twenty-five percent of the standards for the newly listed chemicals were to be issued by 1994, another 25 percent by 1997, and the remaining ones by 2000. To address the possibility that the EPA would fail to meet all these deadlines, Congress also included a "hammer provision" mandating that states eventually incorporate limitations equivalent to MACT into routine air permits of industrial facilities, even if the EPA failed to meet its deadlines.

In 1992, the EPA issued an initial list of over 150 "source categories" that it intended to regulate under section 112 (U.S. EPA 1992). Virtually no major industrial sector was spared. The targeted industries ranged from steel production to dry cleaning, organic chemical manufacturing to commercial fumigation operations, gasoline distribution to magnetic tape manufacturing, surface coating of automobiles to rubber tire manufacturing. Twelve years later, after missing some of the deadlines in the act and settling lawsuits filed by environmental groups to enforce the deadlines, the EPA finally issued its last toxic air emissions standards. In total, the agency established 96 toxic air emissions standards governing 160 different source categories (U.S. EPA 2004). According to the EPA, these standards have led to the reduction of about 1.5 million tons of toxic air pollution (U.S. EPA 2004).

EPA's Information Gathering in Air Toxics Rulemakings

The Clean Air Act's shift from a risk-based approach in 1970 to a technology-based approach in 1990 replaced one set of demands on the EPA's expertise with another. Since Congress listed the chemicals it deemed hazardous and mandated that standards be set based on existing control technologies, the EPA no longer needed to answer the vexing question of "how safe is safe?" for hundreds of different chemicals. However, it now had to learn about the industrial processes in over 150 different industries. EPA regulators needed vast amounts of information about manufacturing equipment and industrial operations in each sector—and in each of their numerous subcategories. The task was daunting. Virtually overnight, EPA regulators needed to become experts in widely divergent lines of business, each of which had varied production methods, equipment, and pollution control options.

How did the EPA overcome its information deficiencies and decide what emissions limits to impose on thousands of different businesses? It sought out this information from business itself. Firms themselves possessed a clear informational advantage over the EPA,[15] so the EPA went right to the source. By considering how the EPA gathered information in its NESHAP rulemakings, we can understand better how information factors into the regulatory game between business and government.

General Rulemaking Procedures   Whenever the EPA issues a binding standard like a NESHAP, it imposes a legal obligation on businesses that can be enforced through administrative or judicial actions and the threat of civil penalties of up to $25,000 per day of violation. In setting air toxics emissions standards, therefore, the EPA needs to follow the rulemaking procedures outlined in the Administrative Procedure Act (APA).[16] The APA outlines a procedure for "notice-and-comment rulemaking," dictating three main steps: (1) publish a notice of proposed rulemaking in the *Federal Register*; (2) allow regulated industry and other members of the public to comment on the proposed rule; and (3) after considering the comments, publish the final rule in the *Federal Register* with a statement explaining the agency's decision and responding to the submitted comments.[17]

The APA's notice-and-comment requirements provide an obvious vehicle for government regulators to obtain information from industry, namely, through comments. These comments, along with all other supporting information, are stored in a publicly accessible docket for each rulemaking, and perhaps for that reason they have been the most studied part of the rulemaking process (Cuéllar 2005; Golden 1998; Kamieniecki 2006; Kerwin 2003; West 2004). In terms of securing needed information from industry, however, the comment period is only a small part of the overall rulemaking process (Kerwin 2003; West 2004). Clearly, before anyone has anything on which to file comments, regulators need information in order to develop a proposed rule.

Methods of Gathering Information In the EPA's air toxics program, the process of gathering information began long before the agency issued any notice of proposed rulemaking. For many sectors, EPA staff knew virtually nothing about the industry they needed to regulate. Yet over the past decade and a half, EPA officials have gathered extensive information about hundreds of industries and thousands of facilities. They have done so using seven main methods.

1. *Informal interactions.* In developing the NESHAPs, one of the first challenges the EPA faced was to identify the firms operating within a targeted industry. The United State has no national, governmental registry of businesses. As a consequence, the EPA staff called people who might know something. They talked with state regulators, industry analysts in the private or academic sectors, and representatives of any applicable trade associations.[18]

After identifying the population of firms, the EPA often faced another informational challenge: a chicken-and-egg problem. The EPA needed to know something about an industry in order to ask intelligent questions and learn more about the operations of that industry. To be sure, EPA staff members did have a general idea of the information they needed about an industry: the types of pollutants firms emitted, the processes generating these pollutants, test data on different technologies and control methods, and so forth. But for those sectors about which the EPA knew little, it needed more specific information just to ask intelligent questions. To find out what processes to ask about and what vocabulary engineers in the industry used, EPA staff would talk with people informally. At times, the agency staff members would consult extensively with trade-association representatives to develop the wording of questions that the EPA later wanted to ask facility engineers and plant managers.

In addition, before developing proposed standards, the EPA would frequently convene informal meetings with representatives from industry. For example, in developing toxic emissions standards for the baker's or nutritional yeast manufacturing sector, the EPA held a series of conference calls and meetings with representatives from the yeast manufacturing sector. Yeast is produced in the United States by ten facilities owned by five different companies. Production involves a fermentation process that results in emissions of volatile organic compounds (VOCs) and acetaldehyde, the latter being listed as a hazardous air pollutant. EPA faced a legion of design choices in establishing its NESHAP for this sector. Should facilities be required to monitor emissions of acetaldehyde directly, or could they use emissions of VOCs, which they already monitored, as a proxy? How often would facilities be required to measure emissions? Should emissions limits be based on concentrations in the airflow leaving the facility or be based on the facility's production volume? To which stages of fermentation would the standards apply? These and a host of other questions required the EPA to obtain a detailed understanding of yeast manufacturing at various plants across the country. Over the course of a series of meetings, conference calls, and other informal contacts, the leading yeast manufacturers, Fleischmann's Yeast and Red Star Yeast, provided the EPA with a wealth of technical data on their industrial operations to help the agency develop its standard. An advantage of such informal opportunities is that they operate through dialogue, allowing the EPA to ask follow-up questions, seek clarification, and ask for additional data.

2. *Site visits.* In the same NESHAP, Fleischmann's Yeast also volunteered to provide the EPA with a site visit of its operations. Site visits have been another way for the EPA to gather information about the

industries it regulates. Through such visits, EPA officials not only see exactly how a plant is operated, but they can talk with plant managers informally and conduct monitoring or testing of equipment on site. For example, in addition to agreeing to an EPA site visit, Fleischmann's Yeast also agreed to have an EPA contractor conduct a weeklong series of air sampling tests at its plant.

3. *Mandatory information requests.* In making voluntary requests for site visits and other information, the EPA's hand has been greatly strengthened by Section 114 of the Clean Air Act.[19] Section 114 grants the agency the authority to issue mandatory requests for information, and the EPA used this authority extensively in developing its NESHAPs. For instance, in the iron and steel foundries rulemaking, it needed information on about 740 foundries located across the United States.[20] To gather this information, it developed a questionnaire asking about "production facilities, production capacity, emission control devices in place and their basic design and operating features, quantity of air emissions, and pollution prevention programs at each plant" (U.S. EPA 1997). The questionnaire spanned nearly thirty-five pages and the EPA estimated it would take respondents about twenty-four hours to complete (U.S. EPA 1997). When the agency received the responses, it entered them into a database and used that information to analyze the environmental and economic impacts of different regulatory options (U.S. EPA 1997). When firms requested that the agency keep secret some of the data they submitted, the agency classified and treated the information as "confidential business information," thereby precluding others from knowing exactly what a firm disclosed.

4. *MACT Partnerships.* After several years of implementing the 1990 Clean Air Act, the EPA grew increasingly concerned about its progress toward meeting the act's deadlines. The agency was falling behind schedule. In 1995, it announced a new strategy called MACT Partnerships that it applied to twenty-five NESHAP proceedings (U.S. EPA 1995). Before conducting extensive industry surveys, the EPA engaged in informal consultations with state regulators and industry representatives to develop a "presumptive MACT" based on already-available evidence. This approach was clearly not feasible for all sectors, but for some of the industries that were already highly regulated the EPA tried to use the presumptive MACT as an intermediate step toward developing a final

NESHAP. The hope was that by collaboratively amassing all available data, the agency could be more targeted and thorough in gathering additional information. The agency also proposed a process called "share-a-MACT," which took place after a presumptive MACT was developed. Under the "share-a-MACT" model, industry worked side by side with regulators, sharing in the EPA's "responsibility for developing the underlying data and analysis from which EPA would determine the MACT emission limitation" (U.S. EPA 1995).

The MACT Partnership program was designed specifically to address EPA's need for information. In 1997, a joint presidential and congressional commission on risk regulation heralded the MACT Partnership program, noting that it "is intended to increase the amount of knowledge, skills, and resources devoted to the development of a MACT standard" (Presidential/Congressional Commission on Risk Assessment and Risk Management 1997). The agency viewed partnerships as an opportunity where, among other things, "industry/association experts could be of particular assistance in addressing specific issues" (U.S. EPA, n.d.). Industry response to the program was, perhaps not surprisingly, generally quite positive (Morss 1996; Siegler 1997).

Notwithstanding the enthusiasm of its supporters, the MACT Partnership program does not appear to have had a long or extensive impact on the EPA's air toxics program. For one thing, the MACT Partnership model never was intended for industries where the EPA lacked virtually any available information on which to base a presumptive MACT. Even where some information was available, the accuracy of that data was an issue. Sometimes the information that was most available information was out of date or of questionable reliability (Traylor 1998). After a few years, the EPA essentially abandoned the MACT Partnership program, although it did continue to work informally with industry trade associations and cooperative firms.

5. *Formal advisory committees.* Most regulatory agencies establish formal advisory committees to enable regulators to learn from outside experts (Jasanoff 1990). Unlike the informal meetings that take place prior to the development of proposed regulations, meetings of advisory committees are announced in advance, are open to the public, and need to include a balanced set of interests in the committee membership (Croley and Funk 1997). In 2005, the EPA had about two dozen advi-

sory committees. While none of these committees focused squarely on air toxics, a few did have subcommittees or workgroups charged with assessing scientific issues related to air toxics.[21]

On occasion, the EPA has also used a special type of advisory committee called a negotiated rulemaking committee in developing a NESHAP. In a negotiated rulemaking, the agency facilitates a negotiation process among a diverse set of interests—businesses, environmental groups, and other concerned parties (Fiorino and Kirtz 1985). If the affected interests convened by the EPA agree on the terms of the proposed rule, the EPA then uses the agreement as a basis for its final rule. This approach has a goal similar to MACT Partnerships, namely to speed up the rulemaking process, but the negotiated rulemaking process is much more formal and explicitly seeks to reach consensus among all the affected interests on a proposed NESHAP.

For three years, from 1993 to 1995, the EPA issued one air toxics standard per year that had been developed using negotiated rulemaking. These were standards for coke oven batteries, leakage from chemical equipment (part of the Hazardous Organics NESHAP), and wood furniture coatings (Coglianese 1997). Agency officials gained helpful information by participating in these negotiated-rulemaking sessions, as they did through informal consultations and meetings. Yet in the end, negotiated rulemaking did not appear to speed up the regulatory process or stave off subsequent litigation (Coglianese 1997, 2001a). In two out of the three negotiated NESHAPs, industry groups still filed litigation challenging the EPA's decisions. The EPA has not used negotiated rulemaking to develop a NESHAP since 1995.

6. *Public comments.* The EPA uses the above methods of information gathering before publishing a notice of proposed rulemaking. After the EPA publishes a proposed rule, industry has an opportunity to submit written comments. The proposed rule provides a credible signal of how the agency intends to regulate, thus giving firms an additional incentive to come forward with information that they once may have preferred not to disclose.

Although scholars have questioned whether comments on proposed rules have much impact on agency decisions (Golden 1998; West 2004), in the air toxics area industry comments did appear to provide additional information that affected the EPA's final standards. This was no doubt in part due to the vast complexity of NESHAP decisionmaking. That complexity, combined with the deadlines imposed by Congress or the courts, often meant that the EPA proposed NESHAPs even when the agency still had a lot of uncertainty about what they would achieve.[22]

7. *Postrulemaking interaction.* Once the EPA issues a final rule, industry still can come forward with additional information. Firms and trade associations often requested that the agency reconsider or amend certain aspects of its NESHAPs. Furthermore, after the EPA published a final NESHAP in the *Federal Register*, industry sometimes immediately asked a court to review the EPA's decision, even before the agency had taken any steps to enforce the standard.[23] As part of negotiations to settle such administrative and judicial petitions, industry would sometimes come forward with additional information showing why the EPA should change its rule. As one industry representative explained, "This litigation [is] just a continuation and a narrowing of the regulatory process. . . . You've narrowed the universe . . . to those who really care, and you can get down to business" (Coglianese 1996). Even though courts have handed down decisions reviewing less than 10 percent of the NESHAPs that the EPA has issued, industry has filed suit and negotiated out-of-court settlements with the EPA in still more NESHAPs.[24] As part of these settlement agreements, the agency has often agreed to make minor amendments that address further industry information and arguments offered after the publication of the final rule.

Information and Interests: Strategic Aspects of the EPA's Air Toxics Rulemakings

As the editors of this book note in chapter 1, lobbying by business has long been viewed in terms of placing pressure on policymakers. More often than not, though, businesses' involvement in regulatory policymaking is really about information, not political pressure. Government regulators need information from industry in order to make effective policy decisions, and so government itself actively seeks out businesses and their data through the very kinds of methods that the EPA has used in its air toxics program. The EPA's approach to information gathering in its air toxics program followed the two main types of strategies used by regulators more generally, namely, exploiting differences in interests and providing incentives for disclosure.

By instructing the EPA to set NESHAPs based on MACT, the 1990 Clean Air Act Amendments made it easier for the agency to exploit differences in interest across firms and break down a unified response within sectors. The MACT principle directs the EPA to base its toxic emissions standards on what the best firms are able to achieve. This encourages cleaner firms to step forward to reveal information to the EPA, so that it will adopt their higher level of performance as the MACT standard and thereby push their competitors to comply equally with high standards. Not surprisingly, industrial sectors at times had difficulty maintaining a united front in NESHAPs proceedings, because some firms cooperated with the EPA and succeeded in obtaining standards that advantaged them relative to their competitors.

The 1990 Clean Air Act's shift to technology-based NESHAPs also gave disclosure incentives to the businesses that sell pollution control technology. Companies selling state-of-the-art control technology stood to gain if the EPA adopted stringent standards that would expand their customer base. As a result, these companies more readily provided data to the EPA. In some NESHAPs, the EPA would rely on data from pollution control vendors to compute the expected costs of its standards.

In addition to exploiting differences across firms, the EPA used rewards and threats to elicit information from companies. The complexity of NESHAP rules gave industry opportunities to gain from cooperation with the agency. It was seldom straightforward how NESHAP limits would be expressed in the final rule and how compliance with them would need to be measured by industry and state regulators. The EPA routinely faced design choices such as whether facilities could measure proxies for the hazardous air pollutants, how frequently facilities needed to take measurements, what monitoring equipment to use, and what protocols to follow, among other issues. Even if cooperating firms could not expect to persuade the EPA to adopt less stringent emissions limits, they did foster greater trust by cooperating, which undoubtedly helped in persuading the agency in certain cases to adopt more practical and less burdensome methods of monitoring.

The EPA also used punishment as a threat to elicit information from industry. Section 114 of the Clean Air Act gives the agency mandatory power to compel the production of data, a power that the agency frequently noted when communicating with firms. In addition, the EPA's use of presumptive MACTs and notices of proposed rulemakings sent credible signals of what the agency was prepared to do if firms did not disclose information, which in effect gave firms a new reason to share information that they otherwise might have preferred not to share. Finally, the Clean Air Act's hammer provision always lurked in the background, as a reminder that industry could not expect to benefit greatly from delay.

Conclusion

Business groups are often said to wield influence over government decisionmakers because they possess greater financial resources and can hire lobbyists, public relations and media experts, and teams of lawyers. While these greater resources are often described in terms of the greater "pressure" that business can exert on the policy process, a key advantage of business lobbying, at least in regulatory policymaking, comes from the information business possesses. In the regulatory process at agencies like the EPA, so-called business pressure really takes place through business information.

From the standpoint of making effective policy, business information is essential. The EPA simply could not have regulated 160 different industries over the span of a dozen years without finding ways to involve business in designing new regulations. For this reason, business holds an inherent advantage over government in the regulatory process. But knowledge does not always mean power. Despite industry's superior knowledge of its products and operations, it certainly does not always get its way in environmental policymaking (Vogel 1989). The EPA's air toxics program has, after all, imposed hundreds of millions of dollars of costs on industry, notwithstanding the daunting technical and analytic challenges EPA confronted. EPA officials do recognize that much information offered by business will be self-serving, and so they know that their challenge is to find ways to elicit information industry otherwise might not be inclined to disclose. In the EPA's air toxics program, the agency's regulators used a variety of methods to secure the information they needed to justify placing strict new standards on almost every industrial operation in the country.

A thorough understanding of how business interests try to influence environmental policymaking requires consideration of the important role of business information. The choices businesses make about what information to disclose—and what not to disclose—are central to business' political strategy. Of course, the government does not remain passive, but affirmatively seeks to ferret out needed industry information by exploiting asymmetries of interest and creating incentives for firms to disclose. As such, the politics of environmental policymaking is, at its core, a politics of information. Anyone interested in the influence of business on the policy process must therefore examine the information needed to make specific policy decisions and consider how the struggle over that information ultimately shapes the decisions that government makes.

Notes

The author expresses appreciation for helpful comments from Sheldon Kamieniecki, Dinah Koehler, Michael Kraft, and Gary Marchant.

1. U.S. Code, title 5, section 706.

2. *Citizens to Preserve Overton Park v. Volpe*, 401 U.S. 402 (1971); *Motor Vehicle Manufacturers Association v. State Farm Mutual Insurance Co.*, 463 U.S. 29 (1983).

3. By "collective silence," I do not mean that businesses would say nothing to the regulator. On the contrary, they often share extensive information—though much if not all of it will be *self-serving* information. By "silence," I simply mean the absence of disclosure of *adverse* information—that is, information that would help the regulator impose costly regulations on industry.

4. Of course, when the "squealers" are individual employees within a company, they face the risk of the type of retribution that any whistleblower might confront, including being fired.

5. In this section of the chapter, I highlight these two main strategies and offer a few examples of specific tactics that are consistent with these general strategies. For a more comprehensive treatment of the information-extraction tactics available to regulators, see Coglianese, Zeckhauser, and Parson 2004, 305–324.

6. Of course, the differences between the firms cannot be so great that the information provided by an informant firm is not capable of being used as the basis for a generally applicable rule. For example, information provided by a firm that uses a unique manufacturing process would probably not help in most cases in deciding how to regulate the other firms in the sector using other types of processes.

7. Data reported under the EPA's Toxics Release Inventory distinguish between on-site releases to air, land, water, and underground injection. In 1989, for example, 2.6 billion pounds of toxic chemicals were released to air, 1.2 billion to underground injection (from just a relatively small fraction of all facilities), and 0.7 billion to all other media (U.S. EPA 2005).

8. U.S. Code, title 42, section 7408(a).

9. U.S. Code, title 42, section 112.

10. *Natural Resources Defense Council v. EPA*, 824 F.2d 1146 (D.C. Cir. 1987).

11. Upon a sufficient showing, the EPA was authorized to de-list a chemical, which it has done for one chemical.

12. Under the act, a business is considered a "major source" if it emits more than 10 tons in a year of a single hazardous air pollutant, or 25 tons in a year of a combination of such pollutants. Smaller sources are sometimes regulated as "area sources" if the combined effect of their emissions poses a special public health concern, such as in urban areas.

13. U.S. Code, title 42, section 112(d)(3).

14. The level of the top 12 percent represented the "MACT floor," but the EPA could go further and impose more stringent limits.

15. As one EPA document put it, "Industry personnel are . . . invaluable sources of technical expertise and data needed to develop MACT standards" (U.S. EPA 1995).

16. U.S. Code, title 5, section 553.

17. Over the years, other procedural requirements have been added, notably a requirement imposed by presidential order since the early 1980s that agencies complete an economic analysis of their proposed and final rules.

18. In more recent years, agency officials have used the Internet to help identify firms operating within a given sector, but they still have consulted with knowledgeable individuals.

19. U.S. Code, title 42, section 114.

20. Whenever the EPA sends an identically worded information-collection request (ICR) to more than nine respondents, the Paperwork Reduction Act requires that the agency receive approval for the ICR from the Office of Management and Budget.

21. For example, at various times the agency has had a workgroup of the Clean Air Act Advisory Committee devoted to urban air toxics, a subcommittee of the same committee on "Permits, New Source Reviews, and Toxics," and a subcommittee of the Science Advisory Committee on air toxics monitoring.

22. This was certainly true to a fair extent for rules issued by both the Clinton and Bush II EPAs. An interesting line of inquiry for future research would focus on the differences, if any, in how the EPA plays the information game with business under different presidential administrations. The existence of statutory deadlines, and court orders enforcing those deadlines, probably mutes some of the differences that might otherwise exist across administrations.

23. Under section 307 of the Clean Air Act, any party seeking to challenge a NESHAP in court must file its petition for review within ninety days.

24. As of September 2005, only eight judicial decisions have been handed down in cases involving the review of one of the ninety-six final NESHAPs promulgated under the 1990 Clean Air Act.

References

Adler, Matthew D., and Eric A. Posner. 2001. *Cost-Benefit Analysis: Legal, Economic, and Philosophical Perspectives.* Chicago: University of Chicago Press.

Andrews, Richard N. L. 1999. *Managing the Environment, Managing Ourselves: A History of American Environmental Policy.* New Haven, CT: Yale University Press.

Bauer, Raymond, Ithiel de Sola Pool, and Louis Anthony Dexter. 1963. *American Business and Public Policy: The Politics of Foreign Trade.* New York: Atherton Press.

Breyer, Stephen. 1982. *Regulation and Its Reform.* Cambridge, MA: Harvard University Press.

Breyer, Stephen. 1986. "Judicial Review of Questions of Law and Policy." *Administrative Law Review* 38:363.

Bryner, Gary C. 1995. *Blue Skies, Green Politics: The Clean Air Act of 1990 and Its Implementation.* Washington, DC: CQ Press.

Coglianese, Cary. 1996. "Litigating within Relationships: Disputes and Disturbance in the Regulatory Process." *Law & Society Review* 30 (4): 735.

Coglianese, Cary. 1997. "Assessing Consensus: The Promise and Performance of Negotiated Rulemaking." *Duke Law Journal* 46 (6): 1255.

Coglianese, Cary. 2001a. "Assessing the Advocacy of Negotiated Rulemaking." *New York University Environmental Law Journal* 9:386.

Coglianese, Cary. 2001b. "Social Movements, Law, and Society: The Institutionalization of the Environmental Movement." *University of Pennsylvania Law Review* 150 (1): 85.

Coglianese, Cary, and David Lazer. 2003. "Management-Based Regulation: Prescribing Private Management to Achieve Public Goals." *Law & Society Review* 37:691.

Coglianese, Cary, Richard Zeckhauser, and Edward Parson. 2004. "Seeking Truth for Power: Informational Strategy and Regulatory Policymaking." *Minnesota Law Review* 89 (2): 277.

Conference Committee. 1990. "Clean Air Act Amendments of 1990, S I–III." *House Report* 101-490 Part 1A. Washington, DC: U.S. Congress.

Croley, Steven. 2003. "White House Review of Agency Rulemaking: An Empirical Investigation." *University of Chicago Law Review* 70:821.

Croley, Steven, and William F. Funk. 1997. "The Federal Advisory Committee Act and Good Government." *Yale Journal on Regulation* 14:451.

Cuéllar, Mariano-Florentino. 2005. "Rethinking Regulatory Democracy." *Administrative Law Review* 57 (2): 413.

Derthick, Martha A. 2002. *Up in Smoke: From Legislation to Litigation in Tobacco Politics.* Washington, DC: CQ Press.

Esty, Daniel C. 2004. "Environmental Protection in the Information Age." *New York University Law Review* 79:115.

Fiorino, Daniel J., and Chris Kirtz. 1985. "Breaking Down Walls: Negotiated Rulemaking at EPA." *Temple University Environmental Law & Technology Journal* 4:29.

Golden, Marissa. 1998. "Interest Groups in the Rule-Making Process: Who Participates? Whose Voices Get Heard?" *Journal of Public Administration Research and Theory* 8:245.

Graham, Mary. 1999. *The Morning After Earth Day: Practical Environmental Politics.* Washington, DC: Brookings Institution Press.

Hamilton, James T. 2005. *Regulation through Revelation: The Origin, Politics, and Impacts of the Toxics Release Inventory Program.* New York: Cambridge University Press.

Hart, David M. 2002. "Business Is Not an Interest Group (And, By the Way, There's No Such Thing as 'Business.')" *John F. Kennedy School of Government Faculty Research Paper,* No. RWP02-032. Cambridge, MA: John F. Kennedy School of Government, Harvard University.

Hawkins, Keith, and John M. Thomas. 1989. "Making Policy in Regulatory Bureaucracies." In Keith Hawkins and John M. Thomas, eds., *Making Regulatory Policy.* Pittsburgh: University of Pittsburgh Press.

Jasanoff, Sheila. 1990. *The Fifth Branch.* Cambridge, MA: Harvard University Press.

Johnston, Jason Scott. 2002. "A Game Theoretic Analysis of Alternative Institutions for Regulatory Cost-Benefit Analysis." *University of Pennsylvania Law Review* 150:1343.

Kamieniecki, Sheldon. 2006. *Corporate America and Environmental Policy: Does Business Always Get Its Way?* Palo Alto, CA: Stanford University Press.

Karkkainen, Bradley C. 2001. "Information as Environmental Regulation: TRI and Performance Benchmarking, Precursor to a New Paradigm?" *Georgetown Law Journal* 89:257.

Kerwin, Cornelius M. 2003. *Rulemaking: How Government Agencies Write Law and Make Policy.* 3rd ed. Washington, DC: CQ Press.

Krehbiel, Keith. 1991. *Information and Legislative Organization.* Ann Arbor: University of Michigan Press.

Leone, Robert A. 1986. *Who Profits: Winners, Losers, and Government Regulation.* New York: Basic Books.

Melnick, R. Shep. 1998. "Strange Bedfellows Make Normal Politics: An Essay." *Duke Environmental Law & Policy Forum* 9:75.

Michael, Douglas C. 1996. "Cooperative Implementation of Federal Regulations." *Yale Journal on Regulation* 13:535.

Morgenstern, Richard D. 1997. *Economic Analyses at EPA: Assessing Regulatory Impact.* Washington, DC: Resources for the Future Press.

Morss, Elizabeth M. 1996. "Clean Air Act Implementation: An Industry Perspective." *Pace Environmental Law Review* 14:63.

Noll, Roger G., and Bruce M. Owen. 1983. *The Political Economy of Deregulation.* Washington, DC: American Enterprise Institute.

Office of Management and Budget (OMB). 2003. *Circular A-4: Regulatory Analysis.* Washington, DC: Office of Management and Budget.

Portney, Paul R. 2000. "Air Pollution Policy." In Paul R. Portney and Robert N. Stavins, eds., *Public Policies for Environmental Protection*, 2nd ed. Washington, DC: Resources for the Future Press.

Presidential/Congressional Commission on Risk Assessment and Risk Management. 1997. *Risk Assessment and Risk Management in Regulatory Decision-Making.* Vol. 2. Washington, DC: The Commission.

Quirk, Paul J. 1981. *Industry Influence in Federal Regulatory Agencies.* Princeton, NJ: Princeton University Press.

Siegler, Ellen. 1997. "Regulatory Negotiations and Other Rulemaking Processes: Strengths and Weaknesses from an Industry Viewpoint." *Duke Law Journal* 46:1429.

Traylor, Patrick D. 1998. "Presumptive MACT as a Regulatory Tool to Streamline the Development of National Emissions Standards for Hazardous Air Pollutants." *Environmental Lawyer* 4 (February): 393.

U.S. Environmental Protection Agency. 1992. "Initial List of Categories of Sources under Section 112(c)(1) of the Clean Air Act Amendments of 1990." *Federal Register* 57 (July 16): 31576.

U.S. Environmental Protection Agency. 1995. "National Emission Standards for Hazardous Air Pollutants Streamlined Development: Announcement and Request for Comments." *Federal Register* 60 (March 29): 16088.

U.S. Environmental Protection Agency. 1997. "Part A of the Supporting Statement for Information Collection Request for Iron and Steel Foundries." www.epa.gov/ttn/oarpg/t3/reports/foun_sps.pdf.

U.S. Environmental Protection Agency. 2004. *Fiscal Year 2004 Annual Report.* Washington, DC: U.S. Environmental Protection Agency.

U.S. Environmental Protection Agency. 2005. *Toxic Release Inventory 2003 Data Update* (June 8). http://www.epa.gov/triexplorer/.

U.S. Environmental Protection Agency. n.d. "EPA Starts Developing Regulations for Combustion Engines Using Consultative Process." http://www.epa.gov/ttn/oarpg/t3/reports/mactmess.txt.

Vig, Norman J., and Michael E. Kraft, eds. 2006. *Environmental Policy: New Directions for the Twenty-First Century.* 6th ed. Washington, DC: CQ Press.

Vogel, David J. 1989. *Fluctuating Fortunes: The Political Power of Business in America.* New York: Basic Books.

Wagner, Wendy E. 2004. "Commons Ignorance: The Failure of Environmental Law to Produce Needed Information on Health and the Environment." *Duke Law Journal* 53 (April): 1619.

West, William F. 2004. "Formal Procedures, Informal Processes, Accountability, and Responsiveness in Bureaucratic Policy Making: An Institutional Policy Analysis." *Public Administration Review* 64:66.

Wilson, Graham. 1990. "Corporate Political Strategies." *British Journal of Political Science* 20:281.

V

Policy Intervention through the Courts

8

Business and Environmental Policy in the Federal Courts

Paul S. Weiland

Businesses, like other interest groups, attempt to influence public policy to advance their interests. Use of the federal courts to influence environmental law and policy is one facet of this broader phenomenon. Although scholars have focused greater attention on interest-group advocacy in the executive and legislative branches of government (e.g., Bickers and Stein 1995; Thurber 1991; Schlozman and Tierney 1986; Lowi 1979; Heclo 1978), case law provides countless examples of advocacy in the courts by the business community. In this chapter, I examine the use of the federal courts by business to influence environmental law and policy.[1]

The chapter addresses four major questions. First, what are the pros and cons of shaping environmental law and policy through the courts vis-à-vis the executive or legislative branches of government? Stated another way, what structural factors must business assess when determining whether to engage in or remain in federal environmental litigation? Second, what roles does business play in federal environmental litigation? Third, what are the types of judicial actions that businesses are involved in as they attempt to shape environmental law and policy? Federal environmental litigation can be a means to resolve discrete, parochial controversies among two parties or complex, recurring conflicts among many parties. Fourth, why do businesses engage in environmental litigation in the federal courts? That is, what goals do businesses hope to realize by engaging in litigation? Throughout the chapter reference will be made to existing case law to supplement the discussion of concepts.

Background

To ensure that there is a common understanding of the parameters of this chapter, below I define the key terms: the federal courts, business, and environmental law and policy. General analyses of the courts and environmental policy may be found elsewhere (O'Leary 2006).

Article III of the Constitution established the U.S. Supreme Court and authorized Congress to establish lower federal courts. Congress, in turn, has established the Circuit Courts of Appeals and the District Courts. At present, there are thirteen Circuit Courts (twelve regional Circuit Courts and the Federal Circuit, which has nationwide jurisdiction over specialized cases) and ninety-four District Courts (Administrative Office of the U.S. Courts 1999). These federal courts are courts of limited jurisdiction—that is, the types of cases they may hear are prescribed by the Constitution and federal statutes. There are both constitutional and statutory limits on the jurisdiction of federal courts. The primary constitutional limits are the standing, ripeness, mootness, and political-question doctrines. The primary statutory limits are federal question and diversity jurisdiction. These limits are discussed in greater detail below.

The business community has wide-ranging, often conflicting interests. For this reason, as discussed in chapter 1, it would be a mistake to treat business as a monolith (Prakash 2000). Businesses vary, most fundamentally, in terms of their purposes. But they also vary in other important ways, such as their structure and ownership, size, leadership, and organizational culture. These differences affect the frequency with which businesses litigate environmental controversies or are subject to environmental litigation in federal courts. For example, air emissions may be a necessary aspect of operations for certain businesses, such as oil refineries, and thus tied to the purpose of those businesses. This, in turn, may affect the likelihood that such businesses will be subject to enforcement actions. By comparison, the leadership of some businesses may make a decision to "green" their organizations (Press and Mazmanian 2006). To the extent that such decisions permeate organizational culture and affect operations, they may be expected to affect the likelihood that the business will engage (either voluntarily or involuntarily) in federal environmental litigation.

For the purposes of this chapter, environmental law and policy encompass federal law and policy. Federal law includes the Constitution, statutes passed by Congress and signed by the president, and regulations promulgated pursuant to the Administrative Procedure Act (5 U.S.C. 551 et seq.) by federal agencies. Federal policy includes courses of action or inaction chosen from among alternatives and adopted either formally or informally by the executive branch (Caldwell 1990; Kraft and Vig 2006). Environment is defined broadly to encompass human interrelationships with the natural world, so that environmental law and policy extend to pollution control activities, natural resource management, and species and open-space (including ecosystem) protection efforts. Defined in this manner, environmental law and policy are wide-ranging, encompassing both formal (for example, laws enacted by Congress and signed by the president pursuant to a process specified in the Constitution) and informal (for example, informal agency practices such as nonbinding protocols developed by the Fish and Wildlife Service for use by biologists when surveying for the presence of species listed under the Endangered Species Act) government actions. The expansive nature of environmental law and policy complicates efforts to categorize and describe the role of the business community.

The Pros and Cons of Shaping Environmental Law and Policy through the Federal Courts

From a business perspective, shaping environmental law and policy through the federal courts is sometimes necessary and often perilous. As a general matter, use of the courts to influence environmental policy is problematic (O'Leary 1993). Environmental disputes often tend to involve multiple parties with multiple interests. The adversarial system is designed to address controversies between two parties—a plaintiff and a defendant—and, even given modern rules of procedure that allow for multiparty proceedings, provides a suboptimal forum to resolve often complex, multiparty environmental disputes. Court proceedings tend to reduce the flow of information among litigants and consume resources (Bardach and Kagan 1982). Additionally, the federal courts can only address claims presented by the litigants; claims not pleaded generally cannot be addressed even if they are central to a dispute. As a result, involvement of the courts in the policy process has been variously described as sporadic, fragmented, and episodic (Rabkin 1989; Shapiro 1988). Furthermore, whereas decisionmakers generally can be identified at the outset of the policy process in the executive and legislative branches (subject, of course, to electoral cycles), business (and other interests) engaged in litigation in federal court cannot identify the decisionmaker in advance because a judge or panel of judges is not assigned to a case until after it is filed.

The structure of the federal courts also imposes limitations on the ability of parties to use those courts to influence policy in the form of constitutional and statutory limits on the jurisdiction of the federal courts. The constitutional limits are all derived from Article III, Section 2 of the Constitution, which states that the judicial power extends to cases and controversies; they include the standing, ripeness, mootness, and political question doctrines. Of these, standing is the most frequently litigated. The burden to establish standing is upon a plaintiff. That party must meet a three-part test articulated by the Supreme Court: (1) did the plaintiff suffer an injury in fact; (2) is there a causal connection between the injury and the conduct complained of; and (3) is it likely that the injury will be redressed by a favorable decision (*Lujan v. Defenders of Wildlife* (1992); *Friends of the Earth, Inc. v. Laidlaw Environmental Services (TOC), Inc.* (2000)). Ripeness and mootness are doctrines designed to ensure that there is an ongoing controversy among the parties (Tribe 2000). Finally, the political-question doctrine provides that the courts will not adjudicate certain alleged constitutional violations, such as challenges to the president's conduct of foreign policy (*Goldwater v. Carter* (1979)).

Whereas the Supreme Court is established by the Constitution, the lower federal courts are created by statute, and Congress and the president have the ability to dictate the subject-matter jurisdiction of those courts. The primary statutory bases for jurisdiction of federal courts are federal-question and diversity jurisdiction. (There are a variety of less noteworthy statutory bases for jurisdiction, such as jurisdiction over admiralty cases and actions against foreign states.) Federal-question jurisdiction allows a plaintiff to bring a case in federal court to enforce a federal right, that is, a right created by the Constitution, federal statute, or a treaty (28 U.S.C. 1331). Diversity jurisdiction allows a plaintiff to bring a case in federal court where the amount in controversy exceeds $75,000 and the action is between citizens of different states (28 U.S.C. 1332). These constitutional and statutory limitations are hurdles to access to the federal courts as a forum to shape law and policy.

The adversarial system imposes certain risks on parties that seek to use the federal courts to influence environmental law and policy that are different from those risks imposed on parties that engage the executive or legislative branch. First and foremost, in litigation there is typically, although not always, a winner and a loser. The ability to compromise is constrained by the structural attributes of the system as described above. Second, because the process of judicial decisionmaking curtails the flow of information to and from judges, the outcome is uncertain. For instance, rules limit ex parte communication between judges and parties during the course of litigation (e.g., Model Code of Judicial Conduct Canon 3) and limit the evidence that judges may consider (e.g., Federal Rule of Evidence 401). Third, in some circumstances, litigants may be required to pay the fees incurred by their adversaries. For instance, the Clean Water Act (33 U.S.C. 1365(d)) and Resource Conservation and Recovery Act (42 U.S.C. 6972(e)) (RCRA) include fee-shifting provisions.

While there are persuasive bases to avoid litigation as a means to shape environmental law and policy, business nevertheless does engage in federal environmental litigation for the purpose of shaping environmental law and policy. Other than due to necessity, there are additional reasons that businesses work to shape environmental law and policy through the federal courts. First, the courts may provide a forum that is less partisan than the executive or legislative branches. The extent to which the courts are countermajoritarian may be limited (Mishler and Sheehan 1993). And there is evidence that political ideology does influence decisionmaking by judges in environmental cases (Austin et al. 2004; Lazarus 2004). But precedent along with the doctrine of stare decisis (that is, the notion that courts are bound by the decisions of their predecessors) function to limit the ability of judges to make decisions solely on the basis of political ideology. Second, as a general matter, the courts do make affirmative decisions with respect to cases within their jurisdiction in a timely manner. For example, in 2004, the median amount of time from filing of a civil matter to disposition was 8.5 months for all civil matters in federal district court (Administrative Office of the U.S. Courts 2005). In contrast, the executive and legislative branches often allow environmental problems to go unaddressed for years or even decades.

The attributes of the judiciary described above influence the decision whether to proceed with a lawsuit as a mechanism to influence environmental law and policy. Yet, the penultimate determinant of whether to file a lawsuit is the likelihood of success. There is little informative empirical data respecting the success of attempts by business to influence environmental law and policy through the courts. One of the few existing analyses is provided by Kamieniecki (2006), who analyzes how successful business interests have been in their appeals of EPA actions in the District of Columbia Circuit Court between 1995 and 2002. According to Kamieniecki, the data indicate that business groups appeal cases addressing a wide variety of environmental laws, though a majority of their appeals involve the Clean Air Act. Companies win more than they lose on legal challenges to regulations promulgated under the Comprehensive Response Compensation, and Liability Act (CERCLA) and the Toxic Substances Control Act. Business groups and the EPA are equally successful in cases involving the Clean Water Act. The EPA, however, wins more appeals concerning RCRA and the Clean Air Act than does business. Overall, according to Kamieniecki, between 1995 and 2002 business interests won as many cases as they lost on appeal to the District of Columbia Circuit.

Available Mechanisms to Shape Environmental Law and Policy through the Federal Courts

There are four major roles business can play in federal environmental litigation: plaintiff, defendant, intervenor, and amicus. The plaintiff is the party that initiates a lawsuit by filing a complaint. The defendant is the party being sued in civil litigation; the defendant is the party accused of a crime in criminal proceedings. Intervention is a procedure whereby an outsider with an interest in a lawsuit may become a party though he or she is not named by the existing litigants (Federal Rule of Civil Procedure 24). An outsider may intervene either as a plaintiff or defendant.

An amicus is "someone who is not a party to the litigation, but who believes that the court's decision may affect its interest" (Rehnquist 2001, 239).

Each role differs in important respects from the others. As the party that initiates the lawsuit, the plaintiff is able to decide when to commence the case and can initially define its scope. The plaintiff also has the ability to choose the initial forum for litigation—that is, the court in which the case will be litigated. Often (although by no means always), the scope of the case and forum for litigation articulated by the plaintiff remain the same throughout the course of the litigation. At the same time, the plaintiff has to fulfill the jurisdictional requirements described above, including through a showing that the court has subject-matter jurisdiction and the plaintiff has standing.

In contrast, the defendant typically has little control over the timing and scope of a case against him or her. There are exceptions to this general rule. For example, agencies often know with a fair degree of certainty when their actions will result in the filing of a complaint. Also, though the initial scope of a case is outside the control of the defendant, through use of federal rules permitting counterclaims against the plaintiff and cross-claims against third parties the defendant is able to alter the scope of the case (Federal Rule of Civil Procedure 13).

An intervenor may enter a suit as a plaintiff or defendant. Like the plaintiff, the intervenor has the ability to determine whether and when to engage in litigation. But like the defendant, the intervenor has limited control over the scope of the litigation. The Federal Rules of Civil Procedure establish two types of intervention—as of right and permissive. The former allows the party to intervene automatically if he or she has met certain conditions, whereas the latter gives the court discretion to balance competing interests for and against intervention. When a district court grants a motion to intervene, the outsider becomes a party to the lawsuit subject to the jurisdiction of the court and lawfully issued court orders, ranging from those establishing briefing schedules to those imposing sanctions for contempt. At the same time, an intervenor "may be subject to appropriate conditions or restrictions responsive among other things to the requirements of efficient conduct of the proceedings" (Federal Rule of Civil Procedure 24 Advisory Committee Notes).

The final major role business can play is amicus curiae, or friend of the court. An entity that is not a party to litigation but desires to participate or is invited by the court to participate may file a so-called amicus brief. Generally, an entity must seek court approval to file an amicus brief (e.g., Federal Rule of Appellate Procedure 29). Because an amicus curiae is not a party to the litigation, the jurisdiction of the court over that party is limited.

In each of these major roles, businesses work to shape environmental law and policy through the federal courts. For example in *In re: Operation of the Missouri River System Litigation* (2004), pro-navigation business interests filed a complaint challenging the operation of the Missouri River system by the U.S. Army Corps of Engineers. The Judicial Panel on Multi-District Litigation (created by statute to determine whether cases in different districts involve common factual issues that should be consolidated and to select courts to hear such consolidated proceedings (28 U.S.C. 1407)) consolidated the case with a number of others challenging the Corps management of River operations, including cases filed by upstream and downstream states, environmental groups, and tribes. The primary legal bases for the challenges were the Flood Control Act, National Environmental Policy Act, and Endangered Species Act.

Initially, the pro-navigation business interests controlled the litigation. But soon thereafter, the legal landscape changed dramatically for the business interests as the forum changed from district court in Nebraska to Minnesota and the number of claims mushroomed to include many by other plaintiffs to the consolidated action. Among the plaintiffs were parties with interests at tension with the pro-navigation business interests including upstream states. Whereas the pro-navigation business interests wanted to ensure adequate waterflow to support barge traffic on the river, the upstream states wanted to retain water in upstream reservoirs for recreation. Ultimately, the federal district court in Minnesota concluded that the United States properly balanced the competing uses of the Missouri River system and upheld the decisions of the Corps of Engineers and Fish and Wildlife Service with respect to the operation of the Missouri River system.

Why Do Businesses Engage in Environmental Litigation in Federal Courts?

Business may attempt to shape environmental law and policy in the federal courts for varying purposes (see table 8.1). On one end of the continuum, a business may engage in litigation with another party over a discrete alleged harm and for the purpose of obtaining a specific remedy. Such litigation typically is parochial, involving narrow interests, and is likely to result in judicial decrees that have limited impacts on broader policies. Litigation of this sort may be referred to as private-law litigation (Chayes 1976). On the other end of the continuum, a business may engage in litigation with the government over a wide-ranging harm and for the purpose of obtaining a general remedy (often, some degree

Table 8.1
Categories of litigation

Category of litigation	Type of injury alleged	Remedy sought	Example from environmental law
Private-law litigation	Discrete harm, particular to plaintiff	Specific remedy (monetary, injunctive, or declaratory relief or combination thereof)	Contract dispute between seller and purchaser of real property regarding liability for on-site contamination
Public-law litigation	Wide-ranging harm, applicable to class of which plaintiff is member	General remedy (injunctive or declaratory relief or combination thereof)	Challenge by trade association to constitutionality of Endangered Species Act
Hybrid litigation	Discrete harm, capable of repetition	Specific remedy (monetary, injunctive, or declaratory relief or combination thereof)	Challenge to issuance of cleanup order by EPA under the Comprehensive Environmental Response, Compensation, and Liability Act (CERCLA)

of reform of a public institution). Such litigation may be—though it is not always—strategic. Litigation of this sort may be referred to as public-law litigation (Chayes 1976). A third category of hybrid litigation combines characteristics of the first two.

In some circumstances a single case may shift between these categories. One example of such a circumstance is *Cooper Industries, Inc. v. Aviall Services, Inc.* (2004). Cooper Industries owned airplane maintenance facilities in Texas. In 1981, Aviall Services purchased the facilities. Subsequently, Aviall determined that the facilities were contaminated with hazardous substances, notified the state authorities, and took action to address the contamination. Aviall then filed a civil action in federal district court alleging breach of contract by Cooper and, in the alternative, seeking contribution under both federal and state law. In its initial stages, this case was a dispute between two former owners of contaminated properties about each owner's fair share of the cleanup costs; the plaintiff Aviall alleged it paid for a disproportionate share of the cleanup costs and was entitled to recover monetary damages from the defendant Cooper.

But the district court rejected Aviall's sole federal claim—that is, the claim for contribution under federal law (specifically, section 113(f)(1) of CERCLA, 42 U.S.C. 9613(f)(1)). Furthermore, the district court refused to retain jurisdiction over the remaining state-law claims. Aviall appealed to the Court of Appeals for the Fifth Circuit, and a divided three-judge panel of that court affirmed the district court. Aviall then petitioned for rehearing en banc (a procedural move whereby the petitioner seeks reconsideration of a panel decision by the entire court of appeals) from the Fifth Circuit, which granted the petition and reversed the district court judgment. In a ten-to-three decision, the majority held that Aviall could seek contribution under section 113(f)(1) of CERCLA even though Aviall was not subject to a prior lawsuit under CERCLA to undertake or to pay for the costs of cleanup.

Cooper Industries sought and obtained Supreme Court review of the decision of the Fifth Circuit. After the Supreme Court accepted review, this case that began as a controversy about the allocation of cleanup costs among two former owners of a contaminated property became a case about the ability of parties that voluntarily cleaned up contaminated properties to recover cleanup costs in contribution from other liable parties. The importance of the case is demonstrated by the fact the amicus briefs were filed in the Supreme Court on behalf of the United States, more than twenty states, a trade group representing major corporations (i.e., the Superfund Settlements Project), and a number of major multinational corporations including ConocoPhillips, Atlantic Richfield, and Lockheed Martin. Absent congressional action, the Supreme Court's interpretation of a statute (in this instance, CERCLA) controls.[2]

As *Cooper v. Aviall* demonstrates, public-law litigation may be initiated for the singular purpose of obtaining the relief requested (or, in that case, recovery of cleanup costs from a joint tortfeasor). To the extent that litigation is pursued by business for the narrow purpose of obtaining a discrete remedy, it may be differentiated from public-law litigation filed with more grandiose goals in mind. Such strategic public-law litigation may be undertaken as part of a larger effort to shift public opinion or public policy. For example, groups have filed strategic litigation to achieve the underlying goal of removing the system of dams on the Colombia River and to have the Endangered Species Act held unconstitutional.

While the categories of litigation identified above demonstrate the breadth of environmental litigation in the federal courts, they offer limited guidance to scholars and practitioners regarding the motivations of businesses engaged in environmental litigation in federal courts. Myriad motives exist for businesses to engage in environmental litigation in federal courts (see table 8.2). Generally, the motives to engage in environmental litigation in federal courts are the same as the motives to influence the executive and legislative branches at other points in the policymaking process. The common theme is self-interest, and the primary interest is to maximize profits (Prakash 2000).

As a general matter, there are three motives to engage in federal environmental litigation: strengthening one's market position, maintaining one's market position, and weakening a competitor's market position. In each case, the motive is relativistic. Any individual business is focused on maintaining or improving its current position. To do so, businesses may pursue strategies to improve market conditions across the board (for example, by reducing compliance costs through litigation to invalidate a regulation that imposes such costs) or improve their individual market

Table 8.2
Motivation for business to engage in federal environmental litigation

General motivation	Specific motivation	Example of action taken
Strengthen market position	Increase the flow of governmental benefits	Defend validity of regulation that provides subsidy
	Reduce costs of compliance	Challenge validity of an existing statute imposing compliance costs
	Reduce liability	Intervene to defend statute that preempts existing state law cause of action that results in liability exposure
Maintain market position	Maintain the flow of governmental benefits	Challenge validity of statutory amendment that reduces tax preference
	Oppose increase in compliance costs	Challenge validity of a recently promulgated regulation imposing compliance costs
	Oppose increase in liability	Challenge statute that alters existing liability scheme and thereby increases liability exposure
Weaken competitor's market position	Decrease the flow of governmental benefits to competitors	Challenge validity of statute or regulation that provides subsidy
	Increase competitors' costs of compliance	Defend validity of regulation imposing compliance costs

conditions (for instance, by intervening to defend a permit issued by a regulatory agency that authorizes construction of a new facility).

As a result of the risks imposed by the adversarial system that were described above, it is often the case that businesses engage in environmental litigation in federal courts only after attempts to influence environmental law and policy through the executive and legislative branches have failed. For example, in December 2000, the International Snowmobile Manufacturers Association (ISMA) filed a lawsuit in federal district court in Wyoming against the National Park Service, challenging a rule to phase out snowmobile use in Yellowstone National Park, the John D Rockefeller, Jr. National Parkway, and Grand Teton National Park

(U.S. Department of the Interior 2001b). The 2000 Rule was the result of a multiyear review of winter use of the parks; ISMA actively participated in that review in an effort to influence the agency decisionmaking process (U.S. Department of the Interior 2001a).

ISMA is an organization of snowmobile manufacturers. In their complaint filed with the federal district court, the manufacturers claimed that the 2000 Rule phasing out snowmobiling will decrease snowmobile use and, therefore, snowmobile sales. Thus, in this circumstance, according to the complaint filed in court by ISMA, the motivation to engage in federal environmental litigation was a desire on the part of the manufacturers to maintain their market position. Specifically, the manufacturers desired to protect the existing benefit to them (principally in the form of snowmobile sales and use) resulting from permissive snowmobile use in the parks.

In June 2001, the Park Service agreed to conduct a supplemental environmental analysis of snowmobile use in the parks, and at that time the district court agreed to stay the litigation. Based on its supplemental analysis, the Park Service issued a rule in December 2003 allowing limited snowmobile use in the parks (U.S. Department of the Interior 2003). Environmental groups filed a complaint in federal district court in the District of Columbia challenging the 2003 Rule. The court held that the Park Service violated the Administrative Procedure Act and National Environmental Policy Act in the course of promulgating the 2003 Rule, and it vacated the 2003 Rule and remanded the matter to the Park Service for further proceedings (*Fund for Animals v. Norton* 2003). The Park Service issued yet another rule in 2004, which is currently the subject of litigation (U.S. Department of the Interior 2004). While litigation over this contentious issue is likely to continue in the foreseeable future absent clear congressional action, it may be expected that ISMA will continue to participate in the controversy in order to protect the interest of its members in continued snowmobile use in the parks.

Whereas in the case described above (*International Snowmobile Manufacturers Association v. Norton* (2004)) the primary motivation was a desire to maintain market position, challenges to agency regulations by business often are motivated by a desire to avoid increased compliance costs. For example, in *Environmental Defense Center v. EPA* (2003), two industry groups—American Forest and Paper Association (AFPA) and National Association of Homebuilders (NAHB)—petitioned the D.C. Circuit for review of an EPA regulation that requires entities to obtain Clean Water Act National Pollution Discharge Elimination System permits for small municipal separate storm sewer systems and stormwater discharges from construction activity disturbing one to five acres. The industry petition was consolidated with two other petitions before the U.S. Court of Appeals for the Ninth Circuit.

The Clean Water Act expressly requires the EPA to regulate stormwater discharges to waters of the United States (33 U.S.C. 1342(p)). In 1990, the agency issued the Phase I stormwater regulations governing large-scale discharges. The EPA proposed the Phase II stormwater regulations in 1998, and finalized them in 1999 (U.S. EPA 1999). Along with the industry petitioners, environmental and municipal petitioners raised numerous challenges to the Phase II regulations. With respect to the industry petitioners, the Ninth Circuit began by considering its jurisdiction. The court concluded that one of the industry petitioners—AFPA—lacked standing to challenge the regulations. As explained above, standing is a doctrine derived from Article III of the Constitution that limits the jurisdiction of federal courts. Here, the court held that AFPA failed to establish that it suffered injury-in-fact because its interest in avoiding future regulation of forest roads through stormwater regulations was not actually or imminently threatened.

The Ninth Circuit determined that NAHB fulfilled the standing requirements and therefore reached the claims contained in the industry petition. The court rejected each of the four industry claims in its decision. The only claim that the court upheld was advanced by the environmental groups. The court agreed with those groups that the EPA could not allow a regulated entity to obtain a permit to discharge pollutants by filing a notice of intent (to seek coverage under the applicable permit) that establishes the standards applicable to that entity absent agency review and public review of the notice.

In the two preceding cases, businesses were motivated by self-interest. In the snowmobile litigation, business is working to maintain the benefit it received as a result of snowmobile access to the parks. In the stormwater case, business worked to oppose regulations that would increase compliance costs. The snowmobile case is particular to a relatively small industry (snowmobile manufacturing) and a limited geographic area (the parks described above). For this reason, it is on the private-litigation side of the continuum. The stormwater case involves a rule of national application that affects significant numbers of municipalities and construction sites. For this reason, the stormwater case is on the public-litigation side of the continuum.

Conclusions

Despite persuasive reasons to avoid litigation, business regularly turns to litigation as a means to shape environmental law and policy. To understand why business engages in such litigation and the variety of roles business plays, it is necessary to understand the context within which business operates—in this instance, the federal courts. The structure of the adversarial system, rules of procedure, rules of evidence, and ethical canons are all part of that context. In addition, the context includes a policymaking process that is variously described by scholars of political science and public administration. One prominent approach is rooted in the garbage-can model of organizational choice articulated by Cohen, March, and Olsen (1972), applied to the federal government by Kingdon (1995), and applied specifically to federal environmental policy by Fiorino (1995). The garbage-can model is, in part, a reaction to the theory of synoptic decisionmaking by bureaucracies. This model posits that organizational preferences are often ambiguous, organizations are characterized by bounded rationality, and organizations drift in and out of the policymaking process.

Application of the garbage-can model to litigation is constrained by the context described above. For example, the ability of organizations to enter and exit litigation to affect policy is limited by the Constitution, federal statutes, and rules of procedure. But the model may be useful in explaining business behavior in the context of federal environmental litigation.

As Kraft and Kamieniecki note in the introductory chapter to this book, numerous studies have concluded that business dominates the policymaking process, but some studies support the contrary position. In the context of federal environmental litigation, the success of business is mixed. In *Environmental Defense Center v. EPA* (2003), business was unsuccessful, while business succeeded, at least temporarily, in *International Snowmobile Manufacturers Association v. Norton* (2004). At times, business is both the winner and the loser in federal environmental litigation, as in *Cooper Industries, Inc. v. Aviall Services, Inc.* (2004), demonstrating the danger associated with treating business as a monolith.

While the work of Olson (1965) and others may provide a basis for concluding that business is well organized and well funded, in the context of litigation the extent to which business is organized and funded is highly variable. In fact, business interests routinely are fragmented in the context of environmental law and policy. *Cooper Industries, Inc. v. Aviall Services, Inc.* (2004)—a case in which the two original litigants were aircraft maintenance businesses—provides a archetype example of that fragmentation. Another example is *National Wildlife Federation v. National Marine Fisheries Service* (2005). This case, which is pending, involves a challenge to the operation of dams and reservoirs in the Columbia River system by the Bonneville Power Administration, Bureau of Reclamation, and U.S. Army Corps of Engineers. In 2004, the National Marine Fisheries Service issued a Biological Opinion to the federal operators for the Columbia River system under the Endangered Species Act. Numerous parties challenged the validity of the Biological Opinion, including representatives of the commercial and sports fishing industries (e.g., Trout Unlimited, Pacific Coast Federation of Fishermen's Associations, and Federation of Fly Fishers). A number of business groups intervened on behalf of the federal defendants, including irrigation (e.g., Washington State Farm Bureau Federation) and power interests (e.g., Public Power Council). Other parties filed amicus briefs in the matter, including the National Association of Homebuilders. Thus, business interests are on opposite sides of the litigation.[3]

Such fragmentation may not be apparent if one or more business interests are not party to the litigation. For example, in litigation involving major river systems, such as *In re: Operation of the Missouri River System Litigation* (2004), it is often the case that upstream pro-recreation interests (e.g., boating and fishing businesses) are at odds with pro-navigation interests over whether and when to release water from reservoirs.

There is a dearth of scholarship regarding the use of the federal courts by business to shape environmental law and policy. Empirical research, in particular, is lacking. Although practical constraints on the availability of data may contribute to this absence of research, it is also the case that analysis of the impact of the judiciary on environmental law and policy is lacking. The major contributors to this area of inquiry can be counted on one hand (i.e., R. Shep Melnick, Rosemary O'Leary, and Lettie McSpadden). Legal scholarship on the subject is more voluminous and varied, yet much of that scholarship is anecdotal and cannot fill the void that is the result of a lack of rigorous empirical research. To the extent that political scientists do focus on efforts by business to influence environmental law and policy through the federal courts, they would do well to focus on the constraints imposed by the structure and procedure of the federal judiciary and resist any effort to homogenize business—that is, to treat business as well funded, well organized, and possessing a single set of well-defined preferences.

Notes

1. The author participated in a number of the cases described in this chapter. The views of the author are not necessarily those of any organization with which he is or has been affiliated.

2. The Supreme Court reversed the lower-court holding that Aviall cannot seek contribution from Cooper under section 113(f)(1) of CERCLA. The Court remanded the case in order that the lower courts could determine whether Aviall properly pled a cause of action under section 107 of CERCLA.

3. In October 2005, the district court issued a final order remanding the Biological Opinion to the federal defendants. Federal defendants have appealed that order to the Ninth Circuit.

References

Administrative Office of the U.S. Courts. 1999. *Understanding the Federal Courts*. Washington, DC: Administrative Office of the U.S. Courts.

Administrative Office of the U.S. Courts. 2005. *Judicial Business of the United States Courts*. Washington, DC: Administrative Office of the U.S. Courts.

American Bar Association. 2003. *Model Code of Judicial Conduct*. Chicago: American Bar Association.

Austin, Jay E., John M. Carter II, Bradley D. Klein, and Scott E. Schang. 2004. *Judging NEPA: A "Hard Look" at Judicial Decision Making under the*

National Environmental Policy Act. Washington, DC: Environmental Law Institute.

Bardach, Eugene, and Robert A. Kagan. 1982. *Going by the Book: The Problem of Regulatory Unreasonableness.* Philadelphia: Temple University Press.

Bickers, Kenneth N., and Robert M. Stein. 1995. *Perpetuating the Pork Barrel: Subsystems and American Democracy.* Cambridge: Cambridge University Press.

Caldwell, Lynton K. 1990. *Between Two Worlds: Science, the Environmental Movement, and Policy Choice.* Cambridge: Cambridge University Press.

Chayes, Abraham. 1976. "The Role of the Judge in Public Law Litigation." *Harvard Law Review* 89:1281.

Cohen, Michael D., James G. March, and Johan P. Olsen. 1972. "A Garbage Can Model of Organizational Choice." *Administrative Science Quarterly* 17:1–25.

Fiorino, Daniel. 1995. *Making Environmental Policy.* Berkeley: University of California Press.

Heclo, Hugh. 1978. "Issue Networks and the Executive Establishment." In Anthony King, ed., *The New American Political System.* Washington, DC: American Enterprise Institute.

Kamieniecki, Sheldon. 2006. *Corporate America and Environmental Policy: How Often Does Business Get Its Way?* Palo Alto, CA: Stanford University Press.

Kingdon, John. 1995. *Agendas, Alternatives, and Public Policy.* New York: HarperCollins.

Kraft, Michael E., and Norman J. Vig. 2006. "Environmental Policy from the 1970s to the Twenty-First Century." In Norman J. Vig and Michael E. Kraft, eds., *Environmental Policy: New Directions for the Twenty-First Century*, 6th ed. Washington, DC: CQ Press.

Lazarus, Richard. 2004. *The Making of Environmental Law.* Chicago: University of Chicago Press.

Lowi, Theodore. 1979. *The End of Liberalism.* New York: Norton.

Mishler, William, and Reginald Sheehan. 1993. "The Supreme Court as a Countermajoritarian Institution? The Impact of Public Opinion on Supreme Court Decisions." *American Political Science Review* 87:87–101.

O'Leary, Rosemary. 1993. *Environmental Change: Federal Courts and the EPA.* Philadelphia: Temple University Press.

O'Leary, Rosemary. 2006. "Environmental Policy in the Courts." In Norman J. Vig and Michael E. Kraft, eds., *Environmental Policy*, 6th ed. Washington, DC: CQ Press.

Olson, Mancur. 1965. *The Logic of Collective Action.* Cambridge, MA: Harvard University Press.

Prakash, Aseem. 2000. *Greening the Firm: The Politics of Corporate Environmentalism.* Cambridge: Cambridge University Press.

Press, Daniel, and Daniel A. Mazmanian. 2006. "The Greening of Industry: Combining Government Regulation with Voluntary Strategies." In Norman J. Vig and Michael E. Kraft, eds., *Environmental Policy*, 6th ed. Washington, DC: CQ Press.

Rabkin, Jeremy. 1989. *Judicial Compulsions: How Public Law Distorts Public Policy*. New York: Basic Books.

Rehnquist, William. 2001. *The Supreme Court*. New York: Knopf.

Schlozman, Kay Lehman, and John T. Tierney. 1986. *Organized Interests and American Democracy*. New York: Harper & Row.

Shapiro, Martin. 1988. *Who Guards the Guardians? Judicial Control of Administration*. Athens: University of Georgia Press.

Thurber, James. 1991. "Dynamics of Policy Subsystems in American Politics." In Allan Cigler and Burdett Loomis, eds., *Interest Group Politics*, 3rd ed. Washington, DC: CQ Press.

Tribe, Laurence H. 2000. *American Constitutional Law*. New York: Foundation Press.

Cases

Cooper Industries, Inc. v. Aviall Services, Inc., 543 U.S. 157 (2004).

Environmental Defense Center v. EPA, 344 F.3d 832 (9th Cir. 2003).

Friends of the Earth, Inc. v. Laidlaw Environmental Services (TOC), Inc., 528 U.S. 167 (2000).

Fund for Animals v. Norton, 294 F. Supp. 2d 92 (D.D.C. 2003).

Goldwater v. Carter, 444 U.S. 996 (1979).

In re: Operation of the Missouri River System Litigation, 363 F. Supp. 2d 1145 (D. Minn. 2004), *aff'd*, 421 F.3d 618 (8th Cir. 2005).

International Snowmobile Manufacturers Association v. Norton, 340 F. Supp. 2d 1249 (D. Wyo. 2004).

Lujan v. Defenders of Wildlife, 504 U.S. 555 (1992).

National Wildlife Federation v. National Marine Fisheries Service, Case No. 01-640 (D. Or. Oct. 24, 2005), *appeal docketed*, Nos. 06-35011 and 06-35019 (9th Cir. Jan. 9, 2006).

Laws and Regulations

28 U.S.C. 1331.

28 U.S.C. 1332.

28 U.S.C. 1407.

Administrative Procedure Act, 5 U.S.C. 551 et seq.

Clean Air Act, 42 U.S.C. 7401 et seq.

Clean Water Act, 33 U.S.C. 1251 et seq.

Comprehensive Environmental Response Compensation and Liability Act, 42 U.S.C. 9601 et seq.

Endangered Species Act, 16 U.S.C. 1531 et seq.

Federal Rules of Appellate Procedure.

Federal Rules of Civil Procedure.

Federal Rules of Evidence.

Flood Control Act, Pub. L. No. 78-534 (Dec. 22, 1944).

National Environmental Policy Act, 42 U.S.C. 4231 et seq.

Resource Conservation and Recovery Act, 42 U.S.C. 6901 et seq.

Toxic Substances Control Act, 15 U.S.C. 2601 et seq.

U.S. Department of the Interior. 2001a. *Record of Decision, Winter Use Plans for the Yellowstone and Grand Teton National Parks and the John D. Rockefeller Jr., Memorial Parkway.* Washington, DC: U.S. Department of the Interior.

U.S. Department of the Interior. 2001b. "Special Regulations, Areas of the National Park System; Final Rule." *Federal Register* 66:7,260–7,268.

U.S. Department of the Interior. 2003. "Special Regulations; Areas of the National Park System, Final Rule." *Federal Register* 68:69,267–69,289.

U.S. Department of the Interior. 2004. "Special Regulations; Areas of the National Park System, Final Rule." *Federal Register* 69:65,347–65,366.

U.S. Environmental Protection Agency. 1999. "National Pollutant Discharge Elimination System—Regulations for Revision of the Water Pollution Control Program Addressing Storm Water Discharges; Final Rule." *Federal Register* 64:68,721–68,851.

9

Industry's Use of the Courts

Lettie McSpadden

Since the founding of the Republic, American businesses have found the judicial branch to be a useful resource for advancing their interests. Without courts there could be no private property or enforcement of contracts needed to conduct normal business operations. Courts have proved highly receptive to business demands for protection from Congresses and administrations that have sought to rein in some business practices. Starting in the 1930s during the Franklin Roosevelt administration, the courts backed away from declaring most federal economic regulations unconstitutional. Since the 1970s when environmental regulations were added to economic ones, business has appealed to courts to reduce the burden placed on it by the new laws. The courts have continued to be receptive to many arguments coming from business to protect private property and uphold the sanctity of contracts.

Another reason business organizations have often appealed to the courts to uphold their interests is the same one that motivates other interest groups to use the courts. In the words of John Marshall, the Chief Justice of the U.S. Supreme Court who best defined that institution, "The duty of the judicial department is to say what the law is" (*Marbury v. Madison* (1803)). By this he meant that no matter how the Congress words its laws, or the agencies formulate their regulations, law courts make the final interpretation of all forms of laws in this country. American judges are as involved with policymaking, including environmental policy, as the other two branches of government. American business, as one of the major political actors in the country, uses the courts as a last resort when it has failed to prevail in the congressional or administrative arenas.

Despite the obvious reasons for doing so, little research has been conducted specifically on how industry uses the American court system. Many questions remain unanswered, such as when and why corporations and trade associations choose to use the courts to advance their interests. What strategies have they developed for doing so? The U.S. judicial system is complex, consisting of fifty state systems as well as the federal system. Industry has many forums to choose from to initiate their cases; why do they choose some over others? How often have they succeeded and under what circumstances? The purpose of this chapter is to examine the strategy and frequency of industry's use of the courts, and to shed some light on the degree to which it has been successful. It is difficult to obtain meaningful quantitative data on how often business interests use the courts for environmental policy and how often they succeed. However, there is a rich supply of studies of particular cases that provide impressionistic and anecdotal evidence for answers to some of these questions.

Historic Overview

After the first wave of U.S. environmental legislation in the 1960s and 1970s, industry did not rush to court, as one would expect, in a policy area that concerned it so vitally. Instead, it observed as pro-environmental public interest groups, from the venerable Sierra Club and Audubon Society to the recently formed Environmental Defense Fund and Natural Resources Defense Council (NRDC), worked aggressively to nudge administrators and the courts to enforce the new laws. However, when the U.S. Environmental Protection Agency (EPA) began issuing ambient air and water quality standards and emissions and effluent control standards for sources of pollution, industry took action. Individual industries soon realized that environmental groups were active in assembling an expert staff of lawyers to supplement what the government was doing. If the U.S. Department of Justice was unwilling to initiate cases against a business, public interest groups often did so in its place because many of the laws contained "citizen-action" clauses that enabled them to enforce the law if the government was not taking action.

As a result, major corporations added environmental divisions to their in-house law offices to defend against both governmental and private-citizen suits against them. Trade associations beefed up their legal staffs as well and often combined with individual corporations to challenge regulations that affected whole industries. Legal foundations such as the Pacific Legal Foundation and the Mountain States Legal Foundation were created to take their own cases against government management of natural resources for conservation. Business soon developed considerable legal expertise in the new field of environmental law and began taking the initiative. Following the old adage that "the best defense is a strong offense," by the 1980s industry was bringing as many suits against government for being overzealous as environmental groups were bringing for lack of zeal in enforcement (Wenner 1982).

Conservation groups were initially eager to take any losses they may have suffered in the lower courts to appellate bodies in the 1970s. By the 1990s they found they had lost so many appeals that it was often not worth the expense to appeal, especially to the Supreme Court. Often the outcome was only made worse. Industry took up the slack and made more business appeals to the Supreme Court as their confidence in a positive outcome grew. In addition, the two sides adopted the tactic of "forum shopping," seeking the most favorable circuit in which to make their demands. For industry it was the U.S. Court of Appeals for the Fourth Circuit in the Southeast. For environmentalists it was often the District of Columbia Circuit because of the philosophy of the judges sitting in the circuit. By the twenty-first century this strategy had changed because of major shifts in personnel staffing those courts. Business interests focused not only on the Fourth and Fifth circuits, but also on the formerly pro-environmental District of Columbia Circuit, while environmentalists took their pleas to the Ninth Circuit on the West Coast.

Data Limitations and Methodological Constraints

As this brief history suggests, business has played an increasingly active role in using the courts to affect environmental policy. Yet it is also difficult to study just how influential business groups have been in these efforts and to determine what factors affect the strategies they adopt for intervening in the courts and whether and how they succeed. To be sure, there are large datasets available to researchers today (e.g., on the Supreme Court (Spaeth 2000) and on the federal circuit courts of appeal (Songer 2000)). Yet these are not intended to answer such focused questions as those I have raised concerning business uses of courts in environmental policy. The scholars who created and use these datasets are judicial behaviorists concerned with broader questions: explaining liberal-conservative divisions among judges and the consistency of individual judges' ideology in large categories of cases such as civil liberties, criminal rights, and economic regulation (Schubert 1965; Segal and Spaeth 1993). Environmental scholars have yet to make use of these large datasets from the federal court system to examine environmental cases undertaken by industry.

Legal scholars who focus on environmental cases are concerned with what they consider the major cases that set precedents for cases to come. They often have a particular perspective on some aspect of the law and choose cases from that perspective. The emphasis is on explicating court doctrine and understanding the rationales judges write for making their decisions with little emphasis on litigants' strategy in bringing the cases or their relative success and/or failure (Findley and Farber 1999; Plater, Abrams, and Goldfarb 1998). It is on these descriptive and analytic studies that much of the data in this chapter relies.

There are two examples of systematic data collected specifically on environmental cases, but neither assessed only industry demands on the courts. In fact, both emphasized the use made of courts by environmental groups. It was shown that industry came to use the courts a little later than its environmental rivals. Yet, once started business organizations and trade associations soon took the lead in the 1970s in challenging any and all EPA regulations for their lack of concern for costs to industry (Wenner 1982). Government tended to win more of these cases than business, but the fact that regulations could be temporarily suspended while the issue was being litigated meant years when industry did not have to comply with the new regulations. An even more subtle method of industry influencing policy occurs when a company or trade association may threaten to sue the EPA or another regulatory agency and the agency backs off the rulemaking action in fear of such a suit taking legal resources away from more important goals.

Another scholar who reviewed a large number of environmental cases extending through the 1980s focused primarily on the cases initiated by environmental groups to force government to meet all the deadlines in environmental laws for setting standards (O'Leary 1993). One such case was started in 1973 by the NRDC to force the EPA to identify toxic substances found in America's waterways and set standards for them. Years of litigation, court decisions, reversals in higher courts, and consent decrees followed. Environmentalists argued the EPA had not identified a sufficient number of toxics in water and its standards were lax. In 1976 the cases were settled by a consent decree negotiated between the EPA and the NRDC. Industry groups moved to have the decree vacated. Multiple modifications followed throughout the 1980s. The EPA has revised its toxic standards for water pollutants so many times that it would be difficult to identify a true "winner" in this case. It ended as do most such conflicts in compromise, and the author concludes by noting how frequently environmental mediation is used to reach solutions. This reveals a pattern of environmental policy through repeated judicial remands and administrative rulemaking through several cycles (O'Leary 1993).

Even if victories were clear-cut, simply counting the numbers of business victories achieved in the courts is not fully revealing either. In some cases, one side may lose the battle but win the war when the court remands the case back to the EPA or another agency to rectify a mistake. The agency may use the opportunity to make the decision more pro-business even when reprimanded by the court. Sometimes environmental groups' lawsuits have backfired to industry's benefit. During the Carter administration the Forest Service undertook a comprehensive inventory of its roadless public lands to determine which would be developed and which would remain as wild land. The state of California, the NRDC, the Environmental Defense Fund, and local environmentalists sued, arguing that the public had not been given sufficient time to comment on the plan. The timber industry joined the federal government's side, but the judge in Northern California agreed with California and environmental groups, and remanded the plan to be reconsidered by the Forest Service to include more wilderness areas. However, by the time this was done, the Carter administration had given way to the Reagan administration, which used the opportunity to rethink the Carter plan to reassess all the acreage that had been set aside for wilderness and label some of that for development (Wenner 1984).

The attempt to assess industry strategy is further complicated by the fact that many court cases do not make it to the casebooks because judges choose not to have them published. Recently, some scholars have attempted to rectify this oversight by systematically collecting unpublished cases, which necessitates researching records in federal courthouses around the United States. Scholars had assumed the unpublished cases were inconsequential and/or similar to the published ones, and therefore could be ignored. However, they have found examples of important precedents in unpublished works and deny that these are little different from the published ones (Rowland and Carp 1996). Some systematic work has been done concerning civil implementation of the Resource Conservation and Recovery Act as well as the Clean Water and Clean Air Acts by the EPA and the Department of Justice, including unpublished cases. However, the research focuses on what causes fines to fluctuate: facts of the case, the political environment, and ideology of judges (Ringquist and Emmert 1999). In these cases industry is the defendant and is responding to government's use of the laws; hence there is little industry strategy to assess. The same kind of analysis has not been applied to cases initiated by business.

Yet another wrinkle in trying to assess how business influences environmental policy through its intervention in the judicial process can be seen in an intriguing argument by Smith (2005) concerning how Congress drafts environmental laws. Smith examines three sets of amendments to the Clean Air Act and shows that members of Congress sometimes "strategically manipulate statutory rules governing the role of courts in regulatory policymaking to help their political supporters and to advance their own policy goals" (p. 139). That is, environmental laws may be written in a way that enhances opportunities for interested parties to take their concerns to the courts if they cannot win in the agencies. Indeed, many proposed regulatory reform bills from 1995 to 2005 clearly have had as a major objective precisely this kind of increased access to the courts to challenge agency rulings, with the presumption that business interests were the intended beneficiaries (Kraft 2006). Some of those recent changes to laws, such as the Data Quality Act of 2000, have been used extensively by business interests to challenge regulatory-agency rulings (Andrews 2006).

The upshot is that the influence of business within the courts may well be growing, but not merely because it is investing more effort or more money in litigation or because it is winning a greater percentage of cases in which it is involved. Its success also depends on access to the judicial venue provided by Congress, a more subtle process that is difficult to study. Along with the other impediments highlighted above that limit our ability to study the role of business in the courts, there are several implications. Scholars need to think critically about the various ways in which the courts can shape environmental policy, and they need to improve the quality of evidence on which conclusions about the role of business are based. This might include examination of a larger number and greater diversity of cases or use of a more expansive set of data that would similarly promote more confidence in the conclusions reached.

This chapter explores two major types of strategies industry has developed to pursue its interests in court. The first involves pollution control cases in which a particular industry attacks the standards set by the EPA before it has an opportunity to apply them and take industry to court to enforce them. In most of these cases industry lawyers argue that they lack the technological means to achieve the standards and/or that the cost of developing such means is not worth any benefits that would be derived from them. The second strategy developed by business lawyers has created a new and expanded meaning of words in the U.S. Constitution. They have reinterpreted "the taking of private property" to include government regulation of land uses by private owners as well as actual physical occupation of the land. Another helpful tool for business to use in both kinds of cases is the division of power between state and federal governments by their laws and constitutions. Sometimes business argues for the states' authority; at other times, for that of the federal government, depending on which is more favorably disposed toward business at the time.

Pollution Control Cases

The Clean Air and Clean Water Acts instruct the EPA to set ambient standards for air and water. In addition, the EPA sets specific emissions allowances for industry to empty its wastes into air and effluent standards for dumping into waterways. Clearly, these standards are interconnected, because the level of pollutants allowed to enter our ambient air and water is dependent on the amount of pollution allotted to industry to dump. The laws also allow for affected parties to comment on regulations as they are formulated by the EPA, and industry has taken full advantage of this process, often writing detailed comments on proposed standards, as do environmental groups. If still dissatisfied with the severity of the regulation, companies and public interest groups can use a different venue, the courts, to challenge the regulations, and both have done so with enthusiasm. Rarely is a new EPA regulation applied in the year it is formulated. Months, and sometimes years, of litigation and appeal may intervene before the standards are ready for application. This has occurred, for example, in the EPA's efforts to increase the standards for particulate matter and ozone.

Both individual corporations and trade associations representing large numbers of corporations in the same business have often argued that the standards set for ambient air and water quality are utopian and unnecessary, downplaying the possible damage to human health. Emissions and effluent standards are attacked as too costly, given industry's limited resources, or as technologically impossible to achieve. In some cases environmental groups have sued government at the same time, arguing the standards were not strong enough, and the suits have been consolidated in the courts. In other cases, business groups have supported government agencies when they were challenged by environmental groups.

An early example of industry's claim that it was impossible to create a device to eliminate pollution occurred in the motor vehicle industry. After years of hearing representatives of the automotive industry swear that a device such as the catalytic converter was impossible to produce, in 1970 Congress decided to specify some goals within the law itself instead of depending on the EPA to set strict standards. It mandated that hydrocarbons and carbon monoxide from motor vehicles must be reduced by 90 percent from 1970 levels by the year 1975. This was considered a technology-forcing strategy, and the automotive industry was eager to have its day in court to prove it could not be done. There was a provision made in the law for a one-year extension of the deadline, and the car manufacturers petitioned for its immediate application. The EPA refused, because the 1975 deadline was several years away. All three of the major car manufacturers—Ford, General Motors, and Chrysler— immediately took their cause to court as the next logical stage in their delaying strategy. They joined in *International Harvester Co. v. Ruckelshaus* to argue that the deadline for meeting emissions control standards was unrealistic because no technology that could reduce car emissions by 90 percent existed or could exist.

Judge Harold Leventhal of the D.C. Circuit Court of Appeals was clearly ambivalent about this case. He acknowledged that neither side had conclusively proven that the technology could or, alternatively, could not be ready by 1975. Scientific studies were much too divided to decide that the balance of the evidence was clearly on one side or the other. Ultimately, the Court of Appeals for the District of Columbia agreed with the automotive industry that the EPA had failed to demonstrate that the technology would be available to meet the 1975 requirements. Hence, it must issue the one-year extension, which was done. This was only the beginning of slippage for motor vehicle emissions standards. Congress passed a law to postpone compliance until 1977, and finally 1981 (Findley and Farber 1999).

Although the goal was eventually reached, the automotive industry reaped the benefit of many postponements and saved millions, if not billions, of dollars in the sale of cars without the higher emissions standards in the intervening years. In addition, many areas in the United States remained out of compliance with ambient air quality standards because of increased number of cars on the road, increased traffic, and the continued use of cars manufactured before the emissions standards were set. Judges proved responsive, as did their legislative and executive counterparts, in listening to the pleas from industry for relief from the economic burden of complying with the original law. Nevertheless, in 1990 the Clean Air Act was amended once again and further goals set for reductions of nitrogen dioxide, carbon monoxide, and hydrocarbons.

Many experts argued that the only way air quality standards could be met, given America's commitment to individual cars, was through clean-fuel vehicles that would emit no pollutants. California took the initiative in this endeavor and mandated that operators of certain fleets of vehicles purchase only new clean-burning or electric cars (Plater, Abrams, and Goldfarb 1998). In *Engine Manufacturers Association et al. v. South Coast of Air Quality Management District* (2004), the automobile industry challenged California's right to forbid local governments and other fleet operators to purchase or lease vehicles that were not powered by clean fuels. The U.S. Court of Appeals for the Ninth Circuit interpreted the federal Clean Air Act liberally to allow California to do this. Industry, knowing the Ninth Circuit's proclivity for pro-environmental rulings, immediately appealed to the U.S. Supreme Court. The latter, by now dominated by justices sympathetic to business arguments, overturned the ruling, saying that California had no authority to force local governments and other fleet operators to purchase only alternative-fuel or hybrid models for their use. This, the court argued, was an attempt to get around the federal Clean Air Act's prohibition against states setting their own emissions standards more stringent than the national ones. The prohibition against the fleet owners buying new polluting vehicles was simply a different way of achieving higher emissions standards for the state.

What was surprising about this case was the author of the majority opinion, Justice Scalia. Normally, he claims to be a champion of states' rights against the encroachment of federal government into state affairs. Yet he wrote the majority opinion reprimanding California for trying to act on its own. Justice Souter, a more liberal justice known for his approval of federal regulation, dissented. As in many environmental cases, it was difficult to explain justices' opinions based on their asserted attitudes toward the division of power between state and federal governments. Instead, it was easier to do so by looking at whether the decision favored industry.

Standards for stationary sources of air pollution also came in for immediate industrial criticism as soon as they were promulgated. In *Portland Cement Co. v. Ruckelshaus* (1973), industry lawyers contended that the U.S. EPA had not sufficiently taken into consideration the cost to industry of achieving the standards. Although the EPA claimed to have considered emissions control costs to a degree, it had not performed a formal cost-benefit analysis to ensure that the gains to society for cleaner air would outweigh industrial costs for emissions control devices. The District of Columbia Circuit Court (at that time environmentally oriented) agreed with the EPA that it had taken costs into consideration. But it remanded the standards back to the EPA to make clear to industry the grounds for its decision.

This decision led eventually to more lobbying in Congress for modifying the act to force the EPA to use more cost-benefit analysis in setting emissions standards. Over the years we have seen Best Available Technology (BAT) gradually replaced by the less stringent Best Practicable Technology (BPT) as the standard in most industries. All three branches of government have proved sympathetic to industry's argument that the costs of emissions controls be balanced by equal or greater benefits to society, which are sometimes difficult to quantify.

One major tactic developed early by industry was the "bubble" concept of controlling air pollution. Emissions regulations apply to new sources of pollution as well as to modifications made in old plants. Hence, when a plant expands, it must control both the new components and the old to meet standards. Industry's imaginary bubble was designed for an entire industrial complex of several plants built at different times. As long as the total emissions from the complex did not exceed total emissions standards, all plants in it were considered to be in compliance. One old plant might well exceed the standards for its type of facility if measured by individual smokestack. But because it was averaged into the newer, cleaner units, it also met standards. Many old plants thus avoided being retrofitted with pollution controls, but this action was generally accepted by the EPA and upheld by the courts.

After the 1977 amendments to the CAA, during the Carter administration, however, the EPA established a rule preventing plants in nonattainment areas (not yet meeting ambient air quality standards) from using the bubble concept. Later in the Reagan administration the EPA changed its regulations again to permit bubbles to be used everywhere. The NRDC sued Chevron U.S.A. Inc. for using a bubble in calculating its emissions from one oil refinery, and the Circuit Court of Appeals for the D.C. Circuit agreed with the NRDC. On appeal to the U.S. Supreme Court in *Chevron, U.S.A., Inc. v. NRDC* (1984), the Court agreed with both industry and the EPA. Bubbles can be used in attainment and nonattainment areas alike. Thus, the bubble concept received the full approval of the Court, and the EPA was freed to make new interpretations of what constitutes one source of pollution. As Justice Stevens expressed it, when Congress does make clear its intent concerning an issue, courts should not insert their policy preferences, but should defer to the administrative agency responsible if its interpretation is a viable one under the law. This deference to the executive branch has not always been honored by the courts; it very much depends on which litigant the decision favors.

Plants discharging effluents into waterways made the same two kinds of arguments that sources of air pollution did: that the technology was not feasible and that the costs were too burdensome. The meat industry's trade association sued the EPA in *American Meat Institute v. EPA* (1975). The EPA had drafted standards for meat-packing plants in 1973 and opened the process to comments by both industry and environmental groups. After considering these, the EPA based its standards on the best existing performances by meat-packing plants throughout the industry. These were essentially secondary treatments using bacteria in lagoons to consume the organic waste matter. Industry argued this type of treatment would not have the desired effect. The court accepted the EPA's standards as reasonable under the language of the Clean Water Act. Best Practicable Control Technology (BPCT) was defined as secondary treatment, due to be in place in all meat-packing plants by 1977. This decision was rendered in 1975 and led to an extension of the deadline. Once again, even though industry did not achieve its desired goal of having the standards struck down, the length of time it took to adjudicate the cases through the courts gave it breathing space and saved it millions of dollars in costs it avoided for several years. Of course, in these kinds of disputes it is also noteworthy that if industry had prevailed against the EPA's position it would have gained even greater benefits, and society would have borne even greater costs.

The chemical industry added the argument that the EPA should provide a different effluent standard for each plant, rather than a uniform rule for the whole industry (*E.I. du Pont de Nemours Co. v. Train* (1977)). DuPont argued that when the receiving waters for the effluent are abundant, the standards for cleaning up should not be severe. It denied that the CWA empowered EPA to set industrywide limits; instead each plant's permit should have its own individual effluent limits. This was despite the fact that the clear language of the law stated that no polluting effluent should be discharged into American waterways after

1985, and the interim standards should be in effect by 1977. The Supreme Court, however, agreed with the EPA's reading of the law. In doing so, the Court recognized the difficult burden it would place on the technical capacity of the EPA to set individual standards for every plant. A Best Practicable Treatment (BPT) standard was, therefore, to be established for each polluting industry, taking into consideration the costs to the industry of applying the controls.

Despite this Supreme Court decision in 1977, other industries continued to challenge the EPA's authority to set effluent limits for them. In 1978, the Appellate Court for the District of Columbia ruled that the paper industry was not entitled to avoid treatment simply because several plants emptied into the spacious Pacific Ocean (*Weyerhaeuser v. Costle* (1978)). In so doing, the court ruled that the EPA did have to take into consideration the costs of compliance and the benefits to be obtained from the standards as well as other factors such as the plant's age. However, it did not have to demonstrate that benefits balanced out costs.

Other industries did not give up on their suits, and each time the EPA issued a new standard it was sued by business interests such as the organic chemical, plastics, and synthetic fibers industries, among others. In 1990 the Ninth Circuit Court of Appeals upheld the placer or dredge mining standards (for mining gold in water, such as a gravel bed in a stream) in *Rybacek v. Alaska Miners Association* (1990). These suits consumed so much time and resources that long after the 1977 deadline for industry to be in compliance, and well after there was supposed to be "no discharge," the EPA was still formulating interim limits.

More recently, in 2000, industry challenged the EPA's authority to amend ambient air standards designed to preserve human health. They are necessary for setting emissions standards, because the condition of the surrounding air is dependent on what is emitted into it. During the second Clinton administration, a successful lawsuit, *American Lung Association v. EPA* (1998), forced the EPA administrator, Carol Browner, to amend the ozone and particulate matter National Ambient Air Quality (NAAQS) standards to mandate cleaner air for the nation than those set in the 1970s. The American trucking industry immediately challenged the EPA's authority to take this action (*Whitman, Administrator of EPA, et al. v. American Trucking Associations, Inc.* (2001)). (By the time the decision was rendered, the Bush administration had replaced Carol

Browner, and the new appointee Christie Whitman's name appears on it.)

The trucking industry argued that the EPA had not taken costs into consideration when it changed the standards. The Court of Appeals for the D.C. Circuit found an unconstitutional delegation of legislative authority to the EPA in the law that allowed the EPA to adjust the standards every five years. This decision ignored the *Chevron* precedent (discussed earlier), deferring to Congress and the executive branch. However, the U.S. Supreme Court overturned and remanded. Although the justices disagreed about the grounds on which they ruled, they all agreed that the Clean Air Act did not illegally delegate legislative authority to the EPA. While the Clean Air Act required the EPA to consider costs in making emissions standards, it was not so constrained when setting standards for the ambient air needed to preserve the health of Americans. Regardless of the fact that 1990 NAAQS had not yet been attained, it was permissible for the EPA to revise the then-existing standards. This decision, by a unanimous court, followed the *Chevron* precedent, giving the benefit of the doubt to the EPA. However, the court did remand the EPA's implementation plan back to the lower courts, and the EPA had to clarify the stages in which these standards were to be met.

Pollution control cases have sometimes been complicated by the question of how power should be divided between state and federal governments. In *Alaska Department of Environmental Conservation v. EPA* (2004), Alaska issued permits for Teck Cominco Alaska to build additional capacity at its zinc mine, despite the fact that it would degrade the air below national ambient air standards. In so doing Alaska rewrote Cominco's permit to allow it to use a process that reduced the pollutants by only 30 percent, even though a process was available that could remove 90 percent of the pollutants. Alaska redefined Best Practicable Control Technology for diesel engines by simply accepting Cominco's statement that they found the stricter standard not feasible. The EPA objected, and when the case reached the Supreme Court it again followed *Chevron* and deferred to the EPA. As in the trucking case the decision went against industry, for the majority argued that Congress had authority to delegate this discretion to the EPA. However, four conservative justices dissented, arguing that the majority was interfering with the states' rights to control use of land. This time the vote on the court was split along ideological lines, with four conservatives—Chief Justice Rehnquist and Associate Justices Scalia, Thomas, and Kennedy—dissenting in favor of industry.

Still, some federalism cases involve states that regulate more stringently than the federal government. As noted above with respect to *Engine Manufacturers Association et al. v. South Coast of Air Quality Management District* (2004), the automobile industry challenged California's right to forbid the purchase by local governments of cars not meeting California's clean-fuel requirement. Overturning the ruling of the Ninth Circuit, the Supreme Court preferred the national government's preemption of state regulations. Thus, a state's attempt to go beyond federal protection of its area was struck down by a court that claims to defend states' rights against federal power.

A similar case that illustrates the way the U.S. Supreme Court treats federalism cases when states try to be more severe occurred in 2000. It came about in response to the largest oil spill in American history by the *Exxon Valdez* in Alaska. After that 1989 disaster the state of Washington passed new restrictive laws against oil tankers coming into its waters. A case was brought by an international consortium of oil-tanker owners (*U.S. v. International Association of Independent Tanker Owners (Intertanko)* (2000)) objecting to state regulation of tankers in its waterways, claiming federal laws had preempted it. The Supreme Court agreed with the tanker industry, and the Justice Department that intervened for industry, that federal law preempted any stricter state standards. This decision followed the precedent set by *Ray v. Atlantic Richfield Co.* (1978) that international treaties and national laws must override any state attempts to control the size and design of tankers entering state waters and the training of personnel on board. The only part of the law allowed to stand was the provision for the recovery of damages to Washington.

By 2005 another major case involving a state trying to exceed federal standards (where business groups were actively opposed) concerned greenhouse gas emissions. In September 2004, the California Air Resources Board approved far-reaching regulations to limit emissions of greenhouse gases by automobiles beginning with the 2009 model year. The regulations were to take effect on January 1, 2006. What the board called a "landmark decision" set California on a collision course with the federal government and the automobile industry. The Bush administration announced that it would side with industry in challenging the California regulations. It argued that the regulations were at odds with exclusive federal power to regulate automobile fuel efficiency. California officials countered that they were regulating carbon dioxide as a pollutant under the Clean Air Act and not automobile fuel efficiency itself even though the chief effect of the regulations would be to promote greater fuel efficiency. In December 2004, the Alliance of Automobile Manufacturers announced a suit against the state, and it was joined by the Association of International Automobile Manufacturers. The case almost certainly will become one of the latest tests of how federal-state relations in environmental policy will be redefined at a time when the states are moving ahead boldly to set the pace for environmental protection (Rabe 2006).

Later still, in 2006, ten states joined forces to sue the EPA over the issue of global warming. These were New York, California, Connecticut, Maine, Massachusetts, New Mexico, Oregon, Rhode Island, Vermont, and Wisconsin. They argued that the federal government should require tighter pollution controls on the newest generation of power plants. Joined by numerous environmental groups and New York City and Washington D.C., they filed in the U.S. Court of Appeals in the District of Columbia, which had already ruled in 2005 that states could not force the EPA to regulate carbon dioxide emissions from cars and trucks in order to reduce global warming (Truthout 2006).

In summary, industry has increased its lawsuits against governmental pollution control laws from the 1970s into the twenty-first century by adopting a preemptive-strike strategy. It has attacked most regulatory standards as excessive and too costly whether developed by the EPA or state governments. Often, its objectives have been balanced by counter-complaints made by environmental groups. Industry must divide its litigation between state and federal courts according to the laws being challenged. However, within the federal system there is some choice, and when possible, business has taken its complaints to the most sympathetic circuits in the federal system. Its choice of the D.C. Circuit has increased as the personnel on that court have become more pro-business (Mooney 2003). Although overall government wins more cases than it loses in federal court, industry has succeeded in many of its cases. In others it has delayed the inevitable, with considerable savings in time and money.

What is lost in one area of public policy may be regained in another. An area in which industry is even more active in lobbying Congress and appealing to the courts concerns the U.S. tax code. The rules regarding what business may consider a cost of doing business and therefore a legitimate tax deduction change often, but the interpretation industry favors argues that any fine imposed by state or federal government is a business expense, and hence deductible. (See U.S. Code, title 26, subtitle A, chapter 1, subchapter B, part VI, section 168). The general assumption on which laws are based is that a penalty imposed for breaking the law will have an inhibiting effect on the wrong-doer and others considering the same action. If, however, the burden of such action falls not on the perpetrator, but on the taxpayer because of lost revenue, then such a fine may lose its effectiveness. Moreover, much environmental litigation ends in negotiated settlements between the government and industry, in which the latter agrees to remedy the situation by installing pollution control devices or cleaning up a contaminated site. The tax code is clear on this: all expenses from environmental remediation costs are tax deductible. (U.S. Code, title 26, subtitle A, chapter 1, subchapter B, part VI, section 198).

Despite these clear tax advantages to industry, it continues to resist vehemently any government suits initiated against it. It has enjoyed great success in this endeavor in the Bush administration, as is evident from the letter of resignation from Eric V. Schaeffer, former director of the EPA's Office of Regulatory Enforcement:

It is no longer possible to pretend that the ongoing debate with the White House and Department of Energy is not effecting(sic) our ability to negotiate settlements. Cinergy and Vepco have refused to sign the consent decrees they agreed to 15 months ago, hedging their bets while waiting for the Administration's Clean Air Act reform proposals. Other companies with whom we were close to settlement have walked away from the table. The momentum we obtained with agreements we announced earlier has stopped, and we have filed no new lawsuits against utility companies since this Administration took office. We obviously cannot settle cases with defendants who think we are still rewriting the law (Schaeffer 2002).

Industry's eagerness to go to court has waxed and waned with the administration in power. When a vigorous EPA took actions to tighten standards during the Carter and Clinton administrations, business initiated an ever-growing portfolio of cases. During the Reagan years and the two Bush administrations, industry could relax its vigilance and file fewer cases, because its influence with the executive branch of government was greater. After the reelection of George W. Bush in 2004, it seemed less likely that industry would need to use its litigation option. Even when industry is well treated by Congress and the executive branch, businesses may nevertheless decide to go to court to improve their situation because the Bush administration has appointed so many radically probusiness judges. It has been amply demonstrated that Republican judges are more sympathetic to industry's pleadings than are Democratic judges (Ackerman 2001; Eilperin 2004).

Regulatory Takings of Private Property

Business interests have shown their clout in federal and state courts even more dramatically on the subject of property rights. Among other rights, the Fifth Amendment of the U.S. Constitution prohibits government from "taking private property for public use without just compensation." Originally directed at the federal government, the same protection was later extended to apply to actions of state and city governments through the Fourteenth Amendment. During the nineteenth century, the courts interpreted this law to apply to government seizing private property to use for public purposes, such as building roads. Under the rule of eminent domain, the authorities must buy the land from the landowner at the market price before converting it to public use. However, in the twentieth century, business interests succeeded in extending this provision to strike down government laws regulating the purposes to which landowners could put their private property on the theory that government was depriving the owner of use of his or her land.

Industry's first successful use of the Fifth Amendment to protect private uses of land came in *Pennsylvania Coal Company v. Mahon* (1922). A state law, the Kohler Act mandated that coal companies should not mine underground coal to cause the collapse of the surface land on which towns and farmers' fields stood. This pitted private landholders against Pennsylvania Coal, which claimed that it had the right to extract all coal under the land because the company legally owned the mineral rights to it. Justice Oliver Wendell Holmes wrote the decision for the U.S. Supreme Court, striking down the Kohler Act and agreeing with the coal company that this regulation took its property without just compensation. Thus was created the concept of "regulatory taking" to supplement the principle that government could not physically take over private property without paying for it.

Sixty-five years later, a majority of the Supreme Court in *Keystone Bituminous Coal Association v. De Benedictis* (1987) revised this ruling. It upheld as constitutional a new Pennsylvania subsidence law requiring that coal miners leave a substantial amount of coal underground to prevent the subsidence of the surface land where homes, towns, and farms are located. Writing for the majority, Justice Stevens claimed he was not overturning *Pennsylvania v. Mahon*, but simply redressing the balance between the public need to protect surface rights and the owner of mineral rights. Chief Justice Rehnquist wrote a strong dissent for the court minority, arguing there is no essential difference between physical taking and regulatory taking of property by government.

Even before the second Pennsylvania coal case, however, *Penn Central Transportation Co. v. New York* (1978) was decided for government. New York had passed a historic-preservation ordinance and designated Penn Central Station a landmark when the Penn Central Corporation proposed building a multistory office building above the station. In this case, the Supreme Court agreed with New York that the public interest in maintaining the original appearance of the station outweighed any economic damage to the company. The law did not deprive the company of all economic use of the land, and its development rights could be transferred to other land in the vicinity.

Since the Penn Central case and the second coal case, the real estate industry has prevailed in several important cases expanding the concept of regulatory taking. New justices appointed by Presidents Reagan and the first George Bush agreed with Justice Rehnquist's dissent in *Keystone* and have expanded property owners' rights to do as they wish with their private property.

In California a couple named Nollan who owned a beachfront lot near a public beach decided to build a house on their land. The California Coastal Commission, charged with keeping public access to the beach, agreed to issue a building permit under the proviso that the Nollans provide an easement for the public to reach the beach from the road. Justice Scalia ruled that this provision constituted a "taking" of the Nollans' property without compensation (*Nollan v. California Coastal Commission* (1987)). If the state wanted to continue public access it would have to buy the easement, just as all public bodies that wish to acquire private land do under eminent domain law. He argued that the public good (access to the beach) could not be directly tied to the easement on the Nollans' property because the public had other access points. Two associate justices objected, saying there was an obvious connection between getting people onto the public beach and the easement, but they did not prevail.

Other private-property owners, developers, and the real estate industry itself lost no time in applying the new ruling to additional city and state land-use regulations to which they objected. In 1988 the South Carolina Legislature enacted a beachfront management law that prohibited owners from building on areas deemed too fragile to sustain more development. David Lucas—who proposed to build two family homes on his parcel of land—argued that the state was now depriving him of all economic use of his property, and the Supreme Court agreed. A new rule was created whereby land-use regulations could be struck down if the law does not advance the public interest or if it denies the owner all economically viable use of his or her land, as in this case where the state denied Lucas the right to build any house on his land (*Lucas v. South Carolina Coastal Council* (1992)). The dissenters argued in vain that a public need was served—conserving beach land to prevent erosion of land on which buildings already stood. The majority of the Court argued that the only way the state could stop Lucas from building there was to purchase the land or prove that the property owner was creating a public nuisance. Amenities for the public are not enough to constitute the public interest. The liberal minority dissenting argued that there is a broader base for public interest in land-use control than simply preventing nuisances. Mr. Lucas won the case and the state of South Carolina eventually purchased the land from him.

In 1994 the Supreme Court decided in the case of *Dolan v. Tigard* (1994) that an Oregon town could not require a hardware store owner to devote part of her land to a greenway with a bicycle/pedestrian path before it would issue a building permit to expand the business. Tigard argued there was a public interest in preventing flooding from the additional paved area. The court found for the business despite acknowledging the benefit the greenway would have for the community. Chief Justice Rehnquist's majority decision added a new requirement for such benefits: the public good must be "roughly proportionate" to the harm done to the landowner. He found for the store owner on both counts. There was no clear connection between the easement the city wanted and the proposed addition to the store. Further, there was no proportional relationship between the greenway's benefit to the public and the burden it would place on the business for allowing a public path on its property. Dissenting justices argued that the majority was raising the bar higher and higher for local and state governments to control land uses for the public good.

Rhode Island, like California and South Carolina, established regulations designed to preserve as much of the wetlands between the ocean and land as possible. The state refused to issue a permit to develop seventy-four units to Mr. Palazzolo. The state defended its actions on the theory that it had not deprived the landowners of all economic use, because they could still develop the upland part of the property. Also, the wetland regulation was law before Palazzolo acquired the land. The Rhode Island Supreme Court found the state laws and action legal. The U.S. Supreme Court overturned the state supreme court, saying that it did not matter that Palazzolo had acquired his title after the law was passed. He still had a right to a reasonable expectation of increased value to his land (*Palazzolo v. Rhode Island* (2001)).

In *Tahoe-Sierra Preservation Council et al. v. Tahoe Regional Planning Agency* (2002), the planning commission had put a moratorium on building permits in order to devise a method to clean up Lake Tahoe. Developers sued, and the district court agreed they were deprived of all economic use of land for a lengthy period of time. But the Ninth Circuit overturned, saying they had gotten their property rights back. The U.S. Supreme Court upheld the Ninth, arguing that if cities/states had to compensate every property owner for every temporary delay in development permits, the planning process would be compromised. The Chief Justice and two other associates dissented, arguing this deprived developers of all use of their land for six years. Temporary taking, they claimed, is just as bad as permanent because the loss of profit may be just as high. While they recognized preserving Lake Tahoe's quality as a public amenity, they believed the cost of doing so should be borne by the taxpayer, not the individual property owner.

Business interests have used the takings doctrine to defend their property against federal as well as state regulations. The Clean Water Act made the U.S. Army Corps of Engineers responsible for issuing permits to dredge, fill, and construct on wetlands—once considered a total nuisance, but now valued as an ecological amenity helpful in cleaning up waterways and providing a barrier against hurricanes and other storms. Generally, property owners have argued that they should be allowed to make the "highest and best use" of their land—that being the most profitable, which requires development and building.

A consortium of waste haulers and disposers in Cook County proposed to make an abandoned sand and gravel pit into a solid-waste disposal site. The Army Corps of Engineers would not give them a permit to fill a wetland. The court found that allowing a federal agency to preempt traditional state and local government's control over local land and water use was not constitutional. The majority of the court said there was no evidence that Congress intended the U.S. Army Corps' power to extend to abandoned quarries. Four justices dissented, arguing that the "migratory bird rule" applied. Traditionally, the Corps was given authority to control permits in wetlands quite distant from other waterways in order to keep the flyways open to migrating birds that need resting places on their journey (*Solid Waste Agency of Northern Cook County v. Army Department* (2001)).

Another court that has been quite responsive to industrial claims to compensation for regulatory takings is the U.S. Court of Claims. It decides cases in which litigants claim they are owed compensation from the federal government for a harm that has been done them. Two cases decided in 1990 are illustrative of the types of environmental cases decided there. Both concerned the refusal of the Corps of Engineers to issue a permit to use wetland areas in a manner that the Corps believed would contaminate aquifers (Epstein 1990).

Florida Rock was denied a permit to quarry limestone on ninety-eight acres. The company actually owned much more land and had already quarried a great deal of limestone. The judge in the trial court, however, held that he would consider only the remaining ninety-eight acres despite the Corps' claim that mining there would pollute an aquifer. In these cases the court had to consider several variables. How much was the land originally worth? How much is it now worth after having a permit refusal? Are there other uses of the property that the owner could sell it for? Government and owners differed widely on their estimates of the land's actual value. Ultimately, the trial judge took the landowner's estimate of the worth of the property after the refusal of the permit and refused the Army's higher estimate of what the land could be sold for.

In *Loveladies Harbor, Inc. v. United States* (1990), a developer wished to fill 12.5 acres for residential use. He had already developed most of the area. The Corps refused to issue a permit, and argued that the court should consider the total value the developer had already gotten from the much larger parcel of land. However, the court focused on the 12.5 acres and agreed with the owner's evaluation of the property.

In both these cases the court accepted the pleadings of the plaintiffs that the public harm that might be prevented (water pollution) was not sufficient to balance the loss to the property owner, despite the CWA that gives responsibility for preserving wetlands to the Corps. This is typical of the kinds of cases the Court of Claims has adjudicated since *Lucas*, in which practically the only way to regulate land use successfully without having to pay compensation is to prevent a public nuisance on the property. The court appears to place most importance on the expectation of gain that the owner had when he or she purchased the land. This doctrine prevails despite the fact that in the intervening years, the Clean Water Act was amended to protect wetlands.

In all these cases judges are asked to weigh the monetary loss to the landowner against public amenities like green space and access to beaches, all of which appear relatively unimportant. When actual harm to the larger community from polluted water, loss of wetlands, and traffic congestion can be shown, more consideration is given the government's arguments. But it is rare when these difficult-to-measure losses outweigh the cost to the landowner. It appears that we are getting closer to Justice Scalia's belief that only a public nuisance is not worth compensation. Perhaps because of the increasing pro-business posture of the Supreme Court and lower federal courts, business interests have become bolder in making demands about property protection. The burden of proof to the government agencies to show that they have a legitimate need to zone and control private uses of land has become so severe as to have a chilling effect on their regulatory activities.

Another federal law that pits the interests of landowners against amenities for the public is the Endangered Species Act of 1973. Its broad language forbids the harming of endangered or threatened species on both public and private land. The Fish and Wildlife Service of the Interior Department, which has responsibility for administering the policy, has interpreted the term *harm* to include not just the deliberate killing or capturing of wildlife, but also the degradation of its habitat to the point of extinction. One of the industries hardest hit by this law is the timber industry, which has been prevented from harvesting wood in certain areas, such as the Northwest's old-growth forests where the northern spotted owl and the red-cockaded woodpecker live. The timber industry as well as other landowners have objected strenuously to this incursion into their discretion about use of land, and it has been the subject of several lawsuits.

One example is *Babbitt v. Sweet Home Chapter of Communities for a Great Oregon* (1995). In this case a number of small landowners and others dependent on the logging industry in the Northwest brought suit to argue that the Fish and Wildlife Service had interpreted the statute too broadly. As in other land-use cases, they argued that if the government wished to ban logging on their land it would have to buy it. The case came before the D.C. Circuit Court of Appeals, because the landowners shunned the more pro-environmental Ninth Circuit where the dispute took place. Although the landowners won in the lower court, the Supreme Court found that the word *harm* could be used to include the reduction in habitat. The Interior Department had the authority to make the broad interpretation it did. There were three adamant dissenters—Rehnquist, Thomas, and Scalia—who are the hardcore defenders of business interests on the Court.

Land-use law is complicated by the federalism issue just as pollution control law is. Industry argues one of two ways in these cases. One is that the states have exceeded their authority when they try to impose higher standards on business than the federal government has, as in the *Engine Manufacturers Association* case. However, when the tables are turned and the state is on industry's side, business interests do not hesitate to argue that states' rights should rule the day. Courts have varied in their decisions about these federalism cases, but at present the regulatory taking of private property is viewed as an important legal doctrine. As the balance on the Supreme Court and other federal courts continues its shift to the right, it is likely to become even more important. We have already seen how a former conservative minority has changed the definition of "regulatory takings" to be the dominant view on the court. Regulators at both the state and federal levels now struggle to identify what land uses are controllable for the public interest.

Conclusions

As noted early in the chapter, data limitations and methodological challenges make it difficult to quantify industry's use of the courts and the degree of success it has enjoyed with environmental cases. However, it is clear that industry's use of the courts has increased over time in both pollution control and land-use cases—at least at the level of the U.S. Supreme Court. Land-use law has a longer history, with some cases dating back to the early twentieth century, whereas pollution cases for the most part began only in the 1970s. That the business litigants have found some satisfaction from the courts is demonstrated by their increasing use of the courts even today. It would be useful to have more systematic studies using the large datasets that are now available to determine patterns at the trial and middle appellate level as well as at the level of state courts. Such research could focus on some of the key questions set out in chapter 1, such as how frequently industry chooses to intervene in the courts and its record of success, and the variation in its intervention and success across different courts and issue areas.

To put the role of the courts into perspective, it should be noted that while the legislative and executive branches of government are subject to frequent changes of personnel and consequently changes in attitudes, courts are not so constrained by public opinion. Because federal judges have life tenure and most state judges are traditionally returned to office, their public policy judgments may be less mutable and more long-lasting. While there is less reason for business to use its legal option when there is a solidly conservative Republican administration in office, it is also true that the federal bench is quite favorably disposed to business arguments and is likely to grow more so in the next few years.

Business interests, like others, are eager to influence the selection of new judges. Given the George W. Bush administration's propensity to listen to business positions on other matters, industry's opinions about judicial nominees are given very serious consideration (Sunstein 2003). Beyond merely influencing the original selection of nominees, industry also undertakes efforts to try to influence congressional action on a president's nominees. For example, in 2005, the Sierra Club charged that the National Association of Manufacturers "launched a multi-million dollar campaign to boost the president's picks—seven of whom were rejected last term as too extreme." Among those rejected by the Senate in 2004 but considered again in 2005 was William Myers III, a longtime lobbyist for the coal and cattle industries, whom the *New York Times* called "an antienvironmental extremist" (Scherer 2005).

This conflict within Congress came to a head in July 2005, when Associate Justice Sandra Day O'Connor announced her retirement from the Court (Toner 2005; Singer and Caruso 2005), and later with Chief Justice William Rehnquist's sudden death. John Roberts, nominated by President Bush to replace Chief Justice Rehnquist, was quickly approved by the U.S. Senate. Given his impeccable intellectual and pro-business credentials it was widely expected that Chief Justice Roberts would simply duplicate Rehnquist's vote, which was normally cast in opposition to those few cases that environmental groups won in the Supreme Court.

The replacement of Justice O'Connor, however, followed a more complicated path. Widely viewed as the swing vote on a closely divided Court (Rosen 2001), O'Connor's announcement led Senate Democrats to promise a more difficult confirmation process if the president nominated someone they considered too conservative (Hulse 2005). Bush first made an abortive effort to obtain Senate confirmation for his White House counsel, Harriet Miers, which was thwarted by the right wing of the Republican Party because they were unsure of her stand on abortion. After that failure, the White House nominated Judge Samuel A. Alito, a man with an impeccable record of conservative leanings as both a federal appellate court judge and a Justice Department attorney. Although twenty-five Democratic Senators made an effort to filibuster the nomination, Justice Alito was confirmed with almost a straight partisan vote, with only one Republican defection while four Democratic Senators voted for confirmation (Kirkpatrick 2006).

President George W. Bush's appointments to federal courts have moved the courts noticeably to the right, not only regarding social issues, but also regulation of business. The confirmations of his two nominees to the Supreme Court in 2006 are sure to give an added boost to industry's interests there. The solid probusiness coalition on the Supreme Court now numbers four instead of three: Antonin Scalia, Clarence Thomas, John Roberts, and Samuel Alito. They need only one vote from the remainder of the court to constitute the majority in a split vote. Anthony Kennedy is the justice who will most likely be the deciding vote. Ruth Ginsburg, David Sutter, and John Paul Stevens generally favor regulation of environmental problems. With easy access to the Justice Department, business will continue to be instrumental in the selection of federal judges at all levels. Combined with the Senate Democrats' seeming inability to stem the tide of conservative appointments, this trend guarantees that the federal courts will continue to be a bulwark for business interests for the foreseeable future.

References

Ackerman, Bruce. 2001. "Foil Bush's Maneuvers for Packing the Court." *Los Angeles Times*, April 26, 12.

Andrews, Richard N. L. 2006. "Risk-Based Decision Making: Policy, Science, and Politics." In Norman J. Vig and Michael E. Kraft, eds., *Environmental Policy*, 6th ed. Washington, DC: CQ Press.

Confessore, Nicholas. 2001. "Should Bush Shape the Bench?" *The American Prospect*, www.prospect.org/2001/04/28.

Eilperin, Juliet. 2004. "Environmental Group Cites Partisanship in the Judiciary." *Washington Post*, October 9, section A, 2.

Epstein, Lee R. 1990. "Takings and Wetlands in the Claims Court: *Florida Rock* and *Loveladies Harbor*." *Environmental Law Reporter* 20:10517–10521.

Findley, Roger, and Daniel A. Farber. 1999. *Cases and Materials on Environmental Law*. 5th ed. St. Paul, MN: West.

Hulse, Carl. 2005. "Amid Vows of Opposition, Senate Braces for Disarray." *New York Times*, July 2, A12.

Kirkpatrick, David D. 2006. "Final Senate Vote on Alito Is Scheduled for This Morning," www.nytimes.com/2006/01/31.

Kraft, Michael E. 2006. "Environmental Policy in Congress." In Norman J. Vig and Michael E. Kraft, eds., *Environmental Policy*, 6th ed. Washington, DC: CQ Press.

Mooney, Chris. 2003. "Circuit Breaker." *The American Prospect* (spring): A14–A15.

O'Leary, Rosemary. 1993. *Environmental Change: Federal Courts and the EPA*. Philadelphia: Temple University Press.

Plater, Zygmunt J. B., Robert H. Abrams, and William Goldfarb. 1998. *Environmental Law and Policy: Nature, Law, and Society*. 2nd ed. St. Paul, MN: West.

Pritchett, C. Herman. 1948. *The Roosevelt Court*. New York: Macmillan.

Rabe, Barry G. 2006. "Power to the States: The Promise and Pitfalls of Decentralization." In Norman J. Vig and Michael E. Kraft, eds., *Environmental Policy*, 6th ed. Washington, DC: CQ Press.

Ringquist, Evan J., and Craig E. Emmert. 1999. "Judicial Policymaking in Published and Unpublished Decisions: The Case of Environmental Civil Litigation." *Political Research Quarterly* 52 (1) (March): 7–37.

Rosen, Jeffrey. 2001. "The O'Connor Court: America's Most Powerful Jurist." *New York Times Magazine*, June 3, Section 6, 2.

Rowland, C. K, and R. A. Carp. 1996. *Politics and Judgment in the Federal District Courts*. Lawrence: University Press of Kansas.

Schaeffer, Eric V. 2002. "EPA Regulator Quits in Disgust," www.Counterpunch .org/2002/3/3.

Scherer, Glenn. 2005. "Full Court Mess: Bush Tries to Stack the Bench with Industry-Friendly Judges." *Sierra*, May-June, 13.

Schubert, Glendon. 1965. *The Judicial Mind*. Evanston, IL: Northwestern University Press.

Segal, Jeffrey, and Harold Spaeth. 1993. *The Supreme Court and the Attitudinal Model*. Cambridge: Cambridge University Press.

Singer, Paul, and Lisa Caruso. 2005. "The Battle Is Joined." *National Journal*, July 9, 2192–2196.

Smith, Joseph L. 2005. "Congress Opens the Courthouse Doors: Statutory Changes to Judicial Review under the Clean Air Act." *Political Research Quarterly* 58 (March): 139–149.

Songer, Donald. 2000. *U.S. Courts of Appeals Database (1925–1996)*. www.cas.sc.edu/poli/facbio/Songer.html.

Spaeth, Harold J. 2000. *United States Supreme Court Judicial Database: 1953–1996 Terms*. San Diego: Social Sciences Collection, University of California, San Diego. http://ssdc.ucsd.edu/ssdc/icp09422.html.

Sunstein, Cass. 2003. "The Right-Wing Assault." *The American Prospect* (spring): A2–A4.

Talbot, Margaret. 2005. "Supreme Confidence: The Jurisprudence of Justice Antonin Scalia." *New Yorker*, March 28, 38–55.

Toner, Robin. 2005. "After a Brief Shock, Advocates Quickly Mobilize." *New York Times*, July 2, A13.

Truthout. 2006. "Ten States Sue EPA Over Global Warming," www.truthout. org/2006/04/28.

U.S. Code, Annotated. 2005, Title 26, Subtitle A, Ch. 1, Subchapter B, Part VI, Section 168, and Section 198.

Wenner, Lettie McSpadden. 1982. *The Environmental Decade in Court.* Bloomington: Indiana University Press.

Wenner, Lettie McSpadden. 1984. "Judicial Oversight of Environmental Deregulation." In Norman J. Vig and Michael E. Kraft, eds., *Environmental Policy in the 1980s: Reagan's New Agenda.* Washington, DC: CQ Press.

Court Cases Cited

Alaska Department of Environmental Conservation v. EPA (540 U.S. 46, Supreme Court, 2004).

American Lung Association v. EPA (34 F. 3d 388, D.C. Circuit, 1998).

American Meat Institute v. EPA (526 F. 2d 442, Seventh Circuit, 1975).

Babbitt v. Sweet Home Chapter of Communities for a Great Oregon 515 U.S. 687, Supreme Court, 1995.

California v. Bergland, 483 F. Supp. 492, Ninth Circuit, (1980).

California v. Bergland, 690 F. 2d 760, Ninth Circuit, (1982).

Chevron, U.S.A., Inc. v. NRDC (467 U.S. 837, Supreme Court, 1984).

Dolan v. Tigard (512 U.S. 374, Supreme Court, 1994).

E.I. du Pont de Nemours Co. v. Train (430 U.S. 112, Supreme Court, 1977).

Engine Manufacturers Association et al. v. South Coast Air Quality Management District (541 U.S. 246, Supreme Court, 2004).

Florida Rock Industries v. United States (21 Cl Ct. 161, 1990).

International Harvester Co. v. Ruckelshaus (478 F2d 615, D.C. Circuit, 1973).

Keystone Bituminous Coal Association v. De Benedictis (480 U.S. 47, Supreme Court, 1987).

Loveladies Harbor, Inc. v. United States (21 Cl. Ct. 153, 1990).

Lucas v. South Carolina Coastal Council (505 U.S. 1003, Supreme Court, 1992).

Marbury v. Madison (5 U.S. 137, Supreme Court, 1803).

Nollan v. California Coastal Commission (483 U.S. 825, Supreme Court, 1987).

Palazzolo v. Rhode Island (533 U.S. 606, Supreme Court, 2001).

Penn Central Transportation Co. v. New York (438 U.S. 104, Supreme Court, 1978).

Pennsylvania Coal Company v. Mahon (260 U.S. 393, Supreme Court, 1922).

Portland Cement Co. v. Ruckelshaus (486 F2d 375, D.C. Circuit, 1973).

Ray v. Atlantic Richfield Co. (435 U.S. 151, Supreme Court, 1978).

Rybacek v. Alaska Miners Association (904 F2d 1276, Ninth Circuit, 1990).

Solid Waste Agency of Northern Cook County v. Army Department (531 U.S. 159, Supreme Court, 2001).

Tahoe-Sierra Preservation Council et al. v. Tahoe Regional Planning Agency (535 U.S. 302, Supreme Court, 2002).

U.S. v. International Association of Independent Tanker Owners (Intertanko) (529 U.S. 89, Supreme Court, 2000).

Weyerhaeuser v. Costle (590 F 2d, 1001 D.C. Circuit, 1978).

Whitman, Administrator of EPA, et al. v. American Trucking Associations, Inc. (531 U.S. 457, Supreme Court, 2001).

VI
Policymaking at the State and Local Level

10

Business Influence in State-Level Environmental Policy

Barry G. Rabe and Philip A. Mundo

The playing field for enacting and implementing environmental policy at the state government level might well be expected to be tilted sharply in favor of business and industrial interests. States need to be attentive to economic development concerns—that is, sensitive to their competitiveness with other states and nations. They may well be reluctant to take any regulatory actions that might deter sustained or expanded private investment. Any state inclination to pursue significant environmental policy initiatives may face considerable organized opposition. For every legislator serving in one of the fifty statehouses in 2000, there was an average of five lobbying groups representing business and industry influence that had set up shop in a state capital (Renzulli 2002; Teske 2004). Surveys of the "most influential interests" in the fifty states have deemed groups representing manufacturing, business, and electricity generation firms to be extremely powerful, regularly eclipsing organizations devoted to environmental protection (Thomas and Hrebenar 1999).

Consequently, business is likely to be highly active and potentially influential in a wide range of environmental policy decisions taken in state capitals. Individual states vary enormously, reflecting divergence in physical and population size, institutional structures for governance, and political culture. But none are likely to be immune to the pressures of business to tailor environmental policies in ways that they prefer. Indeed, as we will see, many dynamics emerge in settings such as Sacramento and Springfield that are quite comparable to those outlined in the introductory chapter for Washington, D.C., and the federal government. In both settings, business is regularly visible and influential in policy enactment and implementation and employs a range of strategies to shape outcomes. But, consistent with the general findings of this book, business is neither equally influential on all issues nor able to speak with a unified voice in many matters.

Mindful of these overlapping themes, this chapter examines some of the most important dynamics of state-based environmental policymaking, with significant attention to factors driving the rapid expansion and diversification of state policies designed to reduce greenhouse gases. It explores the challenges facing businesses that operate with state governments in a federal system of government, in which either environmental contaminants or the cost of reducing them can potentially be shifted to other jurisdictions. This leads to the distinct possibility that very different configurations of organized interests emerge as influential in various states. This chapter considers alternative possibilities for business influence—or lack thereof—in varied contexts, following a broader introduction to the evolving role of state governments in environmental policy.

States in the American Political Economy

A consistent theme in this analysis is that state government leaders and institutions act essentially in rational ways, advancing their own political and professional interests as well as those of their respective state as they discern them. This leads us to depart from more traditional depictions that assume that state environmental policy decisions are routinely dominated by business and industry. Instead, we note that states may often take actions that are either partially or substantially contrary to the views of some home-based businesses or industries, but that they do so, at least in part, for *economic development* reasons. In short, we view states as highly engaged participants in the competitive political economy of the American federal system, just as business is heavily engaged in the national (or international) political economy. State governments will be strongly inclined to maximize the benefits of any actions for their respective state, whether environmental improvement or varied economic advantages. They may face opportunities to export compliance costs to other jurisdictions while containing or internalizing as many environmental and related economic benefits as possible. They may have to choose between competing industrial concerns in weighing long-term economic development options, including alternative responses to the challenge of ensuring the reliability of electricity supply and costs. They may be keen to improve their regional, national, and even international environmental image, even if this means constraining or alienating some state-based business forces.

This internal state political calculus does not mean that states regularly side against business and industry. Instead, we attempt to sort out the differing ways in which business interests might play out on environmental issues in various state capitals. In some instances, such interests may indeed be dominant, particularly in settings in which any potential benefits from proposed policy are likely to be marginal within the state and anticipated costs potentially steep. At the same time, business interests may prove far less influential when intrastate environmental benefits from policy appear substantial, any economic benefits from action can be captured internally, and many economic costs can be exported to other jurisdictions. In turn, other options may also emerge, including cases in which business interests literally collide, and state political officials have to navigate between competing positions. We also explore two additional scenarios for business influence that reflect the unique role of state governments. First, the majority of states offer the option of direct democracy, literally shifting political decisions from representative institutions to ballot propositions, presenting a complex set of opportunities and challenges for various environmental interests. Second, as units embedded within a larger federal system, state governments face inherent constraints. They cannot enact treaties with foreign governments, usurp those powers assigned to the federal government, or take steps that restrain the movement of commerce (which has been quite broadly defined over two centuries of federal jurisprudence) across state boundaries. For business, in short, a decision taken by state representative institutions is not necessarily final, given the very real possibility of "shifting venues" to either the ballot box or federal government institutions on political or legal appeal. The latter venue, as we will see, may become increasingly important as business faces policy reversals in one or more state capitals, and thereby appeals to Congress or the president to "preempt" all state actions in favor of a uniform federal policy.

Our analysis draws on case examples from a wide range of states and environmental issue areas. However, it relies most heavily on a growing body of evidence on state policies designed to reduce greenhouse gas releases. Most conventional analyses of climate policy—and regulatory federalism—have assumed that jurisdictions such as state governments would never consider acting unilaterally to reduce their emissions. Nearly a half-decade after the federal government withdrew the United States from the Kyoto Protocol, virtually all proposed federal legislation to reduce greenhouse gases has continued to be stymied in Congress. At the same time, a growing number of states have actively entered this arena through a wide range of policies designed to reduce emissions. These range from various forms of carbon emissions caps on electric utilities that burn fossil fuels in eleven states to an effort involving ten states to reduce carbon emissions from vehicles.

Our analysis focuses particularly on a climate policy tool that has diffused to more states than any other, the so-called renewable portfolio standard (RPS). RPSs mandate that a specified level of renewable energy (such as wind, solar, geothermal, hydro, and biomass, among others) be provided by any utility that generates and distributes electricity in a given state. The RPS approach is used widely among European Union nations as a central piece of their strategies to reduce greenhouse gases and attempts to meet their Kyoto Protocol obligations (Van der Linden et al. 2005). As of July 2006, twenty-two states had legislatively adopted RPS programs, and at least six more were formally considering an increase of their existing requirements (see table 10.1). At the same time, an RPS was receiving serious legislative attention in six other states, leaving the remaining states either completely inactive on this issue or in the very early stages of consideration.

The RPS issue immediately engages a number of significant business and industrial players, most notably large utility firms that have relied almost exclusively on fossil fuel and nuclear sources historically and may be threatened by a renewable energy mandate. An RPS currently exists in several "strong coal" states, those with very high levels of coal mining and consumption of coal-generated electricity, such as Texas, Pennsylvania, and Colorado, where strong opposition to competition from renewables would be anticipated. The policy also exists in states with little indigenous supply of coal or other traditional fuels. Federal policy does not create any requirements or incentives for states to adopt an RPS, leaving this, thus far, as an area of exclusive state jurisdiction. Review of the evolving RPS experience, involving a fifty-state inventory and subset of intensive case studies supported by the Pew Center on Global Climate Change, was conducted during 2005–2006. The analysis draws on legislative histories, relevant reports and documents, and more than forty interviews with officials representing state government, electricity generating firms, and environmental advocacy groups. More detailed accounts of this work, including detailed case studies, are available at www.pewclimate.org. Key findings from this work are used to examine differing business roles and interest configurations in differing state contexts.

The Evolving Role of State Government in Environmental Policy

Many scholars cutting across the fields of economics, law, and political science have converged in presenting an interpretation of state environmental policy that emphasizes policy shirking to placate regulated parties and maximize their satisfaction. Under such a view, states have enormous disincentives to take unilateral action to improve environmental quality, particularly since pollutants or other contaminants can often be expected to migrate to other jurisdictions. Such analyses naturally focus on cases where a single industry provides a substantial economic boost to a state and a good deal of its environmental impact will be felt outside state boundaries. Indeed, it is difficult to envision a West Virginia or Pennsylvania restricting the mining of coal and its use for electricity, or a Michigan or Indiana prodding for tougher vehicle emissions standards. Yet such interpretation need not apply only to predominant industries within a state. Speaking much more broadly, many analysts contend that "environmental pollution cannot be controlled without a plan that extends across metropolitan areas, states, or even regions" because of the relentless economic pressures to avoid serious engagement below the level of national or even international authority (Peterson 1995, 25). In extreme form, states may even engage in some form of a "race-to-the-bottom," attentive to the actions of neighboring states and eager to enhance their attractiveness to investment by lowering standards and minimizing costs of compliance wherever possible (Esty 1996; Oates and Schwab 1988; Revesz 1992). In theory, such downward competition can be employed either to retain existing industry or to recruit new industry currently operating in other jurisdictions.

Table 10.1
State renewable portfolio standards: Key design features

State	Year enacted	Date revised	Governor partisanship	Legislature control
Arizona	2001	2006	Rep	Split
California	2002	2005	Dem	Dem
Colorado	2004		Rep	Rep
Connecticut	1999	2003	Rep	Dem
Delaware	2003		Dem	Split
Hawaii	2004		Rep	Dem
Illinois	2005		Dem	Dem
Iowa	1991		Rep	Dem
Maine	1999		Ind	Dem
Maryland	2004		Rep	Dem
Massachusetts	1997		Rep	Dem
Minnesota	1997		Rep	Dem
Montana	2005		Dem	Split**
Nevada	1997	2005	Rep	Split
New Jersey	2001	2004	Rep	Rep
New Mexico	2002	2004	Rep	Dem
New York	2004		Rep	Split
Pennslyvania	2004		Dem	Rep
Rhode Island	2004		Rep	Dem
Texas	1999	2005	Rep	Rep
Vermont	2005		Rep	Dem
Wisconsin	1999	2006	Rep	Rep

Sources: DSIRE, EIA, NGA, NCSL, Pew Center on Global Climate Change.
** Senate is Dem Controlled, House is split 50–50.

Preliminary target		Final target		Who's covered	Credit trading
0.2%	by 2001	15%	by 2025	Utility	No
13.0%	by 2003	33%	by 2020	Investor Owned Utility Municipal Utility	Yes
3%	by 2007	10%	by 2015	Utility Investor Owned Utility Rural Coop	Yes
4%	by 2004	10%	by 2010	Utility	Yes
1%	by 2007	10%	by 2019	Retail Electricity Supplier	Yes
7%	by 2003	20%	by 2020	Utility	No
2%	by 2007	8%	by 2013	Utility	No
105 MW		none		Utility	No
30%	by 2000	none		Utility	Yes
3.5%	by 2006	7.5%	by 2019	Electricity Supplier	Yes
1%	by 2003	4%	by 2009	Utility	Yes
1,125 MW	by 2010	1,250 MW	by 2013	Xcel only	No
5%	by 2008	15%	by 2015	Utility	Yes
6%	2005	20%	by 2015	Investor Owned Utility	Yes
6.5%	by 2008	20%	by 2020	Utility	Yes
5%	by 2008	10%	by 2011	Investor Owned Utility	Yes
none		25%	by 2013	Investor Owned Utility	Yes
1.5%	by 2007	18%	by 2020	Utility	Yes
3%	by 2020	17%	by 2020	Electric Retailers	Yes
2,280 MW	by 2007	5,880 MW	by 2015	Municipal Utility Investor Owned Utility Rural Coop Retail Supplier	Yes
none		7.0%	by 2012	Retail Electricity Supplier	Yes
0.5%	by 2001	10%	by 2015	Utility	Yes

At the same time, the experience of recent decades reveals a much more active role for state governments in environmental policy than conventional theory would ever anticipate. During this very period in which the federal government has been largely unable to reach agreement on either new legislation or updating existing environmental laws, states have increasingly become central players in virtually every arena of environmental policy. This is reflected by a growing role in policy implementation and by setting the national agenda through policy innovation in such areas as pollution prevention and waste reduction, public involvement and information disclosure, and groundwater and wetlands protection. Indeed, a growing number of states have begun to move into areas that have generally been assumed to be the exclusive province of federal or international authorities, including greenhouse gas reduction to respond to the challenge of climate change. These policy initiatives vary markedly from state to state and region to region. In some instances, they may be dismissed as largely symbolic and thereby not straying from conventional depictions of state deference to the predilections of industry and business. Collectively, however, they constitute a rather large and expanding body of policy engagement related to environmental protection (Rabe 2004, 2006). All of this experience clearly challenges any depiction suggesting that state governments are lodged securely in the hip pockets of regulated entities. Three broad factors converge to explain why conventional depictions of the role of business in state environmental policy are increasingly limited.

State-Government Maturation

This somewhat unanticipated outcome may be traceable in part to important developments in state politics and governance over at least the past quarter-century (Hedge 1998). These factors may, in a growing number of state cases, converge and result in far more robust policies than might have been envisioned as politically feasible in prior decades. State-government agencies with some degree of jurisdiction over environmental concerns have diversified and generally expanded their capacities of independent analysis and policy development. Many states have also expanded the size and analytic sophistication of their legislative staff, particularly in those states that delegate considerable authority to environmentally focused committees (Rosenthal 2004). State officials are not indifferent to the concerns of business and industry and may indeed prove highly responsive to them. But they have carved out a degree of autonomy and a capacity to hear from other interests and learn from the experience of other states. Recent studies across a range of state regulatory policy arenas, including a number of different spheres of environmental protection, suggest that business and industry influence is consistently discernible but not necessarily dominant (Teske 2004; Engel and Saleska 2005; Ringquist 1993). In turn, many states have established far more barriers, such as strict codes of ethics, that make it far harder for any business to "buy policy retail" through direct gifts or promises of potential employment, to state officials (Rosenson 2005).

Political Ambitions of Elected State Officials

State governments have increasingly been led by elected officials with political beliefs and ambitions that may compel them to part company with at least some well-endowed interests operating within their state's boundaries. Most states elect their attorneys general on a partisan basis and approximately 40 percent of these officials ultimately run for governor. In the past decade, such officials have directly confronted such well-endowed industries as tobacco, securities, and gun manufacturing and have turned their attention in recent years to industries that generate greenhouse gases, mercury emissions, and lead-based paints (Derthick 2005; Provost 2003). In turn, other elected state officials, such as governors, have proven increasingly effective in parlaying their statehouse records into greater national visibility and possible runs for higher office, part of an ongoing jockeying for promotion that is also evident in the ranks of state legislators. A growing number of attorneys general and governors, from both political parties, have attempted to burnish their reputations by "taking on" powerful industries, including those seen as degrading environmental quality. One can even leap ahead to the 2008 presidential primaries and envision a number of gubernatorial contenders who might run in part on their environmental records, including active engagement on combating climate change amid continuing stasis on the issue at the federal level. Still further electoral "wild cards" in the state political process may include elected state treasurers, who have considerable latitude in directing state investment decisions, and the constitutional provision in more than thirty states for ballot propositions, which may allow for very unusual engagement by a diverse array of interests that have been stymied in their efforts with representative institutions. In addition, any state environmental policy decision that leads to litigation and resolution in state courts may also involve elected officials. Unlike the appointment process for judges in the federal bench, approximately one-half of judges serving at the state appellate or Supreme Court levels are selected by the electorate. Consequently, state governments are stocked with democratically elected officials, whose career aspirations may indeed influence their stands on environmental policy issues.

The Environmental Protection–Economic Development Nexus

In recent decades, states may have stepped beyond traditional interpretations and increasingly value environmental quality both as a public health concern and as an essential ingredient for economic development. As legal scholars Henry Butler and Jonathan Macey have noted, "Every state has evinced a strong interest in environmental quality" (Butler and Macey 1996, 6). This can be linked at least in part to securing a level of environmental quality and natural resource protection that fosters a perception of a high quality of life and public health. In recent years, states have increasingly made an explicit link between their environmental initiatives, even if taken in the face of interest opposition, and the need to make their states places that people want to visit as tourists and locate as workers or retirees (Graham 2002). Some states with poor environmental reputations, such as New Jersey and Pennsylvania, have placed significant emphasis on improving environmental quality in recent years, framing the case largely in economic terms. As one prominent environmental policy proposal emanating in 2004 from the Pennsylvania governor's office noted: "In the new economy environmental quality has become important not simply as an end in itself, but as a prerequisite for attracting new talent" (Commonwealth of Pennsylvania 2004).

These factors do not automatically eclipse the views of business and industry. They may indeed lead to some coalescence of views or result in organized interests taking their case to the area of state government that is most likely to do their bidding. This may block or soften proposed environmental policies. Just as some states have become national and even international leaders in such areas as pollution prevention and greenhouse gas reduction, others have taken purely symbolic actions or even steps to preclude any state institutions from acting on the issue. Just as some states clearly race toward the top, others may gravitate toward the bottom or intentionally aim for the middle of the pack (Rabe, Roman, and Dobelis 2005; Green and Harrison 2005). The balance of this chapter examines broad considerations that may help refine our understanding of the varied impact that business and industry—or other interests—may have in the state environmental policy process. This analysis reviews accounts of state-by-state differences and the strategic considerations that any state government and its elected and appointed officials will take in weighing policy options. As noted above, it considers very different outcomes, including those in which business and industry exercise considerable influence and those in which they may be trumped, either by larger environmental concerns, pressure from competing industries and interests, or the decision to take policy to another venue, such as a ballot proposition.

When Business Trumps Environmental Considerations

The prospects for business and industry to deter a wide range of possible state environmental policies may be greatest in those instances in which any environmental benefits are likely to be exported and perceived costs are likely to be steep and concentrated within state boundaries. States may face a significant disincentive if they are uncertain of the intrastate benefits and persuaded that intrastate costs of compliance will be high. This may lead to a number of actions, including successful efforts to moderate or soften existing regulations or to deter or prohibit new regulatory initiatives. Scholars have long noted that the structure of a federal system may indeed "create incentives for states to export pollution" (Gormley 1987; Lowry 1992, 44). This is perhaps most evident for conventional air contaminants, such as sulfur dioxide and nitrogen oxide, but it is also true for a wide range of other environmental problems that may literally migrate across state and regional boundaries and thereby impose costs on another jurisdiction. If there are few environmental or ancillary benefits, the case for imposing costs unilaterally within a state may be vigorously and effectively thwarted by business and industry.

Business and industry are well represented in virtually every state capital, not only with the platoons of lobbyists noted earlier but through the significant ability of professional associations to draft model legislation and provide extensive analysis of the likely impact of any policy proposal. Many of these associations are state-level affiliates of such national organizations as the Chamber of Commerce and the National Association of Manufacturers. Moreover, in recent years, nationally based organizations such as the American Legislative Exchange Council (ALEC) provide direct assistance to state legislators and firms eager to minimize any state government engagement in environmental protection. ALEC's membership base includes nearly one-third of all sitting state legislators and most of its resources are derived from corporations and trade associations. It offers regular conferences and training sessions but is perhaps best known for drafting model legislation that can easily be adopted by an individual state and introduced into a legislature. Such legislation consistently confronts existing policies and seeks to deter new initiatives, often through framing proposals with appealing titles that emphasize "economic impact assessment," "verifiable environmental science," and "environmental literacy improvement" (American Legislative Exchange Council 2003). Some of its proposals, such as the Environmental Audit Privilege and Immunity Act, which shields firms from liability for self-reported environmental regulatory violations, have been widely adopted (Greenblatt 2003). A consistent message from ALEC and related organizations such as the Heartland Institute is that state efforts to promote environmental protection should be extremely modest, given the risks of imposing unilateral costs that weaken private-sector competitiveness in a given state and offer few if any benefits that are likely to be realized internally.

Relieving Regulatory Burdens

In recent years, state-based business and industry and their allied associations have been particularly effective in advancing legislative initiatives that emphasize "regulatory flexibility." Virtually every state with a major manufacturing sector has enacted some legislation that modifies or streamlines procedures for securing state approval under various air, water, and waste management legislation. Much of this focuses on the terms whereby firms maintain compliance with existing requirements, consistently attempting to minimize their regulatory burdens through maximization of flexibility.

One far-reaching initiative that aggressively promotes such flexibility is the 2004 Wisconsin Job Creation Act, backed by a predominantly Republican legislature and Democratic Governor Jim Doyle in the face of strong opposition by a range of leading environmental groups. The legislation integrated a wide set of regulatory flexibility provisions, many focused on the issuance of permits. For some categories of activities, such as hand-dredging, many farming operations, and seasonal structures for fishing, permits would no longer be required. For larger activities, time-lines for agencies to review permits would be shortened, with automatic approval if the agency failed to meet established deadlines. The legislation also imposed an array of constraints that, according to the Wisconsin Manufacturers & Commerce, would "limit the ability" of the Wisconsin Department of Natural Resources "to impose new and unnecessary regulations that apply only to industries in this state" (Buchen 2003). Although the entire legislative debate provided little evidence of likely impact on the economy or job protection, the employment issue proved to be a central rationale, with proponents repeatedly citing the need to "lessen regulatory burdens identified as impeding economic growth and job creation."

Minimizing Impacts

States may also attempt to make their environmental policies as palatable to business as possible, either by avoiding certain areas entirely or offering direct opportunity for drafting amendments and shaping key provisions. In the arena of renewable energy, some Midwestern states, such as Indiana and Michigan, and Southeastern states, such as Tennessee and Alabama, have traditionally relied almost exclusively on fossil and nuclear sources for electricity. In addition to these states, Arkansas, Florida, Georgia, Kentucky, Mississippi, and South Carolina also have had minimal experience with renewables and at best are only at the early stages of exploring programs to encourage their development

(U.S. Department of Energy 2006). Some states have limited programs to encourage the use of renewable energy sources, many of which are purely voluntary in nature. South Carolina, for example, focuses primarily on modest experimentation with such fuel sources as wood, tires, landfill gas, and municipal solid waste. Although U.S. Senator Lamar Alexander (R-TN) has lashed out against federal support for wind power, his home state does operate a wind prospecting program in the Tennessee Valley region. However, these types of programs are very modest in scope and objectives, none approaching the ambitious goals of RPS programs. The lag in the launch of RPS programs in this large portion of the nation may be attributable to such factors as the absence of political leadership with respect to renewable energy sources, a general political reluctance to challenge the dominance of traditional providers, and relatively poor quality of renewable energy potential for those sources that are increasingly proving cost-effective.

As a result, some states have very limited experience with renewables and may view any policy promoting them as a threat. In such cases, predominant electric utility firms have argued aggressively that an RPS could pose a significant economic danger if adopted. They contend that intrastate potential to develop renewables is weak, thereby limiting any in-state economic benefit and likely increasing dependence on energy imports from other states. In turn, they argue that all the costs associated with RPS implementation would be borne by commercial and residential rate payers. This combination has proven a strong impediment to RPS development in a number of states, keeping the issue in deep political storage (Fialka 2005).

But even in instances in which a state goes forward to adopt an RPS, business and industry do not necessarily throw in the towel. In a few states, it is evident that an RPS proposal was initially advanced to foster new sources of renewable energy but was subsequently modified through the legislative process to instead protect and even promote traditional energy sources and providers. In Pennsylvania, for example, an RPS was initially promoted as part of a multifaceted plan to emphasize energy diversification and environmental improvement by incoming Governor Edward Rendell, a Democrat. As the legislation worked its way through the Pennsylvania legislature during 2004, however, the Pennsylvania Alternative Energy Portfolio Standards Act acquired so many environmentally suspect provisions that it ultimately became the first state RPS to be enacted in the face of active opposition from a large range of environmental groups.

Opponents decried the legislation, characterizing it as "without a doubt, the dirtiest RPS in the nation," as they examined provisions that might ultimately result in only limited increase in renewables and might actually increase the state's already-prodigious generation of greenhouse gases (ActionPA.org 2005). One area of enormous contention was the decision to expand the definition of "renewable energy" in the Pennsylvania case to include "waste coal" that was being stored in landfills after mining operations from previous decades. This definitional change was directly linked to formal plans to construct three new power plants in Western Pennsylvania that would burn such coal for electricity, with the renewable label and mandate creating further incentive for plant development. Other definitional changes took the unique steps of also labeling coal-mine methane and energy generated by the incineration of trash and poultry waste from large animal-processing plants as "renewable." In turn, the Pennsylvania law was amended to provide enormous latitude for state officials to weaken or refrain from enforcing the mandate under various scenarios as well as assure all participating utilities that they could expect generous terms for recovering any costs incurred through implementation of the requirement. Such concessions were essential to sustain a political coalition large enough to secure enactment, including provisions designed to boost the prospects for energy sources more conventionally characterized as renewables. Nonetheless, they have led to many questions as to whether this policy will actually promote renewables or instead preserve and promote the status quo. This type of dynamic has also been evident in states with high levels of electricity from large hydro projects, most notably Maine, where major utilities with high reliance on hydro sources back an RPS because it can be used to counter proposals to dismantle aging dams in favor of natural river restoration.

When Environmental Considerations Trump Business

The Wisconsin and Pennsylvania cases involve different issues but demonstrate a common dynamic whereby the leverage of business and industry is likely to be maximized. However, a significant range of policies may respond to situations in which environmental ramifications for a state are substantial and may warrant intervention. In some instances, environmental concerns may be so great that there is an overwhelming consensus that forces business and industry to respond. In others, policy may prove appealing not only because of perceived benefits but also the likelihood that any costs will be minimal or even negligible. These may even present scenarios that allow creative policymakers to devise measures that will concentrate benefits within state boundaries while exporting some or most costs to other jurisdictions.

Triggering Events

Perhaps the most familiar type of state environmental policy reaction that overrides business and industry involves situations in which concerns over environmental quality pose a clear and significant threat to public health (Baumgartner and Jones 1993). Such concerns emerged in many states over exposure to toxic chemicals and wastes in the 1980s, triggering numerous state policies that either supplemented or went beyond federal standards despite considerable opposition from regulated parties. A more recent example involves air emissions of mercury, particularly the nearly 50 million tons of this substance that are released annually from coal-burning power plants. Mercury is a neurotoxin that can cause severe health problems for children, and its impact is supported by an extensive body of scientific literature that examines the serious risks posed at relatively low levels of exposure. Prevailing federal laws, including the 1990 Clean Air Act Amendments, have left many loopholes that have allowed such plants to maintain a high level of emissions. After a period in which many states tinkered with more modest reforms, such as mandatory replacement of household items using mercury, a growing and diverse set of states have begun to impose sharp reductions on mercury emissions from power plants. These provisions have been actively opposed by regulated utilities in most states, but the increasingly compelling scientific evidence concerning the human health threat from mercury exposure has enabled governments in such diverse capitals as Des Moines, Hartford, and Raleigh, among others, to take fairly bold steps in the face of strong opposition.

Exporting Costs

A different dynamic—but similar policy outcome—emerges in instances in which the environmental threat may be less salient or immediate but the calculus of costs and benefits can be modified to make unilateral state action compelling. Cost externalization may be a real possibility in certain instances. This may entail the transferal of compliance costs to business and industry located outside a given state. Another option may entail leveraging the advantage for in-state firms in developing new, greener products and thereby marginalizing the role of out-state providers. Such a pattern is particularly notable as the number of states that are unilaterally taking steps to reduce their greenhouse gas emissions, in the absence of any federal pressure to do so, continues to grow and the level of their proposed emission reduction becomes increasingly ambitious.

States with large populations and economies tend to have the greatest likelihood for far-reaching cost externalization. Were California to secede from the American federal union, it would constitute the world's sixth largest economy. Despite its economic scale and legendary consumption of fossil fuels for transportation, however, California would rank only seventeenth among the world's greenhouse gas emitters. This is due to many factors but can be explained in part by long-standing state-government efforts to pursue energy efficiency and aggressive reduction of conventional air emissions, contributing to a rate of per capita greenhouse gas emissions that more closely parallels the nations of the European Union than most regions of the United States and Canada.

California also has unique powers, sustained through various iterations of the federal Clean Air Act Amendments, to set air emissions standards for motor vehicles that are more stringent than those established nationally. Whenever California takes such a step, the remaining states may then choose to adhere to existing federal law or adopt the California step. This long-standing practice has led to a periodic "ratcheting upward" of vehicle emissions standards widely heralded as the "California effect." In 2002, California decided to apply this power to climate change, becoming the first Western government to legislatively establish carbon dioxide emissions standards for vehicles. This legislation passed through the California legislature on a highly partisan basis and over the active opposition of many vehicle manufacturers. But it has retained considerable political support as it moves toward implementation in the final years of the current decade. Democratic legislators and Republican Governor Arnold Schwarzenegger increasingly tussle over who deserves the most credit for this initiative and, literally, whose name should be directly associated with the legislation. Since California's action, eight Northeastern states and the states of Oregon and Washington have adopted the California standards, with decisions pending in other state capitals. In turn, the legislation is a key element in Schwarzenegger's June 2005 executive order to pledge far-reaching carbon dioxide emissions reductions over the next four decades (Ball 2005; Freeman 2006).

The political attractiveness of such an initiative can be attributed to a combination of cost externalization and benefit maximization. Although Californians purchase a large share of the vehicles sold each year in the United States, they do not manufacture many of them. Despite its massive population and industrial sectors, California had less than 37,000 vehicle-sector jobs in 2003, a fraction of the approximately 220,000 jobs in a much less populous state such as Michigan (Engel and Saleska 2005). Moreover, California has tended to lure vehicle manufacturers, such as Toyota, that have emphasized products promoting emissions reduction and fuel economy far more than American-based counterparts such as General Motors and Ford. A somewhat similar dynamic exists among those states that have emulated California's standards, because none are major players in the motor-vehicle manufacturing sector.

Consequently, this policy option allows California to export a good deal of the economic costs that might stem from implementation, namely, to those states with a higher proportion of their workforce involved in vehicle manufacturing. Its own citizens might pay more per vehicle, should the legislation have such an impact on vehicle pricing, but no more than their neighbors across the country. Californians might also derive significant savings if state policies lead to improved vehicle fuel efficiency and hence lower their fuel costs for transportation. Furthermore, California-based manufacturers might even derive a further boost to lead the nation in the introduction of new vehicle types and technologies. Indeed, a pair of 2006 studies project significant in-state job growth for California in the vehicle manufacturing sector in coming decades through implementation of the carbon dioxide emissions standard (McFarling 2006). At the same time, the projected environmental benefits, including greenhouse gas reductions, from implementation of the legislation is not trivial, especially as the number of states emulating California expands. If all fifty states were to adopt the California standard, American greenhouse gas emissions would decline by 2.6 percent from current projections by 2020 (Engel and Saleska 2005). California also envisions additional environmental benefits from the related reduction of conventional air emissions that are expected to accompany the anticipated change in vehicles. Finally, there are political benefits for leading proponents, including near-celebrity status for some (such as Democratic Assemblywomen Fran Pavley), a boost to seek statewide office (such as Democratic Senator Debra Bowen), and an opportunity to gain national and international recognition as a leader on climate policy (such as Governor Schwarzenegger, who announced the state's 2005 executive order not in Sacramento but rather at the United Nations World Environment Day meetings).

Internalizing Benefits

Not every state, of course, can cast a California-like shadow or possess such significant opportunity to export costs and internalize benefits. But even more moderately sized states have seized on the RPS tool in large part because of the relatively attractive calculus of perceived benefits and costs. Aside from extreme cases like Pennsylvania, the vast majority of remaining RPS states give far less indication of compromising with fossil fuel interests. They are clearly focused on steadily increasing the supply of renewable energy available in coming years and decades at the same time they recognize, and want to capture, potential environmental benefits. All of these programs have been tailored in ways that will most likely concentrate any environmental and economic benefits within state boundaries. A review of the legislative histories of all twenty-two state RPS programs suggests that this environmental-economic convergence is universal, albeit played out differently in particular states. States have attempted to maximize the benefits from this energy transition through various initiatives designed to assure that any new renewable sources are generated and consumed within state boundaries. The American electricity grid divides the nation into regions that, in most instances, assures considerable movement of electricity across state and regional borders. Under virtually all of the RPS programs, electric utilities can either generate their own level of required renewables or acquire so-called renewable energy credits (RECs) through purchases from other generators (see table 10.1). Without state restrictions, it would be eminently possible for an intra-state utility to satisfy its RPS requirement through purchase of out-state electricity credits. In response, states have erected a number of barriers intended to maximize the likelihood that new renewables are truly home-grown and home-delivered products.

Much of the attraction for such a strategy is the anticipated economic development boost from renewables. In contrast to fossil-based sources such as natural gas and coal, renewables do not require acquisition or purchase of fuel. But they tend to be much more labor intensive per kilowatt hour, both in terms of construction and operation. Various studies contend that electricity generated from renewable sources generate between 2.5 and 3.5 more permanent jobs per kilowatt hour than electricity derived from fossil fuels. For states such as Hawaii and Massachusetts, which still rely on imported oil for more than one-quarter of their electricity, the specter of shifting investment from out-state oil supplies to in-state renewable energy developers is regularly advanced to sustain support for their respective RPSs. Similar patterns are evident among other RPS states that currently import much of the raw material that is combusted to generate their electricity.

States have a clear incentive to capture any economic development benefit from such activity and have, in some instances, begun to erect barriers to assure that outcome as part of their effort to promote renewables. In Nevada, for example, RPS development in 1997 has been followed by three subsequent laws that have expanded the program, including amendments enacted in 2005 that further raise the bar for future renewable requirements. All of these laws make clear that, in essence, only electricity generated in Nevada can count toward RPS compliance. Through these deliberations, Nevada has been driven by a series of factors, including a desire to diversify its energy supply and take advantage of abundant indigenous sources of renewable energy. But it has also been very eager to make sure that any new renewables are developed exclusively in that state and not repeat the experience of 2001 in which California tapped into Nevada's supplemental supplies to meet its own severe energy shortfall. In 2001 testimony before the Nevada legislature, one pro-renewable lobbyist illustrated this emphasis: "We all desire to jumpstart and boost the economic development and economic diversity in this state. We certainly don't want to make a bill that allows us to improve the economic diversity and development of Oregon and California and Utah. That's not the intent of this bill" (Wellinghoff 2001). Similarly, as Minnesota has explored expanding its RPS and is particularly intrigued by the possibility of expanding wind turbines in rural areas, a senior public utility commission official noted, "We want that economic development to accrue to Minnesota. We don't want to allow Xcel (the state's main utility covered under the RPS) to get their wind from South Dakota, because that doesn't help Minnesota farmers."

Other states have been somewhat more subtle than Nevada in promoting exclusively in-state development, attributable in large part to their awareness that strict state constraints on electricity distribution could potentially invoke constitutional challenges about violating the rights of interstate commerce. The current range of state strategies includes mandates that any renewable imports may only cross designated transmission lines (which are highly unlikely to be a conduit for renewables), surplus RECs for electricity generated within state boundaries, reciprocal agreements allowing full and equal trade between smaller and contiguous states, and confinement of eligibility to electricity generated within a specified "service territory." These various devices demonstrate the extent to which anticipated economic development benefits are an important driver behind RPS enactment, potential gains that individual states are reluctant to share with others. In fact, an increasing number of states that have enacted RPSs or are considering their creation have tended to heavily emphasize the perceived economic benefits to a state, with environmental benefits, such as reduced release of conventional emissions and greenhouse gases, as an important but largely supplemental benefit. RPS proponents may shift their emphasis of these perceived virtues depending upon the audience being addressed at a given moment (Rabe 2004). Such convergence of forces makes it far more attractive for political figures to select an "environmentally friendly" option while simultaneously making the case that these steps will create new jobs.

When Competing Business Interests Collide: State Environmental Policy Opportunities

Considerable opportunities for state environmental policy development may also exist where the interests of respective businesses and industries differ markedly. Interest group scholars increasingly concur that private interests at the federal level are rarely unified on proposed legislation in a wide range of areas, and this dynamic is clearly evident in state capitals (Smith 2000). Under such circumstances, governments cannot simply adopt "the business sector position" and are certain to alienate at least one side of the divide regardless of what they do. This may create opportunities for firms that can make some claim to assuming greater environmental responsibility, perhaps tipping government support in their direction. In any event, governments will have to make particularly difficult choices in these settings, weighing environmental considerations alongside pressures to favor one type of pollution abatement technology or one form of renewable energy over another.

Allocating Responsibility and Cost

One sphere of environmental policy in which such competing interests are likely to surface is waste management, an area where states generally retain enormous latitude to devise their own approaches for hazardous, biomedical, low-level radioactive, and solid wastes. Every state government faces a series of choices that will likely generate different responses from various business and industry interests. If a state wants to promote reuse of bottles and cans, does it impose a deposit and require all grocers and beverage distributors to cover the costs of accepting returnables? Or does it mandate specific recycling goals, perhaps favoring certain firms likely to dominate business in a state? If it wants to conduct far-reaching cleanup of hazardous waste, does it embrace firms that feature chemical neutralization, incineration, or landfilling as a preferred approach, with potentially huge financial consequences for winning and losing firms? One increasingly contentious area in which states are being "forced to choose" involves the debate in many state capitals over how best to manage the growing tonnage of electronics waste from televisions and computers. Like many areas of waste management, this is one in which states retain considerable latitude. Some states are beginning to follow the example of Maine and place a "take-back" mandate on all manufacturers; this strategy is endorsed by some computer giants such as Dell and HP. But others are following California's lead in developing an "advanced recovery fee" that leaves open the question of final disposal or reuse; this strategy is endorsed by IBM, Apple Computer, Panasonic, and Sony. Environmental analysts can and do debate the merits of competing strategies, but state governments frequently must take a decision that cannot satisfy the preferences of all corporate competitors.

Navigating between Competitors

A similar dynamic occurs in the arena of climate policy, particularly renewable energy, as significant fault lines develop. As states continue to move from electricity delivery systems whereby one provider dominates a state for generations toward one of greater competition among multiple generators, it becomes more difficult to simply pigeonhole the views of disparate firms as uniform. For firms devoted exclusively to development of fossil fuels or nuclear power, renewables may constitute a significant threat. But for those that are diversifying their portfolios, renewable energy may actually be part of a long-term growth strategy. Moreover, there are clearly a growing number of private and non-profit entities in many states that are specializing in renewable energy. As a result, states may often find themselves picking winners and losers between competing businesses that promote different forms of renewable energy.

The existence of organized interests in advocating renewable energy is not new in state capitals but their visibility and clout have clearly increased in many locales in recent years. Such organizations are increasingly visible and influential as renewables continue to move from the fringe of electricity supply to more central roles, especially through "second-generation" RPSs that set higher targets for renewables, such as the ones enacted in Texas and Nevada in 2005 and in New Jersey and New Mexico in 2004. The degree of governmental subsidies for competing fuel sources remains hotly debated by energy analysts but renewable energy providers are clearly becoming better-represented in state government by a combination of locally-based providers as well as state affiliates of such groups as the American Wind Energy Association and the Geothermal Energy Association, among many others. Such organizations clearly lack the resources of traditional providers but are becoming more visible in state policy deliberations. They tend to establish formidable alliances with state agency officials in designing policy and securing needed political support. A review of state legislative hearings on RPS bills and elite interviews indicates that these forces have significant opportunities for input, with broad coalitions that support renewable energy fracturing at times between competing interests that favor generators from one renewable source over another.

Indeed, renewable interests, and the overall appeal of renewables, may have advanced so far that it is no longer an issue in many capitals as to whether a state will mandate renewable energy expansion. Instead, an increasingly salient question involves whether an RPS will be neutral on the type of renewable energy to be developed as long as overall levels are reached, or give preferential treatment to one or more source. A fundamental shift in RPS development was fairly consistent emphasis on source neutrality through 2003 but a growing emphasis on differential treatment by source thereafter. This represents in large part the dramatic expansion of wind capacity versus most other renewable energy sources covered by RPSs, reflecting wind power's significant technological advancement and increasing cost competitiveness with conventional sources. Total installed wind capacity in the United States has climbed from 1,997 megawatts (MW) in 1997 to 4,275 MW in 2001 to 9,149 MW in 2005, followed by consistently high projected expansion over the coming decade. This has triggered a bit of an "antiwind" backlash, with proponents of other renewables pushing for more favorable treatment.

Solar energy is perhaps the best illustration of this phenomenon, since its costs per kilowatt hour remain more than twice that of wind, geothermal, and micro hydro sources in most regions. In a number of states, solar advocates have secured special treatment versus other renewables. These protections range from RPS "solar carve outs" mandating that some subset of a state's renewables must come from that source to "credit multipliers" that provide a given amount of solar-generated power appreciably greater REC credit than other sources. In such deliberations, the broad constituency that emerges on renewables to push for an RPS can quickly splinter, pitting specialized renewable advocates against one another and leaving legislators with yet another set of trade-offs to weigh. Such divides multiply further when regional considerations are taken into account. In Nevada, for example, incentives for solar are most likely to support constituencies in the southern part of the state, whereas geothermal incentives are likely to benefit rural communities, and wind incentives could likely apply across the state. As the volume of electricity provided by renewables continues to increase, one can envision far greater intersource competition between renewable providers, leaving state officials with the growing challenge of favoring some sources and suppliers over others.

Shifting Venues: Opting for Direct Democracy

At the federal government level, legislation can only be made by representative institutions and so business and industry concentrate their efforts intensively on Congress. But the majority of states, including many of the most populous ones, have constitutional provisions that allow for ballot propositions that can produce binding legislation. The particulars of these provisions vary from state to state but one common form of direct democracy, the initiative, allows for direct placement of a proposition before the electorate if a specified number of voters sign petitions calling for such a vote. Certain states, such as California, Colorado, Michigan, Oregon, and Washington, use these tools with particular frequency, and many states have used ballot propositions to pass legislation with major environmental ramifications (Guber 2003). In 2005 alone, state ballot propositions included such topics as bonds for land conservation and water system protection, air quality standards, electricity regulation, commercial fishing rights, and energy taxes.

Many of these state provisions were established early in the Twentieth Century with the direct intent of enabling the general citizenry to circumvent the enormous power business and industry were thought to have over representative institutions at the state level (Cronin 1989). A growing body of scholarly work examines whether direct democracy has lived up to its promise of opening up the political process to direct input from the citizenry (Gerber 1999). For business and industry, the shift of venues may pose particular threats, not only due to possible passage of legislation that they oppose but to their inability to modify the legislation once it is approved for consideration by the electorate. Of course, organized interests can often be extremely influential, either in finding ways to thwart proposals that are initially popular or to advance their own particular interests by sponsoring their own propositions. At the same time, direct democracy often creates opportunities for environmental interests that may be stymied in their efforts in the statehouse; they may elect to literally shift their focus to another venue that is more likely to provide a favorable hearing.

One prominent example of this phenomenon involved the first state ballot proposition enacted with direct linkages to climate change policy. After a coalition involving electric utilities and coal mining interests narrowly blocked proposals in the Colorado legislature for three consecutive sessions to create an RPS, the state seemed highly unlikely to ever adopt such a policy. Indeed, Colorado had been among those states most reluctant to take any steps related to greenhouse gas emissions in the previous decade. However, a diverse coalition of interests converged, secured more than 100,000 petition signatures calling for a ballot proposition, and gained a 54-to-46 percent victory in November 2004. This legislation calls for a steady increase in the level of renewables used in Colorado, ultimately reaching a level of 10 percent by 2015, with at least 4 percent of that total coming from solar sources.

In this instance, the state's predominant utility, the Public Service Company (PSC) of Colorado, a subsidiary of Minnesota-based Xcel Energy Inc., was clearly the main loser. It spent more than $1.5 million in leading the campaign to oppose Proposition 37 through an organization called Citizens for Sensible Energy Choices. This organization emphasized its concerns about potentially high costs that would be transferred to customers and the willingness of PSC to expand its own renewable offerings on a voluntary basis. The company was also clearly concerned about the impact of the proposition on its plans to build a massive coal-burning plant near Pueblo.

As is customary in ballot propositions, industry opposition efforts did close the gap. Polling by the *Denver Post* indicated that Proposition 37 had enjoyed a 28 percent lead one month before the vote. But support was maintained through a campaign that had bipartisan leadership, including the Republican Speaker of the Colorado House and a Democratic Congressman. The campaign enlisted a tapestry of supporters representing numerous renewable energy developers, agriculture and ranching, public health and environmental protection, and various religious organizations in working to sustain voter support. The campaign also received endorsements from most of the major media outlets in the state.

By working so aggressively and effectively to thwart legislation through conventional channels, PSC and its allies took the risk that the RPS proposal would not be converted into a ballot proposition—and lost big. Not only did they spend heavily in the initiative campaign and receive considerable negative publicity, but the RPS that emerged from direct democracy was, in all likelihood, far more demanding of PSC than anything that might have emerged through conventional legislative processes. In particular, Colorado voters imposed significant "cost caps" on electricity customers of any RPS, with any costs of compliance exceeding 50 cents per customer per month to be borne by PSC or any other utility covered by the legislation. In turn, utilities were required under the legislation to subsidize the solar energy "carve out" and enter into contracts with renewable providers that would last a minimum of twenty years. This latter provision was designed to assure renewable generators of a purchase guarantee and is double the length of the longest contract guarantees required by any other RPS state.

Just as policy innovations diffuse across states through representative institutions, there is ample precedent for one state's use of direct democracy to trigger replication elsewhere. The Colorado RPS case has likely received more national publicity than enactments through more conventional means in the twenty-one other states that have established similar policies. RPS advocates around the country have begun to speak openly of "going the Colorado route" and pursuing a ballot proposition—if they cannot get their way with elected leaders. RPS proponents in Oregon and Washington have already begun to set the groundwork for similar initiatives in their respective states, based on careful study of the Colorado experience and with the clear intent of using that case to intensify pressure on legislators to act. Montana's decision to enact an RPS through conventional legislative mechanisms within a few months of the Colorado vote represented a rapid shift in position by the state's utilities, which softened their earlier opposition to negotiate a compromise bill and thereby avoid the possibility of their own ballot proposition. For business and industry, the possibility of shifting venues poses a different set of calculations and risks. In states where the direct democracy option is constitutionally viable and politically feasible, they may prefer to work within the confines of their legislatures to either block policy or make sure it is as favorable to them as possible. In states without direct democracy, business and industry can turn their full attention toward more traditional policymaking venues.

Moving the Intergovernmental Playing Field: The Preemption Option

Federal systems of government inherently allow for ongoing reconsideration of how authority is allocated across various governmental levels. As political scientists Elisabeth Gerber and Ken Kollman (2004, 397) have noted, "In many nations, devolution and centralization occur simultaneously, with some authority shifting to higher levels of government and some shifting to lower levels." In the United States, this reflects repeated shifting and experimentation by both federal and state governments. Where intergovernmental differences of view occur, federal courts often referee, considering the appropriateness of various policies when weighed against the overriding tenets of the U.S. Constitution.

In many spheres of environmental policy, states have expanded their powers in recent decades. This has entailed a wide range of home-grown policy innovations, extended use of powers granted to them by federal legislation, and filling voids left by the inability of respective Congresses and presidents to enact or update existing federal policy. As we have seen, states have now become dominant players in an area conventionally thought to be the province of the federal government and international authorities, through a rapidly expanding set of policies designed to reduce greenhouse gas emissions. At the same time, in other policy arenas, such as homeland security and public education, the federal government has clearly been moving to expand its role and impose ever-increasing restrictions on states in the past half-decade.

There is considerable precedent, not only in environmental policy, for business and industry to reach a point at which they feel states have "gone too far" and seek redress of their grievances by appeal to the federal level for relief (Nivola 2002). This may entail a concern, for firms that operate on a national basis, that their competitiveness may be impaired by having to adhere to a "patchwork quilt" of differing state regulations and policies. It may also reflect a sense that states, in general, are becoming too aggressive in a policy area and generally imposing substantial costs on business and industry, regardless of state-by-state differences. Under such circumstances, business and industry reserve an important option, namely petitioning federal institutions to override—or "preempt"—state authority. This can occur in a number of forms, either through legislation that bundles all state activity under tight federal constraints or federal court invalidation of various state policies that are deemed to violate constitutional principles. The Commerce Clause of the U.S. Constitution is often a central feature in such legal debates, involving questions as to whether certain state actions to promote environmental quality might conflict with the constitutional protection for free movement of goods and services across state boundaries. Preemption challenges have been frequent in recent decades, including a number of cases that directly involve a determination of whether states or the federal government should retain authority over particular areas of air and water quality protection (Zimmerman 2005; Posner 2005). These challenges may be prodded by organized interests and receive a sympathetic ear from federal authorities concerned about state encroachment upon their policy turf.

There are growing indications that as the number of cases in which "environmental considerations trump business" mount at the state level, private firms may indeed reorient their efforts and seek federal usurpation of an entire policy domain. California's legislation restricting carbon dioxide emissions from vehicles will clearly face a challenge in the federal courts brought by many, but not all, vehicle manufacturers. It is also quite possible that the Bush administration will formally back their position in court deliberations. In that instance, a primary focus will be on whether this legislation merely allows California to extend its long-standing powers over vehicle emissions or, as its critics contend, instead encroaches in a stealthlike manner on federal terrain to establish vehicle fuel economy standards. Other state legislation may be similarly vulnerable, including questions over whether renewable portfolio standards designed to favor renewable energy generated within a particular state constitute a violation of the Commerce Clause (Engel 1999). Such a legal challenge might be politically awkward for the Bush Administration, since the Texas RPS signed into law in 1999 by then-Governor Bush is among the most vulnerable to such a charge and the majority of state RPSs have been signed into law by Republican governors (see table 10.1). As is the hallmark of a federal system, these questions defy easy resolution, reflecting the blurry—and often changing—lines that separate federal and state authority. Even the departure of a single Supreme Court Justice could tip the balance, particularly such a staunch advocate of state authority as recently retired Associate Justice Sandra Day O'Connor, a former Arizona state legislator. For business and industry, a strategic question becomes not only how to address issues that emerge within individual states but when to shift tactics and attempt to prod the federal government to trim or even eliminate the role of state governments.

Looking Ahead

The odyssey of American states in recent decades has made them far less likely to be easy targets to do the bidding of business interests in environmental policy than in earlier periods of national history. As we have seen, states can be important sources of environmental policy innovation and leadership, even in areas where business opposition is likely to be significant. This chapter has outlined some of the factors that have fostered a much-expanded state role, even in the arena of global climate change. It also has emphasized that different configurations of interests and policy outcomes can emerge. States will be less likely to act when costs are likely to be concentrated within their boundaries and benefits are somewhat uncertain. Their willingness to engage is likely to grow, perhaps markedly, alongside opportunities to export costs to other jurisdictions and capture environmental and economic benefits. Venue shifting becomes a growing possibility as circumstances and strategy dictate, whether moving toward the realm of ballot propositions via direct democracy or seeking federal usurpation of state authority through preemption or related mechanisms.

Acknowledgments

We are very grateful to Michael Kraft and Sheldon Kamieniecki for their role in organizing this project and their superb guidance at every step of the process. We also benefited from two opportunities to present this work to colleagues, through a panel at the 2005 annual meeting of the American Political Science Association and a 2006 seminar at the Gerald Ford School of Public Policy at the University of Michigan. We very much appreciate the thoughtful comments received from Janna Bray, Jennifer Eckerman, Daniel Fiorino, Melissa Forbes, Elisabeth Gerber, Jessica Goldberg, William Gormley, Lloyd Grieger, Scott Helfstein, Erik Johnson Valenta Kabo, Katherine King, Sumana Rajarethnam, Jessica Wyse, and Jon Zelner.

References

ActionPA.org. 2005. *Dirty "Alternative" Energy Legislation Passes in Pennsylvania.* www.actionpa.org/cleanenergy/.

American Legislative Exchange Council. 2003. *Energy, Environment, and Economics: A Guide for State Legislators.* Washington, DC: American Legislative Exchange Council.

Ball, Jeffrey. 2005. "California Sets Emission Goals That Are Stiffer Than U.S. Plan." *Wall Street Journal,* June 2, A4.

Baumgartner, Frank R., and Bryan D. Jones. 1993. *Agendas and Instability in American Politics.* Chicago: University of Chicago Press.

Buchen, James A. 2003. *Wisconsin Workers Need Job Creation Act to Pass.* www.wmc.org.

Butler, Henry N., and Jonathan R. Macey. 1996. *Using Federalism to Improve Environmental Policy.* Washington, DC: American Enterprise Institute Press.

Commonwealth of Pennsylvania, Office of the Governor. 2004. "Governor Rendell's Quality of Life Proposal." www/governor/state/pa/us/governor/cwp/asp?a=1101&q=436334.

Cronin, Thomas E. 1989. *Direct Democracy: The Politics of Initiative, Referendum, and Recall.* Cambridge; MA: Harvard University Press.

Derthick, Martha A. 2005. *Up in Smoke: From Legislation to Litigation in Tobacco Politics.* 2nd ed. Washington, DC: CQ Press.

Engel, Kirsten H. 1999. "The Dormant Commerce Clause Threat to Market-Based Environmental Regulation: The Case of Electricity Deregulation." *Ecology Law Quarterly* 26 (2): 243–349.

Engel, Kirsten H., and Scott R. Saleska. 2005. "Subglobal Regulation of the Global Commons." *Ecology Law Quarterly* 32 (2): 183–233.

Esty, Daniel C. 1996. "Revitalizing Environmental Federalism." *Michigan Law Review* 95:570–653.

Fialka, John J. 2005. "Senator Is Running against the Wind." *Wall Street Journal,* June 21, A4.

Freeman, Sholn. 2006. "States Adopt California's Greenhouse Gas Limits." *Washington Post*, January 6, D1.

Gerber, Elisabeth R. 1999. *The Populist Paradox*. Princeton; NJ: Princeton University Press.

Gerber, Elisabeth R., and Ken Kollman. 2004. "Introduction—Authority Migration: Defining an Emerging Research Agenda." *PS: Political Science and Politics* 37 (3) July 2004: 397–400.

Gormley, William T. Jr. 1987. "Intergovernmental Conflict on Environmental Policy: The Attitudinal Connection." *Western Political Quarterly* 40:285–303.

Graham, Mary. 2002. *The Morning After Earth Day*. Washington, DC: Brookings Institution Press.

Green, Daniel A., and Kathryn Harrison. 2005. "Racing to the Middle: Minimum Wage Setting and Standards of Fairness." Paper presented at the Annual Meeting of the Canadian Political Science Association, University of Western Ontario, June.

Greenblatt, Alan. 2003. "What Makes ALEC Smart?" *Governing* (October) 18:30–34.

Guber, Deborah Lynn. 2003. *The Grassroots of a Green Revolution: Polling America on the Environment*, Chapter 2. Cambridge, MA: MIT Press.

Hedge, David M. 1998. *Governance and the Changing American States*. Boulder, CO: Westview Press.

Lowry, William. 1992. *The Dimensions of Federalism*. Durham, NC: Duke University Press.

McFarling, Usha Lee. 2006. "Studies Support Emissions Plans." *Los Angeles Times*, January 23, Part B, 1.

Nivola, Pietro S. 2002. *Tense Commandments*. Washington, DC: Brookings Institution Press.

Oates, Wallace E., and Robert M. Schwab. 1988. "Economic Competition among Jurisdictions: Efficiency Enhancing or Distortion Inducing?" *Journal of Public Economics* 33:333–354.

Peterson, Paul E. 1995. *The Price of Federalism*. Washington, DC: Brookings Institution Press.

Posner, Paul L. 2005. "The Politics of Preemption: Prospects for the States." *PS: Political Science and Politics* 38 (3) July: 371–374.

Provost, Colin. 2003. "State Attorneys General, Entrepreneurship, and Consumer Protection in the New Federalism." *Publius: The Journal of Federalism* 35 (2) (spring): 37–53.

Rabe, Barry G. 2004. *Statehouse and Greenhouse: The Emerging Politics of American Climate Change Policy*. Washington, DC: Brookings Institution Press.

Rabe, Barry G. 2006. "Power to the States: The Promise and Pitfalls of Decentralization." In Norman J. Vig and Michael E. Kraft, eds., *Environmental Policy*, 34–56. Washington, DC: CQ Press.

Rabe, Barry G., Mikael Roman, and Arthur Dobelis. 2005. "State Competition as a Source Driving Climate Change Mitigation." *New York University Environmental Law Journal* 14:1–53.

Renzulli, Diane. 2002. *Capitol Offenders: How Private Interests Govern the States*. Washington, DC: Center for Public Integrity.

Revesz, Richard L. 1992. "Rehabilitating Interstate Competition: Rethinking the 'Race-to-the Bottom' Rationale for Federal Environmental Regulation," *New York University Law Review* 67:1210–1254.

Ringquist, Evan J. 1993. *Environmental Protection at the State Level*. Armonk, NY: Sharpe.

Rosenson, Beth A. 2005. The *Shadowlands of Conduct: Ethics and State Politics*. Washington, DC: Georgetown University Press.

Rosenthal, Alan. 2004. *Heavy Lifting: The Job of the American Legislature*. Washington, DC: CQ Press.

Smith, Mark A. 2000. *American Business and Political Power*. Chicago: University of Chicago Press.

Teske, Paul. 2004. *Regulation in the States*. Washington, DC: Brookings Institution Press.

Texas Public Utility Commission. 2005. *Scope of Competition in Electric Markets in Texas*. Austin: Texas Public Utility Commission.

Thomas, Clive S., and Ronald J. Hrebenar. 1999. "Interest Groups in the States." In Virginia Gray, Russell L. Hanson, and Herbert Jacob, eds., *Politics in the States*, 113–143. Washington, DC: CQ Press.

U.S. Department of Energy. 2006. *Energy Efficiency and Renewable Energy*. www.eere.energy.gov.

Van der Linden, N. N., M. A. Uyterlinde, C. Vrolijk, L. J. Nilsson, K. Astrand, K. Ericsson, and R. Wiser 2005. *Review of International Experience with Renewable Energy Obligation Support Mechanisms*. Berkeley: Lawrence Berkeley Laboratory.

Wellinghoff, Jon B. 2001. Testimony before the Nevada Senate Committee on Commerce and Labor, Carson City, April 13.

Zimmerman, Joseph F. 2005. *Congressional Preemption: Regulatory Federalism*. Albany: State University of New York Press.

11
Local Business and Environmental Policies in Cities

Kent E. Portney

The idea that local business might be productively involved in, and supportive of, local environmental policies may strike some people as rather odd, even perhaps as a contradiction in terms. Yet over the last ten to fifteen years, local businesses and business organizations have often joined in an effort to help some cities become more sustainable, with a special emphasis on trying to help protect and improve the quality of the city's biophysical environment (Portney 2003). This chapter examines the role that business has played in local policymaking, particularly in land use and the promotion of local economic development agendas. It outlines some of the major changes that have occurred in cities, changes that have affected the political landscape that has traditionally not been very receptive to the idea of environmental protection at the local level. In the process, it presents an array of case examples from cities that have been fairly aggressive in pursuing local environmental policies such as smart growth, brownfield redevelopment, and ecoindustrial parks, and explores the critical role that business plays in these policies.

This chapter is largely based on examples that come from specific cities that have emerged over the last five to ten years as places where businesses and the business community have played important roles in the pursuit of an environment-friendly agenda. The purpose of this chapter is not to argue that all cities are becoming like these. Indeed, most cities have not had the range of experiences that characterize those discussed here. However, the purpose of the chapter is to begin to delineate the primary characteristics that seem conducive to having local businesses take on a decidedly more cooperative role in the greening of cities than one might find in other cities. Most of the information contained in this chapter comes from research on what are sometimes called "sustainable-cities programs," or programs pursued in cities to sustain or create a particular quality of life. As discussed elsewhere, while sustainable-cities efforts can include a wide array of policies and programs, a huge portion of what cities do in working toward becoming sustainable focuses on efforts to protect and improve the biophysical environment (Portney 2003, chap. 1).

The Politics of Local Policymaking

Perhaps the most important starting point for a discussion of the role of the private sector in local environmental protection is the character of local, especially city, politics itself. One of the essential differences between the politics of city policymaking and policymaking at other levels of government is the fact that, as Peterson (1981, 116) notes, city politics are by and large "groupless politics." What this means is that, unlike federal or most state policymaking processes, city policymaking is not normally dominated by lobbying from large, well-organized and financed, interest groups. Rather, small groups of residents, residents working in the context of local nonprofit organizations, and residents operating alone tend to be more prevalent. This is undoubtedly why the role of businesses in local environmental policymaking has largely been overlooked. And it is probably the reason why prescriptions for reforming local political processes to be more environmentally sensitive almost always focus on the role of participation and engagement of large numbers of residents (Prugh, Constanza, and Daly 2000; Portney 2005).

When interest lobbying occurs, it is often the result of specific businesses or business interests advocating local policies that make the city friendly for the activities of that business. Frequently, real estate interests and developers, the people who have the greatest stake in land-use decisions, are active participants. Sometimes these people participate as officials of their respective companies, and sometimes they manage to work through their local Chamber of Commerce. Rarely are business interests able to organize more broadly than this. In other words, it is somewhat rare to find a single association representing all developers, or all realtors, or any other business interest. Even in very large cities, the critical mass of parties with common political interests is usually nonexistent.

This is not to say that specific businesses are powerless in city politics. Despite the lack of the kind of interest-group or trade-group organization of the sort that might be found at the state or federal levels of government, specific companies often represent business interests and can still exert significant influence over local policymaking. Indeed, it is not uncommon for local city councils, zoning boards, or planning boards to be populated by a healthy dose of people from the business sector. And specific businesses may very well be sporadically active over specific issues as they arise.

The exact way that business interests manifest themselves in city politics varies greatly from city to city. In the jargon of urban studies, the way business operates to influence local policymaking is part of what is sometimes called "the urban governance regime." The urban governance regime encompasses all the formal and informal relationships among the different actors, parties, and interests in local government. As described by Stone (1993), the governance regime influences local policies through three factors: first, the composition of a community's governing coalition; second, the nature of the relationships among members of the governing coalition; and third, the resources the members bring to the governing coalition. One way or another, business is part of the governing coalition in virtually every city. In some places, business dominates the coalition; in others, it is a relatively minor player. When businesses, either working individually or collectively, dominate, it is usually because they possesses relatively large resources and have the ability to exercise leverage, usually by virtue of a willingness to direct capital into the city or elsewhere. Business sometimes possesses substantial leverage by holding the threat of loss of jobs over the heads of elected policymakers. But business does not dominate everywhere. Indeed, there seems to be substantial variation in the ways that business is part of the governing coalition.

The key question here is what kinds of coalitions seem to be most conducive to pursuing environmentally friendly policies. Stone suggests that the character of the governing coalition, especially the way business functions in that coalition, plays a significant role in determining what kinds of policies the city pursues. He uses a typology of cities to summarize different collections of cities' policies. This typology distinguishes four types of cities: cities with "maintenance regimes," where the overriding concern in policy is to maintain the status quo in terms of quality of life and quality of city services; cities with "development regimes," where the economic growth and development dominate the local political agenda; cities with "middle-class progressive regimes," where emphasis shifts to issues such as the environment, equity issues, affordable housing, historic preservation, and imposing linkage fees on development to alleviate the undesirable social consequences of rampant development; and cities with "lower-class opportunity expansion regimes," where equity and social justice issues are paramount.

The role that business plays in the middle-class progressive regime cities, where concern for the environment rises in importance, would be expected to be quite different from the role it plays in the maintenance or development regimes, where the environment gets routinely pushed off or kept off the local political agenda. So what role does business play in such middle-class progressive regimes? What is the relationship between local government and business in such environmentally friendly cities? According to Stone, the relationship tends to be based more on the coercive powers of government and the leverage that government can exercise on specific developers to get them to engage in the kinds of projects the city wants. Of course, some cities—cities with development regimes—either feel they have no leverage, or as part of their "beggars can't be choosers" mentality toward development, feel they shouldn't exercise what leverage they have. Middle-class progressive regime cities, on the other hand, understand that they possess resources—the land and the authority to permit particular uses of the land—that businesses, particularly developers, want. So they use this leverage to push businesses to pursue development in environmentally friendly ways. The primary issue here is whether there seems to be any evidence of a coercive relationship in specific cities where business has partnered with local government to produce what would seem to be environmentally friendly development. Stated another way, is there evidence that business only plays a role in support of environmentally friendly development when the city is governed by a middle-class progressive regime? Although definitive answers would require considerably more evidence than can be presented here, it is still a question worthy of examination. Before addressing this question, it is important to briefly review some of the transitions that, in general, seem to have made the emergence of environmentally friendly development possible.

Local Businesses and Local Public Policies

Perhaps unlike what happens at other levels of government, businesses very often do not engage in lobbying at the policy-adoption stage. Indeed, cities engage in much less broad and sweeping policy adoptions than other levels of government. There are some major types of policies that most, but certainly not all, cities adopt from time to time. These would include a city's long-term and strategic plans (sometimes called "Comprehensive Plans" or "General Plans"), and its zoning ordinances. Businesses have an abiding interest in these types of policies because once adopted, they set the stage for most development activities that occur subsequently. In other words, if a given city adopts a citywide plan that calls for extensive redevelopment in one set of neighborhoods and not others, this can create a significant hurdle for a developer who wants to propose a project somewhere else in the city. Much the same is true of a city's zoning ordinances. Not all cities have the legal authority to engage in zoning, but those that do adopt zoning as their only real legal mechanism for implementing a land-use regulation plan. Indeed, the only legal way most cities have of managing or controlling the private use of the land that makes up the city is through its legal authority to enact and enforce zoning ordinances. Once a zoning ordinance is in place, an added financial and political burden is placed on developers who wish to propose projects that require some sort of zoning variance or waiver. Businesses have an interest in the adoption of these kinds of zoning policies, but there is very little evidence that they explicitly engage the policymaking process at this point. Rather, business leaders are more likely to exert their informal influences to keep such policies from ever being considered if those policies threaten their ways of doing business (Stone 1980).

More commonly, businesses become engaged in the policy process at what might be called the policy-implementation stage. Many of the decisions made by city officials are really about implementation issues.

Sometimes these implementation issues relate to the broader policies adopted earlier, such as strategic plans or zoning ordinances, and sometimes they involve implementation of policies adopted by other levels of government. For example, when a state enacts a statewide or metropolitanwide comprehensive planning requirement that applies to all municipalities in the state, then each city must decide how to implement and comply with this requirement. Often, cities cooperate with other municipalities within their metropolitan area to coordinate services or functions, and city governments subsequently make many decisions about how to implement these cooperative arrangements.

When cities make the many decisions about how planning and zoning policies will be implemented, and indeed how planned development will be implemented, these decisions typically do involve businesses and developers. The case studies developed below largely focus on the implementation processes in specific cities. The proponents of development in these cities did not seem to be terribly interested in influencing the broader policies, including those designed in part to work toward protecting the biophysical environment. However, once efforts got underway to implement these policies—to define in detail how these policies would be put into effect—specific businesses and business leaders clearly got engaged. This chapter does not try to make the argument that businesses have been instrumental in the adoption of local policies designed explicitly to protect the environment. Indeed, most cities that elect to adopt policies to protect the environment do so in spite of the business community. In at least two of the case studies below, the business community appears to have only been interested in the broader environmentally friendly policies to the extent that they served to promote a particular vision of economic development. Once environmentally friendly policies have been adopted, however, the business community has been instrumental in determining how they work.

The Local Landscape of Business and the Environment

If there has traditionally been a role for business in protecting the local environment, it has come mainly from the idea that businesses should keep their own environmental houses in order. In other words, business's role is usually thought of as largely private and internal to the business, with, of course, federal and state regulation where mandated. According to this traditional role, as long as businesses operate with some high level of environmental responsibility and stewardship, perhaps using an internal Environmental Management System, then that business is doing everything it can to promote sustainability (see Shrivastava 1995). Most city governments around the United States are fairly passive about environmental protection, preferring to leave such issues to some other level of government or other organization. Yet as political support for national and state environmental regulation has weakened, local communities have increasingly seen the need to fill the void. Today, dozens of cities around the country have started to become more engaged in efforts to protect and improve their ecologies, sometimes in the context of sustainable-cities programs, livable-cities efforts, climate change initiatives, or just part of their overall planning processes. Local governments have increasing sought to create opportunities to encourage businesses to alter their practices for the betterment of the environment.[1] Business, on the other hand, has not always been a willing partner.

Traditionally, American cities have been thought of as places that create rather than solve environmental problems (Rees 1997; Giradet 1999). As centers of business and industry, particularly manufacturing industry, cities once represented the heart of pollution heaven. Moreover, as the major sources of jobs and economic growth, business and industry were considered the engine that fueled the urban-growth-machine heaven (Molotch 1976). Cities traditionally tolerated high levels of industrial pollution and pollution from related sources as the price to be paid for creating this heaven. Politically speaking, the industries themselves had no incentives to pollute less, for to do so meant that they would likely become less economically competitive. Local political leaders, not wanting to undermine the local economy, not wanting to alienate the businesses that provided the jobs to fuel that economy, and not wanting to drive businesses out of their jurisdictions, would not dare to propose environmental regulation. In other words, maintenance and development governance regimes were dominant. Indeed, this is one of the fundamental tenets underlying the growth of the environmental movement in the United States starting in the late 1960s. Environmental issues would have to be addressed at a national level if the political power of local businesses was to be circumvented or at least counter-balanced.

What, of course, was missing from this traditional relationship between business and industry on one side and the local government on the other was the inevitability that continued pollution would eventually cut deeply into the quality of life that the residents of city experienced. First with air pollution, as in Pittsburgh, Pennsylvania, and Chattanooga, Tennessee, then with hazardous waste sites in cities all around the nation, and with ground- and drinking-water pollution from contaminated rain-water runoff, it has slowly become clear to many people that the quality of the local biophysical environment affects everyone. In many cities, local business leaders have perhaps reluctantly at first come to the real-ization that local economic development becomes difficult or impossible when the local biophysical environment is widely perceived to be pol-luted. When the physical environment deteriorates, fewer people want to live in the city; when fewer people want to live there, it becomes increasingly difficult to attract new businesses and people who might want to work there.

Perhaps equally important in the landscape of local politics is the fact that the character of the local economy in almost every major city in the United States has become transformed over the last twenty years. Up until two decades ago, practically every major city's economy was dom-inated by some manufacturing industry or another. As the federal gov-ernment has made global trade a high priority, the dominance of manufacturing industries has dwindled just about everywhere. The busi-nesses that were once dominant in local politics have all but disappeared. Today, the largest employers in most major cities are government (par-ticularly in state capitals) and service industries, especially health and hospitals. Moreover, many of the largest local employers are local offices of national or multinational firms, and the officials in these local offices no longer seem to have the stake in city politics and policies that their locally owned ancestors did.

What this means is that two major local changes have occurred, one environmental and the other political. Both tend to be positive toward the environment. The environmental impact produced by these changes is that the businesses and industries that were once so clearly responsi-ble for undermining the quality of the environment are largely gone, and so is their continuing pollution. Of course, these businesses often left behind the hazards of their earlier manufacturing processes—stocks of pollution often in the form of Superfund priority sites or brownfields that may make the reuse of the land difficult. And they often left behind an economic disaster area, leaving cities with all the problems they created along with high unemployment levels. As will be discussed later, the need for cities to pursue economic development strategies to replace those lost jobs has motivated many cities to try to become more sustainable—that is, they have tried to envision strategies that would allow them to grow their economic and employments bases without destroying the environment. The political impact is that the strong voices that once stood in opposition to local environmental initiatives—the voices that would certainly never allow environmental protection to get on the local political agenda—are also weakening. This means that cities that once felt they had no leverage to use to coerce local businesses now are increasingly feeling they can exercise this leverage. These two sets of events—the elimination of the sources of pollution and the weakening of the political opposition to environmental protection—have opened the way for a new generation of environmental policies and programs in cities. In many cities, these two events have also opened the door for local citizen groups and nonprofit organizations to fill the void in advocating a cleaner environment. Sustainable Seattle, Inc. in Seattle, the Boston Foundation, Inc. and the Boston Climate Action Network in Boston, and the Jacksonville Community Council, Inc. in Jacksonville, Florida, represent examples of local nonprofit and advocacy organizations that have taken up the environmental protection charge.

But any city-oriented review of environmental policies would be remiss if it did not draw a distinction between the kinds of environmental policies that may be pursued by the federal or even the state governments and those that can be pursued at the local level. Most municipal governments do not have the legal authority to adopt and impose environmental regulations on their residents or businesses. A city cannot decide on its own to impose air emissions standards more stringent than the state or national standards, for example, even if it wanted to. What this means is that cities must pursue environmental policies through the definition of specific programs oriented around municipal government functions that *are* permitted by law. Most of the more aggressive municipal environmental efforts have focused on such issues as comprehensive planning and land-use regulation, usually through zoning, and other programs adopted within the context of accepted municipal services. Rarely do cities articulate an explicit environmental policy per se, although some do. More commonly, cities pursue local environmental policies in the way they go about pursuing their other, perhaps more mainstream policies. One of the municipal functions that has become a prime target for efforts to protect and improve the environment is the broad "economic development" function. In other words, as cities consider how they should go about engaging in economic development, sometimes they elect to do so by trying to protect the environment. Perhaps equally important to note is the fact that most cities do not have the legal authority to compel business to protect the environment per se. The local legal authority that can be used to help protect the environment comes primarily from the authority to regulate land use, particularly through zoning, permitting, and the limited ability to exercise eminent domain. As noted earlier, this legal authority potentially provides cities with leverage they can bring to bear on business. Although most cities do possess this legal authority to some degree, using that authority is rarely cost-free. Businesses that are subject to specific applications of this authority often file challenges in court or elsewhere. The point here is that, to the extent that protecting the environment is a goal, it often requires that cities work with businesses to develop voluntary rather than mandatory programs and initiatives—voluntary partnerships—to get things done.

The most frequent, although not the only, mechanism used in cities to promote local ecologically sensitive policies is the community development corporation (CDC). Community development corporations are nonprofit corporations that are usually created to implement cities' economic development strategies, or to improve the quality of specific human services to residents. Sometimes CDCs are created for very narrowly defined and specific purposes; sometimes they have a broader coordinating function, perhaps facilitating the cooperation among numerous more narrowly defined CDCs operating in a particular geographic or policy domain. CDCs have been a feature of the urban public policy landscape for many decades, but they have only recently become interested in the biophysical environment of the city.

In cities where improving and protecting the environment is a relatively high priority, reliance on CDCs is not uncommon. As will be shown in the four case studies presented later, even CDCs whose primary mission would seem to be oriented around engaging in traditional economic development or redevelopment activities often try to accomplish their goals while promoting principles of environmental protection and sustainability. Cities all around the country are using CDCs for brownfield redevelopment, for urban infill programs and mixed-use zoning projects, for creation of green building programs, for planning ecoindustrial parks, to engage the broader business community in various public-private pollution prevention partnerships, and in many other specific programs thought to be important components of a city's effort to become more environmentally sensitive. CDCs have undoubtedly become a preferred mechanism for pursuing economic development of all kinds because of the federal and possibly state tax benefits that they offer. Yet there is nothing about reliance on CDCs per se that ensures they will be used in efforts to explicitly protect the environment. Indeed, an analysis of the role of CDCs in general would probably find that most have nothing to do with explicit efforts to protect the environment. The CDCs profiled here, however, represent a specific type of organization. They represent partnerships between government and the private sector—a sort of mediating institution—that can be used to pursue common goals of balancing business interests with the public interest of protecting the environment. Four specific partnerships will be profiled later.

Environmental Protection as an Economic Development Strategy

In many cities, especially those that have begun to think about pursuing sustainable-cities initiatives, the growth imperative has been supplanted by a hybrid set of economic development goals. These goals involve achieving economic growth without incurring the negative environmental consequences that were once thought inevitable and acceptable. Sometimes this type of growth is referred to as "smart growth," where cities try to carefully manage the kind of growth they experience. Growth management, or smart growth, is far different from growth controls, where the dominant aim is to prevent further growth within the city's boundaries. In these cities, economic growth is still an extremely important—perhaps the most important—goal. The need to maintain and grow the base of employment in the city must receive attention. But the idea of smart growth looks more and more attractive to cities.

Smart growth presupposes that economic development needs to be planned, using a variety of different techniques and policy instruments, including zoning and land-use management. It can take many forms. Sometimes the focus is on aggressive "brownfield redevelopment," where the city government takes an active role in working with the business community to clean up hazardous waste sites that otherwise would be economically unproductive. Sometimes these efforts focus on the development of ecoindustrial parks—designated economic development areas where low-polluting businesses can be located. Sometimes the focus is on some form of cluster or targeted economic development, where cities try to build on their comparative advantages to lure specific kinds of businesses that are related to each other in some fashion and that would be expected to have very little negative impact on the environment. Sometimes these efforts are the result of collaboration between city planning and economic development agencies; sometimes they are the result of strategic plans developed by the business community itself, often through a local Chamber of Commerce; and sometimes they are the result of collaborative public-private partnerships, often in the form of nonprofit CDCs with specific economic development tasks.

Some case examples of the latter form of public-private collaborations will illustrate in specific, small- to medium-sized, cities how these work. These case studies focus on multisector partnerships designed precisely to advance particular economic development goals of their respective cities in sustainable and environmentally responsible ways. In each case, the partnership takes the form of nonprofit corporations formed on the basis of cooperation between the private sector (specific local companies and local Chambers of Commerce), the public sector (particular local and metropolitan government agencies), and sometimes the broader nonprofit sector (local foundations and universities). In other words, the foundation for these efforts is voluntary collaboration and cooperation between local government and the private sector, where the organizational result is the creation of nonprofit corporations that are tasked with actually doing the economic development projects or activities.

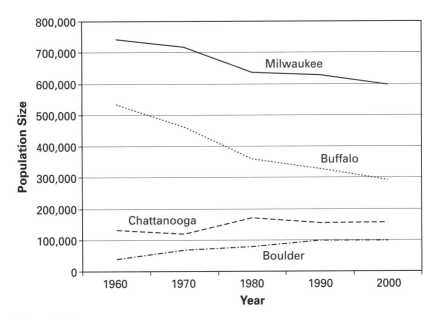

Figure 11.1
Change in population size in four case-study cities

The four cases described below come from Milwaukee, Wisconsin; Buffalo, New York; Boulder, Colorado; and Chattanooga, Tennessee. These cases simply illustrate what is becoming an increasing trend in cities around the country. Cities such as Chicago, Seattle, Portland, San Diego, San Jose, and many others have also seen their respective business communities engaged in the very same kinds of environmentally responsible economic development activities as in these four cities.

Activities in these four cities were selected because the cities are so very different. Aside from sharing a concern for the way economic development is conducted, a concern for ensuring that the future economic development minimizes detrimental environmental impacts, these cities have little else in common. Figure 11.1 shows how the population sizes of these cities have changed over the forty-year period from 1960 through 2000. Table 11.1 provides a brief overview of the change in reliance on manufacturing industries as a source of employment in these four cities. All of this information applies to the cities themselves, not to their larger metropolitan areas. Two of the four cities whose public-private partnerships are profiled here lost substantial population

Table 11.1
Manufacturing employment in four case-study cities

City	Gross population density, 2000 (people/sq. mile)	Percent employed in manufacturing 1970	Percent employed in manufacturing 2000	Manufacturing employment change %, 1970–2000
Boulder, Colorado	3,727	16.4	8.8	–46.3%
Chattanooga, Tennessee	1,254	32.0	16.5	–48.4%
Buffalo, New York	7,138	30.4	18.5	–39.1%
Milwaukee, Wisconsin	6,212	34.8	13.0	–62.6%

over this entire period, with Buffalo having lost nearly half of its 1960 population. Chattanooga lost population in the first ten years, the period when this city's air pollution became extreme, then experienced slight population gains; in recent years, the population size has declined slightly. Of these cities, only Boulder experienced consistent growth.

All of the cities have experienced declines in the proportions of their respective employment bases that come from manufacturing industries, and that is a trend that characterizes the entire nation. Yet some of these cities' declines are quite striking. Milwaukee, which once employed over a third of its labor force in manufacturing, now employs around 13 percent, a decline of over 62 percent in thirty years. The other cities all experienced declines in the 40 percent range. In the face of these challenges, and perhaps because of them, these cities have elected to pursue economic development by emphasizing smart-growth opportunities, and have relied on public-private partnerships and CDCs to accomplish this.

One city, Buffalo, is located in the Northeast, and has suffered more than its share of economic decline and population loss. Buffalo's population currently stands at just under 300,000, but it has been losing population at a rapid rate, having lost over 10 percent of its population between 1990 and 2000 and nearly half of its population since 1960.

Along with this loss has been the loss of industrial jobs. Between 1990 and 2000, the percentage of the labor force employed in manufacturing dropped from 16.2 to 13.1 percent, continuing the long-term trend of job losses. One of its economic development projects, the Green Gold Initiative, illustrates this city's effort to engage in smart growth.

Another city, Milwaukee, located in the upper Midwest, has worked to find innovative ways of compensating for the loss of significant heavy manufacturing industries and their related jobs. Milwaukee is the largest of the four cities discussed here, with nearly 600,000 residents. It has also experienced significant loss of population, although not nearly as large as that in Buffalo. Manufacturing employment has also dropped. In 1990, over 22 percent of Milwaukee's labor force was employed in manufacturing industries. By 2000, that percentage had dropped to 18.5, down from the time when the city employed over a third of its labor force in manufacturing. As the city has examined ways of promoting economic development, the Menomonee Valley Partners nonprofit development company was formed to try to ensure that new development would be consistent with principles of sustainability.

The third city, Boulder, is located in the Rocky Mountains, and is a relatively well-off small city that nonetheless is cognizant of its tendencies to experience significant threats to the environment, particularly air pollution. Boulder's population is a little under 100,000, and has remained fairly stable over time. Boulder's manufacturing employment has never been very large, but even here declines are noticeable. Boulder has been very aggressive in its efforts to protect the environment, and its Partners for a Clean Environment program has impressively tried to tackle one of the thorniest challenges for municipalities, local air emissions.

And the fourth city, Chattanooga, is located in the South, was once a fairly heavily industrial city, and suffered significant environmental consequences. Its population is only a little over 155,000, and after experiencing significant population loss, it is now experiencing some moderate population growth, and has experienced the least decline in manufacturing employment over the ten-year period. Chattanooga's efforts to keep the environment protected while promoting economic growth have led it to an integrated strategy of cluster economic development and related projects.

With these basic city profiles in mind, the issue remains: in what ways has the business community been involved in environmentally friendly economic development? An answer to this question comes from a look at the some of the specific economic development programs pursued in these cities. These programs are not meant to represent an exhaustive description of economic development in these cities. Indeed, there are many traditional economic development activities going on that one might argue are not particularly environmentally friendly. But these do represent examples of how the private sector has embraced environmental protection and improvement.

The Four Cases

This discussion focuses on one major public-private partnership in each city. The examples describe the orientation of the partnerships, and explain how each partnership has attempted to blend the goal of economic development with the goal of maintaining and improving the biophysical environment. They show how the government has essentially joined forces with local business and industry to engage in economic development without ignoring environmental impacts. Moreover, they show that, perhaps contrary to the expectation that such partnerships would tend to arise only when city government can exercise some leverage on the business community, there is evidence only in Milwaukee that such leverage was used or was even necessary.

Menomonee Valley Partners, Inc. in Milwaukee

Menomonee Valley Partners (MVP) is a nonprofit corporation formed in 1999 for the express purpose of promoting and guiding economic redevelopment in the area of Milwaukee known as the Menomonee Valley.[2] The Menomonee Valley is a 1,500-acre area of the city that was once populated mainly by manufacturing industries and that was described in 2005 as "a giant brownfield."[3] As the character of the local economy has turned away from manufacturing, pursuing economic development strategies within the constraints of smart-growth principles has become a priority. The MVP is guided by what it calls "sustainability principles," which simply mean that it tries to promote economic development in environmentally responsible ways. The MVP's mission notes that "the principles of sustainable development guide the efforts of the many partners that work on a daily basis to redevelop the Menomonee River Valley. . . . Sustainable development will be achieved in the valley through environmental stewardship and job creation that benefit . . . surrounding neighborhoods."[4] Projects undertaken by MVP include business parks, open space, infill housing, and others.[5] MVP involves numerous local businesses, the Wisconsin Chamber of Commerce, numerous nonprofit foundations, and city, county, and state government agencies.

In what is an impressive effort to document the environmental, as well as the economic, benefits of the redevelopment projects undertaken by MVP, there is a major "benchmarking project," designed to facilitate explicit measurement of established goals.[6] This benchmarking project, developed with the assistance of faculty at the University of Wisconsin—Milwaukee campus, measures and monitors the wildlife in the valley, the water quality, the air quality, and the quality of the land cover and habitat. Presumably, the benchmarking process will help to ensure that as development progresses, the environmental quality in these areas will not be sacrificed.

Perhaps the reason that this partnership seems to work is the fact that the valley is so large that the development community in Milwaukee cannot seriously ignore it. The city government could simply have taken the view that it desperately needs development, and any development would be welcome. Instead, it understood that it possessed at least some leverage to push developers toward environmentally friendly, or sustainable, approaches. Moreover, because the success of the redevelopment effort requires the exercise of substantial government authority through the powers of eminent domain, zoning and permitting, and legal liability in brownfield areas, among others, everyone seems to understand that the leverage potential of the city is significant. The benchmarking project represents a seemingly effective way to keep that leverage alive as the redevelopment progresses. In other words, if the development projects begin to stray away from being environmentally friendly in some way, presumably the benchmarking project will raise the red flags necessary to push corrective actions.

The Green Gold Initiative/Green Gold Development Corporation in Buffalo

The Green Gold Initiative (GGI) represents Buffalo's effort to pursue economic development strategies that attract environmentally responsible businesses and industries to the city. Combined with the city's extensive efforts to conduct brownfield redevelopment, the GGI represents a relatively new commitment to try to take advantage of a wide range of specific resources. As envisioned by the President of the Common Council, this commitment involves the Greater Buffalo Partnership, the Mayor's Office, the Erie County Industrial Development Agency, Buffalo State College, the Buffalo Environmental Task Force, the Department of Community Development, Vision for Tomorrow, the Common Council, and other organizations.[7] It has also involved a wide array of local "green" businesses, companies whose products or services contribute directly to the protection or improvement of the environment. Clearly, the effort represents an effort to promote economic development while protecting the environment. As James W. Pitts—president of the city's Common Council—put it, "Green Gold is designed to provide interesting, meaningful, well-paying jobs for Western New Yorkers— the kind that will keep young people here when they finish their education."[8]

The brainchild of Pitts, this program's focus is on finding a way to promote Buffalo as a location for only certain kinds of businesses and industries. As Pitts said when he announced the idea,

The key to improving our region is jobs—specifically, jobs that are interesting, fulfilling and that provide a decent income in fields that are likely to grow in the foreseeable future. We all know family members and friends who have left Western New York to seek opportunity elsewhere . . . [and] that the decline of steel and other basic manufacturing industries has devastated our local economy. I believe we need a focused and intelligent strategy to ensure that our recovery from this devastation is swift and complete. Current efforts to market the city to industry in a general way have had only limited success, and I believe that unless Buffalo finds a niche in the world economy, it will be difficult to attract anything but low paying service industries to our area.

It may be a stretch for many of you to see Buffalo becoming a national center for the environmental industry, but that is exactly the type of collective stretch we need to take if we are to rise above our current stagnation. Before telling you why I believe the Buffalo area can become the environmental Silicon Valley, let me describe how I see the Green Gold strategy working. The Green Gold office should be supported by a public–private–university–citizen group partnership. Its mission will be to develop, attract and sustain forward looking businesses that are offering solutions to current and projected environmental problems. The office will:

• Undertake research on the environmental industry and its fit with the local economy and labor force;
• Provide assistance for local companies interested in taking part in the Green Gold strategy and developing a Buffalo Area Green Business Council;
• Work with the School Board and its Environmental Advisory Council to prepare Buffalo's students for participation in the Green Gold business sector;
• Develop a prestigious annual national conference to explore the nature of future environmental problems and the likely economic consequences of those problems;
• Develop and implement a national marketing strategy that identifies Buffalo as "the place to be" for environmental entrepreneurs.

This Green Gold Initiative, therefore, seems to be very much motivated by a desire on the part of local policymakers to merge the goals of economic development with environmental protection. The immediate result was the creation of the Green Gold Development Corporation, Inc., a CDC dedicated to the implementation of this initiative.

Perhaps because the Green Gold Initiative does not yet involve any specific development projects, the city has not found any particular kind of leverage to bring to bear on this initiative's goals. The fact is that Buffalo's population and employment base have been decimated in recent decades, and this has led many in the city government to adopt the "beggars can't be choosers mentality" described earlier. The initiative is motivated primarily by a desire to find some hook to attract businesses to the city. That hook could just as easily have been based on something other than the environment. Nonetheless, this represents an effort to use the environment as a means for providing the city with more leverage than it currently has. Presumably, if the city were successful at attracting environmentally friendly businesses, then it would possess greater ability to exercise leverage over other future development. The true challenge for the city is to find a way to develop this leverage, and the true test will be whether the city is willing and able to use that leverage. To the extent that Buffalo has a maintenance or development governance regime, it might become politically difficult for leaders to exercise whatever leverage they might have, or to avoid using their leverage to prevent development that is not particularly consistent with Green Gold's environmental goals.

The Partners for a Clean Environment (PACE) Program in Boulder
The PACE program, started in 1997, represents an ambitious effort on the part of the city of Boulder's Office of Environmental Affairs, Boulder County, several other area municipalities, and the Boulder Chamber of Commerce to institutionalize pollution prevention (P2) in the private sector.[9] Targeting specific sectors of small businesses, PACE provides extensive technical assistance to ensure that existing and future economic development does not undermine environmental quality. It operates a certification program whereby local businesses of a size not typically subject to regulatory controls can volunteer to participate so that they can be certified as meeting particular pollution reduction goals. There is very little information concerning the decision to develop and adopt this program, although there seems to be general agreement that everyone thought it was a great idea.[10] Clearly, business leaders have readily embraced the program and have been very engaged in the annual implementation and assessment decisions.

Working in several specific business sectors, efforts have focused first on the auto repair, auto body, and printing sectors because of clear-cut pollution prevention alternatives. Additionally, dry cleaners were subsequently added, and the dental and restaurant sectors were targeted because of their impact on wastewater. More recently, the program has also targeted other manufacturing industries, along with landscape and lawn-care businesses. These represent businesses that are usually exempt from the environmental regulations that apply to larger firms, but collectively they often still create significant environmental impacts. In each sector, PACE staff held focus-group interviews with local business representatives to develop sets of achievable and appropriate pollution prevention goals for that sector. These goals then became the criteria for business certification. In other words, once the goals were specified, any specific business in the sector could become certified as a "partner" by meeting all of these goals. A partial certification was instituted for businesses that could not meet all of the goals but could meet at least three of them. In addition to the PACE certification effort, there is also an effort to get local businesses, particularly manufacturing firms, to report on their own hazardous materials usage and generation, and their internal efforts to reduce their streams of hazardous wastes.

The PACE program has reached a very large proportion of the businesses it has targeted, and well over 100 such businesses have been certified. Perhaps equally important, the program claims to have achieved significant reductions in the emissions of pollutants. In 2004, the program estimated that, excluding the manufacturing sector, it had helped to reduce emissions of volatile organic chemicals by some 28 tons, hazardous waste by 5,800 gallons, and polluted water discharges by over 36,000 gallons. Equally impressive environmental results were reported for the manufacturing sector.[11]

Perhaps the most impressive aspect of the PACE program is the fact that it seems to have achieved significant results—reduction in pollution—without overt use of coercion. The program is entirely voluntary on the part of businesses, yet they choose to participate in large numbers. Clearly, the partnership has capitalized on the fact that businesses have been willing to use certification to their competitive advantage when selling their goods and services, but there is very little in the way of coercion at work in Boulder.

A Cluster of Public—Private Partnerships in Chattanooga

Unlike the projects described above, the experience in Chattanooga is representative of a much broader economic public-private collaborative development strategy. Not all of the various projects pursued through such partnerships are explicitly designed to improve or protect the environment, but a significant number are. In a 1997 presentation at a Chautauqua Conference on Regional Governance, the president of the Chattanooga Chamber of Commerce suggested that the reason his organization became interested in what is essentially smart growth was "because the old strategy—low taxes, low cost of land and construction, low wages, and cheap power—wasn't working anymore. We believe some things must grow—jobs, productivity, income and wages, profits, capital, and savings, information, knowledge, education. And that others must not—pollution, waste, poverty, energy and material use per unit of output" (Pierce and Johnson 1998, 3–4). According to his view, the role of the Chamber of Commerce is to help make possible a particular vision where, as he said, "we are going to build the future of Chattanooga by balancing the economy, ecology, and equity" (Parr 1998, 5).

When the Chamber of Commerce president suggested that "the old strategy . . . wasn't working," he was making reference to the environmental nightmare that had befallen the city in the 1960s and 1970s. Chattanooga began this process as a troubled city. With the unfettered growth of the steel, coal, and other industries during the 1960s, Chattanooga developed some of the most serious pollution problems of any city in the nation. Air pollution during the 1960s was the worst problem, with residents frequently required to drive their cars with their headlights on in the middle of the day because pollution had significantly reduced visibility. As L. Joe Ferguson, whose Chattanooga-based company Advanced Vehicle Systems, Inc. was created to build the city's electric bus fleet, noted about the state of air pollution in 1969, "Walter Cronkite announced on the news that we had the poorest air quality in the country, and boy, let me tell you we did" (Graham 1999, 5). So it is in this context that public-private cooperation around smart growth became part of the generally accepted way of "doing business."

The multifaceted smart-growth effort represents Chattanooga's approach to promoting cluster economic development while accomplishing major environmental (brownfield-site) remediation. This case study will highlight efforts to take advantage of the electric- and hybrid-vehicle manufacturing capacity that was developed in Chattanooga for the primary purpose of providing very low or zero-emissions vehicles for the city and regional transit authority. The manufacturing company AVS was joined by the nonprofit ATTI, to advance the use of such vehicles nationwide. Combined with the operations of the nonprofit corporation RiverValley Partners, in cooperation with the Greater Chattanooga Chamber of Commerce, these initiatives account for a significant proportion of the economic development, particularly waterfront development, that has taken place in this city over the last ten years.

RiverValley Partners, Inc. was once described by the Chamber of Commerce as a public-private nonprofit organization dedicated to implementing an economic development strategy that attracts new investment in the city while explicitly seeking to attain quality-of-life goals.[12] RiverValley Partners was created in 1993 after a merger between two predecessor organizations, the RiverCity Company, a nonprofit group established in 1986, and the Partners for Economic Progress, which produced "Target '96," the city's first explicit environmental strategic plan. RiverValley Partners and its predecessors sponsored numerous economic development projects throughout the city and its county, including the Tennessee Aquarium, opened in 1992, the Riverwalk, and the Tennessee Riverpark. By 2001, RiverValley Partners was folded into a larger initiative of the Chamber of Commerce, and essentially became part of the Chattanooga Regional Growth Initiative oriented around what the chamber calls "cluster development." Cluster development focuses on strategically trying to attract businesses in specific industries or sectors of the economy. For example, the chamber has designated health and hospitals, confectionary and baked goods, medical devices and health services, textiles and floor coverings, and a number of other clusters as targets for development. One of these clusters is oriented around the electric-vehicle initiative started for the purpose of providing zero-emissions buses for the city's public transit system. The development of this piece of the economic development puzzle in Chattanooga provides one of the best examples of how the goals of development and environmental protection can be melded.

This story begins in 1992, when the Chattanooga Area Regional Transit Authority (CARTA) decided to request bids for a manufacturer to develop and produce battery-powered electric buses for use mainly in Chattanooga.[13] In late 1992, a decision was made to organize Advanced Vehicle Systems, Inc. (AVS), described by the founders as a public-private partnership, in response. AVS was successful in winning the contract to produce twelve electric buses for a three-mile shuttle system in a renaissance area of downtown Chattanooga; it has since enlarged its line of products to include hybrid vehicles and has expanded its production and sales to other cities. This represents economic development that accomplished the development and environmental goals simultaneously: it created local jobs while at the same time contributing to improving the environmental health of the city. Chattanooga has been able to build on the successes of AVS by starting the Electric Transit Vehicle Institute, ETVI, (now called the Advanced Transportation Technology Institute, or ATTI), a nonprofit organization formed to promote the design, production, and utilization of battery-powered electric and hybrid-electric vehicles.[14] Subsequently, the Chattanooga Chamber of Commerce defined an economic development "cluster" in the area of electric vehicles as part of its regional development initiative.

Clearly, Chattanooga does not possess a middle-class progressive governance regime. Issues of economic development dominate local policymaking. Therefore, Chattanooga would not necessarily be expected to be a place especially conducive to environmentally friendly policies. Yet partly because of the success of the particular economic development strategy they did pursue, and because of the prior environmental problems the city faced, the business community has become a voluntary participant in environmentally responsible development. The danger, of course, is that unless city government leaders are willing to use whatever leverage they might have developed in order to pressure the development community, development can readily revert to a business-as-usual mentality. Indeed, as the city grapples with at least two major brownfield redevelopment projects, there is some evidence that this has started to happen (Portney 2003, 185–193).

Conclusions

While the idea of local governments engaging in environmental protection might seem unlikely, many cities have engaged in efforts to accomplish just that. These efforts have often worked toward achieving this goal through developing partnerships with the local business community. These partnerships frequently take the form of community development corporations created to engage in specific economic development projects that are guided by some conception of smart growth or sustainable development.

This chapter presented information about four cases, or situations, where these kinds of partnerships have been used to great effect. Partnerships in Buffalo, Boulder, Chattanooga, and Milwaukee have all been used as mechanisms for promoting environmentally sensitive economic development or redevelopment. Sometimes this means conducting economic redevelopment in ways that clean up environmental damage done years ago; sometimes it means conducting new development activities—the building of homes and offices, schools and stores—that carefully match the character of that development to the character of the biophysical environment.

The central question remains: what kinds of local conditions seem to be most conducive to having business play a major role in environmentally friendly economic development? Clearly, the character of the local governance regime represents a significant influence on whether and to what extent business plays such a role. While Stone suggests that business is likely to play this role only in cities that have what he calls "middle-class progressive regimes," this is not entirely borne out by the four case studies presented here. Clearly at least two of the cities—Buffalo and Chattanooga—do not have such governance regimes. Instead they have maintenance or development regimes. Yet their emerging public-private partnerships have managed to pursue important programs to help protect and improve the local environment. It certainly may be true that the ultimate success of any of these programs would be greater if all of the cities possessed middle-class progressive regimes, and this is an issue that deserves much more focused analysis in the future. What seems clear is that when cities have the leverage to affect development, and when they have the political will to use that leverage for the benefit of the biophysical environment, environmentally friendly development is possible.

What these four cases demonstrate is that the local business community has played a significant role in the pursuit of local environmental policies in cities, particularly at the implementation stage. The business community may be self-interested in this role, but it is a role that nonetheless looks very different from that which is usually attributed to business. As cities look for new and innovative ways to promote the idea that they need to protect and improve their environments, they will increasingly see that business and industry can be an enormously helpful resource. Only time will tell if these efforts truly result in a greatly improved ecology, but the programmatic results that have been achieved often look very impressive indeed.

Notes

1. A good example comes from Portland, Oregon's, "Businesses for an Environmentally Sustainable Tomorrow" awards program, run mainly out of the city's Energy Office. (See Beatley and Manning 1997, 141.) Another example comes from the many voluntary green building programs that provide extensive technical assistance to architects and contractors in an effort to alter building

design and construction practices to be more environmentally friendly, such as those found in Austin, Texas, Boulder, Colorado, San Jose, California, and many other cities.

2. See www.renewthevalley.org/.

3. Chris De Sousa, Ben Gramling, and Kevin LeMoine, *Menomonee Valley Benchmarking Initiative*, 2005. Found at http://epic.cuir.edu/mvbi/05_report. htm.

4. http://renewthevalley.org/sustainable/.

5. http://renewthevalley.org/projects/.

6. The website for the benchmarking study can be found at www.mvbi.org/.

7. www.ci.buffalo.ny.us/Home/Leadership/City_Departments/Special_ Programs_and_Agencies/Green_Gold_Initiative/TheGreenGoldStrategy   and www.ci.buffalo.ny.us/document_158_31.html.

8. www.ci.buffalo.ny.us/document_295_40.html.

9. See www.pacepartners.com/.

10. www.pacepartners.com/.

11. Partners for a Clean Environment (PACE) and Watershed Approach to Stream Health (WASH), 2003 Annual Report. www.bouldercolorado.gov/ www/pace/index.html.

12. Information about the RiversCity Company and RiverCity Partners can be found at www.rivercitycompany.com. For a description of the accomplishments of this partnership, see www.pps.org/upo/info/design/success_chatanooga.

13. www.eere.energy.gov/afdc/pdfs/chatt_cs.pdf

14. See www.atti-info.org/.

References

Beatley, Timothy, and Christie Manning. *The Ecology of Place: Planning for Environment, Economy, and Community*. New York: Island Press, 1997. www.green-rated.org/prog_bestawards.asp.

Girardet, H. 1999. "Sustainable Cities: A Contradiction in Terms?" In David Satterthwaite, ed., *The Earthscan Reader in Sustainable Cities*. New York: Earthscan.

Graham, Lamar. 1999. "The Reborn American City: A Place Where You Might Want to Live." *Parade*, April 25, 4–6.

Molotch, Harvey. 1976. "The City as Growth Machine: Toward a Political Economy of Place." *American Journal of Sociology* 82 (2): 309–332.

Parr, John. 1998. "Chattanooga: The Sustainable City." In Bruce Adams and John Parr, eds., *Boundary Crossers: Case Studies of How Ten of America's Metropolitan Regions Work*. College Park, MD: Academy of Leadership.

Peterson, Paul. 1981. *City Limits*. Chicago: University of Chicago Press.

Pierce, Neal, and Curtis Johnson. 1998. "A Civic Vignette: The Chattanooga Story—From Troubled Raw River Town to Global Model." In Neal Pierce and Curtis Johnson, eds., *Boundary Crossers: Community Leadership for a Global Age*. College Park, MD: Academy of Leadership.

Portney, Kent E. 2003. *Taking Sustainable Cities Seriously: Economic Development, the Environment, and Quality of Life in American Cities*. Cambridge, MA: MIT Press.

Portney, Kent E. 2005. "Civic Engagement and Sustainable Cities." *Public Administration Review* 65 (5) (September–October): 579–591.

Prugh, Thomas, Robert Constanza, and Herman Daly. 2000. *The Local Politics of Global Sustainability*. Washington, DC: Island Press.

Rees, William E. 1997. "Is 'Sustainable City' an Oxymoron?" *Local Environment* 2 (3) (October): 303–310.

Shrivastava, Paul. 1995. "The Role of Corporations in Achieving Ecological Sustainability." *Academy of Management Review* 20 (4): 936–960.

Stone, Clarence. 1980. "Systemic Power in Community Decision Making: A Restatement of Stratification Theory." *American Political Science Review* 74 (December): 978–990.

Stone, Clarence. 1993. "Urban Regimes and the Capacity to Govern: A Political Economy Approach." *Journal of Urban Affairs* 15(1): 2.

VII

Overview and Implications for the Future

12

Conclusions: The Influence of Business on Environmental Politics and Policy

Sheldon Kamieniecki and Michael E. Kraft

Few would seriously question the proposition that business is a central player in environmental and natural resource policymaking even if disagreement exists over the extent of its influence. Contemporary actions on issues as diverse as national energy policy, clean air and water, management of toxic chemicals, forest conservation, and protection of endangered species suggest that business interests often are pivotal to government decisionmaking. The same could be said of the role of business in major environmental policy decisions over the past four decades, when most of the current laws and regulations were put into place. For these reasons, as we noted in chapter 1, we find it surprising that little systematic research has been conducted on what business interests try to do to influence policy decisions and how successful they are at it. This explains why there are conflicting assertions about the power that business wields in environmental politics and policy.

Most environmentalists consider business interests not only to be exceptionally active players in the policy process but exceedingly powerful. Indeed, they think that business interests are so influential that they constitute a major obstacle to the enactment and implementation of sound policies that can protect the environment and conserve natural resources. They find themselves fighting business interests in nearly every institutional and policy venue, from local decisions on land use to national debates over climate change. They are convinced that corporate America is able to use its vast economic resources to exert inordinate influence in all of these settings. Thus they, and many others, conclude that business often—if not always—gets its way on crucial environmental and resource issues.

Some scholars of interest-group politics offer a contrary view of the role of business in environmental policy. They believe environmental and other citizen groups, which enjoyed enormous gains in membership and resources from the 1960s to the 2000s, have been highly successful in overcoming the power of "big business." Their considerable resources have helped them to battle against business interests for most of the modern environmental era. While not always successful, the enactment of dozens of major environmental policies, from the Clear Air Act to Superfund, attests to the substantial political clout of the organized environmental community (Baumgartner and Leech 1998; Berry 1999; Smith 2000). It has been able to succeed at such policy change by receiving support from the scientific community, galvanizing public opinion, gaining favorable media coverage, and intervening in all of the major institutional venues, from state legislatures to Congress and the federal courts. Its success was particularly evident during the 1970s and, to a lesser extent, during the 1980s. Yet even in the 1990s and 2000s it often has used its resources effectively to bring attention to the issues and to win support for its positions (Duffy 2003).

A third pattern has been evident since the mid-1990s, a period in which environmental groups generally have done less well, especially at the national level, in achieving significant policy change. The political climate has tended to favor their opponents in the business community, and mobilization of the American public on environmental issues has become more difficult (Bosso 2005; Vig and Kraft 2006). One consequence has been an extended period of policy gridlock in which neither environmental groups nor business groups have succeeded in attaining their goals (Kamieniecki 2006; Kraft 2006). Environmental groups have been unable to persuade government to enact major new legislation or reauthorize existing programs, and business groups have been unable to convince government to scrap or alter substantially landmark air and water pollution laws and other major environmental legislation, such as the Endangered Species Act of 1973. This pattern of policy stalemate has sparked disagreement over exactly how much access and influence business groups enjoy in the environmental policy arena at different levels of government (e.g., Brown 2001; Cahn 1995; Clawson, Neustadt, and Waller 1998; Davis 2002; Dryzek 1997; Glazer and Rothenberg 2001; Gonzalez 2001; Korten 1995; Libby 1998; Milbrath 1989).

One other development bears mention in this context. In recent years many large corporations have attempted to change the prevailing impression that they care little about the environment and that they are concerned only about making money. In some cases, businesses have gone well beyond regulatory requirements to develop new technologies and pollution control devices and approaches (Hoffman 2000; Marcus, Geffen, and Sexton 2002; Prakash 2000; Robbins 2001). Other businesses have voluntarily entered into cooperative arrangements with federal, state, and local governments in an effort to seek cost-effective approaches to protecting and enhancing environmental quality (Press and Mazmanian 2006). Although such modes of cooperation have had mixed results to date, they perhaps signal a new, emerging philosophy within the business community even if the extent of this transformation remains uncertain.

Environmentalists are skeptical of such pronouncements and of forecasts about the greening of industry. They see such assertions and actions by businesses and business groups as mere "greenwashing." They are designed, they say, to give the impression of greener corporate commitments when nothing fundamentally has changed. Evidence in support of their argument can be found in the continued efforts by business groups either to block enactment of new environmental laws and regulations or to weaken them to the point where they are ineffective in protecting the public's interests. Environmentalists point as well to the remarkable access to policymakers that business groups have enjoyed in the administration of George W. Bush (Vig and Kraft 2006). At the same time, many urban areas throughout the United States still experience air pollution problems, many inland lakes and streams remain polluted, and numerous species of flora and fauna are threatened with extinction.

These observations bring us back to the purpose of this book. As we said in chapter 1, we set out to investigate the extent to which business groups choose to intervene in the policy process, where and when they do so, and how much influence they have over policy formulation and implementation. The book's chapters have examined different venues in which business has actively sought to shape public attitudes as well as public policy and regulations. They draw from a diversity of evidence, from case studies to survey data, to try to answer these key questions. Along the way we have learned a great deal about the strategies and tactics that business interests have employed, and whether they get what they want. The findings have provided us with a much better understanding of the conditions under which business groups influence environmental policy, and the opportunities and constraints that affect their success.

Because the role of business groups in environmental policymaking, and in the policy process more generally, is relatively unexplored, we believe the book makes an important contribution. It adds substantially to our knowledge about how interest groups try to influence the policymaking process across multiple venues in the American political system. In particular, it tells us much about whether, when, and how business groups intervene in the policy process, and the factors that affect the degree to which they are likely to be successful. In this last chapter we review the major findings of the contributors, discuss the implications of their results based on the themes and conceptual framework outlined in the introduction, and offer several possible paths for future research.

Access Points in the Policymaking Process

One of the distinctive features of this book is the focus on the extent of business influence across varying access points in the policymaking process and different levels of government. Business interests, as well as other groups, generally have the flexibility to select strategically the stages of the policy process at which they try to promote their interests or to fight their battles. Several of the chapters provide insights into where and when corporations try to mold environmental policy and the factors that tend to affect policy outcomes.

As the chapters by Guber and Bosso and by Duffy show, business often attempts to influence public opinion and elections in order to promote or block agenda building. In their analysis of the debate over whether to allow drilling for oil in the Arctic National Wildlife Refuge (ANWR), Guber and Bosso underscore the importance for business to be able to frame issues to their advantage. (Layzer also makes this point in her examination of climate change issues.) Initially, oil companies framed the need to drill in ANWR as a way for the nation to reduce its dependence on foreign oil imports and create new jobs for Americans. The issue of drilling for oil in ANWR became particularly salient when gasoline prices increased sharply in 2005. Reflecting Duffy's data showing huge discrepancies between the amount of campaign spending between industry and environmental groups, oil companies were able to help elect four pro-drilling proponents to the U.S. Senate in 2004. Their addition to the Senate was enough to permit Republicans to narrowly win passage of legislation to allow drilling in ANWR, but not enough to overcome a filibuster by Senate Democrats later. Prodrilling senators are likely to want to continue this battle in the future. Given the relatively small reserves of oil contained under ANWR, however, oil companies may be hesitant to drill in this sensitive area for fear of generating a public backlash. As Guber and Bosso suggest, the ability of corporations to influence public opinion and elections through the media can have a critical impact on agenda building and policymaking in Congress as well as in other venues.

It is possible that business groups decide to challenge environmental regulations at every access point when the issue is not salient to the public and the media, and thus when they might expect little attention to their effort and only token opposition. Such an effort might begin at the subcommittee or committee level of Congress, for example, when bills are first being formally evaluated. Bryner's analysis of the formulation of the Clean Air Act reveals how fossil-fuel producers were able to block critical amendments by preventing proposals from leaving subcommittees and committees in one or both houses of Congress. Likewise, Layzer's chapter indicates how producers of greenhouse gases were able to delay consideration of climate change legislation by arguing for the need for additional scientific research.

These political strategies become less tenable as scientific consensus grows and media coverage becomes extensive, thus raising the saliency of the issues and possibly altering the balance of power. In the case of climate change, as the scientific evidence pointed toward human causes of greenhouse warming, business interests strategically altered their argument and began focusing on the great costs that climate change policy could impose on society. That position was embraced by the Bush administration, which opposed meaningful action on climate change, and it won support on Capitol Hill as well. By late 2005, however, as

Layzer recounts, some business interests signaled their willingness to consider actions to reduce greenhouse gas emissions, and congressional alignments on the issue were shifting toward modest policy efforts in that direction.

The chapters also suggest that on controversial issues business groups may decide to mount limited opposition in the public arena of Congress (or an equally visible venue at the state and local level). Instead, they devote their time and effort contesting environmental rules within regulatory agencies (such as the EPA) or in the courts, where extensive media scrutiny is less likely. If a particular policy affects only one industry or a handful of companies, business leaders may choose to bypass Congress altogether and quietly approach an agency with their concerns. Furlong's study suggests that America's corporations do indeed attempt to influence rulemaking and are often successful in doing so. Depending on who occupies the White House and the level of sympathy on the part of the president's appointees to the agencies, business groups are likely to have success not only in shaping final rules but also in determining which rules are initially proposed (Kamieniecki 2006). Research by Coglianese reported in this book underscores the important role that information plays in the ability of business to influence rulemaking. In many cases the EPA must make a concerted effort to acquire necessary data and educate itself about the amount of pollution being produced and the most cost-effective way of reducing it. Industries can steer the agency to desirable outcomes depending on the kind and amount of information they release.

As Weiland's and McSpadden's examination of the role business plays in the litigation process shows, corporations can and often do influence environmental policy in the courts. They tend to have the necessary resources and legal expertise to take the EPA and other agencies to court on a regular basis. Business groups are most likely to use the court system to attempt to change environmental policy when the stakes are especially high for them. Many of the judicial cases Weiland and McSpadden analyze show that business interests succeed in influencing rules and regulations, and the manner in which they are enforced, a significant amount of the time in critical areas. Just the threat to sue on the part of business can lead to a rethinking of rules and standards being considered for adoption and to a lengthy delay in their final implementation.

It is no secret that agency officials often develop new regulations with an eye on possible litigation. They are likely to consider business interests even before major litigation is threatened or pursued. Both researchers express disappointment with the limited amount of data available on the use of the courts by business within the environmental policy domain. Thus their conclusions necessarily are based on examination of key cases rather than on a broader and representative set of data about judicial decisionmaking.

One would think that business groups would have more influence over environmental policymaking at the state and local level than at the national level. In general, national environmental organizations are more active at the federal level than at the state and local level. Moreover, states and cities tend to differ considerably in the number and size of environmental groups within their borders. Major employers with headquarters and operations in particular states and localities tend to possess significant leverage in state and local politics because of the percentage of people they employ and the taxes they pay. They can cite the negative economic effect that certain regulatory proposals might have on their business, and they can always threaten to move elsewhere if a state or city considers the enactment of laws that are stricter than those adopted at the national level. State legislators and municipal elected officials may receive a substantial portion of their campaign contributions from large industries, and they may be hesitant to pass laws that will interfere with business.

According to Rabe and Mundo as well as Portney, however, officials in a number of states and cities have adopted, or are considering the adoption of, innovative and often-demanding environmental policies that save energy, reduce pollution, and address climate change. One of the most interesting arguments that Rabe and Mundo advance concerns the number of states that have enacted programs involving renewable portfolio standards (RPS). These RPS programs mandate that a specified level of renewable energy (such as wind, solar, geothermal, and biomass) be provided by any utility that generates and distributes electricity in a particular state. They note as well how the RPS approach is currently being used widely among European Union nations as a central piece of their strategies to reduce release of greenhouse gases. Similarly, Portney demonstrates how cities such as Chattanooga, Tennessee, as well as

Buffalo, New York, are forging cooperative relationships between industry and government in order to improve their environmental quality and quality of life.

It is ironic that, initially, American states and municipalities ignored pollution problems within their borders prior to the emergence of the modern environmental movement in the 1960s, or enacted fairly weak policies that were enforced minimally. These deficiencies were among the major reasons for the great expansion of federal authority for environmental protection efforts during the late 1960s and 1970s (Kraft 2007; Vig and Kraft 2006). However, many state and local officials are now out in front of federal efforts to reduce pollution and the emissions of greenhouse gases and improve the nation's environmental quality. Thus analysts find that they can no longer easily predict the role of business interests in these quite different institutional venues. Nor can they foresee the extent of their influence on environmental and natural resource policy at a time when decisions increasingly take place at the state and local level (Mazmanian and Kraft 1999; Durant, Fiorino, and O'Leary 2004).

Implications for Environmental Policymaking

The findings reported in the book have important implications for the influence of business interests in environmental policymaking. The chapters by Guber and Bosso and by Duffy demonstrate that business exerts a great deal of influence over agenda setting in environmental policy, more so than citizen groups. As the other chapters show, this is also true in Congress, the EPA, and the courts. The chapters by Rabe and Mundo and by Portney, however, paint a different picture of the role corporations play in state and local government decisionmaking, especially most recently. At the state and local level business and government leaders are more willing to join forces and support initiatives that integrate efforts to stimulate economic growth and environmental protection simultaneously. Clearly, the same level of cooperation is lacking at the federal level, where the relationship among environmental groups, industry, and government continues to be highly contentious and divisive. This is well documented in the chapters by Layzer, Bryner, Furlong, Coglianese, Weiland, and McSpadden. Analyses by Rabe and Mundo and by Portney suggest that policymakers within certain states and cities are frustrated by the ongoing vitriolic debates at the national level and have decided to move forward on their own in order to improve environmental policy within their borders. This reaction by state and local policymakers has spawned a diversity of innovative policy approaches involving government and business interests (Durant, Fiorino, and O'Leary 2004; Mazmanian and Kraft 1999). Such cooperative arrangements may provide models for future collaborative efforts involving environmentalists, business leaders, and policymakers at the federal level.

Although business interests represent a powerful, countervailing force in Washington, D.C., it is not true that they always get their way at the national level. As Bryner's chapter shows, competing elites in the media and the scientific community, along with environmentalists, often high-light differences between what corporations assert is true and the actual evidence. For example, the media have played an important role in raising awareness of the health problems associated with exposure to certain toxic chemicals. Likewise, the scientific community was instru-mental in convincing members of Congress of the need to control sulfur dioxide emissions to reduce acid rain. In Layzer's view, the scientific community is placing increasing pressure on the federal government to address climate change. President Bush and a number of legislators have been forced to modify their positions on climate change, thereby raising hope that the federal government will soon take action to control green-house gas emissions.

The chapters in this book also suggest why the United States has not made more progress in improving its environmental quality and manag-ing its natural resources. As Bryner, Furlong, Coglianese, Weiland, and McSpadden reveal, government has not enforced existing pollution control laws and regulations as aggressively as possible. Thus many states and localities are still in violation of clean air and water standards, and contamination of inland waterways and coastal ocean regions continues to be a problem. Public lands in the West are increasingly being opened up to mining, drilling for natural gas and oil, and logging. Clearly, industry leaders have succeeded in convincing policymakers that current levels of pollution are tolerable. They also have been effective in arguing that the nation possesses an abundance of natural resources that can be used to support economic development. They seem as well to be persuasive in arguing that further efforts to enhance environmental protection and natural resource conservation may have a negative impact on employment and economic growth in the United States. They also have contended that the nation cannot compete economically at the international level unless it further exploits its natural resources. Their wealth and collective action advantages (Olson 1965) have translated into access to policymakers and the governmental process, providing them many opportunities to present their arguments. In comparison, environmental groups have been less effective in shaping the discourse over environmental protection and natural resource conservation, and they have not convincingly made their case as to why action on various fronts is necessary. As one consequence, the public has failed to take stronger stands on today's environmental issues and vote for elected officials who will improve pollution control and conserve the nation's natural resources (Bosso and Guber 2006). Until environmental groups produce a groundswell of broad public support, business interests are likely to continue to get their way on critical issues much of the time without significantly violating central tenets of democracy.

Interest Groups and Democracy

As students of American politics are aware, James Madison attempted to address the thorny issue of the "mischiefs of faction" within the context of the new U.S. Constitution in Federalist Paper Number 10. A major concern among leaders and citizens at the time was whether the proposed government under the new Constitution would prevent a faction, large or small, from taking control of the country. Madison wrote that factions would naturally arise because of the freedoms granted citizens under the Constitution to associate and form groups. He knew that rational individuals would recognize the advantage of acting in numbers rather than alone. In Madison's view, factions would be a natural product and price of liberty. He argued that government must control them, but it cannot suppress them. According to him, factions would be limited in their power under the new Constitution because the national government would be divided into three separate branches with important checks and balances on one another. "Ambition must be made to counteract ambition," he said. He also explained that elected representatives would have the intelligence and the wisdom to serve the larger interests of the nation and would help control efforts at tyranny from any source. In addition, citizens would have guaranteed civil rights and civil liberties to protect them from the "mischiefs of faction."

The potential danger of excluding certain segments of the population from the political process was a major concern of the founding fathers as well. While Madison believed the causes of factions were rooted in human diversity, he thought inequality in the possession of economic resources was at the heart of the problem:

> But the most common and durable source of factions has been the various and unequal distribution of property. Those who hold and those who are without property have ever formed distinct interests in society. Those who are creditors and those who are debtors fall under like discrimination. A landed interest, a manufacturing interest, a mercantile interest, a monied interest, with many lesser interests, grow up of necessity in civilized nations, and divide them into different classes, actuated by different sentiments and views. (Hamilton, Madison, and Jay, 1961, Federalist Paper Number 10, 79)

Madison argued that all individuals and groups, including the poor and the affluent, would be equally protected by the Constitution.

Even though Madison wrote his essay more than 200 years ago, many of the issues he addressed remain relevant to American politics. At least since the early 1960s, presidents and members of Congress from both parties have complained vociferously about the undue influence of interest groups in Washington, D.C., primarily because of the rapid growth in the number, size, and resources of these groups. The general public, too, has grown increasingly cynical about the role of interest groups in the political system. Today, interest groups are blamed for legislative gridlock on vital issues such as health care reform, education reform, energy policy, and environmental policy, as well as for the increased politicization of the judicial nominating and approval process.

In particular, the size and wealth of business lobbying organizations have grown dramatically since World War II, prompting some observers to argue that they are now too powerful and are undermining democracy and threatening the well-being of society (e.g., Korten 1995). The weakening of the political parties, the rising costs of media advertising and election campaigns, and the increasing contributions by Political Action Committees (PACs) to candidates and parties have led to calls for reform in the way American elections are financed. Business interests, among others, are key targets of critics who demand the enactment of meaningful campaign finance reform at the federal level. The campaign finance reform legislation enacted in 2002 bans "soft money," among other things, and is a significant attempt to level the playing field. Loopholes in the act exist, however, and it will be necessary to adopt additional regulations in the future in order to correct inequities in the financing of campaigns. Thus, despite Madison's assurances, the question of how we allow business and other interest groups to form and participate but control their influence remains a dilemma in modern times. We continue to grapple with the question of whether the amount of influence business has is proportionate to other interests in society and is appropriate in view of the competitive needs and well-being of a large, complex, and democratic society. How one addresses this issue in relation to the environmental policy sphere depends on one's assessment of the role business is playing in persuading government to take actions that protect and promote its interests, often at the expense of public well-being. Is the cost of protecting the rights of business interests to participate fully in the political process too high? This depends on how much the nation values environmental protection and public health as well as how one appraises both the actions of business groups and their actual influence on policy decisions. We hope that, taken together, the chapters in this book help shed light on these concerns and provide at least some tentative answers to the questions.

Future Research Paths

The findings reported here point to a number of possible avenues for future research. With the exception of the chapters by Rabe and Mundo and by Portney, this book focuses primarily on issues at the federal level. In light of the findings reported by Rabe and Mundo as well as by Portney, scholars should explore in greater depth the influence of business over environmental policy at the state and local level. It would be fruitful to examine how much business affects agenda setting and policymaking in the executive, legislative, and judicial branches of state and local governments. While competition from environmental groups is far less evident in some areas of the country than others (the South comes to mind), certain companies and industries are quite dominant in particular regions. One would therefore expect to find that corporations have considerable influence in certain states and cities and less influence in others. What accounts for the differences? In addition, strategies and tactics used by business may differ between the federal level and the state and local level as well as among states and cities. Little systematic research has been pursued in this area, and an exploration of business influence over government institutions at the subnational level could further understanding of interest-group politics and public policymaking.

As Weiland and McSpadden observe, additional research is needed as well on how successful business interests are in the adjudication of disputes over environmental and natural resource issues. More data are needed on the participation of corporations in the federal courts, including the U.S. Supreme Court. Furthermore, almost no research has been done on out-of-court, negotiated settlements by the EPA and polluters. How the EPA approaches this process and what types of outcomes are produced should be addressed. Of course, obtaining data on these deliberations and on other informal contacts between business interests and policymakers or regulators will not be easy.

Likewise, we know very little about the communications and negotiations that take place between business groups and members of Congress *prior* to the formal introduction of legislation (Kamieniecki 2006). What is the nature of the communications between business interests and congressional representatives on environmental issues at this very early stage of the legislative process? How much influence do business groups have in writing legislative proposals or blocking the introduction of certain legislation? Since no public records are kept concerning these interactions, it might be difficult to collect accurate and reliable data on the influence of business over the actual writing of legislative proposals.

Similarly, almost no research exists on the lobbying activities and level of influence of foreign corporations involving environmental and natural resource legislation, and nearly all the work that has been done has focused almost exclusively on the lobbying activities of domestic groups in the U.S. Congress (Kamieniecki 2006). This is true for research that specifically addresses lobbying efforts by business groups (e.g., Baumgartner and Leech 1998; Smith 2000). In recent years, however, many foreign and domestic companies have increasingly pressured

Congress and the president's foreign policy advisors to open up new markets abroad (e.g., in Asia and Central and South America) and to endorse multinational and international free-trade initiatives. At the same time, American industry has placed considerable pressure on the federal government not to sign international agreements that will undercut its profits and compromise its interests both here and abroad (e.g., the transfer of technology). Such lobbying activities have been largely ignored by American political scientists in their research on the role of interest groups in policymaking. No doubt, only certain kinds of businesses, principally large companies and multinational corporations, attempt to persuade government to join or not to join international regimes. The frequency and success with which domestic-based citizen groups (e.g., consumer, social service, and environmental groups) affect American policy at the international level are also unknown.

We do know that American companies have been heavily involved in shaping U.S. policy on the depletion of the ozone layer and climate change, but with opposite results. Despite pressure from a certain sector of the chemical industry, the U.S. government played a leadership role in forging a series of successful international agreements to reduce chlorofluorocarbon (CFC) emissions and protect the ozone layer. In contrast, the U.S. government, especially during the George W. Bush administration, has been roundly criticized by environmental groups and nearly all advanced industrialized and developing nations for doing too little to reduce greenhouse gas emissions, principally carbon dioxide (CO_2) emissions. The United States is the largest emitter of CO_2 in the world. Nevertheless, as Layzer shows, the American energy companies, led by the fossil-fuel industry, have been quite successful in blocking government action. As a consequence, the U.S. government has not signed the Kyoto climate change treaty, nor has it formulated and implemented a comprehensive plan of its own. Of course, the economic impact of reducing greenhouse gases will be broader and deeper on industry, consumers, and the nation than the economic impact of reducing CFC emissions has been.

Although Layzer discusses the role of energy companies in shaping U.S. policy on climate change, further empirical research needs to be conducted on the ability of domestic-based companies (and citizen groups) to influence U.S. involvement in international regimes, including those that address environmental and natural resource concerns. Specifically, future studies should at least address the following questions: Do the tactics and strategies of foreign companies differ from those of their American counterparts and, if so, in what way? How often do they get their way in the legislative process? Do they lobby various units of government for favorable treatment or just Congress? Do foreign companies tend to form coalitions among themselves, or do they form coalitions with American companies within the same industrial sector (e.g., automobile manufacturing)? Answers to these questions will add to our understanding of legislative outcomes involving environmental and natural resource policy.

In recent years research institutes or "think tanks" have played an increasingly important role in policymaking. Smith (2000) analyzes their role in his study of business influence over agenda building in Congress. As Guber and Bosso as well as Duffy note, polluting industries, in particular, have established and funded such organizations in an effort to influence media coverage and public opinion on salient issues. Such organizations often present themselves as neutral, third parties conducting balanced research and offering objective views. Exactly how effective they are in shaping public opinion and the government's agenda concerning environmental protection is unknown and should be studied.

In addition, more research should be conducted on the environmental beliefs and attitudes of business leaders, as well as those working in environmental audit and compliance offices inside companies. In-depth, carefully crafted surveys of business leaders and managers should be able to tell us a great deal about how they view the responsibility of their company to meet environmental laws and regulations and their commitment to improving environmental quality and conserving natural resources. Such interviews can also provide insights into how business leaders select the policy venue in which to oppose regulation as well as the tactics and strategies they employ. Empirical studies of this kind are challenging, and response rates for surveys of business officials on environmental management decisions are notoriously low (Coglianese and Nash 2006; Stephan, Kraft, and Abel 2005). Yet there are so few rigorous studies of this kind that they are very much worth pursuing.

Finally, researchers should strive for greater clarity in their analyses of business interests. Business is not a single entity. Rather it comprises many different people, individual companies, industries, and associations having different missions, priorities, and goals. How can these important differences best be described and categorized? What kinds of typologies might be suggested that would assist us in understanding the diverse ways business groups seek to influence policy decisions? At the same time, as the various chapters in this book suggest, there needs to be further study of the particular conditions under which business groups become politically active and succeed or fail in influencing public policy. This will probably require the development of new theories of interest-group access and influence related to business. Given the important role business plays in American politics, it is surprising that few researchers have closely examined its activities and level of influence.

We have not offered a comprehensive research agenda for the study of business and environmental policy, nor do we wish to do so. Instead, we have suggested a number of neglected areas of study that we believe will be of great interest to students of environmental policy and politics. The individual chapters in this book hint at many other potentially fruitful lines of inquiry. In nearly all instances they suggest that scholars might want to analyze additional case studies, seek out new sources of data, and build new insights from theoretically informed investigations of business actions across a range of environmental policy issues in different venues.

Much the same could be said for the study of comparative environmental politics and policy. To what extent are the patterns identified in this book also found in other developed nations? What best accounts for the variation from one nation to another, or business influence in the European Union nations compared to what one finds in the United States? How do the activities and influence of business groups in developed nations compare to those in developing nations? Some of the best recent work on cross-national environmental politics and policy offers a good starting point in addressing these questions (Desai 2002; Vig and Faure 2004; Vogel 2005; Vogel and Kagan 2002).

We are convinced that such research, whether focused on the United States or other nations, can provide a richer and deeper understanding of the role of business interests in environmental policymaking than is now available. We also place a high value on research that reflects the unique circumstances of our time. The nation and the world will confront unprecedented environmental and resources challenges over the next several decades. For that reason alone, it is imperative to learn more about the diverse demands made on government, how conflicting demands are assessed and acted on, and how well the resulting environmental policies promote the public interest.

References

Baumgartner, Frank R., and Beth L. Leech. 1998. *Basic Interests: The Importance of Groups in Politics and in Political Science*. Princeton, NJ: Princeton University Press.

Berry, Jeffrey M. 1999. *The New Liberalism: The Rising Power of Citizen Groups*. Washington, DC: Brookings Institution.

Bosso, Christopher J. 2005. *Environment, Inc.: From Grassroots to Beltway*. Lawrence: University Press of Kansas.

Bosso, Christopher J., and Deborah Guber. 2006. "Maintaining Presence: Environmental Advocacy and the Permanent Campaign." In Norman J. Vig and Michael E. Kraft, eds., *Environmental Policy*, 6th ed. Washington, DC: CQ Press.

Brown, Lester R. 2001. *Eco-economy: Building an Economy for the Earth*. New York: Norton.

Cahn, Matthew A. 1995. *Environmental Deceptions: The Tension between Liberalism and Environmental Policymaking in the United States*. Albany: State University of New York Press.

Clawson, Dan, Alan Neustadt, and Mark Waller. 1998. *Dollars and Votes: How Business Campaign Contributions Subvert Democracy*. Philadelphia: Temple University Press.

Coglianese, Cary, and Jennifer Nash, eds. 2006. *Leveraging the Private Sector: Management-Based Strategies for Environmental Protection*. Washington, DC: Resources for the Future Press.

Davis, Devra. 2002. *When Smoke Ran Like Water: Tales of Environmental Deception and the Battle against Pollution*. New York: Basic Books.

Desai, Uday, ed. 2002. *Environmental Politics and Policy in Industrialized Countries*. Cambridge, MA: MIT Press.

Dryzek, John S. 1997. *The Politics of the Earth: Environmental Discourses*. Oxford: Oxford University Press.

Duffy, Robert J. 2003. *The Green Agenda in American Politics: New Strategies for the Twenty-First Century*. Lawrence: University Press of Kansas.

Durant, Robert F., Daniel J. Fiorino, and Rosemary O'Leary, eds. 2004. *Environmental Governance Reconsidered: Challenges, Choices, and Opportunities*. Cambridge, MA: MIT Press.

Glazer, Amihai, and Lawrence S. Rothenberg. 2001. *Why Government Succeeds and Why It Fails*. Cambridge, MA: Harvard University Press.

Gonzalez, George A. 2001. *Corporate Power and the Environment: The Political Economy of U.S. Environmental Policy.* Lanham, MD: Rowman & Littlefield.

Hamilton, Alexander, James Madison, and John Jay. 1961. *The Federalist Papers,* assembled by Clinton Rossiter. New York: New American Library.

Hoffman, Andrew J. 2000. "Integrating Environmental and Social Issues into Corporate Practice." *Environment* (June): 22–33.

Kamieniecki, Sheldon. 2006. *Corporate America and Environmental Policy: How often Does Business Get Its Way?* Palo Alto, CA: Stanford University Press.

Korten, David C. 1995. *When Corporations Rule the World.* West Hartford, CT: Kumarian Press.

Kraft, Michael E. 2006. "Environmental Policy in Congress." In Norman J. Vig and Michael E. Kraft, eds., *Environmental Policy,* 6th ed. Washington, DC: CQ Press.

———. 2007. *Environmental Policy and Politics,* 4th ed. New York: Pearson Longman.

Libby, Ronald T. 1998. *Eco-Wars: Political Campaigns and Social Movements.* New York: Columbia University Press.

Marcus, Alfred A., Donald A. Geffen, and Ken Sexton. 2002. *Reinventing Environmental Regulation: Lessons from Project XL.* Washington, DC: Resources for the Future.

Mazmanian, Daniel A., and Michael E. Kraft, eds. 1999. *Toward Sustainable Communities: Transition and Transformations in Environmental Policy.* Cambridge, MA: MIT Press.

Milbrath, Lester W. 1989. *Envisioning a Sustainable Society: Learning Our Way Out.* Albany: State University of New York Press.

Olson, Mancur. 1965. *The Logic of Collective Action: Public Goods and the Theory of Groups.* Cambridge, MA: Harvard University Press.

Prakash, Aseem. 2000. *Greening the Firm: The Politics of Corporate Environmentalism.* New York: Cambridge University Press.

Press, Daniel, and Daniel A. Mazmanian. 2006. "The Greening of Industry: Combining Government Regulation and Voluntary Strategies." In Norman J. Vig and Michael E. Kraft, eds., *Environmental Policy,* 6th ed. Washington, DC: CQ Press.

Robbins, Peter Thayer. 2001. *Greening the Corporation: Management Strategy and the Environmental Challenge.* London: Earthscan.

Smith, Mark A. 2000. *American Business and Political Power: Public Opinion, Elections, and Democracy.* Chicago: University of Chicago Press.

Stephan, Mark, Michael E. Kraft, and Troy D. Abel. 2005. "Information Politics and Environmental Performance: The Impact of the Toxics Release Inventory on Corporate Decision Making." Paper presented at the annual meeting of the American Political Science Association, Washington, DC, September 1–5.

Vig, Norman J., and Michael Faure, eds. 2004. *Green Giants? Environmental Policies of the United States and the European Union*, Cambridge, MA: MIT Press.

Vig, Norman J., and Michael E. Kraft, eds. 2006. *Environmental Policy.* 6th ed. Washington, DC: CQ Press.

Vogel, David. 2005. *The Market for Virtue: The Potential and Limits of Corporate Social Responsibility.* Washington, DC: Brookings Institution Press.

Vogel, David, and Robert Kagan, eds. 2002. *Dynamics of Regulatory Change: How Globalization Affects National Regulatory Policies.* Berkeley: University of California Press.

Index